D1278327

Educational Psychology

• • • • • • • • • • • • • • • •

Robert M. W. Travers . .

The Macmillan Company, New York / Collier-Macmillan Publishers, London

..........Educational Psychology

A Scientific Foundation for Educational Practice

LB1051
T668

Copyright © 1973, Robert M. W. Travers

Printed in the United States of America

All rights reserved. No part of this book may be reproduced or
transmitted in any form or by any means, electronic or mechanical,
including photocopying, recording, or any information storage and
retrieval system, without permission in writing from the Publisher.

The Macmillan Company
866 Third Avenue, New York, New York 10022

Collier-Macmillan Canada, Ltd., Toronto, Ontario

Library of Congress catalog card number: 72-80076

Printing: 1 2 3 4 5 6 7 8   Year: 3 4 5 6 7 8 9

This book attempts to bring to the undergraduate student of education some of the aspects of the behavioral sciences that appear to have important implications for education. It is not a cookbook of recipes for effective education. Such a cookbook probably could not be written at the present time. It is a compilation of scientific conclusions about the nature of learners and the nature of learning that, I believe, have value in guiding the behavior of classroom teachers. A knowledge of the nature of the human learner is essential to the teacher, if he is to behave as a professional person and make professional decisions. The behavioral sciences are viewed in this book as having the same role in the practice of teaching as physiology and biochemistry have in the practice of medicine. Of course, the physician may practice medicine by doing no more than prescribing pills on a rule-of-thumb basis, and the teacher may teach by handing out packaged materials for the pupil to master, but one must hope that both the physician and the teacher, through proper training, may be able to practice their arts at a higher level. In both fields, a basic knowledge of relevant findings from the related sciences seems to be of fundamental importance in providing a foundation for practice.

Texts on educational psychology differ widely in content. Some do not endorse the position taken here and use little of the knowledge presented by the basic sciences. This practice hardly seems reasonable when one considers that sweeping changes in educational practice have been brought about in the last few decades through the basic research of such individuals as E. L. Thorndike, J. Piaget, and B. F. Skinner. Even to understand some of the important changes taking place in schools, one has to have some familiarity with the work in the behavioral sciences that has provided the foundation for such change.

Textbooks on educational psychology that attempt to give the student of education a scientific foundation for teaching also vary in what they include and the traditions of research on which they draw. A part of this variation is a result of the fact that research literature is so vast in quantity today that no single person can be expected to be acquainted with more than a small fraction of it. The author of a textbook has to make judgments about the lines of research that seem to have the most important implications for education and then confine his study of the research literature to those areas. I must admit to having had to make such decisions, and the book reflects the areas of basic science that I think have the most important implications for education.

The task of selecting subject matter for this volume has been made doubly difficult by the fact that the behavioral sciences appear to be undergoing a revolution. Considerable disillusionment is widely expressed with the accomplishments in the stimulus-response form and the operant form. At the same time, research in psychology is being revitalized by forces emanating from outside itself. Among these forces are those that derive from the combination of biology and epistemology embraced by Piaget and his associates, from the new conceptualizations of language and language development that have come from linguistics, and from the contribution of computer technology to models of human thinking.

Within psychology, advances in the areas of perceptual learning and human information processing have produced radical changes in our conception of how learning takes place. The renewed sources of life given the behavioral sciences by these influences show their impact even in an elementary textbook such as this one. This does not mean that these new influences have wiped out the contributions of the older approaches. Conceptions of learning based on classical and instrumental conditioning still have contributions to make to practical enterprises such as education, but they are recognized not to be the universal panaceas they were claimed to be. They are seen to apply within limited boundaries, but within their boundaries to offer valuable techniques for changing behavior.

A main result of this scientific revolution is a changed conception of the nature of man. In many ways, the new and most widely endorsed conception of man in the behavioral sciences, in contrast to that in neobehaviorism, comes quite close to the predominant conception of man found among contemporary educators. This conception of man views him not as a passive organism acted on and controlled in a simple way by environmental circumstances but as an organism that acts upon the environment, continuously scanning the world for information that is then internally organized and reorganized. This active organism, man, also has great capacity for ignoring and not being controlled by immediate circumstances in order to achieve long-range goals. Whereas at midcentury the predominant theme of psychology held the free man to be a myth, the present trend involves attempts to build models of autonomous man. The new conception of man that is emerging from the revitalized behavioral sciences may revitalize the educational enterprise.

R. M. W. T.

. . . .

Contents

The activities engaged in by teachers today in the classroom are very different from those of a century ago. Although teachers of the last century differed among themselves in their practices, they still tended to show a characteristic pattern of instruction that has been well described by those who visited their classrooms. A substantial emphasis was placed on drilling children in what were believed to be the fundamentals of a good education, and slowness in achieving the goals set by the teacher was typically punished. Joseph Mayer Rice, who described the schools he visited in the late 1890s, was appalled by the fact that some teachers might spend as much as five hours a day drilling children in spelling. A similar intensive drill was found in arithmetic. School subjects were often taught just because they were believed to be hard to learn, because it was thought that a subject had to be difficult to master in order for it to be

Introduction

valuable for training the mind. Failure to master the tasks required for the performance of a particular lesson usually resulted in punishment, often in the form of keeping the child in school during recess or after school. Failure in school was treated largely as moral failure. Children who did not learn were regarded as children who just did not want to learn. In contrast, the teacher today spends very little time in organizing recitation–drill situations in which skills such as spelling are pursued to the exclusion of all else. Subjects are selected for study not because they are difficult but because they are expected to have some subsequent utility, or because they provide an understanding of the world, or because they provide enjoyable activities or experiences worthwhile in themselves. Failure of a pupil to master a task leads to questions about the adequacy of the teaching materials or the teaching methods, and the question is sometimes asked whether the source of the difficulty might be some disability in the pupil. Failure of the pupil raises issues about instruction and learning and not moral issues.

The enormous changes that have occurred in the behavior of teachers over the past century can be attributed to various causes, but the most basic of these is the discovery of significant facts about the nature of man. In the intervening years, the development of psychology and sociology has provided a picture of the nature of man that has radically changed the way the young are treated in the classroom. This new picture would not alone have been sufficient to produce the striking changes in classroom management, for the evolution of education required also that teachers be educated in the discoveries of the newly emerging behavioral sciences. Perhaps as important as the emergence of the new sciences themselves has been the improved standards of teacher education. Teachers today are not only more able and better educated than their predecessors, but they have also been exposed to some of the findings in the behavioral sciences, particularly the findings that have important implications for the management of learning in the classroom.

It is all too easy to write devastating criticisms of the schools today and to overlook the improvements that have come about in the way teachers, particularly at the elementary level, handle their day-to-day problems. Sweeping criticisms come not only from those who would like to see a freer and more stimulating school environment but also from those who advocate a greater degree of control and enhanced regimentation. The former critics are represented by such a writer as Silberman (1970)* and the latter by Bereiter (1966) and Skinner (1971). Both radicals and conservatives have their plans for the reform of the schools, and these opposing plans advocate changes in opposite directions. Both attempt to initiate change through the wholesale condemnation of what is happening in schools today.

One cannot deny that the schools are in serious difficulties and that much can be done to improve teaching, but only some of the problems

---

* Complete bibliographical information for references in the text is to be found in the References section at the back of this book.

can be attributed to the inadequacies of teachers. The extraordinary amount of disruptive behavior engaged in by pupils, both inside and outside the classroom, must be viewed as a result of other aspects of turmoil in our society over which the teacher has virtually no control. The widespread criticism that the curriculum lacks "relevance" cannot be interpreted as a criticism of teachers, for teachers make few decisions concerning what is taught in schools. Also, there is no unanimity concerning what *should* be taught. Proposals for curriculum change are not only varied but are often in opposite directions. Amid the disruption of education produced by social problems of the day and the intense struggle among outside political forces to produce change in the schools, little recognition has been given to the improvement in teaching that has taken place over the last half century. Indeed, the teacher has often become a scapegoat for those who would tear down the schools.

The professionalization of teaching has resulted in a great increase in the number of functions that the teacher performs in the classroom. The modern teacher is expected to have some competence in organizing learning activities as well as to have skill in the traditional teaching functions of explaining, demonstrating, informing, and evaluating. In addition, the teacher must diagnose learning difficulties of children, energize children's behavior and help them to direct their energies into desirable channels, select materials appropriate to the level of attainment of particular children, and identify handicaps that need treatment by other specialists. Teachers are also acquiring enlarged professional roles related to activities outside of the classroom through participation in committees that set objectives and develop curricula. Let us consider some of the many different activities engaged in by teachers in the course of a day in school.

Routine management activities: A classroom is a complex society and cannot provide maximum opportunities for the development of each child unless there is management of the activities. Management at the simplest levels involves making arrangements for children to begin work, to move from room to room when necessary, to clean up the room, to pass out materials, to collect materials, and to listen to announcements. Teachers vary to an enormous extent in the time they devote to such matters, but these activities should occupy less than 10 per cent of the time of an efficient teacher. Less efficient teachers may spend 50 per cent or more of their time in such activities. For a few teachers, routine classroom management may become an end in itself, and much of the class time may be spent in grouping and regrouping the children and in distribution and collection of materials. Unnecessary management activities are readily manufactured, and teachers, like anyone else in a managerial position, can invent unnecessary routines. The author can recall a teacher who had invented a complex routine for obtaining permission to go to the toilet. Two students were in charge of toilet passes, which consisted of two red cards for the boys and two blue cards for the girls. A child who wanted to go to the toilet had first to obtain the permission of the teacher. Then, after entering his name on a roster along with the time of day, the child went to the student in charge of passes and obtained a pass. On returning to the classroom, the child went through the reverse procedure. Other phases of classroom activity were organized with equal precision and equally wasted energy.

Although some time has to be spent on management activities, these should not become an end in themselves, though sometimes they do. The teacher should remember that every minute spent unnecessarily on management activities is a minute taken away from activities more closely related to learning. Although a minimum amount of time has to be spent on activities related to organization, any time spent beyond this minimum is unlikely to add to the amount learned by the pupils. When teaching is skillfully conducted, the management activities take place unobtrusively, with little fuss. Such activities should never be used merely to hold the pupils in front of their work (which they may not be doing). The previously described teacher who devoted his day to routine management matters did so largely to hold reluctant pupils in front of very dull classwork. Also, management does not mean that the teacher makes all the decisions. One aspect of management is seeing that decision making is distributed among as many individuals as possible.

Activities related to bringing pupils into contact with materials and ideas from which they can learn: The teacher was formerly sometimes little more than a classroom policeman who distributed printed materials and then saw to it that the pupils remained with their noses glued to the materials. Today there exist such rich sources of materials that a substantial body of professional knowledge is necessary in selecting materials to be used. The teacher is likely to have a limited choice of textbooks, if he has any choice at all, but the day has long passed when pupils engaged only in the study of books prescribed by a central authority. Many teachers are able to consult a media specialist, who can advise on films, tapes, slides, and other such materials that can be used to add flesh to the skeleton of education provided by the usual classroom materials. The teacher must also use professional knowledge in selecting materials for children who are having particular difficulties in mastering certain aspects of the curriculum. In addition, pupils have to learn to find information for themselves. Although schools at the turn of the century spoon-fed pupils with materials in textbook form, increasing pressure is being placed on the pupil to dig out knowledge for himself. Such an emphasis is highly reasonable, for when the pupil leaves school he will have to find whatever knowledge he needs through his own efforts. In the past, schools too often had programs designed as if based on the wholly invalid assumptions that what pupils learned in school would be the knowledge they needed throughout life and that learning after leaving school would be quite unnecessary. Much of education today has to be based on the valid assumption that school is, to a considerable extent, the place where students learn to derive knowledge from suitable sources all by themselves.

There is now available for schools an increasing supply of concrete materials that children can use, including kits for conducting scientific experiments, geological specimens, living creatures to be kept for demonstrating particular phenomena, and other equipment to provide special demonstrations. The existence of such materials means that modern teachers have knowledge that permits them to use these materials efficiently.

The directing and redirecting of the energies of pupils: Closely related to the selection of materials through which pupils learn is the problem of directing and redirecting the energies of pupils. This problem is sometimes referred to as the **problem of motivation.** It is also the problem of discipline in that the pupil who is being disruptive in the classroom is one whose energies are being directed into nonproductive and nonuseful lines. The traditional approach to the problem of how to direct pupils' energies into useful learning activities has been to threaten to punish those who did otherwise. To some extent, this is still a solution commonly observed. Several alternative solutions to this problem exist. One is to make the materials so interesting and attractive that they command attention, but this is not always so easy to do. Another solution is to provide a system of rewards to pupils for staying in the learning situation. Educators have long been hesitant to offer rewards for learning and have tended to make the assumptions that children enjoy learning and that learning should be a reward in itself. In recent times, a few psychologists have advocated the alternative position and have even suggested that children in high school be paid for learning, much as any other worker is paid for his work. Such suggestions appear radical and impractical, but it should be remembered that, not very long ago, the idea that punishment should be kept at a minimum in schools was also considered radical.

The energizing of behavior in the classroom is not only dependent on the learning opportunities provided but is also closely related to the background that the pupil brings to the learning situation. Study of ghetto children has shown all too clearly that they tend to have values that conflict with those of the school. The result is that the children do not progress according to the school's expectations. Close cooperation between school and home seems necessary if children's energies are to be directed along productive lines. The problem of motivating children can no longer be considered to be one for the teacher to solve single-handedly. The problem is complex and requires the help also of both the home and the community.

The identification of special handicaps in children: A century ago, a teacher might have been expected to take note of the fact that a child was blind or completely deaf, but the more common handicaps were rarely noted. A partially deaf child typically was dubbed as stupid because he answered every question with "I don't know." This is the way children who cannot hear properly what is said to them manage to get the teacher off their backs. A modern teacher will recognize the symptom immediately and will probably arrange for the child to visit an audiologist. Teachers are vastly more responsive to cues of this kind today than they were even fifty years ago.

Teachers are also professionally trained to recognize a greater number of symptoms of learning difficulties than they were a generation

Professionally trained teachers can help to solve many problems that poorly trained teachers would never even recognize.

ago. Such training is made possible because of increased knowledge of factors that interfere with learning. For example, it now seems clear that some children suffer brain damage at birth and that such damage may produce difficulties interfering with the recognition of visual forms such as is required in learning to read, and these children typically also have other behavioral symptoms including general physical restlessness and high distractibility. The modern teacher is not equipped to diagnose the existence of brain damage in a child, but he is trained to recognize enough symptoms to be able to identify the child who needs to be referred to a diagnostician. If the diagnosis is brain damage, and if special facilities for the education of the child are not available, the teacher today can still handle the child more effectively than could the teacher of a generation ago.

Teachers are also trained to recognize the symptoms of autistic children, who were often described in the past as being just uncooperative because they are characterized by an inability to respond to other human beings. The teacher may be able to do little with such a child but refer him for diagnosis and treatment. However, this is a vastly better procedure than to allow him, as in days past, to remain a nagging source of irritation in the classroom.

There is no clear line of demarcation between the child who has some serious deficiency that interferes with classroom learning and the child who encounters a particular difficulty in mastering some aspect of the school curriculum. For example, the child who has difficulty in learning long division may simply have developed some misunderstanding that the teacher has to identify and correct. In such a case, the attitude of the teacher is one that leads to an understanding and solution of the problem. The teacher's most important single role is that of solving the learning problems presented by the thirty or more children in the classroom. Some of those problems the teacher can solve, but others require the help of other experts. A good school system provides teams of experts who can assist in solving most of the problems presented by the children in school.

Explaining, demonstrating, and informing: The traditional role of the teacher has been that of **explaining, demonstrating,** and **informing.** Dreeben (1973) points out that teachers have as many as 650 interactions with pupils during the course of a school day. About two thirds of the teacher–pupil interaction time is spent in responding to pupils' questions. There are enormous differences in this respect among teachers, some spending as little as 10 per cent of their time on this type of instructional activity. On the average, about half of the teacher's time is spent in disseminating information.

The role of the teacher as a source of information or explanation has probably declined in recent years, though perhaps not as far as it should have. Teaching materials have improved so much over the last quarter of a century that they typically provide more easily understood information and clearer explanations than the teacher can provide. A clearly written account of how the Indians lived in the West before the arrival of the white man is likely to inform the child more accurately, and perhaps in a more interesting way, than an account given by the teacher. Before writing, the author of the textbook probably made a detailed study of how the Indians lived. In addition, the manuscript of the book was reviewed by another competent historian in order to ensure accuracy. The teacher's account of how the Indians lived is likely to be based on vague memories of a course in college and cannot have the historical authenticity of a well-written text prepared by a competent authority. In the modern classroom, teachers have much more important things to do than provide rather poor accounts of material much better presented in texts. There was a time, back in the Middle Ages, when students had no books and the teacher had to be the main source of information. In those days, the teacher took up the practice of giving lectures, because he was the major channel through which pupils acquired knowledge. Then came books, and the practice of lecturing became unnecessary, but teachers had come to enjoy the role of imparters of knowledge and were not willing to give it up. So today teachers often lecture as though students had no books covering the same material.

Although the teacher can have only a limited role as a source of information, he still has important functions to perform in the area of explaining and demonstrating. A teacher engages in explaining when he relates one item of knowledge the student has acquired to others. A teacher may point out that the human body and an oil-burning heater are both warm for similar reasons. The student may never have realized that both derive their warmth from the burning of materials. The teacher explains the similarity by bringing out the common underlying basis of the heat that both produce. Explaining is a much more difficult task to perform than is informing, and this is probably why teachers often prefer to devote their time to informing.

Providing a model of behavior for pupils: There is very substantial evidence that children tend to perform in ways similar to those of the adults they observe. Long ago, research workers demonstrated that aggressive teachers tend to have pupils in their classes who also show a high incidence of aggressive behavior. The kind of control that the teacher exerts over his own behavior is likely to provide a basis for pupils acquiring a similar form of control. Educators have long assumed that the intellectual habits of pupils are also influenced by the intellectual habits of the teacher. Teachers who are willing to admit that they do not know the answer to a question and who tell the children that they will have to find the answer in some authoritative source may be expected to have pupils who are willing to search for knowledge. All too often, teachers fail to provide a proper example of intellectual performance for pupils to follow. Teachers who say "That is the right answer because I say it is" or "That answer is right because it is in the book" are providing pupils with deplorable intellectual examples to follow. Teachers who shout at pupils are teaching them that if one has enough power, one can put everybody else in his place. In contrast, teachers who ask questions when some unusual object is brought to school by a pupil can demonstrate how inquiry is a means of arriving at knowledge.

Programs of teacher education do not generally attempt to provide the teacher with a list of behaviors he should try to manifest in order to exert a desirable influence on pupils. Perhaps the main reason for this omission from the teacher education curriculum is that there are a vast number of ways of behaving that may provide a desirable model for the pupil to emulate. Unfortunately, the omission of this topic from teacher education has led beginning teachers to underemphasize the important influence they have as models.

Establishing objectives and developing curricula: The role of the teacher in establishing objectives and developing curricula has changed from the day when he saw his function as primarily that of teaching the three Rs. Today, more than ever before, there is controversy concerning what should be the central objectives of education as well as how they should be achieved. The question of who should decide on the objectives is not settled, but there is a widely held belief that in a democracy there should be broad participation in the activity. Teachers do not set the overall objectives of the school program, but they may have important roles in connection with the task. The teacher is in a good position to advise on what objectives can be achieved with children at particular ages, as well as to help committees recognize the fact that the time a child spends in school is sufficient only to achieve a limited number of these goals. Although committee members discussing the objectives of education commonly hold the belief that the school exists only to prepare children for fitting into the adult world, the teacher knows from his professional studies that the schools have a still larger task. Education can do much more than merely prepare children to carry on the business of the world as it is known in the present. Education can shape the world so that it becomes a different place from what it is today. The task of education in shaping the future is a concept familiar to the teacher, but it is one quite unfamiliar to the typical citizen who participates in the planning of educational programs.

The teacher can provide committees concerned with the establishing of educational objectives a broad view of the issues that are involved and some professional advice on what can be accomplished and what cannot. In this respect, the teacher is somewhat like a judge who advises a jury on issues to be considered in arriving at a decision and on what are the relevant facts to be considered, although it is up to the jury to arrive at the decision after being fully informed. Teachers and other professional persons connected with education have vital roles to perform in helping groups to understand the issues involved in arriving at educational decisions.

Although the teacher may have no direct role in setting up the broad overall objectives of the educational system, he must work on the establishment of the day-to-day goals through which the objectives are achieved. The teacher also makes important decisions related to how the objectives are to be achieved. Skill in writing the English language can be achieved through such varied activities as composing formal written themes, helping to publish a newspaper, writing a letter to a friend, and preparing a speech on some important issue. The teacher has to make decisions concerning the most appropriate means for achieving these day-to-day goals.

Providing a source of concern for the pupil's welfare: Jackson (1968) has pointed out that a crucial function of the teacher is demonstrating concern for the pupil. Without such a concern, the school as an institution, run like a machine, may appear to be an inhospitable environment for the child. Even a smoothly running school where the work of each pupil is carefully planned on an individual basis may give the pupil the feeling that he is only a forced participant unless he knows that the teachers have a personal concern for him as a human being. One of Jackson's chief recommendations for improving the contemporary school is that greater attention be given to the development of such concern. The present mood of many pupils, which often leads to disruptive behavior, may make it difficult for teachers to feel warm concern for the welfare of each individual pupil, but developing it may be vital for improving the social climate of the school.

Determining the extent to which each pupil is making progress: Every teacher is responsible for finding out whether pupils are making progress at appropriate rates. If the teacher does not have this information, then he will not know which pupils need special help. The teacher also has responsibility in this respect for reporting to parents how their children are progressing. In addition, the administrative staff may need such information for many purposes, including that of identifying aspects of the curriculum that need to be changed.

Providing a guide for the development of values: Providing a guide for the development of values is an aspect of the role of the teacher long stressed by Raths (1969) but long neglected in the training of teachers. Classrooms may be chaotic and wholly lacking in any social order based on concepts of fairness, equality of rights, and respect for the dignity of others, or they may reflect the very essence of the humaneness of man. Over a century ago, Horace Mann wrote of the hundreds of schools that had to be closed during a single year in Massachusetts because of the disruptive behavior of pupils and of a smaller number that had to be closed because of the incompetence of teachers in maintaining an orderly school community. Similar examples of anarchy, and complete lack of moral values, are not hard to find in classrooms today. The problem of establishing a social order in the classroom that reflects basic moral principles remains one of the most important ones in education. A good educational climate is a highly moral climate, where the participants are dedicated to helping one another and where no one infringes on the rights of others. Only a little is known about how teachers can develop such a social climate, but it is known that it is all too easy for teachers to be unfair without even realizing that they are. For example, numerous studies show that teachers tend to give most help to the students who need help least, because teachers find such students more congenial than those who are struggling with academic failure (see Bidwell, 1972).

Helping children interact intellectually and socially in ways that enhance their maturity: The world children are being prepared to live in is one where groups explore problems and arrive at decisions. It is not like the world of the individual study carrel or of the desk at which the student sits forbidden to talk to other students. Preparation for the real world requires that pupils learn to interact constructively with each other. Unfortunately, such interaction among pupils is quite rare, the interactions in many classrooms being limited to those between each pupil and the teacher. A part of the teacher's art is arranging for constructive pupil interactions.

Research on Common Forms of Teaching

The obvious way to conduct research for the purpose of improving teaching is to go into the classroom and discover which aspects of teacher behavior have the greatest impact in producing pupil learning. Tests can measure the extent to which pupils have learned one or another aspect of the curriculum, and teacher behavior can be observed and recorded. What could be simpler than to find out which aspects of teacher behavior are correlated with pupil achievement and which appear to depress it? This simple formula for improving teaching has attracted research workers for nearly half a century, but today, after such inquiries have involved thousands of hours of observation in the classroom, only very meager knowledge has resulted. The enterprise has been a very expensive one on which millions of dollars have been spent, and much of the work has been undertaken by research workers of competence. The lack of a sizable and useful product from such research cannot be attributed to either lack of money or incompetent research workers, but rather it must be attributed to difficulties that are inherent in the enterprise. These difficulties are only slowly being identified.

Anyone who wishes to conduct a study of teachers and the effects they produce on pupils must begin by making some decisions concerning what aspects of teacher behavior he is going to observe and record. Classrooms are places filled with an immense richness of events. Teachers do thousands of different things and perhaps never quite repeat themselves, always performing even routine activities with a wealth of variation. In a sense, a particular act on the part of a teacher is a unique event, never to be repeated. Also, division of the behavior of the teacher into a set of acts is necessarily artificial, for the behavior involves a continuous flow.

In traditional kinds of educational research, rather broad categories of teacher behavior have been rated for the extent to which they occur or do not occur. Categories that have been used in many studies include warmth, praise, flexibility, enthusiasm, the extent to which the teacher talks, the extent to which the teacher clarifies, and the teacher's knowledge of the subject matter being taught. A very large number of studies indeed have been undertaken in which teachers were rated on such variables and the ratings were then compared with measures supposedly related to effectiveness of teaching. In the older studies, the measure of the effectiveness of teaching was typically a rating provided by the principal. Such measures are no longer used, because the overwhelming weight of evidence shows that the ratings of principals concerning the effectiveness of teachers in their schools are virtually worthless. When studies have been undertaken in which the ratings of principals were compared with the gains in achievement test scores made by the pupils, there was virtually no relationship between principal ratings and pupil gains in achievement. This finding is really not very surprising, because principals do not spend much time in the classrooms of their teachers, and when they do spend time there both teachers and pupils behave rather differently from the way they behave when the principal is in his office. An outside observer, who has nothing to do with the administration of the school system, is much more likely to be able to see typical conditions in classrooms than is the principal.

Most research workers today agree that the measure of teacher effectiveness that has the greatest and most direct validity at the present time is derived from the measured performance of the pupils. If one can demonstrate that pupils show a genuine gain in scores over a year on an achievement test related to the objectives of the school, then one has evidence that some aspect of the teaching situation has been effective. The effective aspect may be the materials used, the behavior of the teacher, or the influence of the home. The teacher's contribution may be drowned in the overwhelming weight of other contributions, which is why the effect of the teacher is not always detectable in studies in which different teachers are compared on the basis of pupil gains in achievement. At the best, only small relationships can be expected, because of the overwhelming effects of other conditions that influence learning.

The results of such studies are typically of limited utility for another reason. Suppose one finds that teachers who are rated high on enthusiasm are those who by and large produce the greatest pupil gains in achievement. This is an interesting piece of information, but what does one do with it after discovering it? Not much is achieved by telling the apprentice teacher that enthusiasm is probably a good thing to have, for he is likely to ask "What do I have to do to show enthusiasm?" The word *enthusiasm* describes a very broad category of behavior and represents only a rather vague idea. Some investigators believe that more can be accomplished by conducting research in which such broad categories of behavior are avoided. What they suggest is that the broad category be broken down into components such as the teacher showing interest in what the pupils do, expressing interest in their work, holding up to the class the work of pupils that is particularly noteworthy, and encouraging students to pursue further ideas they have. If enthusiasm can be broken down into such components, sometimes referred to as **specific behaviors,** then one can tell the trainee something about the ways he should behave if he wants to be perceived as an enthusiastic person.

Although one may attempt to break down the category of enthusiasm into smaller categories, this may not necessarily be a useful thing to do. It may be found that different teachers express enthusiasm in different ways and that there is no single pattern of expressing enthusiasm that has any universality. If the analysis leads to this type of conclusion, then it may be difficult to tell teacher trainees just how they should express enthusiasm. Breaking down large categories into small categories does not necessarily provide the solution to any problem. Broad categories have generally provided the best predictions of the measured gains of the pupils, but these provide the least useful information for the selection of teachers or for teacher training.

Rosenshine and Furst (1971) have summarized the results of the kinds of studies of teaching that we have been discussing. They find that there are several categories of behavior that show a quite strong and consistent relationship to student gains in achievement. These are described as clarity, variability, enthusiasm, task orientation and/or business-like behavior, and providing the student with opportunity to learn. In addition, teacher indirectness, a complex of behavior that involves the extent to which the teacher uses student ideas, also shows up as a positive attribute of teaching. Some of these categories have a commonsense relationship to pupil achievement. Certainly, if the teacher explains clearly whatever the pupil does not understand, then the pupil is going to achieve more than when the explanations are confusing to him. Equally obvious and noninformative are the relationships of student achievement and the business-like quality of the teacher or the opportunities provided for learning. These relationships simply tell the teacher to do the things that have long been recognized as the marks of a good teacher. Much less obvious in their relationships to learning are the categories of variability and enthusiasm. Apparently, teachers who show variability in their approach and in their plan of instruction have pupils who make greater gains than do teachers who follow a consistent and uniform pattern. This finding fits well with what is known about maintaining attention, for variability is the key to maintaining attention, as will be shown later in this book. The virtue of variability is almost certainly in the effect it has on the attention of the pupil.

In addition to the factors already discussed, which are quite firmly established as being related to student achievement, there are some conditions that appear to have a much weaker relationship to student gains. One of these is the extent to which the teacher uses student ideas. The relationship of this variable to pupil learning, if it is a genuine relationship at all, is quite obscure. Its impact on the pupil is probably complex. The teacher's use of student ideas may energize pupils, may function as a reinforcement, and may tie whatever is to be learned in with what has been previously learned. The discovery of this kind of a variable adds little to our knowledge of teaching, but perhaps it provides something in the category one might call "tips for teachers." Does a teacher's knowledge that using pupils' ideas makes a positive contribution to the classroom influence his behavior and subsequent teaching effectiveness?

13

. . . .

Research on Common
Forms of Teaching

One really does not know the answer to this question. Knowing what one should do is an entirely different matter from doing what one should do. Giving advice may not help as much as one would like it to.

Another variable showing a weak relationship to student achievement is the extent to which the teacher uses criticism. The relationship is a negative one; that is, the most critical teachers tend to produce lower achievement in students. This is just about what might be expected in terms of what is known about learning. Criticism is likely to depress performance. Criticizing a student may make him stop doing what he is doing, but what he was doing was probably the most adequate response that he had to the situation. Criticism may block the student from making what was already his best response, and his alternative responses for coping with the situation may be even less adequate. One suspects that if criticism of the student is also accompanied by helping him to perform more adequately, then a positive effect might be found, but criticism alone is likely to lead to an even poorer response.

Other variables that probably have some relationship to pupil gains are the extent to which the teacher uses structuring comments (states clearly the ideas the pupil has been groping to state), the extent to which the teacher moves from one level of discourse to another (usually from a complex explanation to a simple explanation), and the extent to which the teacher probes the ideas presented by students. These again are fairly obvious kinds of relationships between what teachers do and what pupils learn, and they are variables assumed to operate within the usual pattern of teaching found in American schools today. In schools that depart from this pattern, one would not expect to find such relationships. In the kinds of school programs based on the idea that the materials, and not the teacher, should do the teaching, they would have no relevance at all. A strong case can be presented by those who take the position that the materials should teach and that well-designed materials should not require the teacher to clarify, because the materials should be clear in the first place. Within such a program, the variable of the level of discourse would have no place because the materials would set the level of discourse and the teacher would not. If a pupil had difficulty in understanding the assignment given to him, he would be given an assignment at a simpler level. The task of the teacher would be to recognize that the pupil was having difficulties with the materials and to find simpler materials. The teacher would use his knowledge not to explain the materials but to find appropriate materials.

Thus it is evident that the variables related to effective teaching are never more than variables that pertain to a particular system of teaching. They are not universal variables, descriptive of all good teaching.

Rosenshine and Furst (1971) point out that the variables found to be significant in contemporary teaching cannot be written off simply as those that common sense says are important. They point out that common sense tells us that many other conditions should be important, but most of these other conditions do not show significant relationships to achievement.

They point out that among the other nonsignificant variables are the number of incidents of praise, the rated warmth of the teacher, and the rated amount of student participation. What is not known is whether these conditions are just nonsignificant, or whether they do not occur sufficiently frequently to leave a measurable mark on student achievement. This is the problem one always encounters when studying the effect of numerous conditions all operating at the same time under natural conditions. This is the advantage of studying the effect of the same conditions in a laboratory, for one can arrange an experiment so that only a few of the conditions are varied and so that the effects of each condition can be separated. Observation under natural conditions is limited in the information it can supply.

Interaction Analysis

The traditional approach to the analysis of teaching has been that of relating ratings of the way teachers behave, or the detailed counting of how often teachers do this or that, to estimates of how much pupils are learning, but ratings or the counting of behaviors are not the only procedures that the research worker can use for the study of teaching as it is. Some research workers believe that the crucial element in teaching is not so much an act or collection of acts on the part of the teacher as it is the interaction the teacher has with the pupils. Of course, teaching can involve a lecture with virtually no interaction with pupils, but in the elementary grades, and also in high school, the typical recitation procedure involves a continuing interaction between teacher and pupils. Observers of teaching typically agree that the very essence of good teaching is to be found in the nature of the teacher–pupil interaction. It is quite evident that the quality of interaction and the potential for learning are small when a teacher responds to a pupil by saying "What you are saying sounds silly." They are substantially greater when the teacher says "I know you are trying to say something important, but I am not yet clear what you have in mind, so try asking your question in another way." The one pronouncement can nip the student's idea in the bud, but the other can make the student's idea blossom forth. The two interactions are vastly different in quality. Many research workers believe that if they could study carefully the interactions taking place in the classroom, then they could discover the key to effective teaching. The study of these classroom events is referred to as **interaction analysis.**

Let us consider briefly this approach to the study of teaching. Numerous different methods exist for studying the interactions of teachers with students, as is evident from the volumes by Simon and Boyer (1970), who list seventy-nine of them. The best known of these systems is that of Flanders (1970), which has been used in hundreds of researches. Attempts have also been made to adapt the system so that it can be used for the training of teachers.

Let us consider the Flanders system quite briefly. In order to study classroom events, data have to be collected by a classroom observer, who sits in the classroom, usually toward the back. Several visits may be required to habituate the students to the presence of the observer, and data cannot be collected until this habituation has taken place. When it has, then the observer records his data. He cannot record everything going on in the classroom but restricts his observation and records to certain limited events. Indeed, he limits himself to recording only ten different kinds of events, denoted by the numbers 1 to 10. Of these, seven are what teachers do, two are what pupils do, and the tenth represents the occurrence of a silence or confusion in the classroom. The following is a list of the categories used, described in an abbreviated form:

Teacher Talk

1. Accepts and clarifies in a nonthreatening way an attitude or feeling tone of a pupil.
2. Praises or encourages.
3. Clarifies or uses the idea of a pupil.
4. Asks questions.
5. Lectures.
6. Tells a pupil what to do.
7. Criticizes, exercising authority.

Pupil Talk

8. Pupil answers teacher.
9. Pupil initiates talking.

Other

10. Silence or confusion.

The observer sits in the classroom and every three seconds writes down one of the numbers 1 to 10 to indicate the major event going on. Suppose the following dialogue took place:

Pupil: The book says iron gets bigger when it gets hot. I want to do an experiment to show that. How can I do it?
Teacher: Let's talk about this experiment. Let's say you have a piece of iron rod, about three feet long. What might you do then?

The observer, recording such a dialogue, would record 9 9 9 9 3 3 3 3. What the pupil said occupied twelve seconds, and for each three-second interval a 9 would be recorded, indicating that the pupil was engaged in self-initiated talk. The teacher then began to help clarify the pupil's idea concerning doing an experiment and spent about twelve seconds doing this, so four 3s are recorded. Now the record shows a 9 followed by a 3, that is, a pupil-initiated activity followed by a helping act on the part of the teacher. If the record were filled with such 9 3 sequences, a typical pattern of teaching in that classroom would be described. In another classroom, more typical of American classrooms, the pattern would be one with many 4 8 sequences in the record, indicating a pattern of teaching in which the teacher asks questions and the pupil gives answers. One can thus see that the data provided can give some indication of the pattern of teaching taking place in a particular classroom.

The technique has provided some evidence concerning the characteristics of teaching that produce the most favorable attitudes of pupils toward their schoolwork. Teachers who are indirect in their approach to teaching, whose pupils are most likely to initiate activity, are those most likely to have pupils with favorable academic attitudes. The technique has provided little information that has helped identify patterns of teaching that produce high pupil achievement, but it has provided some indications concerning how favorable pupil attitudes can be produced. The technique also has some possibilities of identifying features of a teacher's performance that may be responsible for poor student attitudes, and hence it has some potential for providing a basis for guidance and in-service training of teachers.

The findings from interaction analysis also have their limitations in that they have been derived from observation of very conventional classrooms. The teaching conditions that produce favorable pupil attitudes in classrooms where recitation techniques are concentrated on may be different from the conditions that produce favorable attitudes in open classroom types of situations in which the pupils exercise considerable freedom in choosing what they want to do.

Classroom Research: Limitations and Alternatives

The research considered up to this point represents one approach to the discovery of conditions that make for effective teaching. Perhaps a major limitation of this research is that it focuses on conditions in conventional classrooms and tells us something about how to improve conventional teaching. Such research does not generally provide a basis for the design of radically new, or different, or unconventional forms of teaching. Nevertheless, the research has made significant contributions.

Now let us turn to another research approach that has had a long history of providing knowledge useful for improving education—the approach of the laboratory scientist. The approach assumes that aspects of natural phenomena can be studied much more easily in isolation in the laboratory than they can be under natural conditions. A familiar example is that the chemist was never able to understand the intricate pattern of chemical processes taking place in nature until he was able to study some of these isolated in the laboratory. Many modern psychologists argue, by analogy, that only a limited amount about learning and teaching can be discovered by observing these in the infinitely complex web of events that constitutes a classroom. A better way to achieve understanding, it is proposed, is to bring into the laboratory small portions of the learning and teaching taking place in the classroom and to study these under carefully controlled conditions. The assumption is made that what is discovered in the laboratory can then be applied to improving teaching and learning in the classroom. At least, most of the older laboratory sciences have had success in applying laboratory knowledge to the solution of problems in the real world, and the anticipation is that the behavioral sciences will have similar success.

There is not the clear distinction that there superficially seems to be between direct classroom observation and laboratory experimentation. Sometimes the research worker may experiment with new techniques of teaching using classrooms as if they were laboratories and using observers to record what happens in the experimental and control classrooms. Such experiments in classrooms are difficult to undertake and have yielded rather limited results. When an experiment is conducted in a classroom, the experimenter has difficulty in controlling a large number of conditions that influence the outcomes, and the results are often clouded by these uncontrolled conditions.

Basic research, including laboratory research, has made substantial contributions to education. It has shown, for example, that the gifted child is typically a very normal child and is not characterized by weakness of personality and physique, as earlier generations believed him to be. This discovery does not show the teacher exactly how to treat the gifted child, but it does tell the teacher to respond to him as a perfectly normal child who has assets that most other children do not have. Research has shown that what is learned in one subject in school may do little to help a child learn another subject and even less to develop a generally disciplined mind. The teacher who knows this fact can then see that there has to be a good reason for introducing any subject into the curriculum and that a vague hope that a subject will improve the mind is not a good reason. The research does not tell the teacher what subjects or aspects of knowledge should be included in the school program, but it does tell him not to teach Latin merely because of some hope that it may help the child with English and not to teach mathematics in the hope that it may improve reasoning skills. A good reason for teaching Latin to a few children is that it opens the door for them to a magnificent literature. A good reason for teaching mathematics to most children is that it provides a practical and useful skill and opens to them a wide range of occupations.

Thus the laboratory sciences have potential for providing the teacher with knowledge he can use in making wiser decisions than he would be able to make without it. These decisions are made in a great many different areas of professional activity, including those involving the selection of curriculum material, the selection of the best point of time to intervene to help a pupil struggling with difficulties, the identification of means of resolving a pupil's learning difficulties, and the planning of ways to promote learning. Professional knowledge is used not only in making decisions about broad policies to be followed in the classroom but also in the minute-to-minute activities involved in teaching.

Observation of teaching provides information about teaching as it is, but experimental studies of learning can suggest new approaches to instruction.

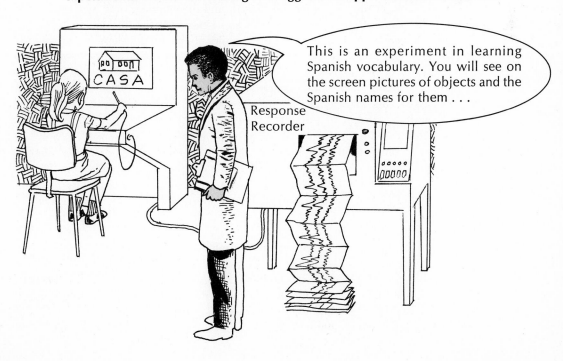

Knowledge derived from laboratory research has impact on the design of the equipment and materials through which education is improved. Sometimes this activity is referred to as educational product development, but this term is misleading, because educational materials and equipment are not so much educational products as they are educational tools. Educators have long realized that the design of books and other materials used for teaching students is a matter of critical importance, but until the present century design was largely a matter of common sense. Medieval educators, for example, were deeply concerned with the importance of arranging subject matter in an efficient sequence. For this reason, they attempted to prepare catechisms that fitted each item into a suitable sequence of ideas. Much of the teaching of the period was undertaken through catechistic procedures, and immense effort was directed toward designing these sequences. One may note that many modern educators have been similarly concerned with finding the "best" sequence for teaching particular aspects of subject matter and have designed programmed texts and programmed materials for use in teaching machines incorporating sequences that seem to be particularly effective for instructional purposes. The problems related to how to sequence subject matter still remain largely unsolved, but they are real and important problems. Our present interest in sequencing derives largely from laboratory research concerned with what is known as **operant conditioning.**

Efforts to improve the design of educational materials have not been confined to the age-old problem of sequencing subject matter, though that has been one of the major preoccupations of educators. Laboratory research on the psychology of growth and development has now evolved to the point where it seems to offer some basis for the design of curriculum materials. Much is known, for example, about the development of vocabulary and language in the child, and verbal materials can be designed in terms of this knowledge. Some information is also available on the kinds of thinking operations that children can and cannot perform at different ages. This knowledge can be incorporated in the design of schoolbooks and the design of problems based on concrete situations. In addition, there is emerging a science of perceptual psychology focused on how the child obtains information from the environment. This emerging science provides the knowledge necessary for designing an environment for the child such that he can readily abstract information from it. The psychology of perception also provides some knowledge that can be used in the design of audiovisual aids and concrete demonstrations of important phenomena of the real world.

Scientific research has prompted explorations of ways of teaching that are alternatives to the traditional methods of instruction used in most schools today. Teaching machines represent one experimental outgrowth of this kind of research. Although such devices are viewed here as experimental, they may ultimately lead to new ways of conducting instruction in schools. Attempts to make radical changes in the tools of the class-

20

· · · · · · · · · · ·

Introduction

room—the books, the displays, the equipment—represent an important impact of research and scientific knowledge on the process of education.

The Limits of the Role of Science in Changing Education

It is all too easy for the person who has had a taste of what scientific research can do for education to jump to the conclusion that all problems of education can be solved through taking a scientific approach. Such an unbalanced view fails to recognize that the central and most important problems of education are philosophical and not scientific. Whoever would attempt to develop an overall plan for education must first decide on the kind of society he wants education to build. Such a decision cannot be arrived at through scientific inquiry, because it is basically a judgment concerning the values to be achieved through living. Many scientifically based attempts to plan education make hidden judgments about the values to be achieved in living. Many of the plans for education based on experimental psychology make the implicit assumption that the main purpose of education is to shape the behavior of the young so that they will fit into the kind of industrial society that already exists. Such a view implies that education has the static role of maintaining society as it is and that behavior has to be shaped to conform to what society at present prescribes.

Others view the school as preparing children to make fundamental changes in the nature of society. Those who take such a position do not view the school as serving the mere function of shaping little human components of the great industrial machine but rather as preparing builders of a new social order. Those who take such a position do not deny the importance of teaching the traditional fundamental skills of reading, writing, speaking, calculating, and so forth. Indeed, many would emphasize the importance of these skills, but they would also want to teach children other skills such as those related to critical thinking in relation to social problems, willingness to embrace change, flexibility in thinking, and a host of other skills that would not be considered by those concerned solely with teaching children what they need to know to fit into current social structures. All too often psychologists have attempted to design programs of education without considering what the basic philosophical issues are in choosing one educational program rather than another. Indeed, some psychologists write as though educational programs should be judged in terms of the efficiency with which they do the things that have been traditionally done in schools.

This leads to consideration of the values that the author considers to be of prime importance and whether his values influence the content of this volume. The hope of the author is that readers of this volume can use the information provided to achieve more effectively whatever goals they believe to be the major ones of education. This is not a book on how to teach basic skills effectively, nor is it a book on how to teach children how to want to change society and the skills needed for actually changing

21
• • • • • • • • • •
The Limits of the Role
of Science in Changing
Education

it. It is a book on how to foster learning in children whatever the goals may be. At least, that is the intention of the author. Despite this intention, the personal philosophy of the author will inevitably show through between the lines, and sometimes in the lines themselves. On every page there is likely to at least be one sentence that tips off the reader about the personal values and prejudices of the author. Indeed, it is difficult to write a sentence that does not do so.

The way in which the teacher relates to children, and what the teacher does in the classroom, depends on tradition, on the prescriptions of the school system, on the books and materials available, and especially on what the teacher conceives to be the basic nature of man. Most teachers never pause to think in detail about their conception of the nature of man, despite the fact that this concept is of enormous influence on their behavior. One teacher attempts to control every aspect of pupils' behavior. Such a teacher assigns particular tasks to be undertaken at particular times. At the assigned time, that task is to be undertaken and no other task. Any behavior not directed toward the accomplishment of that task is discouraged, and perhaps even punished. The teacher makes judgments concerning the adequacy of pupils' performance and decides whether they shall take further work related to that task or move on to another task. The teacher, in this case, makes the assumption that learning has to be under the control of the teacher and that, indeed, for the school to function effectively the entire behavior of pupils must remain under teacher control. The learning that pupils undertake is believed by such a teacher to be controlled externally.

Another teacher shows an entirely different pattern of behavior in the classroom. This teacher permits some discussion of the goals to be achieved and some of the means through which these goals can be achieved. If the goal is to acquire speed in reading, then the teacher may explain that this goal is most readily achieved by extensive practice in reading interesting materials. Pupils may be encouraged to set up their own reading programs with the help of the school library and librarian and to establish dates by which particular reading tasks are to be undertaken. Children may be encouraged to integrate the work of achieving this goal with other goals they may have, as when a child interested in working with animals chooses to improve his reading skills with books on animals. The teacher, in this case, makes the assumption that children make important decisions in relation to what they learn and that learning is best accomplished when they make these decisions. Such a teacher may also encourage pupils to come and seek help whenever learning does not seem to be moving smoothly forward. The teacher is then making the assumption that pupils can tell when they are or are not accomplishing what seem to them to be significant goals and can make decisions about when they need help. On the other hand, the first of the two teachers considered here is likely to make the assumption that, if a pupil needs help, then something is wrong with the instructional materials for learning, which, if properly planned, should provide complete control over what the pupil accomplishes.

The two teachers have fundamentally different conceptions of the nature of children. The one teacher views children as if they were plastic pieces of material to be molded into shape, much as pieces of raw material are molded into shape as they pass through a factory. The other teacher views children as having some degree of internal control and as being capable of making some decisions concerning the kind of development that is going to take place in them. The extent to which children can be *correctly* viewed in the one light or the other is a matter one should be able to decide through research, but the fact is that psychologists have not yet succeeded in devising experiments to determine which of these two ways of looking at the human being and his behavior is most in accordance with reality.

Psychologists have been divided on this issue as long as teachers have. Some psychologists have defined the task of psychology as discovering the conditions that control behavior and have assumed that the conditions always lie in the external environment. The father of American behaviorism, John B. Watson, took this position. For him, a science of behavior consisted of discovering the conditions and events that had to be controlled in the environment in order that behavior could be controlled. For John B. Watson, control of behavior involved only the presentation of the right stimuli in the right order on the right occasions so that they would elicit the particular responses desired. In theory, at least, one person could learn to control completely the behavior of another person simply by exercising control over the stimuli presented to that person.

In more recent times, B. F. Skinner has taken up this theme and coined the term **stimulus control** to describe the state of affairs that exists when a particular stimulus elicits, or tends to elicit, a particular response. For example, familiar friends tend to elicit the response "Good morning" when they are encountered before 10 A.M., and the response is said to be under the control of the stimuli provided by the presence of friends. Skinner, in a series of works beginning with his classic *Behavior of Organisms* (1938), has attempted to describe the conditions wherein a response is brought under stimulus control. These conditions will be described later, for there are occasions in educational settings when one can successfully follow the recommended procedure and bring a response under stimulus control.

The idea that there are simple formulas that can be used to control behavior has widespread appeal. Because the world includes in its communities many individuals who would like, very much, to be able to control the behavior of many other individuals, whoever claims to have a formula for doing this is bound to have a following. The idea is guaranteed at least limited popularity, despite the fact that we all should be alarmed by the thought that a few men, armed with a simple formula, might be able to control the behavior and destinies of the rest of mankind. Fortunately, as will become evident later, any formula discovered up to this point seems to have quite limited utility for such purposes. Indeed, a simple formula with wide utility may never be found at all.

The main criticism of the conceptions of behavior that imply that

23

• • • • • • • • • •

The Limits of the Role
of Science in Changing
Education

behavior can be controlled through simple manipulations of stimuli comes from those who view the human learner not as a simple system of inputs and outputs but as a very complicated information-processing and decision-making system. Although it is true that the only way in which one human being can ever influence the behavior of another is through arranging for certain stimuli rather than other stimuli to be presented to him, the effect of a stimulus will depend partly on how the information contained in it is interpreted by the person whom it is intended to influence. Say to a child "Stop what you are doing," and one child takes this to mean that the time has now come to do other things. Another child, exposed to the same statement, reacts defensively, for the child takes it to imply that he is doing something he should not be doing. The information-processing systems of the two children have come out with different interpretations. In the last few decades, extensive knowledge has been developed concerning the nature of the human information-processing system, and this knowledge tells us a great amount about how information has to be presented in order to be recorded, stored, or used.

Many models of behavior assume that there is some decision-making component of the individual that has to be reckoned with when any attempt is made to influence behavior. Many branches of psychology have long had difficulty in accepting the idea that the human personality includes an element that actively makes decisions, though in recent times such an idea has become far more acceptable, because all computers include an "executive" unit that makes various decisions about what operation should be undertaken next.

Decisions may be either empty or nonempty — a distinction first made by the famous economist Shackle (1961). A decision is empty if it is one that does not really change the course of events. Some educational programs claiming that the work of each pupil is self-initiated may actually involve only empty decisions. The type of program in which each pupil works through a series of assignments at his own pace is of this character. In one such program, when the pupil finishes assignment number 248, he has a choice of repeating a similar assignment or of going on to assignment 249. The choice is a trivial one, for it is really determined by his test score. If it is low, then he does the same kind of assignment over again. If it is high, then he moves on to the next assignment in the sequence. In a sense, the work of the pupil is self-initiated in such a program, but only very trivially.

Nonempty decisions, on the other hand, are consequential decisions. They change the direction of what a person does in some significant way. An example of a significant decision on the part of a child is one that leads him to explore some area of knowledge new to him or one that makes him decide to master an assignment rather than just produce a minimal performance. Many schools that concede that children should make decisions permit the children to make only empty decisions. Relatively few schools encourage children to make nonempty decisions of consequence.

Summary

1 Substantial changes have taken place in education since the last century, when the schools were characterized by intensive drill in subjects chosen because they were hard and were believed to train the mind. The changes that have taken place are largely a result of changes in our concept of the nature of man.

2 Proposals to reform education come from many directions, but the main programs come from those who take extreme positions, advocating either increased emphasis on control or increased emphasis on reducing controls.

3 Major activities engaged in by the teacher include performing routine management functions and functions related to bringing pupils into contact with materials and ideas, directing and redirecting pupils' energies, identifying special learning handicaps, explaining, demonstrating, informing, and providing a model for pupils. In addition, some teachers may become involved in establishing objectives and developing curricula. An activity in a rather different category is that of providing a source of concern for pupils' welfare.

4 Many have long believed that the best way to improve education is to conduct research in the classroom. If there is something wrong with the schools, the obvious approach is to go into the classrooms, find out what is wrong, and then put it right. Although a great deal of research has been undertaken on this basis, the results have been somewhat disappointing. One of the difficulties of the approach is that the teacher is only one factor of many, and it may be difficult to determine whether educational inadequacy is due to the teacher, the textbook, the curriculum, or something else. There are also difficulties in applying what has been learned from research. If it is discovered that teaching would be improved if teachers were more enthusiastic, then how does one drum up enthusiasm in teachers? Attempts have been made to overcome this difficulty by breaking down broad categories of behavior, such as enthusiasm, into components. The components, because they are more identifiable, should be more teachable, but the fact is that this approach has not been too productive.

5 From the numerous studies of teacher effectiveness that have been undertaken, several broad categories of behavior have shown a consistent and strong relationship to student gains in achievement. These are described as clarity, variability, enthusiasm, and task orientation. There is a certain commonsensical relationship of these characteristics to teaching,

but common sense has been wrong as well as right. In addition, a much weaker relationship has been found between the amount pupils learn and the extent to which teachers use student ideas and the extent to which teachers use criticism of pupils. Criticism tends to depress student performance.

6 Studies of the classroom tell us how to improve teaching as it is. They tell us little about how to design fundamentally different and more effective ways of teaching.

7 In recent years, extensive effort has been devoted to the analysis of the interactions between teachers and pupils. A very large number of different systems have been developed for the study and recording of the interactions taking place in the classroom. The commonest in use is that developed by Flanders, which has the advantage of great simplicity and ease of data collection. The system has provided considerable evidence concerning some of the conditions that produce favorable attitudes toward learning, but it has done little to identify conditions that produce pupil growth in knowledge and understanding.

8 Because classroom research has been somewhat limited in what it has achieved, alternative approaches have been sought. One obvious alternative is to do what other areas of social service such as medicine have done, conduct research in the laboratory. Most medical research is not conducted in the physician's office, though some is. Most great medical discoveries are made in the laboratory, and perhaps great discoveries concerning how teaching can be improved also must be derived from laboratory studies. Laboratory science has some potential for doing this and has a record of producing important ideas that have influenced teaching in the past. Laboratory research also has a record of improving the design of equipment and materials through which the student learns.

9 The emerging science of growth and development is providing important information about the ways in which a well-designed environment can facilitate learning in the child.

10 Science always has certain limitations. Most scientific attempts to improve education make hidden judgments about what is worthwhile in life. What the scientist believes to be worthwhile may not be what others judge to be worthwhile. Some scientists wish to develop a school system in which children are molded to fit into a social system, but others would like to see children develop in such a way that they will want to change the social system. Issues of value are not solved by scientific research. A major issue is whether education should bring men under control or whether it should free them from immediate controls.

A good place to begin the study of learning related to schooling is the early life of the child, long before he enters elementary school. What happens to the child in the early years does much to determine what happens to him in school and in life. During the early years, his appetite for learning is either whetted or dulled, and the foundation is laid for the attitudes that constitute such a large part of the adult personality. In addition, in the early part of life the adaptive behavior of the infant and child illustrates many forms of learning that play an important role in subsequent development.

A distinction is sometimes made between the terms **growth** and **development.** Growth refers to an increase in the physical dimensions of the body, and particularly in the skeletal and muscular structures. On the other hand, development refers to an increase in specialization or

2

Basic Learning Processes in Infancy

organization either of the functions performed by the various bodily organs or of behavior. Thus while growth takes place in infancy and the body increases in strength, there is also a development of function. By the end of the first year, the legs and arms no longer simply perform uncoordinated motions, but the legs have become instruments for walking and the arms and hands have become tools for grasping and manipulating objects. This change in the use of the limbs represents development and involves more than a sheer increase in size. The process of development involves differentiation of function (the legs come to do something different from the arms), and the activities involved become part of a coordinated system of behavior.

Many fine textbooks have been written for teachers about human growth and development. These include books by Gordon (1969b), Mussen et al. (1969), and Stone and Church (1968). This chapter cannot do what these texts do; its purpose is much more limited, to introduce the reader to some of the learning processes that control development.

Let us begin by considering the child at birth. The newborn child, that is, the **neonate,** is born with a nervous system in which many basic structures do not yet function or do not function with full effectiveness. The neonate has difficulty in regulating his temperature. The structures related to crawling, walking, and otherwise moving about in the environment have not yet reached a level of development where they can function at all, and many of the fibers of the brain have not acquired the sheath of myelin that insulates them from other fibers and permits them to function as independent units within a system. The neonate is not a simplified adult with a brain lacking traces of experience with the world. The infant is a very different creature from the adult, not just in the experience he has stored but in the equipment he has functioning in his brain.

Hutt et al. (1969) have brought together the information available on the behavior of the child shortly after birth. Unfortunately, there are problems related to the study of infants at birth, because the circumstances of birth, and often the drugs given to the mother, may have a disturbing effect on the infant's behavior. Study of the behavior of the neonate is somewhat analogous to study of the behavior of an adult immediately after an automobile accident in which his entire nervous system was badly shaken. Sometimes as long as three days or a week may pass before the behavior of the infant ceases to show the traumatic effects of delivery.

The human neonate has a limited repertoire of behavior, which does not suddenly appear at birth but has slowly emerged during the period of gestation. Some responses to touch have been recorded in embryos only eight to ten weeks old. The hand will show signs of closing on objects before the embryo is fifteen weeks old, the response of withdrawing the leg appears at about the same time, and sucking behavior occurs at about twenty-four weeks. Babies have been born with calluses on the thumb from thumb sucking before birth.

The determination of the responses that the infant can make to particular stimuli is not the simple matter it might appear to be on the surface, for the response of an infant depends very much on the state it happens to be in. In a broad sense, one can say that the infant has two states, sleeping and waking, and that he spends about 70 per cent of his time in the sleeping state. This is a gross oversimplification of what happens, for the infant may be in any state between the two and may remain so for long stretches of time, much as an adult may spend the early hours of the morning in a twilight stage in which he is half awake and half asleep. Hutt et al. adopt a system of five states, varying from a state in which the eyes are closed, the breathing is regular, and there are no movements except occasional startle responses to a state of maximum activity in which the infant is crying. The intermediate states are the state of having the eyes closed but with irregularities of breathing and heart rate and with small muscle movements, the state of having the eyes open but with no gross movements, and the state in which the eyes are open and gross movements occur. The states are claimed to be distinct conditions, and each represents a characteristic cluster of behaviors that tend to go together. A baby may spend a few minutes in moving from one state to another but does not stay long in a condition between one state and another, though he may stay for long periods of time in one state. The state in which the infant happens to be depends on an interaction of internal circumstances and external conditions. The temperature of the environment is one of the most important conditions determining state. Noise has the opposite effect on an infant than it has on an adult, in whom it produces an aroused and awakened state. In the infant, moderate amounts of auditory stimulation tend to produce a state of sleep. Surrounding the infant with blankets and clothes tends to decrease the activity of the baby and to lower the respiratory rate and the pulse. Internal conditions also affect the state of the infant, including the schedule of nursing, and there appears to be a certain degree of cyclic activity built into the very young child. In the study of what the child can do during the first few weeks of life, the common practice is to experiment with him when he is either awake and passive or awake and making gross bodily movements, though some studies have been conducted on sleeping infants and on infants that are in a more active state of fussing. The infant spends about eighteen hours of the twenty-four hour day in sleep. For two to three hours a day the baby is awake and quiet, and for one or two hours a day he is awake and active. For the remaining one to three hours, he is awake and either crying or fussing. The infant may spend an hour or more in one state at a time, but only a few minutes in moving from one state to another.

Early in the first few weeks of life, a number of other behaviors occur that are under a high degree of stimulus control. The infant will, for example, fixate with his eyes for short periods on a small bright source of light. Turning of the head in the direction of a sound is also claimed to occur early in life and perhaps shortly after birth, if not at birth. The infant also shows a great many reflexes, some of which are similar to those of the adult and some not. For example, reflexes of the pupil of the eye

The sucking behavior of the infant is partly under the external control of the stimuli provided by the bottle.

Internal controls coordinate the activity. The internal schemata develop as the activity is pursued and involve experiences such as those of touching the bottle and seeing the mother.

are the same as in the adult, but reflexes of the foot when the sole is touched lightly are not. This point is raised to indicate that the nervous system of the child has similarities to and differences from the nervous system of the adult.

A particularly interesting response is that termed the **orienting response.** This is a response first discovered by Pavlov, who referred to it as the what-is-it reflex. American psychologists have sometimes called it the **attending response,** a term that loosely describes its functions. The orienting response occurs when a new stimulus is presented and responded to by the infant. The response includes a cessation of on-going activity, dilation of the pupils, dilation of the blood vessels in the forehead, a respiratory pause, and other characteristic responses. In the adult, the orienting response occurs on occasions when the individual says that he is attending to some object or event. The response occurs not only in the typical neonate but even in the embryo only twenty-six weeks old. The early development of the orienting response suggests that the embryo is, in a sense, ready to respond to environmental events at a very early stage of development. Components of the orienting response have been used to determine the stimuli to which very young babies will respond. The newborn infant shows an orienting response to a wide range of stimuli and by the fourth month shows a stronger orienting response to an unfamiliar complex stimulus, such as the face of a stranger, than he does to a familiar complex stimulus such as his mother (see Fitzgerald, 1968).

There are now ways of demonstrating that infants, in the first few weeks of life, retain information about what they see. It can be shown, for example, that an infant fixates on a pattern presented to his field of view. Later, when the same pattern is presented together with another pattern, the infant fixates on the new pattern for a longer time than the original one. This means that the infant has retained information about the original pattern (see Walcher and Peters, 1971).

Despite the fact that the newborn infant behaves, in many ways, as if he were ready to pick up information from the environment, as is evident from his orienting response, his stage of development is still such that he is greatly limited in the information from the environment that he can use. For example, the region of the brain that handles the analysis of visual information appears to be very incompletely developed until about three or four months after birth. Ellingson (1967) points out that, up until three or four months of age, the electrical rhythms of that part of the cortex of the brain (the occipital areas) are rudimentary, but after that age the normal rhythms of the older person become well established and the infant begins to show a capability of performing visually related tasks such as grasping at objects he sees.

The facts that the infant is able to fixate on a bright light and is able to respond to a moving light (Wickelgren, 1969) do not imply that there is any analysis made of the information. Even simple attending responses to moving lights are primitive in that they may involve only one eye and do not involve two-eye coordination.

This picture of the infant drawn up to this point is that of a living creature whose behavior is controlled to some degree by the stimuli provided by the environment. Stimuli control simple behavior such as that of sucking, for the baby generally does not suck unless it is appropriately stimulated from within or without. Stimuli also control general states, such as that of sleeping and waking, for sleep can be produced in a wide-awake baby by patting him rhythmically and a loud noise will wake the sleeping infant. On the other hand, some behavior does not seem to be the result of any particular set of events in the environment. The typical fussing or crying of the infant seems to be quite unrelated to environmental circumstances and to such matters as whether the child does or does not receive much attention. The idea that attending to a baby who is crying will increase the amount of crying is probably false, for crying behavior is triggered by circumstances within the child. Such behavior can be brought under temporary control by patting the baby and changing his general state to one of sleep, but the control is only temporary.

Before further facts about the behavior of the infant are presented, let us consider a few terms widely used in contemporary psychology. When a behavior occurs in the presence of certain stimuli, that is, in the presence of certain events in the environment, it is said that the behavior is under **stimulus control,** as described previously. This simply means that the behavior can be turned on or turned off by the presence or absence of the particular stimuli. Behavior naturally under stimulus control, that is, simple behavior that occurs in the presence of a stimulus without any learning first having to take place, is commonly referred to as a **reflex.** The eyeblink of the infant that occurs when a mild puff of air strikes his eyelid is a reflex. A reflex is called a simple behavior because its major characteristics can be described in simple terms and not because it involves simple physiological processes. Indeed, the processes in a simple reflex response may involve many million nerve cells located in parts of the nervous system both near and far from the physical location of the reflex action.

An event that produces a reflex is called an **unconditioned stimulus.** This term means that the stimulus produces a uniform and predictable response, but it is a response produced without any learning taking place first. A reflex is often described in parallel terms as an **unconditioned response.** The infant shows a great number of unconditioned responses, that is, responses directly under the control of unconditioned stimuli.

A great range of reflex responses that occur in very early infancy have to do with basic biological functions necessary for maintaining life. Thus sucking is necessary for nutrition, the dilation and contraction of the pupil of the eye are necessary for protecting the internal eye, the eyeblink has other eye-protecting functions, salivation is necessary for digestion and preventing the mucous membranes from drying out, coughing removes foreign matter from the throat and bronchial tubes, and so on.

Among the early organized responses, one of the most striking and interesting is smiling. Scott (1967) finds that this response does not occur before the end of the fifth week but that nearly all infants show the response by the third month. Research in this area is made difficult by smiling-like responses that occur during the first few weeks after birth but are more like muscular spasms of the face than they are the familiar smile. In Scott's summary of research, he reaches the conclusion that the response belongs in the category of **primary socialization** and that it is an inborn social response unique to man. He notes that it is primarily a response to the human face but that any facelike object may elicit it. He suggests that the response is not elicited in the first few weeks because the infant does not have the perceptual skill needed to differentiate faces from other objects. Scott also cites evidence indicating that the association of the smiling response with the presence of a face is not because the presence of a human face has been associated with feeding. He cites an experiment in which babies were fed by individuals wearing masks, but the masks did not acquire particular properties of eliciting smiling responses.

Although the smiling response is unique to man, other species have responses that are related to early socialization. The dog, for example, has the tail-wagging response, which begins to appear at about the third week after birth and seems to be primarily a social response, though it occurs both in contacts with other dogs and in contacts with human beings. The dog's social contacts with human beings are very similar to the contacts it has with other dogs. The latter involve walking and running together, romping, nipping with the mouth, and so forth. The human primary social response appears to be confined to behavior toward other human beings.

The smiling response lays the groundwork for future social development. Because the smile of the baby arouses a positive social response in the adult, it forms a basis for future social interactions.

Within a few weeks of birth, many responses, triggered originally only by a particular stimulus, come to be triggered by new stimuli. For example, sucking behavior is triggered at first only by stimulation of the lips; then it comes to be triggered by the baby being picked up and later by the appearance of the mother. This is a case of **Pavlovian conditioning** or **classical conditioning,** which most readers of this text will already know something about. As the reflex responses of the baby become triggered by an increasing number of stimuli, Gagné (1970) would say that the baby comes to learn that certain events come to **signal** other kinds of events, as when being picked up comes to be a signal for eating.

Let us depart here briefly from the main trend of the discussion to describe the general nature of classical conditioning. Pavlov demonstrated nearly a hundred years ago that if a reflex is triggered by stimulus X, and if stimulus Y occurs at about the same time as X, then Y acquires the property of triggering the reflex. A puff of air produces the typical eyeblink response, but if the puff of air is always accompanied by the sound of a bell, then the bell acquires the power of setting off the eyeblink. The bell has become the **conditioned stimulus** for the eyeblink. The phenomenon is usually demonstrated through the use of some response involving a reflex, but it probably does not have to involve a reflex. Presumably, a stimulus that accompanies a response (whatever its source) acquires some capability of eliciting the response, and the conditioned reflex is a special case of the phenomenon. The essential characteristic of classical conditioning is that a stimulus occurs at about the same time as a response and acquires the property of eliciting the response. Sometimes this is described as **contiguity learning,** denoting that the stimulus and the response it is to be tied to must be contiguous, that is, must occur at about the same time. Some psychologists have attempted to maintain that all learning is of this character, but most psychologists would probably maintain that this kind of learning is probably only one of several kinds. The issue is highly controversial. One can say that classical conditioning can take place even before birth (see Brackbill, 1967) and that it continues to be an important form of learning throughout life.

An interesting case of conditioning in infancy is that commonly described as **conditioning to the stimulus of time.** This description is confusing because time is not a stimulus in the sense in which a bright light or a bell or pressure on the skin is a stimulus. Let us illustrate the phenomenon with an example. Suppose that a two-month-old child is lying on his back in his crib and that he is in a waking state, showing some random movements of his arms and legs. Now let us suppose that the experimenter arranges for there to be a marked increase in the brightness of the illumination for a ten-second period at the beginning of each minute. Each time the light goes on, the pupils of the baby's eyes promptly contract and then expand again after the added illumination is turned off. After many trials with the increased illumination, the mechanism is turned off. However, a minute after the last time the light was turned up, the pupils of the baby's eyes contract as though there had been an increase in illumination, despite the fact that there was none. The phenomenon represents time conditioning and clearly illustrates that infants have what might be called a time sense. It shows a primitive capability on the part of the infant to show behavior related to anticipation or expectancy, though we are not saying here that the infant expects or anticipates the presence of the bright light. This kind of conditioning represents a quite complex form of behavior. Strangely enough, this kind of temporal conditioning of the pupillary reflex does not seem to take place in the adult. The adult probably has a much better time sense than the infant, but it seems to be dependent on other mechanisms. The adult lives in a world in which events occur at particular times, and these events become time signals. Under such conditions, primitive mechanisms probably do not have to function.

Some of the activity of the very young infant is organized to a considerable degree. Sucking and eating behavior shows such organization from the start. Fixation of the eyes on bright objects that stand out against the background is another area of organized behavior. Later, **prehension,** that is, grasping with the hand, shows organization. Piaget (see Flavell, 1963) takes the position that underlying these behaviors are what he calls **schemata,*** that is, structures in the nervous system that permit the primitive organization of behavior. Thus Piaget speaks of a schema for sucking and a schema for sight. The schema also represents a focus around which subsequent experiences and memories of the experiences become organized. Similar kinds of psychological organizations are proposed by those investigating the development of language. Such research workers, called **psycholinguists,** have proposed that the baby has potential for organizing speech sounds he hears, and, although they do not refer to the underlying organizing structures as schemas, the basic concept is very similar.

Now let us turn to another form of learning in infancy not primarily related to reflexive behavior. Let us take as an illustration findings from a study conducted by Sheppard (1969) on his own three-month-old infant. The data of interest to us here consist of the leg-kicking movements of the infant. All normal infants kick their legs spontaneously from time to time. Sheppard was able to arrange a device in a special plexiglas crib in which the infant lived so that each kick of the legs tripped a switch and recorded the motion. Sheppard observed how frequently this happened under conditions prevailing before the experiment. He then arranged the equipment so that each leg kick was followed by a flashing light and the playing of a short recording of the mother's voice. The record of the mother's voice had been made during breast feeding, and a short section of this recording was played, monotonously, after each leg kick. When this procedure was followed, the leg kicks began to take place more frequently. Then Sheppard turned off the voice recording and the flashing light, and the leg kicking tended to slip back toward the original rate. The point to note is that the sound of the mother's voice and the flashing light exerted some control over the leg kicking. Perhaps leg kicking is not the most significant response in the world, but the experiment is useful to us here in illustrating some learning phenomena that occur later in more significant contexts.

Before discussing this experiment and its implications at greater length, let us introduce a few terms that will simplify much of our discussion. First, let us consider the leg-kicking form of behavior. This is an activity in which infants engage. It is not produced by any particular stimulus that one can identify. A baby just kicks from time to time. Such behaviors that are not initially under any kind of stimulus control are sometimes referred to as **emitted behaviors.** The rate at which the leg kick occurred before the mother's voice and flashing light were introduced is the **baseline rate.** The experimenter was able to arrange conditions so that he could increase the rate of kicking above the baseline rate, and he could then cause the rate to decline again.

* Piaget uses *schemata* for the plural of *schema.* Many American authors use *schemas* for the plural. In each case, that author's preference has been used in this book.

Are these instances of classical or instrumental conditioning?

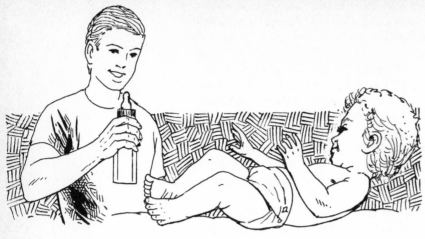

The baby begins to suck as soon as she sees her father with the bottle!

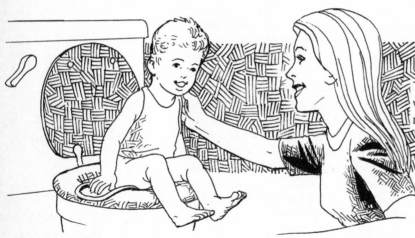

The baby has a bowel movement when placed on the toilet. The mother pats him affectionately.

The baby cries at the sight of the diaper safety pin.

The combined playing of the mother's voice and the flashing of the light are referred to as a **reinforcer** or a **reinforcing event.** This means that it has the property of increasing the frequency of the particular behavior that it follows. Sometimes it is said that a reinforcer strengthens a response. In the particular experiment described, it could be said that the reinforcer was contingent on the leg-kicking response or that the leg kick was the contingency reinforced. After the frequency of the leg kick has been increased, through being followed by a reinforcer, the leg kick is then said to be an **operant.** Skinner coined this term because the behavior "operates on the environment to generate consequences" (Skinner, 1953, p. 65).

This form of learning is sometimes called **instrumental conditioning** or **instrumental learning,** because the behavior involved is the instrument for producing particular events in the environment. The baby learns that the leg kick turns on the mother's voice and flashing light.

Now certain characteristics of reinforcing events must be noted. The reinforcing event just discussed involved a combination of a recording of the mother's voice and a flashing light—and surely the reader must think of this as an odd combination. One can readily understand intuitively that the voice of the mother might be reinforcing, but why the flashing light? The answer to this question is given by Sheppard in his paper. He states that he found by trial and error that a combination of these two events was a strongly reinforcing happening. No doubt he was also influenced by other studies showing that in the case of the very young infant a flashing light does act as a reinforcer. There is also a very large experimental literature in the field of animal psychology showing that a mere increase or decrease in illumination may provide a reinforcement for animal behavior. The point to be brought out by this is that one discovers reinforcing events, to some extent, by experimentation. Intuition may help one to discover some of the reinforcers of child behavior, but it cannot be the sole basis for discovering reinforcing events, and sometimes it is not even a sound basis. Sometimes teachers are wrong in the judgments of what is and what is not reinforcing. Once there was a teacher who thought she could help the work habits of a child by letting him out on the playground for a short time after the completion of each assignment. The reinforcement did the opposite of what it was intended to do. The reason was that the child had learned to avoid the playground because there he was mistreated by other pupils. When the teacher sent the child to the playground, she was punishing him. Experimenters have found a wide range of unexpected reinforcing events in the case of the very young human infant. Some studies use sound for this purpose, generally a tone about an octave above middle C. Other studies have used a vibrator that provides a rather mild tickle. Still others have used the appearance of a picture of a human face as a reinforcer, or even facelike illuminated signs (Watson, 1969). The kinds of events that have reinforcing properties for infants are varied indeed, and they are also large in number for older children and adults, but probably different in kind.

The Sheppard experiment brings out another phenomenon of considerable importance. Recall the fact that when the reinforcer was withdrawn, the infant began to show a reduced rate of kicking his leg. In technical terms, one would say that the response was becoming extinguished. In time, the operant will return to the baseline rate from which it started. **Extinction** is a set of circumstances in which behavior that has been acquired through reinforcement is allowed to occur but without the occurrence of the reinforcer.

Extinction may occur also in the case of classically conditioned responses. Let us return to the case of temporal conditioning of the infant exposed to a bright light that flashed on once every minute. The pupillary response of the infant became conditioned so that it occurred at the beginning of each minute, even though there was no increase in illumination, but this response would not continue once every minute for the rest of the child's life. Each time it occurred, it would be less marked, until it would ultimately fade away. This represents extinction of a classically conditioned response.

Many responses that have been extinguished are rapidly relearned when favorable learning conditions are reintroduced. If the leg-kicking activity of the infant is reinforced again, after perhaps only a single reinforcement he is kicking as rapidly as at the end of the previous set of reinforcements. This is a very important point, for it means that responses that may appear to have been reduced in strength or eliminated may have been just temporarily inhibited. Indeed, many psychologists would take the position that extinction procedures perhaps inhibit a response only temporarily rather than produce any actual reduction in underlying strength. Some psychologists would even go so far as to say that whatever is learned is learned permanently and irreversibly. This is quite a frightening thought, and it may well be not far from the truth.

Operants are brought under the control of reinforcing contingencies by the kind of process that has been described. This kind of process represents a form of learning, just as classical conditioning represents a form of learning. It comes within the definition of learning in that learning is generally defined as being relatively enduring modification of responses produced by encounters with the environment. In the case of the kicking response, the modification involved an increase in frequency of the response. The events that led up to this change in response frequency are commonly referred to as the acquisition phase of learning. Acquisition and extinction are usually contrasted, because they appear to have opposite results, but extinction is not quite the opposite of acquisition, for during the extinction phase the response learned during acquisition is blocked from appearing rather than eliminated.

In summary, then, one can say that neonates and very young infants already have a repertoire of responses under stimulus control and that, through simple forms of learning, new stimuli in the environment acquire the property of also controlling many of these responses. The mechanisms involved are those of classical conditioning and instrumental conditioning, both of which continue to play a role throughout the remainder of life. These are not the only mechanisms involved, but they are the ones that play roles in the early stages of infant development and perhaps sometimes even before birth. Examples will be discussed later of obvious instances of both of these mechanisms influencing the behavior of the schoolchild, even though they tend to become overshadowed by other forms of learning. In addition, the infant has some capacity for learning through mere exposure to events, as is evident from the studies cited earlier.

Some psychologists have attempted to reduce all learning to the categories of instrumental conditioning and classical conditioning, but many suspect that this is a gross oversimplification of human behavior. Many forms of behavior that are learned, particularly verbal behavior, are not readily squeezed into these categories, though attempts have been made to do so. Nevertheless, classical conditioning and instrumental conditioning are important categories of learning, and knowledge gained through the study of these forms of learning has provided important keys to the understanding of many forms of behavior. Of interest is the fact that an understanding of these forms of learning has done much to develop ways of handling behavior problems, both in and out of school, and has even led to the development of new techniques of psychotherapy.

Schedules of Reinforcement

Laboratory studies of operant conditioning since midcentury have focused to a very great degree on the problem of the effect on behavior of what are known as **schedules of reinforcement.** Obviously, a person or machine controlling the reinforcement of a living creature may provide a reinforcing event every time a particular class of behaviors occurs or only on certain occasions. When the reinforcement occurs on every occasion, it is commonly described as **continuous reinforcement.** When the reinforcing event occurs only on some occasions when the behavior occurs, but not on others, the condition is known as **partial reinforcement.** Psychologists long ago established that, in laboratory experiments with both animals and human beings, the partial reinforcement situation produces both slower learning and slower extinction. This interesting discovery did not settle all the issues involved, for there are many systems that may be used for scheduling when a reinforcement is to occur and when it is not. The study of the effects of these various systems on learning constitutes a problem to which we must now turn.

The classic work on schedules of reinforcement is that of Ferster and Skinner (1957). Here, as in most other research conducted since that time, the concentration of effort was on work with animals, partly because automated laboratories permit the collection and collation of vast amounts of data on the topic without consuming much of the experimenter's time. The findings have to do largely with the maintenance of behavior rather than with the modification of behavior.

Most of the schedules studied can be classified either as reinforcements occurring after a particular interval or as reinforcements occurring after a particular number of responses. Let us consider first reinforcements after a particular interval. A pigeon learns to peck at a small white disk on the wall of its training box, referred to as a **key.** The experimenter decides to reinforce the animal for a response occurring at the end of each minute, and no other responses are reinforced. This procedure is referred to as a **fixed-interval schedule.** Under these circumstances, the animal shows a typical pattern of behavior. As the schedule of reinforcement is applied, the pigeon's behavior settles down into a pattern. After each reinforcement, the pigeon stops pecking at the disk until nearly a minute has elapsed, then it will peck rapidly at the disk until it receives the next reinforcement. Then it stops pecking again for about another fifty seconds. The behavior of the animal is intermittent. The schedule of reinforcement is not suitable if the experimenter desires to maintain behavior, for when the reinforcement is withdrawn, extinction takes place rapidly.

Let us now consider a second major category of reinforcement schedule referred to as the **variable-interval schedule.** The reinforcement is set to occur at responses taking place at particular intervals of time, but the intervals are variable. The interval between any two reinforcements may be set by drawing a number at random from a set of numbers representing the various intervals to be represented. Animals trained on a variable-interval schedule of reinforcement show a uniform output of behavior. The pigeon thus trained to peck at a key continues to peck very uniformly and for long periods. If the intervals between reinforcements are too long, then the behavior is extinguished. However, the intervals can be *slowly* lengthened until they are so far apart that the animals appear to maintain the pecking behavior with almost no reinforcements at all. Animals will, of course, give up a particular form of behavior for reasons other than extinction. One such reason is sheer fatigue.

In contrast with the fixed-interval schedule, the variable-interval schedule can produce behavior quite resistant to extinction, particularly when the intervals are gradually increased.

A third type of schedule is the **fixed-ratio schedule,** in which the reinforcement appears after a particular number of responses. The animal exposed to such a schedule shows a very uniform output of behavior. The pigeon pecks consistently, and almost with rhythm. The response is also very readily extinguished. The omission of just three or four reinforcements may be sufficient to produce at least a temporary cessation of the response. Because the nervous system is particularly sensitive to identifying almost any kind of regularity in events, the pigeon is able to identify almost immediately a change in circumstances and adapt its behavior to the new circumstances. The operant-conditioning psychologist, in discussing this situation, prefers to say only that the behavior of the pigeon on a fixed-ratio schedule is readily extinguished.

A fourth type of schedule is a **variable-ratio schedule.** Just as in the variable-interval schedule one of many different systems can be used for determining each time interval, so too in the variable-ratio schedule the number of responses between each reinforced response is varied in some way. The number of responses between two reinforced responses may be derived by drawing a number at random from a selected group of numbers, and it may also be increased as the series goes on in order that the response may become progressively less dependent on the reinforcement. The variable-ratio schedule, once it is turned off, may result in behavior highly resistant to extinction.

The different effects of different schedules of reinforcement have long been claimed to have implications for education. The main application they have in a school situation would be the maintenance of general habits of behavior such as orderliness, neatness, and courteousness. In order to maintain such trends in behavior, or even to improve on them, teachers have long provided reinforcement on a variable-ratio or a variable-interval basis. They have not done this by design, but they have adopted such schedules because their contacts with each pupil, on a personal basis, are necessarily limited, and it is through such contacts that reinforcements are supplied. The typical reinforcer is praise, though nobody knows just how good a reinforcer this is at different educational levels. Social psychologists have long believed that at the age of adolescence praise from the adult is almost worthless but that endorsement by other adolescents has powerful reinforcing properties. Among very young children, praise and warm supportive behavior on the part of the adult appear to be an effective reinforcer, particularly for the behavior of girls (see Nickell and Travers, 1963).

Development of New Behavior

Up to this point, consideration has been given to some of the ways in which a baby's initial repertoire of behaviors is controlled. Through classical conditioning, stimuli that did not originally initiate a particular response acquire the property of initiating it. In addition, through the use of reinforcements, some control can be exerted over the frequency with which particular responses occur. By adjustment of the schedule of reinforcements, frequencies of responses above the base rate can be maintained. However, classical conditioning and instrumental conditioning procedures, discussed to this point, tell us almost nothing about the way the infant acquires new ways of responding, as he most evidently does.

One mechanism involved in the development of new responses, not only in infancy but throughout life, is known as **shaping.** Consider the case of a nine-month-old child who has been given a spoon for the first time. The infant holds it awkwardly in his clenched fist and, with a little guidance, manages to place the spoon in the oatmeal. He lifts the spoon out of the oatmeal, but by the time the spoon reaches his mouth most of the oatmeal has run off it. Very slowly, and over many weeks, he improves his performance, until he has acquired the new skill of bringing the spoonful of oatmeal from the bowl to his mouth without spilling any. The question to be considered here is how the child slowly learns this skill. The skill represents a new response he has learned.

The account given according to operant-conditioning theory of how this skill is acquired is as follows: Whenever the infant, by chance, holds the spoon in such a way that some of the oatmeal reaches his mouth, that way of holding the spoon is reinforced and strengthened. Also, whenever he holds the spoon, by chance, in such a way that the oatmeal slides off the spoon and nothing reaches the mouth, the related responses tend to become extinguished. Because behavior shows a natural variability, each attempt to take a spoonful of oatmeal varies from the previous one. Features of the variable performance that are effective tend to be reinforced and retained, and features that are not effective tend to drop out.

This process, through which behavior is slowly modified and new responses and skills are acquired, is known as shaping behavior. The word *shaping* draws on an analogy between the modification of behavior and the way in which natural materials are tooled to conform with specifications in a factory or workshop. The emphasis is on the control of behavior by external means.

One can demonstrate in some situations that new skills can be developed through the well-planned use of reinforcements, but this is far from demonstrating it to be the only means through which new responses can emerge. An alternative proposal, long favored by many psychologists, including Piaget, is that individuals are inventive of new responses and can generate new behavior through processes within themselves. There are difficulties in testing this view of human behavior, which is why many psychologists are reluctant to accept it. Also, it is a view that many did not like to embrace until recent times because it has been difficult to develop mechanical models of how this could happen. Psychologists have been able to develop mechanical mice that can learn as a result of reinforcement, but building a mechanical mouse that can generate new solutions to problems within itself is a much more difficult engineering task to undertake. Nevertheless, it has become possible, in a sense, in recent years, though the mechanical mouse is now a computer. One can program a large computer so that it can discover solutions for problems that it has not already learned to solve and so that it can store the solutions for use in solving subsequent problems. When the computer discovers the solution to a problem, such as proving a geometrical theorem, it is acquiring a new skill that it can later use (in proving other theorems). A computer has a great capacity for generating new operations (responses!) that it was not originally programmed to undertake. The computer shows that there is nothing mystical about the idea that the human being may have the capacity for inventing and producing new responses, on his own initiative, without the operation of reinforcement and extinction. These play a role, but other processes are also important.

The clearest examples of new behavior being generated from sources within the individual involve the development of language. This is a

42
. . . .
Basic Learning
Processes in Infancy

matter that will be discussed in greater detail in later chapters. In the meantime, it is sufficient to point out that a young child experiments with language, putting together combinations of words he has never heard. He does not learn language through the slow shaping of his infant's babble. He may suddenly say a word or expression without going through any slow process of making closer and closer approximations to the correct form. Language development cannot be understood through any simplistic account involving only reinforcement and extinction. Language is learned, but the process of learning involves the invention of new sentences and sometimes even the invention of grammatical forms. This illustrates how new behavior can be generated internally, much as the computer can generate new proofs of theorems internally.

In any case, the slow shaping of behavior is not a very efficient way of generating new behavior once the child has reached a stage in which verbal communication is possible for him. In the first year of life, one may slowly shape behavior related to toilet training, but just a very few years later one may help the same child to produce a new behavior by simply telling him how to do it. Sometimes one may give the same child a few prompts and then expect him to invent the new behavior needed to solve a particular problem. Much controversy in education is related to the matter of the extent to which a child should be given an opportunity to generate new behavior and the extent to which his behavior should be kept under teacher control or under the control of the educational materials.

Infant Behavior and Information Analysis

Up to this point, the discussion has focused on very simple forms of behavior in which, with a few exceptions, the stimulus is a very simple event that produces a rather simple response. The learning processes described have also been at a relatively simple level, with new simple stimuli in one form or another coming to control behavior. Psychologists have long hoped that the complicated learning undertaken by the older child and adult could be understood in terms of these simple processes. Many impressively ingenious attempts to do this have been made by American psychologists, including J. B. Watson's classic work *Behaviorism* (1924) and B. F. Skinner's *Science and Human Behavior* (1953). These works attracted a large following, partly because of their scientific ingenuity and partly because they offered a promise of providing means of controlling behavior during the period of development. Perhaps they were embraced also because they gave the impression that behavior was not really unpredictable, as it often appears to be in daily life. For at least the first half of the twentieth century, American psychology was dominated by the view that complex learning could be understood in terms of simple conditioning processes, but some psychologists came to doubt the usefulness of this position. Other important processes appear to be involved in learning in early childhood that are not usefully described in the terms of the traditional language of psychology derived from physiology, such as *stimulus* and *response*. The infant soon ceases to be an organism whose behavior can be readily described in terms of the relationship of simple stimuli to simple responses. Rather, the infant comes to resemble more an information-processing system in which there are inputs of information and outputs that may be either adjustive behaviors or outputs of information.

Consider an infant who is the subject of an experiment. The infant has learned to lie still when a certain kind of light display is shown above his head, but when another kind of light display is turned on he kicks his legs. The baby is receiving information that determines whether he will be in one state or in the other. In order for the baby to respond to the information provided, he must have some kind of information analyzer that will decide whether he is faced with the one input of light or the other, one situation or another.

Now let us consider the case of the infant who fixates on a point of light. He does this in the first few weeks after birth but very soon begins to show discriminations in what he fixates on. Thomas (1965) gave infants aged two to fourteen weeks the opportunity of fixating on patterns of different complexity. He found that there was a very strong tendency for the infants to fixate on the more complex of the patterns presented. Now consider what this means. The finding carries with it the implication that the infant has a capability of discriminating between less complex and more complex patterns. Of course, he has no capability of saying to himself "This pattern is more complex than that one" or "I prefer to look at the more complex pattern." The infant does have the inborn capacity to make the discrimination and, hence, the mechanisms necessary for responding to the dimension of complexity. This means that the infant has some capacity to make an analysis of incoming information and that the analysis results in some displays being stared at longer than other displays. The visual behavior is not just a random scanning of the visual world. Data from other sources also suggest (see review by Travers, 1967) that, if a great range of complexity of visual displays is shown to an infant, the infant will probably choose to fixate most frequently on one of medium complexity. A study providing evidence related to the latter point has been undertaken by Haith et al. (1969), who were able to show that limb movements and sucking behavior were related to the level of complexity of a visual display and that the greatest activity in this respect occurred when the displays were of medium complexity in terms of the range of complexity provided. The displays had high attention–attraction qualities in that they involved the presentation of a light that moved in a pattern of varying degrees of complexity. Complexity also is a factor at all ages in determining attention–attraction properties, a fact that can be used in attracting the attention of older children.

Kagan (1970) has made an analysis of the processes involved in the development and control of attention in infants and points out that attending behavior moves through a number of stages. In the earliest stage,

44
• • • • • • • • • • •
Basic Learning
Processes in Infancy

it is determined by quite crude properties of the stimulus itself. In the case of visual stimuli, the extent to which the object shows contrasts of illumination is crucial. An object that contains black lines on a white surface, or bright white lines on a black background, has high attention-attracting properties. The reason for this is that when a bright line or a bright spot moves across the retina it turns the light-sensitive cells on and off as it moves over them, and the infant has a tendency to attend to those events that produce a high rate of change in his sensory system. An object that presents soft contrasts of shading does not have the property of producing the same marked on–off states in the retinal cells and does not have the same property of eliciting an orienting response. Because boundaries and edges are of greatest importance in producing contrast, objects that have sharply defined and contrasting edges are the ones that attract attention best. However, there is also evidence that as the number of edges is increased an optimum point for attracting and holding attention is reached. If the number of boundaries is increased still further, attention to the object declines. It seems that there is an optimum amount of turning on and off the cells in the retina. The very young child avoids overstimulation, as does the adult. Even the adult can become overwhelmed with the amount of contrast and variation in the environment and may want to withdraw. Combinations of flashing lights and blaring music may become unbearable.

As the infant grows, new processes are involved in the attention process. The infant who repeatedly is exposed to, and attends to, a particular pattern retains information about that object or pattern. That information is retained can be readily demonstrated, for the infant's reaction to the same repeatedly presented pattern changes. The data suggest that the infant is capable of taking in and storing information that has some degree of regularity to it and is presented on repeated occasions. The internal representation of the object is referred to by many workers as a schema, meaning only that there is an internal representation of the object. This internalization of information must be considered to be entirely **automatic** (a term originally used by Clark Hull in relation to learning); that is, it has nothing to do with whether the infant decides to attend or not to attend to the object involved. Kagan (1970) takes the position that schemas represent records of information in the nervous system and do not have action components tied to them. Piaget (see Flavell, 1963) has taken the opposite position and suggests that every schema has components that lead to action. Kagan would say that after the infant has had considerable experience with his mother's face a schema containing information about the face is set up. But Piaget would suggest that a schema has action components and includes a tendency to look at and direct attention toward the face.

The formation of schemas in relation to common objects playing a significant role in the life of the infant is said by Kagan to take place during the age of about two to four months. After that time, the schemas become elaborated, other schemas are formed, and some interrelationships among schemas are developed. In addition, a new process emerges.

Toward the end of the first year, an infant will respond particularly to objects for which he has developed a schema, but he will also be particularly attentive toward those that have been modified in some way. He will explore the change if he is able to do so. A mother who presents herself to her one-year-old with a Band-Aid on her face is likely to have it pulled off. Objects that show some deviation from their presentation in the past arouse and prolong the attending response to an unusual degree. Kagan takes the position that in the third stage the child shows evidence of forming hypotheses about the change and sets about testing the hypotheses. If the child cannot test his hypotheses, or has no hypotheses, then he is likely to withdraw from the situation.

Kagan (1970) proposes that all three factors involved in early perception—high contrast, internalization of information, and hypothesis testing—are processes that dominate attention through the school years. He points out that the books used in the lower grades are illustrated with bright colors and show high contrast, new objects are presented enough times to develop internalization of the information, and variations of objects are selected for presentation that are within the child's grasp (that is, the variations are selected so that the child is able to formulate hypotheses about the nature of the variation).

Let us now further consider inborn information analysis mechanisms. An infant aged one year is placed on the floor on a porch raised about eighteen inches above ground level. The porch has no rail around it, and the infant crawls to the edge of the porch, looks over the edge, and withdraws. The infant then moves over to another part of the porch, approaches the edge again, and once again withdraws. This is repeated many times. In such a case, the infant is confronted with a very complex situation. From what the infant sees in this complex situation, he is able to abstract important information that results in a withdrawal response. We know, from other data, that the information to which the infant is responding is that of the drop from the porch to the ground and that he is able to abstract this important information from the vast wealth of information confronting him as he looks over the edge. The infant is not just responding to depth cues; he is able to analyze the total mass of information presented to him and is able to analyze out from this mass of data a small amount of information of particular importance. The response of the infant is an **adjustive response,** that is, an avoidance of danger response, as is seen in his withdrawal from the edge.

Infants avoid attempting to move over places where there is a sharp drop in elevation, as do members of a number of other species from turtles to rats (see the review of research on this problem by Walk and Gibson, 1961). The phenomenon is known as the **visual-cliff phenomenon.** Gibson and Walk (1960) have explored this behavior with young infants, using an arrangement in which the visual cliff consisted of a small ravine, perhaps two feet deep at the deep end and a few feet across. The

46
• • • • • • • • •
Basic Learning
Processes in Infancy

ravine was covered with a piece of plexiglas that could easily support the weight of a one-year-old infant. An infant was placed on one side of the ravine, and the experimenter was on the other. The experimenter attempted to encourage the infant to cross the ravine on the plexiglas. Under these conditions, the infant would advance until he reached the edge of the visual cliff, but he would not cross over it even though he might place his hand on it and could see that it provided firm support. The infant would skirt along the edge of the cliff, never resting his weight on the plexiglas, and could eventually reach the experimenter by going around the visual cliff.

The visual-cliff phenomenon appears to be a clear-cut case of the nervous system having built-in mechanisms for extracting certain kinds of information from the environment. In this case, the mechanism helps the infant to survive. Many such inborn information analysis mechanisms have been identified in animals. For example, frogs have visual analyzer mechanisms that permit them to identify and catch with their tongues small moving objects that have certain characteristics, including that of size. It is not just that the frog has a response triggered by a particular stimulus. Such a simplistic interpretation fails to recognize the fact that the eyes of the frog are exposed to an enormous quantity of information from which it can extract some small amount of highly significant information. The information analysis mechanism in the nervous system has to be fairly complex in that the information extraction process is complex. The complexity of the process is evident when one considers that it would be quite difficult to develop a mechanical or electronic device that would scan the surroundings and indicate when a small fly was in range of an artificial tongue.

Another very interesting example of inborn information analysis mechanisms is found in the case of some birds that can orient themselves to the stars. Presumably, in these birds the direction of migratory behavior is controlled by this kind of mechanism. The nervous equipment of these birds has to be able to identify the position of particular stars and to discriminate them from other stars, and then there must be a mechanism to orient the birds toward the stars. The phenomenon has been demonstrated by bringing birds into a planetarium with stars displayed on the ceiling. The birds orient themselves in relation to particular stars and as the display of stars is moved change their orientation. Ornithologists suspect that many different mechanisms exist through which birds manifest appropriate migratory behavior. Some birds, for example, orient themselves to magnetic fields (see Matthews, 1968).

We are only just beginning to understand the inborn information analysis systems of human beings. Indeed, until recently the assumption was made that there were no such mechanisms. The discovery of the visual-cliff avoidance response occurred because such a mechanism had been well established in many other species and finally somebody had the curiosity to determine whether a similar mechanism existed in the case of young human beings. It did exist, and the way was opened up for the search for other innate information analysis systems. Some evidence was soon found to suggest their existence and that they might be much more extensive than had previously been thought. An example of such discoveries is found in the work of Bower, (1966a,b) on what is referred to as **size constancy.** Let us consider this work briefly.

The child of elementary school age, or older, knows perfectly well that an object seen in the distance is the same object as when it is seen close up. He is not fooled by the fact that the distant object makes a very much smaller image on his retina than does the same object close up. A man does not look smaller when he is forty feet away than when he is twenty feet away, despite the fact that the man far away produces an image on the retina half the height of the image when he is close. This is the phenomenon of size constancy. Psychologists long believed that size constancy was entirely a learned form of behavior. It certainly makes a lot of sense that the infant should slowly come to recognize that his mother is the same person whether she is seen across the room or beside the crib. He should also soon learn that the bottle is the same whether it is seen close to his mouth or at a distance of several feet. There are numerous opportunities for the infant to learn early in infancy that objects are the same regardless of whether they are near or far. Bower (1966a,b) investigated the extent to which young infants were able to recognize particular objects regardless of distance. The infants were aged two to twenty weeks, and the technique used for studying such matters in infants is operant conditioning. The usual form of the technique is roughly along the following lines: The infant first has to learn to discriminate between a large square piece of board and a much smaller square piece of board held at the same distance. One can do this by teaching him that when the large square appears he can obtain milk by turning his head. He also learns that when a small square is shown he cannot obtain milk by turning his head. After he has learned this task, then he is shown the large square object, but at such a distance that it produces on the retina an image the same size as that produced by the small square. Now the crucial question is how does the baby respond? Does he respond as if it were the small square, which would indicate a lack of size constancy, or does he show through his behavior that he recognizes it to be the same object as the one shown close to him? The answer is fairly clear. He responds to the large square held at a distance *not* as though it were the small square but as though it were the large square held at a distance. The evidence indicates that the infant already recognizes the phenomenon of size constancy, but it seems unlikely that the infant has managed to master this difficult skill through learning during the course of his short life since birth. He has had some opportunity for such learning, because he has seen his mother and also numerous different objects both near and far, but size constancy should be quite a difficult matter to master. It seems much more likely that the infant has some inborn capability for interpreting information related to this phenomenon in appropriate ways. We know, from the visual-cliff phenomenon, that the nervous system has a built-in mechanism for judging distances, and such a mechanism would be an important component of the size constancy phenomenon. Undoubtedly, there are some aspects of size and shape constancy that are learned. Consider some of the complex constancy phenomena related to the one considered. One recognizes a round object, such as a plate, as being round even when one views the object obliquely and has an oval image projected on the retina. The rim of a cup "looks" round even when it is viewed across the table. A person who learns to draw, and who wants to draw a cup viewed obliquely, has to learn to see it as it really is. The child in elementary school typically draws a cup by drawing first the sides of the cup and then a circle on top of them to represent the rim. He doesn't draw a picture that much resembles the image projected on his retina, but he draws a conceptualization of the cup.

There is still another phenomenon related to depth and size constancy that illustrates very clearly a built-in mechanism for information analysis. In order to understand this mechanism, the reader must be introduced to a case of visual perception in which an adult is placed in a position of obtaining visual information in a form probably very similar to that presented to the infant. The only case, so far, in which this can be done is with adults who have been blind all of their lives but are able to gain sight for the first time through a corneal graft operation. The first person to recognize the psychological importance of the reports of these postoperative patients was a German ophthalmologist, von Senden (translated 1960), who wrote a book about the entire topic based on his study of his own surgical cases.

Von Senden operated on his patients in order to give them vision, and this he did successfully, but for a long time after they could see they did not have useful vision. Such a patient, after the eye had healed, could be presented with a common object, held up in front of him, and he would not be able to identify it. The necessary machinery in the nervous system for object recognition had not developed, and the patient could not undertake the simplest visual task such as telling the difference between a square and a triangle, despite the fact that he was able to do this easily through touch. However, the visual mechanism did operate at a very primitive level, for he was able to say that an object was held in front of him. It would seem that his native equipment related to vision did make it possible for him to see objects as distinct objects, even though the characteristics of the objects could not be identified. These individuals, with their naive and untrained visual apparatus, did not see the world as just a disorganized confusion. The primitive analyzer mechanisms permitted them to recognize the fact that there were distinct objects in the environment and that there were many distinct objects, but the analyzer mechanism still had to develop before it would permit them to be able to look at an object and identify its relevant characteristics. A primitive kind of object identification is an inherent capability of man's nervous system, but the analysis of object characteristics is learned.

Von Senden also conducted studies to find out something about how his patients developed the capability of recognizing objects. He found that the development of this capability was extremely slow. For example, a patient might take daily training on learning to discriminate a triangle from a square, but even after three months of training he might be able to make the discrimination only by counting the corners. Immediate identification still was not possible.

The implication of von Senden's work is that the nervous system has a crude innate capacity to perceive that there is some kind of organization in the world, that is, that the world consists of things. However, the attachment of meaning to the things requires a long period of learning that involves the development of more sophisticated information analysis systems. Hebb (1966), who did all the pioneer thinking on this matter, came to the conclusion that one of the major tasks faced by the child or by any growing organism is the development of a system of information analyzers that will identify the detailed characteristics of objects so that the objects, crudely perceived as objects by the basic inherent nervous machinery, can be given meaning and significance. Hebb called this process of developing analyzer mechanisms **early learning.** It is a very slow process and perhaps the most significant learning process that takes place during the first two years of life.

A very important information system that plays a significant role in the performance of most skills involving movement is the cerebellum — a mass of tissue that is a distinct organ lying at the rear of the brain. When the child begins to walk, as he does at about the age of twelve to fifteen months, he can do this because the nervous system is able to keep track of a great amount of information concerning where his legs are at any particular time, the position of other parts of his body, and his orientation with respect to the gravitational field. The cerebellum appears to be an organ that collates all this information and makes adjustments permitting the individual to stay right side up to the world. It seems fairly clear that children do not *learn* to walk, though learning may refine the crude walking act, and hence children must be endowed with the nervous machinery required to keep track of all the information that has to be kept track of if walking is to take place. The cerebellum functions very much like a computer designed to control a complex program of activity in which information about many components must be used to make adjustments in the activity of other components (see Eccles et al., 1967).

Although the information analysis systems related to walking are innate rather than learned, information-handling systems have to be acquired through learning so that many learned skills can be adequately performed and controlled.

An area of great significance related to the existence of innate analyzer mechanisms is the development of speech. Before the child begins to speak, he learns to identify a great many speech sounds. Some of the sounds he hears he may suddenly produce himself, as when the child who has not said the word before suddenly says "Bye-bye," a word he has heard others say hundreds of times. The child shows substantial evidence of being able to isolate the sounds of speech and later produce them. For those of us who have heard the sounds of our native language all our lives, there is nothing remarkable about this because we have the illusion that each spoken word is generally said fairly distinctly. Such is not the case at all. Studies of speech show that one sound slurs into another sound and what appear to be distinct sound elements in particular words are overlapping components that cannot be separated in terms of the sound waves they involve. The adult hears words as being separated one from another, but such a separation is strictly an illusion. The sound of speech, as it is recorded, shows no breaks between words. In typical speech, several words are spoken as a continuous stream of sound and then there is a short break followed by another unbroken stream. We learn the illusion that there are breaks between words and that each word consists of a set of separate and distinct sound elements. The young infant appears to have some capacity for making this kind of analysis of sound elements in language. If he did not have some innate capacity to do this, it is doubtful whether he would achieve the extraordinary mastery of language he does during the first two years of his life. Some psychologists also take the view that the child may have some innate ability for discovering the basic structure of language.

Organization of Information

The theme of the previous section of this chapter has been that the infant has an innate capacity for extracting and using some of the information about the world around him. In addition, the infant has some capacity for organizing information, even at this early stage. He does not simply store many small items of information about the environment, pigeonholing each in a separate little compartment of memory. Piaget (see Piaget and Inhelder, 1969) has long stressed that much of the information that the infant acquires is related to such basic functions as feeding, excretion, and social responding. He suggests that children have a capacity to organize the experiences they have around these functions and that the nervous system may have an inherent capacity for doing this. As the perceptual systems develop, and as the nervous system develops, they show an ever increasing capacity to extract, organize, and store information about the environment. A considerable amount of space in subsequent chapters is devoted to a discussion of the expanding capacity of the growing child to handle information about the world around him.

Facilitators and Inhibitors of Intellectual Development in Infancy

In many parts of the world, the education of the child begins shortly after birth, when the child is brought to facilities where he is largely reared. The Kibbutzim in Israel were some of the first to develop on any systematic scale this form of institutionalized child rearing, though some groups of American Indians had developed small-scale communal nurseries. The reader interested in a thoroughly readable psychological analysis of child rearing in the Kibbutzim is referred to Rabin's (1965) excellent study of the matter. The Union of Soviet Socialist Republics has also developed a system for providing child-rearing facilities through infancy and beyond (see Cole and Maltzman, 1969) in order that women might be released from individual child-rearing duties. These kinds of activities have raised questions about the best environment for the rearing of children and whether systematic education can profitably start in infancy. These are questions that are also being raised by those concerned with the problems of poverty in the United States, where one proposed step toward solving the problems involves establishing child-care centers. These child-care centers supposedly have the purpose of releasing the mother for productive work outside the home, and they also have potential for stimulating intellectual development in the young children assigned to them.

There can be no doubt that children born in poverty have considerable difficulty in mastering the school curriculum. They are at a disadvantage when they enter school, and this disadvantage tends to increase, rather than diminish, as they advance through the grades. Two major factors appear to be responsible for this initial and increasing scholastic deficiency. One is nutrition, and the other is the deprived intellectual environment in which children raised in poverty find themselves.

If anyone doubts the significant effect that nutrition can have on the development of intelligence, he should read the excellent summary of the evidence provided by Green et al. (1973). These authors begin with the well-known facts that the children of disadvantaged groups achieve less than middle-class children and that these children fall further and further behind as they go through school. These authors go on to point out that the child born in poverty is at a disadvantage even before birth. The mother is likely to be malnourished and also probably lacks adequate prenatal care. When born, the child of a malnourished mother weighs less than the average and his brain is somewhat shrunken within the skull, indicating that cell multiplication has not proceeded to an optimum extent. An undue proportion of the children of the disadvantaged are born prematurely, which often brings with it mental retardation. Children born prematurely achieve somewhat lower intelligence test scores than children born at full term. Even without the effect of prematurity, low birth weight is associated with a depression in intelligence test scores. The frequency of children being born with a weight below that normally expected is actually on the increase among nonwhites, a fact that should arouse the consciences of all.

The children of the poor also have less well developed thymus glands and suffer from the fact that their mothers often have vitamin-deficient diets. There is some evidence that merely giving mothers a vitamin supplement during pregnancy increases the intelligence quotients of their children measured at the age of four years. In addition, malnutrition during infancy appears to have serious effects on the brain. These effects are probably permanent and cannot be remedied by later improved conditions. Thus when the children of the disadvantaged grow up, they in turn provide unfavorable circumstances for the next generation.

The circumstances of growth in a state of poverty are unfavorable not only nutritionally but also in terms of intellectual stimulation. Bosco (1970) has pointed out that the problem of such a child is not so much understimulation as chaotic stimulation. When a large family lives in very cramped and crowded quarters, conditions are inevitably as stimulating as those of a busy city street, but the infant is not able to learn much from being exposed to such chaos. Living in a room with many other people, most of whom are too busy or too tired to give the infant the kind of attention he needs, provides very inferior circumstances for intellectual development. What the infant needs is a much simpler environment from which he can extract information necessary for his development. For example, in order to begin to differentiate the sounds of speech, he needs to be spoken to by someone who will repeat the same words again and again. The infant can then slowly begin to differentiate the component sounds within these words. This does not mean that the infant will begin to understand what those words mean; the differentiation of speech sounds has to come before any meaning can possibly be ascribed to words. In addition, when the child is a little older, there is little dialogue between him and the other members of the crowded community. He is sporadically talked to and given commands such as "Stop that!" or "Put it down!" but there is little of the give and take found in the conversation of child and parent living under more propitious circumstances. The culture of the underprivileged does not provide for the intellectual development of the child through such conversation.

A number of studies have been undertaken in which underprivileged infants were exposed to an "enriched" environment, but the difficulty in such studies is determining the effect that the "enrichment" has on the baby. Babies have a rather limited repertoire of things they do. For this reason, infants given an enriched environment may have to be followed up for some years to determine whether advantages have been gained.

An interesting study of the effect of attempting to improve the environment of the infant is provided by Gordon (1969a). In this study, mothers of babies in poor rural communities in Florida were given instruction in how to provide an intellectually stimulating environment for their infants during the first and second years of life. The babies were studied at the end of the first and second years to determine how they compared in their behavior with a control group of children who had not received the special stimulation. The mothers were instructed to play certain games with their children involving such varied activities as holding out objects for the very young infant to attempt to grasp, giving the names of objects in the case of the older child, and engaging in simple verbal interactions with the child.

The main findings of the Gordon study were that the children of mothers given training in the program showed enhanced development at the end of the first year of the program as compared with a group of control children. The enhancement was also shown at the end of the second year, provided the mothers kept up the program. Such programs generally seem to show that they produce intellectual advantage. The results also suggest that through such enhancement some of the disadvantages of an impoverished environment can be offset. That such infant training can be provided in the home by women who have somewhat less than a high-school education is a matter of considerable significance. Apparently, infant education does not have to be provided by a well-trained professional staff.

Outputs of the Infant

Outputs of the infant in the first few months of life are very limited. Most of them represent little more than random behavior, that is, behavior with almost no organization or structure. A few exceptions to this have already been mentioned and include feeding, excretion, the orienting response, fixation of the eyes on particular objects, and following of a light with one or both eyes. Crying behavior represents one form of coordinated response shown from birth, but the function of crying is not really understood. At one time, the unlikely theory was propounded that crying provided essential exercise for the lungs, but the passage of time has not provided any great crop of more plausible theories. Smiling behavior also emerges in the first two months of life. Vocalization in the first three months is very limited in the range of sounds produced. Lenneberg (1967), in his discussion of the development of language, describes the early sounds of the baby as "squealing–gurgling" sounds (p. 128) but also notes that some of the cooing is vowel-like in character. A point of interest to note is that these early sounds are produced by completely deaf babies as well as by those who can hear. By six months, the cooing has changed to a babbling, but the noises have greater structure to them and resemble single syllable sounds. By eight months, the baby begins to repeat certain sounds, as when he lies in his crib and says "ma-ma-ma-ma." The intonation of the infant at this stage may be influenced by such states as frustration and fear. The development of speech at more advanced levels will not be discussed here, and what has been said has been introduced only to indicate the limited nature of the behavioral outputs of the young infant. Behavioral outputs are extremely limited until the infant has developed the necessary mechanisms in his nervous system for the analysis of inputs. Indeed, one can make the generalization that the machinery for the analysis of inputs must generally precede the production of corresponding outputs. Thus the production of speech lags behind speech comprehension.

Since the work of Arnold Gesell early in the century, attempts have been made to describe the development of the motor responses and other responses of the infant. One of the more interesting attempts to do this, in recent years, has been that of Bruner (1969), whose study of motor development focuses on responses related to feeding and sucking. The baby starts out with complete and complex responses related to feeding, these responses being organized within a schema, according to Piaget's terminology. The responses include two forms of sucking, the orientation of the head and the lips to the nipple, and a holding action with the hands. The baby arrives in the world equipped with a complete program of responses that take place when he is both hungry and presented with a nipple or a nipple-like object. Bruner points out that in the first few months of life the baby cannot perform this act and some other act at the same time. If he is distracted by some visual object, then he will orient his eyes toward the visual display but will stop sucking. Later, he will become capable of looking at an object and producing the feeding response at the same time. The repertoire of hand and arm responses increases rapidly. In the first month, the baby can grasp firmly if the palm of his hand is touched. Then the grasping action becomes extended so that when the back of his hand is touched the baby will turn his wrist and grasp at whatever is touching it. Later, the baby shows swiping movements that become slowly more refined and he eventually becomes able to grasp objects, but the use of vision as a guide for the grasping hand has to be learned.

The infant appears to have, initially, gross patterns of movement, which he can perform as complete acts. These become broken down into components, called **modules,** and he learns to combine the modules into various instrumental acts. An analogy is a computer program for, say, calculating logarithms. Such a program consists of many subprograms involving addition, subtraction, multiplication, and square-root extraction. One could cut up the logarithm program and put some of the components together in such a way that tasks other than calculating logarithms could be performed. The infant has a complete program for holding its mother's breast, involving raising the arms, touching, flexing the fingers, and so on. Later, the infant learns to control these components separately and combine them in different ways for performing other acts. In addition, the infant learns to *substitute* one response for another.

A particularly important kind of output that has great significance for the development of information analysis systems in the nervous system is known as exploratory behavior.

Within the first few months of life, the infant ceases to be just a passive recipient of whatever information the environment happens to provide. A few months after birth, the infant is an active explorer of the environment and manages, through his own efforts, to reach sources of information to which he would otherwise not have had access. By the age of four months, he may grasp at a small wooden cube and manage to bring it to his mouth. The grasping of the object he sees enables the infant to coordinate the information derived from vision with the information derived from touch. That such a coordination of the two sources of information needs to be learned is very evident from the von Senden data on patients recovering from corneal grafts, who could see but had no way of knowing what the objects they saw would be like if touched. Inputs of information through the various perceptual systems have to be coordinated, and this coordination occurs largely through the explorations the infant makes of his own accord. Because the activities of the hands of the infant are highly related to feeding from the bottle or breast, it is hardly surprising that almost every object touched tends to be moved in the direction of the mouth. Such a tendency will persist for a long time, indeed, until the infant reaches the point where it becomes displaced by a tendency to view with the eyes any new object that is grasped.

Most of those who have observed the young infant emphasize the significance of exploratory behavior. Piaget does, and claims that it is vital for normal intellectual development—as undoubtedly it is. An important point to note is that exploratory behavior is not just a set of random movements but a highly coordinated activity that has the effect of increasing the information input to the child.

Basic Learning Processes

In this chapter, we have reviewed some of the basic learning processes that begin to operate early in life and represent important learning mechanisms. An understanding of these processes permits the teacher to gain some control over some aspects of learning. How the teacher gains this control is a matter to be expanded on in subsequent chapters. Although these processes permeate all learning in later years of the child's life, they cannot be considered to represent a complete inventory of all learning mechanisms. An example of a learning process that emerges later, and could not be considered in relation to the life of the infant, is that involving reasoning. The mature person solves many problems in his daily life through the application of reasoning, and solving a problem is a form of learning. The solution of a problem gives him a new skill, that is, the skill involved in solving the problem. Problem solving by means of reasoning involves the generation of a new form of responding, and it is one of the mechanisms that permits the production of new responses.

Summary

1 A distinction is commonly made between growth and development. Growth is increase in size, but development is increase in specialization of components. For example, legs develop as they are used by the infant for turning over and later for walking.

2 At birth, many components of the nervous system do not function in the way they will later function, and thus the infant cannot be considered to be a miniature adult whose brain is devoid of acquired knowledge. Infants at birth show the traumatic effects of birth itself, and some days elapse before the nervous system can be studied to determine which components are functioning. The neonate has a limited repertoire of behavior that has slowly emerged during prenatal development.

3 The response an infant makes to some aspect of the environment depends on the state of arousal in which he happens to be. There appear to be at least five discriminable stages between full waking and deep sleep. Noise and strong stimulation put the baby to sleep, a response opposite to that of the older child. The neonate spends about eighteen hours a day in sleep states. The infant has a repertoire of reflexes and also some fairly complicated responses such as fixation on a bright light and the orienting response. Although the neonate appears ready to take in a great amount of information from the environment, his nervous system is not developed to the point where it can handle all the different kinds of information that the environment presents. Also, responding to the environment is not the same as analyzing and storing the information that the environment presents. The behavior of the infant is controlled to some degree by the stimuli the environment presents.

4 Fussing and crying by the infant appear to be unrelated to whether the behavior brings attention.

5 If behavior occurs only under certain given environmental circumstances, it is said to be under environmental control. Some behaviors that are naturally under stimulus control are called reflexes. Stimuli that naturally produce reflexes are called unconditioned stimuli. Many reflexes have to do with meeting the infant's needs. An interesting unlearned response that occurs before the end of the fifth week is smiling, and it represents what is called primary socialization. The smiling response lays the groundwork for future social behavior.

6 Many naturally occurring responses come to be triggered by stimuli that did not originally trigger them. The learning involved is called classical conditioning, and the stimuli that come to trigger these responses are conditioned stimuli. Some regard classical conditioning as a special case of contiguity learning. Classical conditioning is possible before birth. Conditioning to the passage of time is an interesting case of conditioning in infancy.

7 The behavior of the infant shows an increasing amount of organization centered on particular activities such as sucking and grasping. Piaget suggests that the nervous system includes means for organizing knowledge about particular areas, and he calls these schemas.

8 Different responses occur at particular rates. The rate at which they occur at the beginning of an experiment is the baseline rate. An event that increases the rate of responding is a reinforcer. One discovers reinforcing events by experimentation. After the rate of responding has been increased through the operation of a reinforcer, the withdrawal of the reinforcer results in a reduction in the rate of responding. This reduction is called extinction. Classically conditioned responses may also be extinguished.

9 A response that comes under stimulus control is an operant. The process of bringing it under stimulus control is acquisition.

10 Some psychologists have attempted to reduce all learned behavior to the categories of instrumental and classical conditioning, but this reduction is of very doubtful validity.

11 The schedule of reinforcement has relevance to the time taken to acquire a response and to the rate at which a response is extinguished. Four main categories of schedules are fixed-ratio, variable-ratio, fixed-interval, and variable-interval. A variable-interval schedule has the property of maintaining behavior without reinforcements. The same is true of a variable-ratio schedule. Teachers, by force of circumstances, provide a variable schedule of reinforcements for pupils.

12 One mechanism that produces new behavior is shaping. Tendencies to perform the desired behavior are reinforced, and tendencies to depart from the desired behavior are extinguished. Shaping is probably not the only means through which new behaviors are acquired. Piaget takes the position that the child has the internal capacity for generating new behaviors, much as computers can be built to generate new solutions to problems. Language acquisition illustrates how responses may be internally generated, for the child may produce sentences he has never heard anyone say.

58

. . . .

Basic Learning
Processes in Infancy

13 Infants have some inherent capacity for analyzing information from the environment. Visual attention is first attracted by areas of sharp contrast in the visual field. However, the infant shows evidence of retaining some information about the patterns he observes, and to do so he must have analyzed the visual information and have retained memory of some of the attributes of that information. Later, the infant shows sensitivity to changes in objects he has previously seen. He then shows behavior indicating that he is testing hypotheses about the changed object.

14 Not only are there inborn information analysis systems but there are also related inborn response systems. One of the best studied of these is shown by what is known as the visual-cliff phenomenon. Most of the inborn mechanisms closely studied have been in animals; bird migrations provide dramatic examples of such responses. However, beginnings have been made in exploring inborn phenomena and mechanisms in children. Studies of size constancy in infants represent steps in such a direction. Studies of patients who gain vision for the first time as adults provide evidence that there is a very rudimentary inborn mechanism of object perception. Such patients can shortly after surgery see an object as an object even though they cannot identify it. The nervous system has some kind of inherent capability of organizing information about the outside world.

15 A unit of the nervous system that has specialized capabilities of organizing information is the cerebellum. This organ keeps track of where the limbs and the other parts of the body are located and stores information about events in the environment in relation to which movements have to be made. The cerebellum develops a program of movements that make it possible to execute particular acts.

16 In the initial stages of learning to understand language, the child learns to discriminate certain sound components. After he has learned to discriminate among the various sound elements and can identify them, he acquires the capability to produce language.

17 Information begins to be organized within the nervous system from the start.

18 The education of the child begins in infancy, but only in recent times has recognition been given to the intellectual significance of the early years. The nervous system can show normal intellectual development provided that proper nourishment is provided. The lack of proper nourishment may have devastating effects on intellectual development, and severe damage in this respect may take place before birth. This is one of the central problems of ending the poverty cycle. In addition, poor nutrition of the mother may result in premature birth, a condition very damaging for future intellectual development. An environment of poverty is also unfavorable as a source of intellectual stimulation, partly because it is an environment overcrowded with people and events. In addition, the poverty environment provides few opportunities for verbal interactions, of a positive kind, between child and adult. Attempts to enrich the environment of the child born into poverty have demonstrated that help can be provided by quite simple means.

19 The infant has limited outputs of behavior, mainly related to basic biological functions. As the infant develops, he becomes more and more an organism exploring and scanning his environment.

60

· · · · · · · · · · · ·

Basic Learning
Processes in Infancy

Some Additional Concepts
Necessary for Understanding
Learning and Development

The previous chapter provided a brief introduction to operant conditioning, a concept of learning that is of central significance to those who refer to themselves as behavior modification psychologists. In the brief presentation, the concepts of reinforcement and extinction were introduced, and it was implied that some behavior of young children can be modified through providing reinforcements or withholding reinforcements. Certainly, some behavior can be modified by these manipulations. There is also a related concept, involving reinforcement and extinction and called shaping of behavior, that gives particular power in the modification of behavior.

3

· · · · · · · · · · ·

Learning in
the Preschool
Years

Consider the case of a child who is beginning to learn to color drawings in coloring books. The child, at first, takes a crayon in a fistlike grip and then scribbles over the entire outline. He does not, as yet, color within the lines. Soon, and probably with some prompting, he will limit his scribbling so that it falls *roughly* within the contours of the objects colored. Any improvement in this respect will be reinforced with praise and encouragement to help establish this as a habit. When the crayon strays outside of the area to be colored, the teacher will probably ignore it and, in that way, hope to extinguish it. Thus, by a process of reinforcing behavior that shows improvement and extinguishing behavior that is inappropriate, one can slowly teach the child how to color objects drawn in outline. Learning by this procedure is rather slow, as anyone knows who has worked with a three-year-old child engaged in this kind of activity. This is the process of shaping behavior by extinguishing inappropriate behavior and reinforcing any tendency for behavior to become more appropriate.

Some of the behavior of the young child is acquired in this way, particularly in the early stages when the child has little skill in copying a demonstration given by the adult and an insufficient understanding of speech to be able to make use of an explanation of how a task should be performed. As soon as the child has acquired some mastery of language, his behavior can be modified quickly and efficiently.

The process of shaping behavior as described by Skinner is basically a very inefficient procedure for developing new behavior in the human being, though the procedure may be resorted to when all other more efficient techniques have failed. For example, a large proportion of children learn to read without much difficulty, but there are still many who acquire little of the skill and remain virtually nonreaders. For some of these children, the central problem is that they have never seen an adult in their homes either look at or read or enjoy a book. Such children do not pick up books, look at the pictures, attempt to interpret the words, or ask the teacher to read. Books have little or no significance to them as objects. The behaviors of looking at, deriving significance from, and attempting to interpret may have to be shaped in such children. Small rewards may be offered for the occasions when the child engages in the activity. Sometimes special situations may be concocted that will make activity related to books especially attractive for such a child. For example, the teacher may ask the child to tell a story about what he has done. The teacher types out the story in large type and helps the child to make it into a book by stapling on a cover that the child has decorated with fingerpaints. The teacher may then help the child to read his own story, and perhaps later he may attempt to read it to the class. By such a procedure, all kinds of rewards are introduced into the situation to keep the child in a position where he will have the opportunity of acquiring some mastery of reading. It should be noted that the procedure used in this case is far more elaborate than that of the teacher who, after seeing a film on the shaping of the behavior of pigeons, used small candies in an attempt to control the reading behavior of the child reluctant to come into contact with reading materials. The system of rewards and incentives likely to be effective must almost certainly be quite complicated.

Sometimes a token system has been used to control the behavior of children who for various reasons are reluctant to come into contact with educational materials. The tokens are handed out to the child as reinforcements, and, when a sufficient number have been accumulated, they may be turned in for some special privilege or some desired toy or other object. Token systems are not without problems. Their main success has been in institutions that handle seriously disturbed patients or in schools for children who are otherwise difficult to handle. Token systems may solve some problems, but they also create other problems. These will have to be considered in connection with problems involved in teaching children of elementary school age.

The shaping of behavior sounds like a fairly precise technique for producing behavioral change, but, in fact, it is not. Consider the first-grade room recently observed by the author in which the teacher's aide was seen to move among the children and pass out miniature marshmallows to those whom she thought were "attending" to the teacher. She said she was reinforcing attending behavior on the part of the pupils, but what did she consider this to be? When asked this question, her answer was that a child was attending if he was watching the teacher, not talking to other children, sitting quietly, and doing what he was told. Now what was the teacher's aide really reinforcing? Was it a tendency to attend to the teacher, or was it just a matter of looking in the direction of the teacher and being generally quiet and subdued. One could well make out a case for the proposition that the teacher's aide was reinforcing inactivity rather than anything else. One could also forcefully argue that the teacher's aide was reinforcing docility and conforming behavior on the part of the children and a tendency to do whatever the teacher wanted them to do. What is being reinforced in such a situation is not clear at all.

The application of reinforcement procedures in the classroom often involves a great amount of wishful thinking. The person who undertakes the reinforcement believes he is reinforcing whatever it is that he wants to reinforce. He is likely to forget that a great amount of behavior is taking place and that all the behavior is likely to be strengthened by the reinforcements provided.

Reinforcement theory grew up in the laboratory on a foundation of data provided by animals that have a very limited repertoire of behavior. In the case of a pigeon reinforced for pecking at a small electrical switch mounted on the wall, one can be fairly sure about what is being reinforced, for the repertoire of behavior of the animal is extremely limited. On the other hand, the behavior of a child is extremely complex, and the complexity makes it difficult to identify all the simultaneous characteristics of behavior that are being reinforced.

The point that has just been made perhaps accounts for the fact that reinforcement procedures for the control of behavior have had their most

63

. . . .

Some Additional
Concepts
Necessary for
Understanding Learning
and Development

successful application at the human level in the case of those human beings who are functioning at relatively simple levels. The procedures have been particularly successful in the training of the severely mentally handicapped, who previously could not be trained to take any part in their own care but many of whom today are trained to handle such matters as clothing themselves and going to the toilet on appropriate occasions. Very young children also belong in the category of human beings functioning at a relatively simple level, and they too often have been found to be highly trainable by operant techniques. The approach has been successful with some classes of mental patients who also must be regarded as operating at a relatively simple level of behavior. Relatively little success has been achieved in the use of such procedures at the elementary-school level, and, indeed, the theory on which such procedures are based is of very dubious validity at that level of human behavioral complexity.

The mechanisms of operant and classical conditioning have limitations even in early childhood. An area in which these limitations are becoming particularly obvious is that of language learning, to which our attention will now turn.

The Acquisition of Language

In terms of subsequent education, the most important single achievement of the child in his early years is the mastery of speech. How speech is acquired has long been the source of considerable speculation, and, although much is known today about how this accomplishment takes place, much still has to be learned. Attempts have been made to apply very simple conditioning principles to understanding how speech develops. Some of these attempts have been highly ingenious and persuasive, and some psychologists would take the position that they are along the right line. The most notable attempt to do this has come from the pen of Skinner (1957), who has written a charming book on the subject, full of delightful anecdotes and skillfully used humor that carries the reader from page to page. The persuasive power of the book is seen in the fact that it has attracted a large following, who teach Skinner's theories as though they were fact, but the truth is that the book is highly speculative and lacks any firm foundation in research studies of human speech.

Skinner regards speech as consisting of a set of operants, that is, behavior that has been learned through positive reinforcement. The general picture of learning presented is of the infant emitting sounds at random, with the vocal behavior slowly shaped so that it conforms to the sounds of the words used in the community in which the infant is being raised. Thus the child who at the age of eighteen months says "cookie" in the presence of his mother is engaged in instrumental behavior that has the effect of obtaining a cookie. Skinner would see little difference between the behavior of a rat that has learned to press a bar to obtain a pellet of food and the behavior of a child who has learned to say "cookie" in the presence of his mother. Both sets of behavior are instrumental in achieving particular goals, and both have been, presumably, learned through reinforcement. Skinner also has his own classification of parts of speech, which include **tacts** and **mands.** A tact—a term derived from the idea that such verbal operants represent contacts with the environment—is a word or expression that draws attention to some aspect of the environment. A two-year-old sitting on the floor who says "doll" in the presence of a doll is exhibiting a tact. Any verbal operant elicited by an object is a tact. A mand is a different part of speech from a tact. The word *mand* comes from the root of such words as *command* or *demand.* A parent who says to a child "Stop that" has given forth a mand. The child who says to his mother "Give me cookie" has also produced a mand. From Skinner's point of view, mands are operants that have established their utility for controlling other people.

Such classifications of items of speech are of dubious value and have absolutely no explanatory value whatsoever. They serve the purpose primarily of suggesting that some speech functions as a verbal operant and represents a successful mode of instrumental behavior. Skinner also has a host of other terms, many of which are no more than the renaming of familiar activities. For example, reading is referred to as **texting.** Incidentally, the general theory of reading implied in Skinner's book is almost certainly wrong. He implies that the understanding of printed words requires that the individual undertake certain subvocal responses; that is, the subject says each word under his breath. This just does not occur in efficient and effective reading, which is far more rapid than even the most rapid speech. Most reading experts would take the position that reading can take place without any activity of the vocal cords.

Although some verbal behavior clearly functions as an instrument for manipulating the environment, as when we flatter the boss, this does not mean that speech is learned by a process of slow shaping. Skinner bases his theory of the development of speech on data, derived mainly from subhuman species, that have nothing to do with speech. The burden of proof is on him to show that some supposed principles of behavior based on entirely different data do actually apply to the speech area. Most psycholinguists would say that they do not.

The early development of language is far from understood. Mention has already been made of the fact that the infant in the first few months of life begins by making various noises and that he makes these regardless of whether he can or cannot hear. Lenneberg (1967) states that the early sounds are vowel-like and that at six months the sounds become more like single syllables, but even at this stage there is no very fixed recurrence of particular sounds. By eight months, the baby shows a tendency to duplicate sounds and to say the same sound over and over again. At this stage, the child also alters the intonation of sounds and reflects in his intonations various emotional conditions, and he begins to show signs of distinguishing between various commands. At twelve months, sound sequences such as "dada" and "mama" are emerging, and by eighteen months the child has a repertoire of anywhere up to fifty words. A point of great interest is that most of the sounds used in most languages are not naturally emitted by the infant. The repertoire of sounds emitted by the infant is rather small. This fact immediately throws considerable doubt on the theory that vocalizations of the infant are slowly shaped by reinforcement and extinction. There is also no evidence that these sounds slowly become shaped into speech sounds. Although there is no doubt that the baby does spontaneously emit some sounds in the first year and that these are fairly uniform across different cultures, the sounds are far from sufficient to provide a basis for a language.

A particularly damaging piece of evidence against the theory that language is mastered through the gradual shaping of speech comes from cases of individuals who never learn to speak but who manage to master the language in terms of comprehension. One such individual is reported by Lenneberg (1967), who studied the child over a period of five years. The child had the capacity of making the normal sounds produced in infancy, including crying and laughter. He also made some unusual sounds when playing alone that sounded like yodeling, but he had no capacity for bringing the speech mechanism under voluntary control. Thus it is clear that having a knowledge of a language is not the same as being able to speak it. Perhaps the case of such a child is the opposite of that of the talking parakeet, which has absolutely no knowledge of the language but can speak it. The human being is able to use language in many ways to guide his behavior, not because he can speak it but because he understands the nature of language.

Another piece of evidence of some significance related to how language is learned, also cited by Lenneberg (1969), is that infants raised in institutions, whose main contact with language is through the television set that often runs all day, may acquire a considerable mastery of language. Such children are often left all day to play on a bare floor with a minimum of toys, and the supervisor may have as many as forty or fifty young children to supervise. The conditions are incredibly lacking in features that make for effective learning. Most of these children do not acquire effective language comprehension, but the fact that some do suggests that mere exposure to language may provide a sufficient base for acquiring some mastery. An operant-conditioning approach to language learning simply cannot account for the fact that these children do learn.

This raises the question of how word sounds come to be produced. One could perhaps expect to find some clues concerning this problem from the study of primates other than man. When a difficult problem related to the understanding of man's behavior arises, a good place to look for the same phenomenon at a simpler level is in the behavior of related species, but in this case the results of studying the vocal behavior of other primates are extremely disappointing. Although extensive, concentrated, prolonged, and sophisticated efforts have been made to teach chimpanzees to speak, the efforts must be regarded as failures. Chimpanzees can be made to use certain sounds to ask for food, water, and other objects, but the enunciation is generally so poor that only the trainer can recognize the words. Also, even after training for as long as a year, the chimp can rarely use more then ten words. The evidence also seems clear that, although the chimp can come to understand simple commands given to it by a trainer and will learn to interpret correctly many of these commands, it probably has little comprehension of how words are put together or the significance of a sentence, but this is a separate problem, to be taken up later.

Excellent descriptions are now available of the early development of language in children. For a description written with implications for education, the reader is referred to Jones (1970). Bloom's (1970) careful case studies of the development of grammar are also of considerable interest. Although the single word is the common beginning of the use of speech, the single word functions as a sentence. When the eighteen-month-old child says "cookie," the mother interprets it immediately as "I want a cookie" or "Give me a cookie." The mother does not interpret the infant's single word as "Do you want a cookie?" or "There is a cookie." The single word functions as a sentence because the mother understands it as a sentence and is able to interpret it as the right sentence. Later, the child removes some of the ambiguity in his pronouncements by constructing two-word sentences. As the child grows older, his constructions become progressively more elaborate and longer.

Now let us move to the issue of what language is, an issue well discussed in the monograph by Deese (1970). Deese points out that language is not a sequence of conditioned responses in which each word is somehow a conditioned response to previous words or to other aspects of the situation. Language is also not a short program of muscular contractions. A sentence is generated in terms of a set of rules, and it is the existence of these rules that makes language more than just a string of sounds. Parrots do not generate new sentences according to a set of rules but say the complete sentence they have learned. Chimpanzees have difficulty in producing single words and probably have little capacity to generate a sentence. Man is the only creature that has capacity to generate sentences in terms of a set of underlying rules. Speech, as we have defined it here, is unique to man.

Although all of us are successful in generating sentences that others agree are well-constructed sentences, we are not able to state with any precision what the rules are. Traditional English grammar is an attempt to state rules supposedly determining what the acceptable sentences are that can be generated, and scientists, including the notable linguist C. C. Fries, have attempted to formulate more precise grammar systems. These rules are very crude representations of the rules that guide the behavior of the adult speaking English, for one can formulate sentences that follow the rules of English grammar yet are in a form that nobody would ever use. The rules of English grammar are only very rough approximations to the system of rules used by individuals to produce sentences. One of the major problems that psycholinguists are trying to solve is the nature of the rules governing language and how these rules are acquired.

A point to be noted is that the rules governing the sentences that can and cannot be generated cannot be explicitly stated by the person who generates them, although his behavior demonstrates that there are such rules stored in him. Speaking and writing involve rule-governed behavior. How the rules governing the production of sentences come to be acquired is a very significant question that also must be answered in order to understand how language is learned.

Some clues concerning the source of speech-production rules can be picked up from studying the acquisition of speech during childhood. Lenneberg (1969) points out that one of the very significant findings about how children learn speech is that they do not progress from words strung together at random to strings of words that conform closer and closer to those of adult grammar. On the contrary, the early groups of words have a definite structure invented by the child, and the invented structure is closely parallel across cultures. A typical grammatical structure of the two-year-old is for the child to say a word such as "boy," which functions as a pivot, and connect it with a great number of other words in such combinations as "boy-good," "boy-small," "boy-eat," and "boy-run." The infant may lie on the floor and give forth long trains of such combinations. Pivot words vary from occasion to occasion. The behavior involves a very simple rule for the construction of an utterance, the selection of a pivot word, generally a noun, and the pairing of that word with almost any other word that comes along. Adults do not construct utterances along this line at all. The language of the two-year-old has other features suggesting that the child produces his own structure. His language is very much like that of the adult writing a telegram, as is seen in such typical utterances as "go toilet," or "food all gone," or "you play." The two-year-old produces language that can be described as pivotal and telegraphic.

Chomsky (1965), who may be regarded as the originator of much in modern linguistics, takes the position that the child confronted with speech seeks to find rules that give it orderliness. This does not mean that the child tells himself that he should look for rules but rather that, in the language area, the human being is uniquely endowed with the capability of finding rules and inventing rules. The early stages of speech production are very largely inventive, but as the child grows older he becomes capable of discovering the rules that permit the generation of sentences similar to those used by adults.

Through a combination of his inherent capabilities and the language to which he is exposed, the human being is able to develop, within himself, a set of rules that permit him to generate sentences acceptable to the rest of his community. If he has limited experience with the sophisticated use of language, he may never reach the point of developing a complicated rule system, and his development may cease with the discovery of rules at a much simpler level.

Let us consider some of the kinds of rules that might be included in a grammar. Let us go back to the two-year-old who takes a pivot word and then adds other words to it in a series of pairing operations. The grammar of this language involves two rules. A basic rule is that the sentence or utterance, generally designated as *S*, must generate a pivot word, *a*. The second rule is that the pivot word can then be combined with other words. However, these rules alone do not form the complete grammar of the young child in the category described.

Another example of a simple rule applied by children and adults alike in generating language is the recursive rule. The application of the recursive rule results in the repetition of particular words or phrases. Examples of the application of this rule in the generation of language are found in expressions such as "long, long, ago," and "He moved very, very, slowly." Such a rule could be written formally with the following notation:

$$S \longrightarrow a$$
$$S \longrightarrow aS$$

The kind of grammar being discussed here is called a **generative grammar;** that is, it is a grammar describing the rules involved in the generation of sentences. A complete grammar must be able to generate all the sentences that could be used in the language. It must be evident to the reader that the rules controlling adult utterances must be very elaborate and complex and that a very long road of research lies ahead in the discovery of these rules. Some beginnings have been made in the work of Chomsky (1965).

A major contrast between the operant-conditioning approach to the study of language and the psycholinguistic approach is that the former involves what is called a left-to-right approach, in that each element in the chain of sounds involved in speech production serves in some way to initiate the next element. However, neither the comprehension nor the production of speech is undertaken in this way at all. Speech cannot be fully analyzed, little bit by little bit as one hears it, but a sizable chunk has to be taken in before any real analysis can be made. Consider the utterance, discussed many times by Chomsky, that, at the beginning of a sentence, would read, "The shooting of the professors. . . ." Just what meaning can be ascribed to such a set of words depends on the circumstances in which it is used. If these words were encountered at the beginning of an article, the reader would have to wait for the rest of the sentence, or perhaps until even later on in the article, in order to identify the meaning. It makes an immense difference whether the sentence is concluded with the words "was poorer than that of the students" or with the words "shocked the entire country." Information provided by language has to be taken in and held in quite large chunks before an analysis can be made, for the meaning of particular words depends on context. After a chunk of verbal information is held in temporary storage in memory, it can then be analyzed for meaning. The analysis requires that the listener identify the structure of the material so that meaning can be properly assigned to it.

Psycholinguists make a distinction between **deep structure** and **surface structure.** Two sentences may have very different surface structures but have the same deep structure. For example, the sentences "John is easy for us to beat at chess" and "It is easy for us to beat John at chess" have very different surface structures, but their deep structure is the same. That is, they have almost the same meaning. A sentence, in order to be understood, has to be analyzed at the deep structure level. The deep structure of a sentence reflects a set of rules that are applied in order to extract meaning. Here again, it must be pointed out that research on the nature of the deep structure is only just beginning to disclose the nature of such structures.

Considerations other than grammatical rules influence the structure of sentences. A very important factor is the amount of information that can be held in temporary storage at one time. Very long sentences can be written or said that represent perfectly acceptable constructions, but these are not likely to be used in any practical communication. Such long sentences tend to be quite unintelligible because the numerous thoughts embedded in them cannot all be considered at one time. The sentences stretch out far beyond the limits of the span of attention. In order for such verbal constructions to be made comprehensible, they have to be broken down into components, each one of which can be considered separately. This is what the editor of written material often has to do. Authors can very easily write complex communications in which phrases are embedded within phrases. These are quite intelligible to him because he knows the material so thoroughly. A reader who has less mastery of the material is likely to be unable to cope with it.

Children generally have a much smaller capacity than adults for holding information in temporary storage. The effect of this on their language is that the younger the child, the shorter is the sentence he is likely to construct. In his second year of life, he is likely to produce many sentences that consist of only one word, as when he says "no" meaning "Stop doing that," or when he says "lollipop" meaning "Give me a lollipop." The length of the sentences used increases steadily with age, but in the elementary-school years, and beyond, length is often limited by the child's inability to use more complex constructions. For this reason, the uneducated adult continues to use very short sentences.

A very important implication of the psycholinguists' contribution to the understanding of the development of language is that they view language as a creative act, undertaken within the boundaries set by the rules determining the kinds of utterances that can and cannot be generated. Language is far from the dull routine skill, to be learned through drill, that some teachers have regarded it to be. Just as the young child acquires considerable mastery of language through being exposed to it, so too may he extend that competence and acquire rules permitting the production of more complicated and sophisticated statements by being exposed to language that incorporates such rules. Exposure to traditional English grammar probably does little to raise competency, but, as many teachers of English have long recognized, further mastery is produced by exposure to suitable models of English. Although this recipe for the development of language skill seems to be a simple one, in practice it is not. At least one difficulty is that material with all the characteristics necessary for good teaching may not attract the attention of students. Exposing the student to appropriate examples of language is difficult in a world where inappropriate examples often have more attractive qualities. For the same reason, a student who enters high school or college speaking a dialect that involves only quite limited structures may prefer to spend his time with others who speak that dialect. Human beings often take pride in the particular dialects they speak, and the dialects may give them a certain self-identity in which they rejoice, but the good features of dialects have to be balanced against the fact that the speaking of a dialect *may* sometimes limit linguistic development.

Compensatory Education and Language Development

Educational programs have long been in existence that attempt to compensate for culturally deprived conditions of child rearing. Some of the earliest of these appeared nearly half a century ago in Israel, where it was noted that the children from the poorest homes lacked the language skills necessary for profiting from school. In particular, these children lacked vocabulary, never having had contact with common objects such as a fork or scissors. Since the days of these early schools, compensatory forms of education have been provided for preschool children in many different countries, and the focus of these schools has been typically on the development of language skills. A short and readable book edited by Denenberg (1970) summarizes the inadequacies of the culturally deprived child and the areas in which he needs special help before entering school, Denenberg stresses the overwhelming inadequacies manifested in the language area.

Schaefer (1970) has gathered together a substantial amount of evidence suggesting that the lack of verbal skills of underprivileged children results in intellectual inadequacies manifested in deficiencies in problem-solving skills and also poor performance on intelligence tests. He points out that there is some evidence that children exposed to programs of compensatory education show an increase in intelligence quotient and that the increase may be very substantial over a number of years. Although the position of Schaefer, in this respect, is widely accepted, there is also some evidence that verbal behavior may not be as critical to thinking as some people believe it to be—at least not during the preschool years. For example, Furth (1971) has gathered together evidence showing that deaf children, who are generally very inferior to hearing children in their comprehension of written language, nevertheless do about as well as hearing children on most problems of the type that Piaget has used for probing the thinking processes of the preschooler. Apparently, deaf children are not at a disadvantage in undertaking many thinking operations. However, the disadvantage may exist in adolescence, when they begin to engage in formal abstract thought.

The disadvantages of the underprivileged child with respect to language are many. Foster and Newman (1971) note that the child from a poor background not only has a smaller vocabulary than the middle-class child but many of his words have special meanings. They cite a study in which children in a particular group were found to define *fish* as an ugly girl and the word *deep* as *good*. Although teachers may be able to learn to understand, and even use, such vernacular in communicating with children, it is unlikely that textbooks will be translated into their language. Thus the children have to learn to understand English as it is printed. Their difficulty in this respect is also increased by the fact that their syntax differs from that used in the material they are required to read. Spoken language generally differs, to some degree, from the written language, but ghetto spoken dialect and written English represent extremes of difference, which can create great learning problems.

Baldwin et al. (1971) observed children perform a task in which the children had to communicate with one another. They found that children of low socioeconomic status were less accurate in their communications than were children of high socioeconomic status. The low-status children seemed unable to communicate all of the information called for by the task.

Much of compensatory education for handling such problems is clearly going to require a one-to-one relationship between child and teacher and hence is likely to be very expensive. Consider, for example, one phase of the development of the child's language successfully handled by middle-class mothers. Dale (1971) points out that these mothers expand as many as 30 per cent of their children's sentences. Consider the following interchange:

Child: Go.
Parent: Go for walk.
Child: Go walk.

In this exchange, the child has made a single-word sentence, which the parent expands to a three-word sentence. The child does not repeat the three-word version, but he does expand his original single-word sentence to a two-word one. In this way, the child slowly learns to expand what he wants to say to include the necessary words, and the parent seems to play an important role in this slow expansion. One can readily understand that a teacher might have to spend an hour or more a day with an underprivileged child in order to provide the child with equivalent language training in a school setting. This can be undertaken only when classes are very small. Such classes are costly to operate.

Faced with this dilemma, many concerned with child development believe that the mothers of such children are going to have to be trained to play a new role in the training of their children. Such mothers have been found to be very willing to participate in such training and have generally been found to help their children in this way. Such training programs also seem to be of benefit to the mothers, who are often desperately frustrated with their inability to do anything except raise their children to become another generation of poor and underprivileged people.

The effectiveness of programs of compensatory education has been difficult to estimate. Numerous studies have been undertaken for this purpose, some mentioned by Denenberg (1970). It is a foregone conclusion that children will benefit from planned learning experiences. The children cannot help but learn more in preschools than they would learn in the disorganized environment from which they come, but there is another much more crucial question that has to be answered—whether, once such training has been given, the children will then have advantages similar to those provided by a middle-class background. Attempts to answer this question involve conducting a follow-up study of the children after they leave compensatory education and enter ordinary school programs. The results indicate that the gains made in compensatory education cease to be evident a year later. Such results are easy to understand. Children living in deeply deprived conditions, undernourished and undercared for, often unable to sleep at night because of the continuous hubbub of noise, can hardly be expected to perform at the level of children living in comfortable suburbia. Such comparison could be meaningful only if both groups of children lived in comparable circumstances. For this reason, one must conclude that the long-term usefulness of compensatory education has not yet been determined.

Those concerned with compensatory education suspect that, if it is to be effective, it probably should cover many years of a child's life and perhaps even be coupled with nutritional and medical therapy. Some have even suggested that it may be necessary to have educational programs such as those in the Israeli kibbutzim, where the children receive all their care and education in a center but spend some hours each day with their parents. Many different procedures need to be tried out so that the poverty cycle can be broken forever.

Perceptual Learning Mechanisms

In the discussion of the child's learning to comprehend speech, emphasis was placed on the natural capacity of the child to receive complex inputs through the perceptual systems and to organize the inputs. From the garbled noise that fills the environment, the infant learns to hear distinct sounds and components of speech. Gibson (1969) describes this process as one of extracting information from the environment. In her book, she emphasizes this capacity of the nervous system to extract information from the data presented to the perceptual systems by

A simple environment with sounds the baby can learn to differentiate.

A chaotic environment, too complex to teach the baby anything.

the environment. One of the experiments she describes richly illustrates some of the processes involved in the case of a task much simpler than that of acquiring a new language. Let us consider her experiment.

Gibson obtained a series of scribbles, very similar to those that young children might make, but smaller. Most of them covered an area no larger than a fifty-cent piece. The subject of the experiment was told that he would be shown a sample scribble that he was to examine carefully. Then he was told that the particular scribble he had seen would be taken away and he would be shown a series of scribbles, some of which would be the same as the one he had seen and some different. The task of the subject was to identify the scribbles that were the same as the one seen. The subject was then shown the new scribbles, one at a time, and he had to judge whether each was the same as or different from the original one. The subject was not told whether he was right or wrong after each guess. After he had been through the pack, he was shown the sample again and then went through the pack once more. After several trials of this kind, the subject could perform the task with considerable skill.

The experiment makes several very important points. First, despite the fact that there was no reinforcement provided and the subjects were never told whether they were right or wrong, all showed steady improvement in the task. If the number of right responses for each time they went through the deck is plotted on a graph, a typical learning curve is obtained. This learning curve is not the product of reinforcement and feedback but of the individual's ability to extract usable information from the task. When a subject is first confronted with a scribble, it looks just like any other scribble. In other words, he is not yet able to extract any information from it about its characteristics. As he views further scribbles, he begins to identify the characteristics of scribbles. This means that he is able to extract information from the scribbles that he can use in identifying them as either the same as the original or different from the original. Indeed, it is possible to trace the learning of specific characteristics by observing the kinds of errors made. Some of the distinctive features of the scribbles are more easily learned than are others.

The data on the scribbles parallel well many common experiences. Consider an illustration from the auditory field. In a foreign country where one does not know the language, the speech of the inhabitants first appears to be a babble of unrecognizable sounds. Slowly one begins to recognize that the speech is made up of certain common sounds. A few common words are then identified that stand out clearly from the rest of the flow of speech. One is learning to extract information from the flow of sound, and this skill in extracting information becomes more and more developed as one is exposed to the language. Now consider a parallel case from the visual field. If a person who has an elementary knowledge of electricity is shown the wiring diagram of an automobile, his immediate reaction to the diagram is likely to be one of bewilderment at the network of wires, which appear to form a maze of extraordinary complexity. If he is given no instruction but rather a whole series of very simple problems to solve such as "Where is the starter switch?" and is not told whether his answers are right or wrong, then after he has worked a few of these the wiring diagram ceases to be the incomprehensible tangle it appeared to be in the first place, and it becomes quite readable. With enough practice, he will see it as a very simple wiring diagram. He has learned to derive information from it.

Second, the Gibson experiment shows that it takes time to extract information from the inputs to the sensory systems. Subjects were not immediately able to identify the characteristics of the scribble shown initially and to match them with the characteristics of subsequently shown scribbles. The series had to be shown several times before the task could be performed well. What the data show is that it takes time to extract information from inputs. The time taken depends on the complexity of the input. For a very complex input, a considerable amount of time may have to be expended in study in order to extract information from it. For example, the first time one hears a very complex and long symphony by a modern composer, one may not be able to find the themes, and one is likely to say "I just don't understand the piece of music." Then one hears the symphony several times on a record. Gradually, the music begins to have some form and structure. It no longer seems just a jumble of notes played, as it were, at random, but it is perceived as an organized musical composition. Those who have a deep understanding of music will always achieve such understanding more rapidly than the less sophisticated. When one says that he understands a piece of music, it means that he can hear it and recognize organization in it and specific features that characterize it. In terms of the language used in the rest of this chapter, the understanding of a piece of music involves extracting information from the music.

The reader must also note that an input can be too complicated for the person to whom it is presented to be able to extract information from it in a given time period. Educational materials have to be designed so that the pupil can extract information from them in the time provided.

A third point to note about the Gibson experiment is that learning to extract information took place without any reinforcing event. The subjects were never told whether they were right or wrong in deciding whether a scribble was or was not the same as the one shown initially. They improved their performance from trial to trial and showed learning without any kind of reward, reinforcement, feedback, or related event. This does not mean that reinforcing events play no part in learning, for sometimes they do. What it does show, as in many other studies, is that reinforcement is not an essential condition for learning. The experiment can be described as involving what is called **perceptual learning.**

An additional condition must also be considered within the category of perceptual learning, related to classical conditioning. The essential nature of the phenomenon is that when two inputs of information are received by the perceptual systems at approximately the same time, any property the one may have for eliciting action is acquired by the other. In crude terms, the two inputs, or stimuli, become **associated.** Psychologists as far back as Aristotle believed that this was a genuine principle of learning and traditionally described the phenomenon as association of one idea with another. The experimental demonstration of this phenomenon in a simple and pure form had to await modern times, when it was demonstrated through what is known as **sensory preconditioning.** In this type of demonstration, the basic procedure is to present together two neutral stimuli, a light and a buzzer, in a long series of trials. One of these, say the light, is then used as the unconditioned stimulus in a typical classical conditioning experiment. For example, the light might be paired with a puff of air on the eyeball, which produces an eyeblink reflex. The light then becomes a conditioned stimulus for the eyeblink response. After all this has been done, the experimenter finds that the buzzer has also acquired the property of eliciting the eyeblink response, although the buzzer was never paired with the eyeblink, only the light was. Nevertheless, the buzzer acquired the property of eliciting the eyeblink because it had been previously paired with the light. This type of experiment, which has now been carried out many times in many different contexts, shows rather clearly how two inputs that occur together can acquire from one another any response-eliciting effects they may have. In crude terms, it might be said that the two inputs have become associated, but when one says that experience X is associated with experience Y, one means that whatever responses tend to be aroused by the one will also be aroused by the other.

The kind of perceptual learning mechanism under consideration appears to be the kind involved in learning pairs of words consisting of English words and their equivalents in a foreign language. If the two items of information can be introduced into the perceptual system, one after the other, then there is a chance that associative learning will occur. The introduction of small rewards such as candy and other events usually classed as reinforcing are not a crucial condition for this kind of learning, though they may determine whether a pair of words is ever attended to.

Teachers generally make the assumption, and rightly, too, that if two items of information can be introduced simultaneously into the student's perceptual system, the items will be associated. Thus a common procedure for teaching spelling is for the student to say the word and then to spell it either aloud or under his breath. The expectation is that the same child engaged in writing a composition will say a word to himself and will then have associated with it the spelling of the word. Countries and their capitals are repeated together for the same reason.

When two items enter the perceptual system simultaneously, they are said to become associated because they are perceived contiguously, that is, at the same time. In some psychological writings, this type of learning is called **learning by contiguity.** Although experiments demonstrating contiguity learning are many, including those of classical conditioning, the condition of contiguity is not sufficient to produce learning that has any degree of permanence. Nuttin and Greenwald (1968) have demonstrated that one essential condition for such learning to occur in verbal learning experiments is that the individual involved have the expectation that the learning is going to have value in the future. Older books on educational psychology would have said much the same thing by saying that learning is improved by intent to learn.

Perceptual Training

Many important questions related to education concern matters of perceptual training. The assumption has been made by reading experts that a child, in order to be able to read, must have the perceptual skills that the task requires. One of these skills is, presumably, the ability to discriminate one word from another. A child who is perceptually unable to make such a discrimination must be assumed to be unable to learn to read.

Perceptual deficiencies, that is, lack of perceptual skills, are regarded as having two main sources. On the one hand, they may result from brain damage. On the other, they may be a product of an environment that has failed to provide the child with favorable circumstances for developing his perceptual systems. Perceptual deficiencies due to brain damage are believed to be quite common, but they can arise from several different causes and have many different consequences. A common cause is believed to be circumstances of birth that deprive the child's brain of needed oxygen. Mechanical injury to the brain during birth is much less likely to be a source of difficulty than is oxygen deprivation, which may occur when the umbilical cord becomes tangled or birth is prolonged and involves complications. Oxygen deprivation results in the death of brain cells. These cells have only the shortest life without an adequate oxygen supply. The results of this kind of deprivation may be extremely varied. The most easily observed consequences are those that influence the control of muscles and produce cerebral palsy. The victim of such a condition may have difficulty in performing the simplest motor acts such as feeding himself or grasping an object or walking, yet his intellectual ability may be unimpaired. Such individuals are commonly mistaken to be stupid and mentally defective because they lack the muscular control necessary for expressing themselves, but many have been found to have, behind their clumsy exterior, brilliant intellects. A central problem in educating them is finding means through which they can express themselves. The teacher has to be able to find at least a small section of the musculature sufficiently under control so that it can be used as a channel for providing contact between what may be a rich inner life and an often unsympathetic and un-understanding outside world.

Brain damage resulting in disturbances of perception is much less likely to be detected than is that producing motor disturbances. Indeed, just a few decades ago, a child with such problems was unlikely to have them identified and might have been classed as unmotivated or unintelligent. Today there are a number of tests that are administered to young children who have difficulty learning to read, and some of these tests are used for identifying brain damage. The best known is the Bender–Gestalt test, which requires the child to copy a number of outlined figures. The claim is that the child with perceptual difficulties resulting from brain damage will show a striking disability to undertake such tasks. It is this kind of disability that is believed to be related to difficulties in learning to read.

A problem of importance is whether a child who has a perceptual difficulty associated with brain damage can overcome this problem with training. Marsland (1970), who has reviewed related research, comes to the conclusion that such perceptual difficulties are not directly remediable. A main argument in favor of Marsland's position is that brain damage occurring early in childhood has lasting and marked effects. This is in marked contrast with the finding that the nearer a person is to adulthood when he suffers brain injury, the less marked are the consequences. Marsland does suggest that, although training may not remove the deficiencies, the difficulties may be circumvented. For example, a child may have difficulty in discriminating an *M* from an *N*, though the difference may be quite obvious to other children of his age. Although he may not be able to obtain an immediate recognition of the difference, he still may learn to discriminate the two by counting the number of strokes in each letter. In this way, the difficulty is circumvented but not directly overcome. The extent to which such devices are effective is not clear. Some children do show recovery, but it might be argued that the original diagnosis of brain damage was wrong. The diagnosis is, at the best, an educated guess.

A second type of perceptual difficulty can derive from abnormal or defective circumstances of living. Most of what is known about such phenomena has been inferred very indirectly. An example of an extremely deficient environment for the development of visual perception is that provided by institutions for foundlings. In such institutions, babies are exposed to a highly uniform white visual field. The ceiling above them is white, the curtains are white, the adults who care for them are clothed in white, the sheets are white, and so forth. Investigators have long noted the behavioral abnormalities of such infants as they grow, pointing out that they are inactive and unresponsive. Experiments with animals suggest that serious perceptual inadequacies may be the result of such an environment. A study by Riesen (1970) indicates that animals exposed to a uniformly lit environment undergo deterioration of the visual mechanism. The retina of the eye ceases to function properly. In addition, research by Valverde and Ruiz-Marcos (1970) suggests that failure to provide proper stimulation for the developing eye may actually produce a degeneration within the brain of some of the structures associated with vision. Whether such degenerative changes are reversible is not known. If they are, then the reversal is probably slow and tedious.

Although one may infer, with some reservation concerning the validity of the inference, that foundling-home children lack adequate perceptual development, direct evidence concerning the effect of perceptual deprivation is hard to find. One can point to the fact that children who have a turned eye (strabismus) are likely to lose the use of vision in the eye not used. In this case, the effect is quite dramatic. Flom (1970) has presented evidence indicating that treatment of such visual problems has to be begun very quickly after the one eye ceases to be used. Particularly in younger children, failure to provide treatment produces a permanent defect that cannot be remedied. This leads to the question of whether perceptual defects caused by living in surroundings unfavorable for perceptual development result in permanent deficiencies that cannot be reversed. The Hebb (1966) studies of animals raised in perceptually deprived conditions indicate that these conditions tend to produce a quite stable deficiency in the ability to use a particular perceptual system. However, man probably has a greater flexibility in adapting to new circumstances and may not suffer such permanent damage.

The problem discussed here is one of considerable significance to teachers. Most educational programs have been developed on the assumption that deficiencies of the child resulting from his background can be remedied. Education has to be based on optimism concerning the modifiability of human nature.

The Addition of Information to Storage

The perceptual systems have some inherent capacity to extract information from a bewilderingly complex environment, although most of the information has only a transitory life. Some of the information extracted becomes integrated with that already stored, and two different processes are involved in this. Piaget has been largely responsible for identifying and describing these processes (see Flavell, 1963), which he has called **assimilation** and **accommodation.** Assimilation involves a process of extracting information from the environment that fits in some way with the information already stored. Even philosophers of science have long recognized that information is not derived from the environment with any great objectivity by the observer. He is always biased in what he notices and what he rejects, and the information is always slanted in the direction of his immediate needs. This is only one aspect of the assimilation of information, but all information that is taken in and becomes a part of the memory structure is assimilated to that structure.

Assimilation is always accompanied by a second process, accommodation. Information taken in through the perceptual systems may modify what is already stored, and the modification is referred to as accommodation. Any information assimilated involves some degree of accommodation, for one cannot add information to a system without, at least to some small degree, changing the overall nature of the total body of information. There are certain dramatic examples of accommodation having great significance for education that may be cited to indicate the importance of the process. One notable example is in the case of attitude education, in which it is desired to change the internal attitude of an individ-

This infant sitting next to his mother, who is driving the car, is already learning to drive the car.

When he reaches the age when he first can take the driver's seat, he will apply the knowledge of driving he has already acquired.

ual by providing him with some information. Let us suppose that the person whose attitude one wants to change lives in a community of people known as "Prejies," among whom there is a small persecuted group of "Minories." Suppose that one knows that the Prejies have a vast amount of misinformation about the Minories, so the plan is to provide the Prejies with some correct information in the hope that it will correct their misinformation. The Prejies appear to listen, but with quite varied responses. Some listen and say to themselves "Of course, there are a few Minories who are the way he says they are, but most are just the bums we know them to be, so there is no reason to change our impression." Such an individual is engaged in the assimilation of the information provided by the speaker, but he has given the information a twist so that it can be added to his store of information without making any major change in it. Other Prejies receive the information and use it in an entirely different way. They say to themselves "Maybe we were wrong about the Minories. Perhaps we ought to think of them in a different light." This is accommodation. In all educational programs involving attitude change, the objective is to change the viewpoint of the receiver of the information, that is, to produce an accommodative response. The accommodation thus taking place always also involves some degree of assimilation. Conversely, those who slough off the information by saying that it applies only to a few have made a minor accommodative change.

Piaget maintains that from the earliest days the infant shows both accommodation and assimilation in building his internal information store. The schema he possesses at birth related to sucking and other basic activities becomes expanded to encompass the variety of experiences in which sucking takes place. Each expanding experience not only adds to the schema but also to some degree modifies it. The processes of accommodation and assimilation always move hand in hand.

Piaget takes the process of internal organization one step further. Internal organizations of information are also continuously being changed, even without the intervention of any new experience. Both child and adult have the capacity of reorganizing the information they possess. The information stored in the nervous system is not stored as it is in a computer, in particular positions and in static form, but is stored in a quite diffuse form, so that the same information is stored in different places, and the system can to some degree reorganize itself.

Almost any theory of behavior, either Piagetian or along the lines of the more traditional behaviorists, has to assume that behavior has an inherent property of variability. Behavior could never be shaped along the lines described by Skinner if it were not variable. Variability introduces behaviors to reinforce that were not initially present. In addition, the inherent variability of behavior continuously brings the infant, child, and adult into new relationships with the environment, and these new relationships result in the development of schemas by both assimilation and accommodation. The young human being thus has basic mechanisms that permit the development of his internal information system.

Which child is learning mainly by accommodation, and which is learning mainly by assimilation?

The source of the variability in behavior is obscure. Piaget, like many contemporary psychologists, refers to an exploratory tendency, but one can make some more precise statements about the nature of the mechanism involved. Because the topic is of such vital concern to those involved in education, a separate chapter will be devoted to it.

The years before the child enters school are also the years when the foundation of many social attitudes are formed through the mechanisms discussed. Of particular interest at the present time is the development of attitudes of racial majorities toward minorities and of minorities toward majorities. When the groups involved are black and white, the first step in the development of interracial attitudes involves recognition of difference in skin color. Goodman (1964) summarizes numerous studies showing that children distinguish between blacks and whites by the age of three, but the ability to make such discriminations does not imply that prejudice has already developed. Once color discriminations of skin have been made, prejudice is not long in developing. Goodman states that during the ages of four to six not only are skin discriminations made, but children are already beginning to ascribe to members of racial groups stereotyped roles. By the age of seven, well-formed attitudes appear in many children, and by the age of twelve, children may reach the peak of their prejudice against minority groups. There is also some evidence that the prejudiced individual does not direct his hostility toward a single minority group. For example, those prejudiced against blacks tend to be prejudiced also against Orientals and Jews.

Goodman suggests from her data that children showing early prejudice were suspicious and mistrustful of the world in which they lived. There is some evidence that such children fail to learn a basic trust of the world in their early life. Such children also show a high degree of preoccupation with social conventions and with conformity. They may claim that color of skin has nothing to do with their choice of friends, but their behavior betrays the development of deep-seated prejudice. Thus development of prejudice against minorities is not a matter of the development of an isolated personality trait, but it reflects a part of a quality of character.

The Development of Operations

Up to this point, stress has been placed on the fact that in infancy behavior can come to be elicited by new stimuli through classical conditioning. Behavior can also be modified or changed to some degree by means of operant procedures. In addition, the perceptual system manages to extract and assimilate or accommodate a vast amount of information from the environment, particularly information related to the acquisition of language. Most formal education, such as takes place in schools, requires that the child be able to undertake much more than these basic processes. Education requires that the individual be able to undertake what Piaget refers to as **operations.** The concept of an operation in the

Piagetian sense is difficult to elucidate, but it is essentially a process of thinking logically.

Before the child can undertake operations, certain prior learnings are necessary. One such prior learning involves classification tasks, which can vary considerably in complexity. The simplest classification tasks, such as sorting colors, involve only simple perceptual processes that permit the individual to recognize identical elements. At a more complex level, they involve the identification of classes, as when a child is given many objects differing in size but consisting of only a few shapes and is required to categorize the objects in terms of shape. The square objects in such a task may differ in size, and thus the child has to recognize the existence of a class of square objects. This is a more complex process than that involving the recognition only of identity. Another skill the child has to master involves seriation, that is, the arrangement of a set of objects in terms of size or weight or hue or some other characteristic. Madame Montessori recognized nearly a century ago the importance of the development of these skills and created many tasks for teaching them to children. She developed tasks involving, among other things, scales of size and roughness. In one such task, the child had to arrange a series of pieces of sandpaper in order from the smoothest to the roughest. Tasks involving seriation lead to the development of the concept of whole numbers and hence pave the way for undertaking operations involving addition and subtraction. The tasks that lead to operations are called **preoperations.**

The development of curricula for modern nursery schools and kindergartens has been highly influenced by the concepts that Piaget developed in relation to intellectual development. One would have a hard time finding such a program that did not include many tasks involving classification, seriation, and so forth. The dominance of Piaget's ideas in this respect is attributable not only to the strength given them by the research on which they are based but also to the fact that useful alternative descriptions of intellectual development in the preschool years have not been developed. Most of the operations discussed by Piaget and derived from his observations on children involve mathematical or logical operations, for he has found that the languages of mathematics and logic are highly suitable for describing the thinking behavior of the young child.

An important category of operations extensively studied by American psychologists is **conservation.** The concept of conservation is simple for the adult, which is why psychologists long failed to recognize the difficulty that children have in acquiring it. The adult knows full well that if one has a small heap of pennies and then divides them into two heaps, the total number of pennies is the same. A person who knows that the division of the pennies into smaller heaps or the consolidation of the smaller heaps into larger heaps does not change the number of pennies has a knowledge of conservation. A child at the age of three years may divide up candy between himself and another child, but the division shows no regard for number or for the idea that there are only a certain number of candies in the total pile to be divided up. Such concepts have to be acquired before the child can arrive at the concept of conservation. The child may be quite satisfied if the other child ends up with ten candies and he ends up with six. He does not have the capacity to arrange the two sets of candy in lines so that for each candy in one line there is a corresponding candy in the other line. He may look at two lines of candy, with the candy pieces touching one another in the one line and spread out in the other, and judge that the two lines of candy have the same amount in each because they are of the same length. He is quite unable to arrange two arrays or sets so that they have a one-to-one correspondence. The operation of conservation requires that he be able to do this.

Conservation, as an operation, is not confined to the concept of number. Conservation can also be found in other concepts such as that of space. The child eventually understands that in dividing up an area nothing is added or subtracted from the area, or that in adding one quantity of liquid to another the amount of liquid is not changed.

Numerous studies have been made of the conditions in which children can form conservation concepts. Probably no operation has been more intensively discussed than conservation. Nevertheless, exactly what the prerequisites are for acquiring this concept is still controversial (see Halford, 1970).

The child becomes capable of the operations discussed at just about the time when he typically enters elementary school. At this stage, and until about the age of eleven or twelve, the operations he performs are referred to as **concrete operations,** because they are always tied to concrete events. At a later stage, the he becomes capable of performing **formal operations,** which are logical operations and can be undertaken in abstract terms. The thought of the child of elementary-school age is tied to concrete events, but he may be able to represent the concrete world within himself. The child, at this stage, is able to think about the world around him but only in quite specific and concrete terms.

Piaget, who describes operations in the language of algebra and logic, finds nine operations related to the groupings of objects. For example, the child of elementary-school age learns that not only can a class of objects be divided into groups but each group can be divided into subgroups. Thus a group of persons can be divided into blacks and whites, and each of these groups can then be subdivided into those who are short and those who are tall. The child also learns operations related to dividing the same class of objects in different ways. The people in a community can be divided into classes by color, income, religion, or sex. He learns to perform other operations related to groupings, as when he finds out how many in the community are both male and Catholic, and can perform operations related to multiplication and division with classes and groupings in concrete situations.

How skill in the performance of operations is acquired is a matter that has been the focus of controversy. The position taken by Piaget (see Piaget and Inhelder, 1969) is that a particular operation can be performed when the nervous system develops to a point where the necessary internal mechanisms exist and the necessary prerequisite experiences have occurred. Learning is not really the key to the appearance of the skill, but the skill will appear if the individual is confronted with situations that permit the exercise of the skill. In the absence of appropriate situations, the child may not manifest the particular operation. This position leads to the expectation that there is little value in attempting to accelerate the time when the child will show an ability to perform a particular operation. This appears to be a matter that could be settled experimentally, and very extensive research has been undertaken in an attempt to determine whether very young children, such as three-year-olds, can be taught conservation skills. Halford (1970) has reviewed many of the studies that have tried to do this, but it is quite evident there are difficulties in planning such studies and interpreting the results that make the task of testing this central thesis of Piaget very difficult. There seems little doubt that children can be taught to say that when a pile of pennies is divided into two piles the number of pennies does not change, but how does one distinguish between the child who is just taught to use those particular words and the child who has some comprehension of conservation of quantity as a principle?

Various techniques have been devised to overcome this difficulty. One is to use a task in which water in a tubular container is poured into a narrower and taller container. The typical child of five years of age will then say that there is now more water. The child can then be corrected and be taught to say that there is still the same amount of water in the new container as there was in the original container, but this does not mean that he has grasped the idea. One may then try and probe what the child has learned by now pouring the water into a broad and wider container. The chances are that the child will now insist that there is now less water. He learned what to say in the first situation but did not grasp the idea that water does not change in quantity by merely being transferred to a new container. The reader can now understand that it is not entirely easy to differentiate the child who has learned what words to use from the child who has grasped the idea of the conservation of quantity. For this reason, the results of numerous studies of the problem of how to accelerate the acquisition of the concept of conservation of quantity have tended to yield inconsistent findings. They do not provide any strong support for the idea that special training will accelerate the development of the concept of conservation of quantity. Piaget insists that the child will discover the concept through his daily transactions when he is ready to acquire it but that special training will not help.

The transition from the preoperational phase to the phase of concrete operations that takes place around the age of six or seven is characterized by the fact that thinking becomes what is called **reversible.** The essential feature of reversibility is that of being able to carry out a logical process forward and then backward. A five-year-old may be able to figure that two things added to two things makes four things, but he cannot understand what happens when two things are taken away from four things. He can solve the problem forward but not backward. Reversibility becomes a property of thinking during the stage of concrete operations.

During this stage, the child can learn addition of single-digit numbers and then move easily to the subtraction of single-digit numbers. There can be no doubt that without reversibility, thinking is extremely limited. Psychologists such as Vinacke (1952) and Johnson (1955) who studied problem solving a couple of decades ago noted that when the problem is difficult the problem solver may first try to solve the problem in the forward direction and then try to solve it backward, starting at the end. Problem solving typically involves a process of going forward and then backward and then forward again. A person whose thinking could only move forward would be extremely limited in the problems he could solve. More recent work on the subject hardly mentions this, though computer systems of solving problems often involve both forward and backward procedures.

The nonreversibility of thinking in the preoperational phase may be accounted for, at least partly, by the fact that the memory span of the young child is limited. Just as the young child does not use long sentences, because if he tried to use them he would forget the first part of the sentence before he could finish it, so too does he have difficulty in taking a statement he has made and working the argument backward. To do this, he has to hold a lot in mind, more than he can at his stage of development.

The distinction has been made between concrete operations and formal operations—a very important distinction in terms of Piaget's concept of the development of intelligence. The preoperational phase prepares the child for the stage of concrete operations. The kinds of examples given in the previous pages fail to stress one important feature of the operations that can be performed by the child of elementary-school age: The operations have to be tied to concrete situations to be performed at all. Presumably, the tie can be of many different kinds. At the kindergarten and first-grade level, the child may learn to count and perform simple arithmetical operations with beads, often arranged in an abacus type of frame. Later, the child may substitute some form of counting on his fingers, and still later he may count on his fingers but with almost imperceptible movements of his hands.

The transition from concrete operations to formal operations is a transition from being able to undertake thinking operations only in terms of concrete events to being able to handle highly abstract concepts. Another way of describing this transition is as a change from thinking dominated by actual situations in the outside world to thinking very free of such a setting.

What has been said does not imply that during the stage of concrete operations, behavior involves only the manipulation of the outside world, for that is not so. Thought can be tied to the real world without it involving the manipulation of the world. In the stage of concrete operations, there is what is called **internalization of the environment**—that is, aspects of the environment become represented internally in the child through the use of words and schemas, but these representations are not abstract concepts if they are to enter into concrete operations.

Relationship of the Development of
Language to Thought

The relationship of language development to thought has long been a matter for speculation, but in recent times it has also become the focus for experimentation. The problem is a difficult one to tackle, because first the term *thought* must be defined somehow. The definition is commonly taken care of by identifying thought as an internal activity taking place when a problem is confronted. On this basis, lower animals think at simple levels, for they can be confronted with problems that are within their capability to solve. It is also clear from this that some problem solving can take place without the intervention of language. Nevertheless, in the case of the human problem solver, language is quite intimately associated with problem-solving behavior. Herriot (1970) has summarized some of the knowledge derived from research in this area and points out that research on children has shown that the talking aloud they do in solving problems is related to their performance. Children who are least adequate in problem-solving performance are those who manifest considerable confusion in the language behavior that goes on while they are working. Children at the preschool age typically talk aloud when solving a problem, whether they are alone or being observed. Presumably, the talking aloud is more than a by-product of the problem-solving process.

A great advantage of language in problem solving is that it permits a precise statement of the problem. Indeed, one can hardly imagine any other mechanism that would permit the precise statement of a problem except the language mechanism. There are some puzzling aspects of problem solving suggesting that processes other than those involved in the deliberate use of language play a part. The fact that the solution to a problem may pop into one's mind, as if from nowhere and some time after the problem has been forgotten, indicates that there are other important mechanisms operating. Of course, the individual may have some capacity for manipulating words and other symbols at levels of his nervous system where he has no direct control. If a computer can perform logical operations with words, then perhaps various levels of the nervous system can do this too, besides the level that has to do with conscious behavior.

The Development of a Control System

The change in performance from the preoperational level of behavior to the level of concrete operations is paralleled by another change of great interest. The change is most clearly seen in the work of Kendler and Kendler (1970), which they have pursued for a number of years. Their experiments involve a choice-discrimination task involving four objects—a large white square, a large black square, a small white square, and a small black square. One of these appears in a window on a screen in front of the child, who must decide whether it is a "right" object or a "wrong" object. If he is correct in his response, he obtains either a small candy or a token he can later turn in for some prize chosen from a group of prizes. Let us suppose that in the learning series, or what is commonly called the **acquisition series,** the experimenter decides that black, and not size, is to be the feature that is to make an object right or wrong and that the child must learn to identify to obtain a reward. Soon the child learns the correct discrimination. At this point, the experimenter switches the rules on him. There are two switches possible, as follows:

1. The experimenter may decide that white, and not black, will be right from now on. This is the opposite of what was right previously, and the shift in rules is referred to as a **reversal shift.**

2. The experimenter may decide that the large square, regardless of color, will now be correct. This is a shift to a new dimension—size—that was not relevant previously. The shift in rules is referred to as an **extradimensional shift.**

Let us consider the case in which there is a reversal shift. For a typical three-and-a-half-year-old who has learned that black is correct, his first response is to continue to call the black shapes right. In terms of the language of instrumental conditioning, the response to black is slowly extinguished. A response to white may then be acquired. The change in the behavior, from responding to black to responding to white, is slow. In contrast, the behavior of the six-year-old is quite different. Very soon after the rewards for black are removed, the child stops responding to black and shifts his behavior to correspond with the shift in the rules.

An important point to note is that the behavior of the three-and-a-half-year-old is very similar to that of a subhuman subject confronted with a change in rules. The previously acquired response has to be slowly extinguished. No such slow extinction takes place in the case of the six-year-old, who is capable of making a quick and rapid adjustment to changing circumstances.

The data on this point seem to be very clear. A change takes place around the age of five or six, and the simple principles of operant conditioning cease to apply in the way they have applied earlier. Just what is the internal nature of this change is not clear, but it appears to involve the development of a new decision-making system. With the development of such a system, the child no longer has to continue to make a response that has no instrumental value but can just block that response and experiment with other responses that may turn out to be more effective. Gladstone (1969), who conducted a study in this area and also showed that responses of four-and-a-half- to five-and-a-half-year-old children were more rapidly extinguished than those of children only a year younger, points out in his conclusion that a great variety of interpretations of the internal change have been suggested. Some psychologists say that it is due to a change in what they call cognitive control, suggesting that knowledge begins to facilitate extinction. Another explanation is that the younger children were unable to discriminate between the condition involving reinforcement and the one not involving reinforcement. This seems to be a very unlikely explanation, because the absence of the reinforcing event is likely to be missed even by a three-year-old. Indeed, in such experiments, children typically comment on the absence of the reinforcement during extinction even though they still continue to perform the task. The child continues to work as though he had no control system that could arrest the unrewarding behavior in which he is engaged.

There is some agreement that the development of a control system is closely related to the development of language. Sometimes it is said that language functions as a **mediator** that causes the unreinforced behavior to be stopped. This, also, is not a very clear conception of the underlying mechanism. Suppose that the child has learned a verbally stated rule that "If the rewards that follow what one is doing stop, then stop doing it and try doing other things." It is still difficult to imagine a mechanism that would invoke this rule on appropriate occasions. All one can say with any certainty is that the development of verbal behavior is related to the development of a decision system that makes it possible to short-cut the extinction process. One may speculate that what is called the control system has sets of rules, from which some selection is made for application. The selection may be in terms of such factors as the rule most recently successful or the rule that logically applies in terms of the facts available.

The evidence cited of a radical change in behavior taking place at around the age of five, or sometimes a little later, is not confined to simple extinction phenomena alone. Another very interesting example of the developmental change being considered is what is known as **the Humphreys phenomenon.**

In order to describe the Humphreys phenomenon, let us consider a simple laboratory experiment in which a rat runs down a straight alley and, at the end of the alley, has a choice of turning either left or right to reach a goal box. This situation is called a T-maze. A hungry rat is used, and ordinarily one would be interested in finding out some condition related to the ability of the rat to learn to find the food in one arm of the maze, so food will always be in that arm of the maze. In order to demonstrate the Humphreys phenomenon, a different condition is introduced. On a certain percentage of the occasions, the food is at the end of the right-turn alley and on a certain percentage it is at the end of the left-turn alley. How would one expect the animal to perform under these new conditions with, say, the right alley rewarded on 70 per cent of the trials and the left alley rewarded on 30 per cent? According to traditional reinforcement theory, because the right alley is rewarded on 70 per cent of the trials the right-turn habit will become the stronger and hence the rat will turn consistently to the right, but this is not what actually happens. If the right alley is rewarded in the proportion stated, the rat will go to the right alley 70 per cent of the time and to the left alley 30 per cent of the time.

One can arrange a situation so that a child is reinforced for pushing a right-hand button on 70 per cent of the occasions and reinforced for pushing a left-hand button on 30 per cent of the occasions, and three-year-old children will behave much like rats. Older children perform differently. They are likely to settle down to pushing the button that has the highest payoff, which is the rational approach to the problem. The maximum payoff is achieved by responding only to the button that gives the maximum payoff and neglecting the other button. However, many children work on the development of some kind of system that they hope will beat the system. They attempt one strategy and then another. They will not believe that the reinforcements are assigned strictly on the basis of chance. They behave as if they believed that they lived in an orderly world in which events do not occur on a random basis. Indeed, those who have worked with children in such settings are impressed with the fact that it may be impossible to convince them that the events are chance events and that there is no rule they can possibly discover to beat the system. The behavior of the children is very similar to that of gamblers who attempt to discover some system in the way in which the ball stops on a roulette wheel.

The decision-making system grows in complexity and in the number of conditions taken into account in arriving at a choice of action. If Piaget's description of the stage of concrete operations is correct, then one would expect the decision-making system to have a limited capacity during the elementary-school years for taking into account events in the future or conditions not strictly observable. Such speculation needs to be replaced by experimentation.

Feedback and the Structuring of Behavior

Behavior is quite obviously modified by its consequences. A particular instance of this modification is found in the typical experiment in which a reinforcing event changes the frequency with which a certain class of behaviors occurs. The consequences of behavior also provide information that, in turn, becomes assimilated as a part of the inventory of information stored by the learner. If one takes the position that the nervous system is a mechanism that extracts information from the inputs through the sensory systems, then it must also be acknowledged that the manipulation of the environment results in new information influencing the information store of the system. Information resulting from a person's own activity is commonly referring to as **feedback.** Thus, when the teacher informs a pupil that he is right or wrong in the answer he has found for a problem, the teacher is providing feedback. The information provided by the teacher can be thought of as a reinforcing event in that it has effects on whether the pupil will or will not solve the problem in the same kind of way in the future. However, the broad classification of all events as reinforcing because they have the same consequence is a practice of dubious utility. Indeed, there is rarely much utility in using consequence as the basis for classification. For example, what use is there in classifying all death-producing events in a single category? One would never learn much about the causes of death if this were done. The only reason for such a broad classification is the trivial one that it does not make much difference how a person dies to the person who dies. From the point of view of preventing death by understanding its causes, such a broad classification is useless. For this sort of reason, information provided as a result of the individual's activity will not be referred to here as a reinforcing event. The term *reinforcing event* will be reserved for events that influence the probability that a particular form of behavior will be repeated but are not intrinsic to the task. Thus when a child is given a piece of candy for pressing a particular button, the candy is not an intrinsic part of the task, for many different reward systems could be used. In a sense, of course, a child may interpret the receiving of candy as informative, as the experimenter's saying "You have pressed the right button and I am giving you a candy to let you know that what you have done is right." But a child does not necessarily have to interpret the task in this way. He may view it as a situation in which the goal is to obtain candy. The arrival of the candy is simply the achievement, or the partial achievement, of the goal.

Many psychologists would not speak of the candy, in the experiment just cited, as a reinforcing event. They would call it an **incentive,** that is, an event that has the property of energizing behavior. In this respect, the use of the candy functions differently from the information provided a pupil when he is told that he has the right answer to an arithmetic problem. When he is told that he has achieved the right answer, the information provided permits him to reflect back on how he solved the problem so that the information can be used in solving other problems. The candy merely strengthens the tendency to push the particular lever that resulted in its delivery, but, in contrast, the same arithmetic problem might never be encountered again.

The situation is complicated by the fact that there is evidence to show that saying "right" when the pupil obtains the correct answer has incentive value as well as information-giving value. A pupil who never worked a problem correctly in a particular class might give up trying.

The information provided through feedback varies in its utility from situation to situation. A teacher who tells a child "Johnny, your general way of solving the problem was right, but you made a mistake in the arithmetic, here" is providing information that is potentially highly useful, if the child listens and then thinks about what is said. The information tells him that he can use the same procedure successfully on problems of the same class, and it also tells him to watch out for arithmetical errors. On the other hand, in learning to throw a basketball into a basket, the feedback is whether the ball does or does not go into the basket, which does not give the person who threw the ball very precise information about how to throw it next time, although he may squeeze out a few clues such as that he should throw the ball harder or less hard. In some sports, the player may not be able to use the information without the help of a coach.

Both boys may be learning to throw the ball into the basket although only one is performing the task. Also, one may help the other to correct his faults.

Even professional golf players, with years of experience, may need the help of another experienced person to correct their own errors in performance.

One of the real difficulties in identifying errors of performance in athletic skills is that each play is executed so quickly that the person cannot keep careful track of what he does. In other words, he cannot both perform and monitor his performance successfully at the same time. What he needs is an observer who will monitor his performance for him and help him to use the feedback information.

The form of feedback in relation to verbal tasks that is most utilizable is verbal feedback. Such information is not only precise but it can be written down, as it is when the pupil's work is corrected. If the feedback is recorded, it can be referred to again and again, and its use is not limited by whether the individual can or cannot remember what was said to him. However, not all verbal feedback is sufficiently precise that a person can make direct use of it. A child who writes an English composition and receives on it the comment "Not well organized" may not know how to use the information. The child thought it *was* well organized. A very important problem in instruction is providing feedback in a form that can be used. The reader interested in more extensive study of problems of feedback, reinforcement, and incentives is referred to the excellent paperback book by Annett (1969).

95
· · · · · · · · · · ·
Feedback and the
Structuring of Behavior

Summary

1 In the preschool years, some skills are acquired through the reinforcement of effective aspects of skills and the extinction of ineffective aspects. Although reinforcement and extinction sound like simple ways of shaping behavior, they are undoubtedly complex phenomena. Also, what a teacher believes he is reinforcing may not be the behavior that is actually reinforced. A teacher's attempts to reinforce behavior are often colored with a great amount of wishful thinking. In the laboratory, precisely defined behaviors can be reinforced, but in the classroom there is little control over exactly what behaviors occur.

2 A particularly notable aspect of development during the preschool years is the acquisition of the native language and grammar. Two main theories have been proposed concerning language development, one by Skinner and the other attributable mainly to psycholinguists.

3 Skinner approaches language development as the acquisition of a set of operants. He views language as a form of instrumental behavior. The child makes statements in order to manipulate the environment. In Skinner's terminology, a statement is a verbal operant, a word produced in response to an object is a tact, and a word that represents a command or a demand is a mand. These terms are attempts to evolve a new way of classifying words on a psychological basis and are to be contrasted with conventional word classifications such as noun and verb. Skinner proposes that reading involves subvocal responses. A major difficulty of Skinner's approach is that linguistic behavior is not slowly shaped. Children say whole words correctly the first time they use them and do not slowly learn to use adult grammatical constructions. Sometimes words are used as forms of instrumental behavior for manipulating the environment, though language is also used for other purposes.

4 Children learn language even under conditions that provide few reinforcements for correct language behavior. Psycholinguists have long been puzzled by this fact and have sought to find alternative descriptions of the development of language. A first point to note is that language is an activity generated in accordance with certain rules. Traditional English grammar is a rather inadequate attempt to formulate such rules, but some much more precise formulations of grammar have been produced. Young children in the preschool years first evolve their own grammar that does not

resemble adult grammar at all. A common construction of the young child is a pivot word connected with one word after another. In early stages, language has constructions very similar to those used in telegrams. The child does not derive telegraphic language from adults. He generates this kind of language himself.

5 A major contrast between the operant approach to the study of language and the psycholinguistic approach is that the operant approach involves a left-to-right production of language and interpretation of language, but the psycholinguistic approach requires that utterances be analyzed as a whole. A sentence is understood not just because of the particular words it contains but because it has a particular structure. Large chunks of verbal communications have to be held in memory before enough is there to be analyzed.

6 Psycholinguists make a distinction between deep structure and surface structure of language. Deep structure represents a set of rules that permit the extraction of meaning. Sentences can be written that are grammatically correct but are so complex in structure that their meaning cannot be extracted except with the greatest of difficulty. Children can extract information and meaning only from rather short sentences, because they cannot remember much at one time.

7 The acquisition of language is a creative act. Utterances and sentences are created within the individual.

8 Compensatory education has typically focused on problems of language learning. There is considerable evidence that the language deficiencies of the culturally deprived child result in intellectual inadequacies. The child raised in deprived conditions typically has a smaller vocabulary than the middle-class child. For such a child, common words may also have special meanings and hence he may have difficulty in communicating with children raised in more affluent circumstances. Ghetto dialect has a somewhat different structure than standard English, a fact that adds to the problems of the ghetto child when he enters school and finds that textbooks are written in a language he has not really mastered. These children also show deficiencies in accuracy of communication. Mothers of such children do not have proper techniques for helping them to master language. The mothers are poor teachers.

9 Studies of perceptual learning provide clear evidence of learning without reinforcement. These studies show that the individual has great capacity for structuring and organizing information. Time is required to extract information from inputs to the senses. The more complex the information, the greater the time required to extract it. If information is more

complex than can be handled, no information will be extracted by the perceptual system.

10 An important aspect of perceptual learning is learning by association. Learning a foreign vocabulary is a common case of associative learning. Such learning is sometimes called learning by contiguity. An essential condition for this form of learning to take place is expectation of future use.

11 Perceptual difficulties may arise because of inadequate training or because of brain damage. The latter occurs mainly at birth from oxygen deprivation. Cerebral palsy is also a result of brain damage and represents damage to the motor system. There is some controversy whether perceptual difficulties due to brain damage can be remedied. If they cannot be remedied, at least they can be to some degree circumvented.

12 Perceptual difficulties that can be attributed to cultural deprivation are probably of common occurrence. The foundling institution is a classic example of an environment that provides minimum perceptual stimulation. Infants raised in such a uniform all-white environment show behavioral disturbances, including inactivity and unresponsiveness. Failure to provide proper stimulation may well result in irreversible brain damage. Experiments with animals provide evidence of the permanence of the perceptual deficiencies thus produced.

13 The infant and child extract information from the environment, and the information produces quite permanent changes in the memory system. Piaget emphasizes that information extracted from the environment is added to the information already stored by either assimilation or accommodation. Information assimilated is information already consistent with what is stored, and it is added to the store in an organized way. When information is added by accommodation, some modification is produced in the information already stored, and there is always some change in the schema to which the information is added. The two processes of assimilation and accommodation always occur simultaneously, and a pure example of the one without the other cannot be found. The information stored in the memory system is also in a continuous state of reorganization, even when no new information is being added.

14 Behavior shows variability. Some aspects of variability of behavior are described as exploratory behavior, in that attention is continuously directed toward new features of the environment.

15 Learning during the preschool years also involves the acqui-

sition of prejudices. Included in these prejudices are those between different cultural groups.

16 During the preschool years, the child undertakes many forms of learning that are necessary for the later performance of intellectual operations. Piaget has outlined a series of tasks that children have to learn to do in the first five or six years of life, and these tasks have been used as a basis for designing nursery-school programs.

17 The ability to perform operations appears during the elementary-school years. An example of such an operation is conservation. When the child is ready to perform such operations and the opportunity arises to learn them, then he will perform them. The key to the acquisition of operations is the presentation of situations calling for them. Research has not been successful in developing teaching techniques through which the ability to perform operations can be expedited. An important feature of the phase of concrete operations is reversibility, that is, being able to perform operations both forward and backward. Nonreversibility of thinking in the preoperational phase greatly limits the intellectual tasks that can be undertaken.

18 The final stage of intellectual development is that of being able to perform formal operations. Formal operations involve abstract relationships, whereas concrete operations are always tied to real events in the surrounding world.

19 Language plays an important role in problem solving, though its detailed function in this respect is not fully understood. Language does permit the precise statement of a problem, an important prerequisite for discovering a solution.

20 The preoperational phase of intellectual development is characterized by the development of an internal decision-making system. The very young child shows problem-solving behavior closely similar to that of lower animals. Older children show very different problem-solving behavior, because it involves internal processes that do not occur in younger children.

21 Behavior is obviously modified by its consequences. The consequences of behavior provide information concerning the adequacy of behavior, but they also provide rewards and incentives that may have the effect of energizing behavior.

In the previous chapters, a general account has been given of the major mechanisms involved in learning and some of the learning that forms the background of the child entering elementary school. Much of this description has had to be sketchy, as it has been in the case of language learning, not just because of limitations of space, but because the knowledge available is far from complete. The information provided has led to the identification of a number of learning mechanisms, including operant conditioning, classical conditioning, sensory association, and perceptual information extraction. Illustrations have been provided of how these mechanisms account for some of the learning that takes place in the early years of life. Attention must now be turned to the implications of current knowledge of learning to the acquisition of perhaps the most important single skill that the child is expected to master in elementary school — reading.

4

Reading: A Study in Perceptual Development

Research on reading has involved a process analogous to attempting to run before one can walk. Nearly all of the research of the last half century on the topic has focused on attempting to determine which method of teaching reading is the most effective. The research has been reviewed by Chall (1967). There is a time when such research is effective, but it cannot be genuinely effective until a sound basis has been established for designing a good teaching method. Methods of teaching reading in the past were developed on the basis of a logical analysis of what reading involves and sometimes only on the basis of an intuitive analysis, for there was virtually nothing else to guide the developer of a new method. A scientific analysis of what reading involves has had to await the development of techniques through which the processes of reading can be systematically probed. In the last decade, such an analysis has been begun (see Smith, 1971) and will be discussed here.

Most of us can read. Why then do we not have sufficient knowledge about reading to describe what it involves? The main reason seems to be that the skill, even in the case of a slow reader, involves many processes that take place at lightning speed and therefore cannot be easily or directly observed. Although the task of reading may seem to be a simple one to the skilled reader, it is extremely complex. Even performances that take place at a relatively slow speed may be very difficult for the performer to describe. Ask a skilled bowler how he throws the ball so that another can learn to perform with the same skill, and he is likely to provide very little useful information. He is quite unable to describe what he does, and his inability is not just due to a lack of the language skills needed to describe the throwing of the ball. A part of the difficulty is that his complex performance runs off quite automatically, once it is set in motion, and most of his preoccupation has to be with the target and not with the performance itself. In a parallel fashion, the reader has to concentrate not on the skill itself while he is reading but on the meaning he wants to derive from the words. Nobody can be a good observer of what he does when he reads, and, for this reason, intuitive descriptions of what reading involves are useless. But an understanding of what reading involves has been made possible through the development of psychological techniques that permit, somehow, the slowing up of the process of perception to the point where components of it can be identified. Scientific attack on the problem of how people read is relatively new, dating back to the classic work of Gibson et al. (1965). This work was immediately followed by a considerable number of studies on the mechanisms involved in reading.

A point to note in beginning this review is that one may conduct studies of the reading of the adult and find out little about how children in the first grade read. Although much has been learned from study of adult reading performance, the techniques that the adult has evolved may be quite different from those that the child uses. Fifteen or more years of daily reading may develop strategies of reading far beyond those that the child could master.

The skill of reading is developed through a number of stages. The

102
. . . .
Reading: A Study in
Perceptual Development

first of these involves learning to differentiate graphic symbols from all the other visual forms found in the environment. Second, there must be recognition either that single letters differ from one another or that words differ from one another. Third, there must be comprehension that the symbols, or groups of symbols, correspond to particular sounds. Finally, there must be some kind of analysis of what the sounds mean, for the child may say the words but not follow the meaning. These stages do not take place one after the other but are inextricably intertwined.

The first of these stages requires that conditions exist that call the child's attention to the graphic symbols. A child living in a slum where nobody ever reads and where his rooms are almost devoid of any written symbols may reach school age without ever having recognized that there are graphic symbols in the world or that adults do attend to them or that the attention of the adults to the symbols has various consequences. The development of the ghetto child in this respect is to be contrasted with that of the middle-class white child, who learns, perhaps as early as the age of two years, that adults who look at graphic symbols are able to do things such as tell stories, find out the name of a street, get news about other people through the mail, and so forth. The well-to-do child perceives graphic symbols as objects of great importance early in life and will attend to the symbols long before he can read. Such a child will commonly be observed with an open book in front of him and making reading-like noises. Soon he will ask the adult what the symbols say. Such a child recognizes the concept that the symbols correspond to sounds but perhaps has not yet learned that particular symbols represent particular sounds or even that there are a series of different symbols involved. Nevertheless, in terms of what has been said in previous chapters, one must assume that repeated exposure to the symbols results in a gradual differentiation of them. Repeated exposure results in an increase in the information that can be extracted from them, including their distinctiveness and the differentiation between them.

One can study the factors that make for discriminability of alphabet letters as Gibson et al. (1965) have done by developing artificial alphabets and then determining the extent to which one letter tends to be confused with another. This can be done with children and adults. These workers found that some discriminations are much harder to learn than others. One of the simplest discriminations is between curved and straight lines. Differences between letters involving rotations, such as the difference between *n* and *u*, are very difficult for four-year-olds, who do not apparently use the orientation of the letter to the viewer as a cue. By the age of eight years, this cue can be readily handled, as can most of the others included in the experiment. In a summary article published in *Science* (1965) describing the research, Gibson concludes that somewhere between the ages of four and eight children learn most of the characteristics of letters that differentiate them. The findings with the artificial letters were also substantiated in a study of five-year-olds using the familiar Roman alphabet.

In late kindergarten and early first grade, the teacher will attempt to introduce children to written speech and to show those who have not had any experience with it that it can have considerable utility in their lives. In kindergarten, children learn to discriminate their written name from other written names and hence find a means of identifying their possessions. Somewhat less meaningful tasks for the children are identifying the words for each day of the week and month of the year. Special tasks often have to be developed for children whose attention cannot be readily drawn to written symbols simply because they have never had any experience with any that had any consequence for them. One task, developed by Ashton-Warner (1963), has been used in which the teacher types out, on a large-type typewriter, a short story made up by a child. The child can then take the story home, have others read it to him, and perhaps even learn to read it himself. The preparation of shopping lists and lists of materials for special projects, and so on, provides other opportunities for the child to learn that printed materials are useful. In this way, the child who has not learned to respond to the printed word may slowly come to do so. Interactions with the printed word should be, above all, enjoyable and of the kind that the child will want to prolong. The child who sits on the floor with an open book, babbling as if reading, is probably interacting with written words in an attempt to reinstate the enjoyment of having stories and nursery rhymes read to him. The young child in kindergarten should have learned a similar desire to interact with written words, for this is the way that primitive shape discriminations are learned.

There has long been controversy over whether the basic discriminations in reading should best be learned first at the letter level. The problem is quite a complex one, for what may be an efficient process in the early stages of reading may result in the child being bored by the task, and this may interfere with the development of further skill. Bishop (1964) conducted a study in which subjects were taught to recognize unfamiliar orthography, that is, Arabic script, either through a letter-recognition process or through a word-recognition process. After completing training on either the letter- or the word-recognition process, subjects were tested on both word and letter recognition. The data showed that those trained on letter recognition learned, at the same time, how to recognize words, but it was also found that those trained with words learned something about the shape of individual letters. However, letter training was more effective in producing word recognition than word training was in producing letter recognition. The reason for the transfer from word to letter is probably that the cues used to discriminate words are often the cues used to discriminate letters. This is not always the case. For example, two words may be discriminated by length, but length of word is not a cue used to discriminate letters. On the other hand, two words may be discriminated in terms of the fact that one word begins with a letter involving an open loop, such as *n*, and the other begins with a closed loop, *o*. Most word characteristics involve letter characteristics, and hence learning to discriminate between words inevitably involves learning the characteristics that permit letter discrimination.

Old techniques did little to arouse interest.

Newer techniques may produce eagerness to learn.

Decoding the Message

The development of the ability to discriminate words or letters, or both, is a necessary prerequisite for reading, but it is not reading. Reading requires that the individual be able to convert the visual code on the printed sheet into a sound code. At least, this is the requirement in the early stages. In the later stages, a different process *may* be involved. The conversion may be learned in many different ways, even when all pupils are provided a uniform instructional procedure. Consider the case in which children in a class are taught to decode the words *boys* and *girls*. They all learn to do this successfully and can read these words. Some children learn to read these two words by noting that one word is longer than the other. Other children note that one word begins with a letter extending above the line, but the other word begins with a letter extending below the line. All have learned the same skill in terms of what they are actually able to do, such as choosing the right sign on an unfamiliar door, but they accomplish the goal through different internal processes, called **mediating processes.**

If children have learned to decode two words such as *boys* and *girls*, it cannot be assumed that they have learned all the letters in the words or that they have learned to attend to all of the possible cues that discriminate one word from the other. Word discriminations take place on the basis of the minimum of information necessary to make the discrimination, and not on the basis of all the information provided. This is true of adult readers as well as of children learning to read. This is the reason why, in reading rapidly, one may not notice gross spelling errors. As a matter of fact, the adult reader may not only fail to attend to particular letters, but he may not even notice particular words and fail to notice when some have been omitted in the printing of a sentence. Whether reading is at the letter level, the word level, or the sentence level, the reader is unlikely to use more than the minimum amount of information he needs in order to read.

The task of decoding is complicated by the fact that, in English, there is no simple relationship between letter names and sounds. A larger unit than the letter usually, but not always, corresponds to the sound. Even when the individual letter is the basic key to the sound to be produced, the appropriate sound is also likely to depend on the context of the letter. Consider the case of the *e* in the two words *e*at and *e*arly. The two sounds are different, despite the fact that the written symbol is the same. This is the difficulty involved in learning to read by beginning with the discrimination of letters and some alleged sounds that go along with them and then proceeding through single-syllable words to multisyllabic words. This kind of a progression has a plausibility to it that is quite persuasive and has guided the practices of generations of teachers. There may be merit in learning to discriminate between the letters of the alphabet because this facilitates the discrimination of groups of letters, but it does not provide a basis for the pupil learning the decoding operation.

Although in the English language there is no simple relationship between groups of letters and particular sounds, some languages do have a very close and precise **phonetic fit,** as it is called. One such language is Russian, in which, once one has learned the sounds that correspond to the particular groups of letters, he can "read" the language. One may not understand what he is reading, but the written symbols can be easily coded correctly into sounds. Japanese has a vastly more complicated system in that it involves two separate systems of orthography that are often intermingled. One system is a phonetic system, with a good correspondence between the symbol and the sound. The other is a form of picture writing in which a symbol represents a complete word. The picture symbol may facilitate reading in the early stages, because there is a quite obvious correspondence between the symbol and the spoken word it represents.

The child faced with the problem of learning to read English is faced with an extraordinarily difficult task because of this lack of simple rules for relating print to sound. As Gibson et al. (1963) have shown, the child has to discover certain higher-order rules that go far beyond simple script–sound relationships. The design of materials for teaching children to read requires that they be selected to present simple decoding rules at first. In technical terms, one would say that the rules should involve simple **grapheme–phoneme** relationships. The grapheme is a letter or a small group of letters that represents a simple sound, the phoneme. For words such as *man, ran, pan,* and *tan,* there is a simple rule for converting the printed word into sound, but there is none for *can, call,* and *cart,* because the *ca* in each of these is pronounced differently depending on what follows. Gibson et al. have shown that as children grow older, during the first to the third grades, the rules they are able to use increase in complexity. Presumably, the materials in a reading program should involve progressively more complex rules for the decoding process as the child matures.

Another point to note in the design of materials is that they have to provide what may be termed **perceptual constancies.** The materials must present similar patterns of input again and again. Through such repetitions of a constant element, accompanied by variations, the child is able through his perceptual processes to tease out the recurring constant elements (such as the constant element in *man, ran,* and *pan*). Constancy becomes the key to the learning of a simple phonetic system for the interpretation of new words.

Methods of Teaching Beginning Reading

There has long been controversy concerning the best ways of teaching beginning reading. Much of the controversy is of a political nature in that it is part of a general attack on schools by parents who have become anxious about the possible failure of their children to achieve adequate standards in reading. The attacks have been typically based on fear that their children might fail rather than on any facts showing that the methods used in schools are ineffective.

Numerous studies have been undertaken comparing one method of reading with another, but despite this extensive research effort no very useful recommendations for the teaching of reading have evolved. Chall (1967) has reviewed these studies in considerable detail and points out the confused nature of the results. In a later article on the subject, Chall (1970) states that methods can be arranged in a line from those that involve the initial teaching of the alphabetic elements and the gradual learning of more and more complex units to those that start by teaching the child word recognition or the recognition of even larger units and then take him through the task of learning to recognize syllables and letters. The evidence is clear that children learn to read by either extreme of method. The difference in the rate of learning by the method at one extreme compared with the method at the other extreme is very small indeed. Studies comparing the two methods sometimes show an advantage for the one method and sometimes an advantage for the other. Chall concludes that, if there is any superiority of one method over the other, then the slight advantage rests with the method that begins by teaching the alphabet. The author suspects that some methods may have advantages with some children but not with others. If there is such an interaction between pupil and method, then teachers should adapt their teaching methods to the characteristics of the pupils. It might be that the method beginning with the alphabet is better for the middle-class pupil, because he is highly motivated to learn to read and does not mind mastering some of the rather dull skills involved in the approach. This is speculation. One can also speculate that the whole-word method of learning to read may have advantages with children who have little incentive to read, because it brings them quickly to the point of actually reading with considerable speed.

Most teachers use a combination of methods. A typical kindergarten teacher will encourage the children to recognize their names on the bulletin board and will also give them opportunity to recognize the day of the week and other common words. The teacher will also probably teach the children to recognize the letters of the alphabet. Once they have had this kind of background in kindergarten, they may be expected to learn to read quite quickly in first grade, regardless of the method of instruction used.

There is another factor that tends to minimize differences in results between methods. Pupils adapt to poor learning conditions by putting out more effort, by obtaining help elsewhere, by asking the teacher and other children questions, and so forth.

Various devices have been developed for the purpose of helping children to read, and the most extensively used is that involving a special alphabet. There can be no doubt that the child who speaks English has difficulty in learning to read because there is no simple relationship between symbols and sounds. Reading would be greatly facilitated if the writing of the English language could be changed so that each written symbol always corresponded to the same sound. This would mean having a somewhat different alphabet from the present one. Various attempts have been made to do just this. Downing (1971) points out that attempts to write English phonetically go back as far as 1570, when John Hart developed a phonetic alphabet. Over the centuries, many different phonetic alphabets have been proposed, and more than a hundred years ago some were in use throughout school systems for teaching children to read. Such systems are said to be **transitional;** that is, they provide, supposedly, a quick means of teaching children to read, but then the children have to make a transition to the ordinary alphabet. The transition is necessary because it seems unlikely that a phonetic alphabet will become universally used, as Melvil Dewey had hoped when he wrote his books in a simplified spelling system. Downing (1967) has written an interesting account of such enterprises.

The present-day version of a simplified spelling system for the teaching of reading is known as the **Initial Teaching Alphabet,** or ITA. It was developed by Sir James Pitman, a famous publisher, and has been made available for all who wish to use it. Although it was developed only in 1961, ITA has been used extensively in schools both in Great Britain and in the United States. Nearly a thousand books have been translated into it so that the child who learns the system is not limited to the classroom textbook in what he can read. Downing (1971) has summarized the data available on the utility of the system. On the good side, he reports that children who learn to read with ITA learn to master the system more rapidly than children who learn conventional orthography. That is to be expected. When the children make the transition to the ordinary alphabet, they encounter difficulties and slip back, but they rapidly gain skill in reading material presented in the conventional alphabet and soon surpass to a slight degree children who received initial instruction with conventional materials. However, Downing does note that slower children seem to have great difficulty in making the transition. This is also to be expected, since slow children have difficulty in transferring what they have learned from one task to another.

Alternative ways of providing a phonetic system of printing that does not use special characters are also being developed. For example, the Educational Research and Development Center at the University of Pittsburgh is experimenting with a system in which the same letter is printed in different colors to denote different sounds. Thus, a silent *e*, as in *E*instein, might be printed in red, the *e* in *e*at might be printed in black, and the *e* in *b*e*d* might be green. As the child learns to read, the colors can be removed. They could also be faded out. Such a system may offer an easier transition to ordinary print than does ITA, but it will not work for 5 per cent of boys and 1 per cent of girls who are color blind.

Robinson (1971) notes that culturally deprived children, who are slow in learning to read, encounter difficulty because they see little value in reading. For such pupils, every effort has to be made to show that reading can be fun and useful. Such children are also often confused by the fact that written speech is different from words that are spoken. Nobody ever says "See Dick, see the ball. Look, look Jane," and so on. Even storybook language is very different from spoken language. In addition, many children are brought up to speak a dialect that may be almost a different language from conventional written English (see Matteoni, 1971).

Reading Readiness

Teachers recognized long ago that some children entering school do not seem ready yet to undertake the task of learning to read. Many reasons were given for this difficulty. Back in the 1930s, the common belief was that the eyes of many children had not matured to the point where they could handle close work, but this is not a credible argument, because infants in the first year of life have the capacity for focusing on close objects. Others suggested that the nervous system had to reach a certain stage of development before reading could be undertaken and that children did not generally reach such a stage of development until they were six or seven years old. This argument is not supported by the facts, either. Fowler (1965) has reviewed many studies showing that very average children, two or more years younger than the usual age for entering school, are quite capable of learning to read. There are, in addition, many well-documented cases of prodigies who learn to read in their second year of life. These are probably quite extraordinary children, but it is possible that ordinary children may be able to begin reading in the third year. The evidence suggests that the nervous system has matured to the point where reading is possible by the age of two or three, and that the difficulties encountered by many children in mastering this skill cannot be attributed to any such lack. There are, of course, a few children who have suffered brain damage through problems of birth or malnutrition and whose nervous systems limit the skills they can acquire. Such children may encounter extraordinary difficulties in the acquisition of reading skill.

Other causes must be found for most of the children who are classified as "not ready to read" when they enter first grade. The most plausible hypothesis, at this time, is that they either lack the motivation necessary for making efforts to acquire the skill or that they have not developed the necessary perceptual skills. One can easily demonstrate that, for some children, the latter is the problem. Such children can be shown, on tests, to be unable to discriminate complex shapes, and, if brain damage is ruled out, the diagnosis must be that they have not acquired the perceptual skills needed for reading.

Problems of motivation have already been considered, together with some of the ways in which young children can be interested in undertaking reading tasks. The reading task itself probably provides excellent training in quite basic perceptual skills. Nevertheless, children who have not already acquired such skills may find that learning the prerequisite skills and then the actual reading skills may be a long and tedious process.

Finally, the point should be stressed that the teacher who encounters

Materials of 75 years ago were often poorly designed for many purposes.

Materials have now been developed for many specific purposes.

a child having reading difficulties should not put off for long having the problem investigated. All too often nothing is done about the child who has a reading problem. The first-grade teacher hopes that the problem will clear up when the child reaches second grade, but it rarely does. Teachers trained in remedial reading techniques have strategies for handling such cases that the classroom teacher does not have. Time is of the essence, for a child who experiences failure during two successive years may sit back and become resigned to a life of failure.

The Recognition Process

What has been said up to this point has been a description of what happens in the early stages of reading. It should be noted that we have not been concerned with reading for meaning, but the problem discussed is much the same as would be involved in teaching a person to read printed Japanese words without teaching him the Japanese language. The reader could probably learn to read aloud most of what is printed in the Japanese papers, but without understanding a word, in perhaps a month of daily practice sessions. The task would involve only the decoding of the graphemes into phonemes and not the understanding of the Japanese language. We have been concerned up to this point with the problem of the American or English child who is struggling to decode printed English and to convert it into sounds that correspond to spoken English. The problem of reading for meaning is different, involving quite different processes, and this problem will have to be discussed later at much greater length after the discussion of the nature of simple recognition processes.

Let us consider the problem of a child learning to recognize the letter *A* and to discriminate it from other letters. In learning to do this, he does not necessarily learn to name the letter, although to name the letter he has to be able to discriminate it from other letters. In most actual learning situations, the child actually learns to name the letter as he learns to discriminate it from other letters, but letter recognition and letter naming are two quite different tasks. In order to demonstrate that the skill of letter recognition is different from that of letter naming, one would have to train the young child in quite artificial situations. One could, for example, develop a button-pushing task in which one of four letters appeared on a screen in front of the child, and his task was to press the button on which the same letter was printed. If the child pressed the right button, the device would produce a marble, or a trinket, or a piece of candy. Through the use of such a device, a four-year-old child can readily learn to discriminate the letters of the alphabet. The task is perceptually not a very difficult one, for even relatively simple animals, such as the laboratory rat, can learn to make such discriminations, at least between pairs of letters, though the task is a very difficult one for animals that have such small brains. The child can learn this discrimination without ever giving a name to a letter. One can begin to understand how a child learns such a discrimination by giving oneself, an adult, a similar task, namely that of learning to discriminate the letters of a foreign alphabet, such as the Chinese or Arabic.

The adult who begins to learn to discriminate a foreign alphabet has the impression, when he first glances rapidly at the characters, that they are all very much the same and not clearly distinct as are the familiar letters in which English is printed. Soon he begins to notice particular features that make one letter different from another. Such features include size—some letters are just bigger than others—and the number of strokes involved. Some characters have closed curves and others open curves. Some have lines that cross, some lines that meet but do not cross, and some lines that never meet. In learning this discrimination task, the adult has to be able to identify the specific features or characteristics that differentiate one letter from another. If he cannot identify the distinguishing features, then he is never able to differentiate the letters. This discrimination learning task requires that he be able to identify the unique combination of features that characterizes each letter of the alphabet. In the early stages of learning the task, a learner is quite aware of the role played by such distinguishing features, and he may say to himself "I must remember this letter by the fact that it involves three horizontal straight lines and a vertical stroke down the middle." After he has completely mastered the task, his analysis of a letter takes place so rapidly that he cannot tell the experimenter how he recognizes a letter. An American can look at a printed letter *A* and push immediately the corresponding letter on the typewriter keyboard. Once discriminations have been thoroughly learned, they are made very rapidly, indeed, perhaps taking place within as short a time as thirty or forty milliseconds. The beginner is slow and may require several seconds for the recognition process to take place.

There are experimental techniques permitting the process of recognition to be slowed up so that one may discover what it involves. Certainly, there is little value in showing a person a word or a letter and asking him what is involved in recognizing what it is. The recognition process takes place in a flash, and the details escape. The main technique for slowing up the recognition process for research and study involves making recognition a difficult task. Laboratory psychologists have developed a piece of apparatus, called a **tachistoscope,** that permits words, letters, or other visual displays to be shown for very short intervals of time, usually down to one thousandth of a second. If the screen on which the material is displayed is very brightly lit and has strong contrasts of black and white, the exposure of a single word for that short duration is sufficient for a word or a letter to be quite legible. The task becomes more difficult as the illumination is reduced, and, at the level of illumination typical of reading in the home, the word cannot be read when it is presented for a single exposure of a few milliseconds to a person who does not know what word to expect. Let us suppose that in an experiment we have the latter level of illumination for a word to be presented on the tachistoscope, and we show it to our subject in a single brief flash. We then ask him what he saw, and he is likely to say "nothing." We then give him some encouragement and ask whether all he saw was a screen uniformly lit. He is then likely to say that he did see something, and perhaps he might tell us that there was a blur in the middle of the screen but he could not tell what word it represented. We then ask him whether it was a short or a long word, and he may be able to tell us that it was a short word.

The point to note in all of this is that the person looking into the tachistoscope was able to derive some information about the word, including its position and length. These are the features that are first identified and are most easily picked up.

Haber and Hershenson (1965) did just what has been described here, with interesting results. If the illumination was low and the flash short, then, on the first flash, the subject was usually quite unaware that there was any word present. When the same word was shown a second time for the same duration, the subject might begin to report that he saw parts of letters or even whole letters. As further flashes of the word were presented, additional letters would appear. Finally, the whole word would be seen, clearly and distinctly. In this way, Haber and Hershenson were able to trace the development of the perception of a word and the cues as they emerged. The cues appear to emerge to some extent in a sequence, as shown by Dick and Dick (1969). For example, very crude cues such as the position of the word and whether it is located horizontally or vertically emerge before letter details, and letter details generally emerge before words. Subjects tended to recognize first and last letters in words before the other letters, indicating that these provide crucial cues in word recognition. Standing et al. (1970) found that merely knowing what the word was, in advance of the tachistoscopic presentations, did not change the slow emergence of the percept to any degree. The fact that the person knew that he was going to see the word *man* did not facilitate the perception of the word as it was presented through successive flashes. Another interesting finding of Standing et al. was that the perception was facilitated either when the subject imagined the word in his mind's eye or when he was asked to say the word under his breath at the time when the word was flashed on the screen. This suggests that perception of a word depends on the existence of some inner representation of the word.

The research reviewed up to this point suggests that the recognition of a word involves an analysis of the various characteristics of the word as it is presented. These characteristics provide cues concerning what the word is. In the case of many words, very few cues are needed in order to recognize it. Almost anyone can read the word W _ _ _ _ _ _ _ _ D.C. without having to have the missing letters. Now try N _ w Yo _ _ N.Y. and W _ _ _ _ pool Corp.

For the adult, reading apparently does not involve recognizing each letter of a word in sequence. Reading is not at all like spelling a word letter by letter. On the contrary, the entire word is scanned for cues. Presumably, when sufficient cues have been picked up, the word is recognized and read.

It is easy to see how this can result in the misreading of a word. One is glancing through a book and glosses over a paragraph heading that he reads as *Child Rearing* when the actual heading is *Child Reading*. The mistake occurs because the word is read before all the information provided by the printing has been assimilated. The reader quite probably may see no more of the second word than the letters *R   g*, but these cues are sufficient for him to jump to the conclusion that the heading presents the familiar combination of words *Child Rearing*. If the reader were to derive all the information from the printed word necessary for interpreting it with complete certainty, then reading would be a very slow process indeed. The mature reader guesses a lot in order to save time. Indeed, high-speed reading is to a great extent a process of guessing what is on the page from very minimal cues.

All this implies that a word, when it is viewed in order to be recognized, is not scanned from left to right but is viewed as a whole, and then information is extracted that will permit the identification of what is there. Studies of eye movements fit well with this concept of word recognition and reading (see Yarbus, 1967). When material such as a column of newsprint is being read, the eyes do not move slowly over the material but are engaged in alternating moves and pauses. The eyes will fixate on a group of words, then they will rapidly move forward, and then fixate again on another group of words. This can be shown by means of a special camera designed to record eye movements photographically. There are also electrical devices that will record eye movements, but with much less precision than the eye camera. Records of effective readers show a clear pattern of movement–fixation–movement–fixation. Most of the time is spent in the fixation stage. This is when information is actually received by the eye and the brain. The sweeping movements are very rapid, in fact, so rapid that the eye could not possibly pick up information from the blurred image that the sweeping movements provide.

The efficient adult reader makes longer sweeps than the slow reader, a finding that leads one to believe that the fast reader is able to take in several words simultaneously and to find meaning in the words. The fast reader is also probably able to conjecture on the basis of fewer cues and a shorter glance the meaning of the words in a group that he fixates. His fixations may also last no longer than half a second, whereas the slow reader may fixate on a single word for as long as several seconds. The fast reader is able to process information internally more rapidly than the slow reader, and that is why he requires such a short fixation period and can take in several words at a time.

As words are read in a sequence, the reader does not approach each word or collection of words as though he had no idea about what the word meanings were going to be. When he fixates on a group of words in context, he needs to have very few cues in order to interpret the material with a high probability of correctness. The more experienced he is as a reader, the less information he is going to need in order to interpret the words correctly. Such a mature performance is to be contrasted with that of the beginning reader, who responds to each word, and even to each syllable or each letter, without making much use of the other information he has in decoding the printed form. This suggests that as the person learns to read and has experience with words, he slowly builds up a body of information about which word follows which word. The information he has stored in this respect is probably quite complex. Consider the following incomplete sentence:

The process of reading involves the extraction of

Now guess the next word. The reader will probably guess *information*, which is the word used in the original context and is the word that would have been there if the complete sentence had been reproduced the way it was in the source. Most of those who have read the first part of this chapter would have guessed this word, perhaps as many as 80 per cent. Those who expected the word *information* would have read this word if they had been confronted with the whole sentence by perhaps noting no more than two or three letters of the word as it was actually printed. Indeed, some rapid readers might note only the first letter of the word *information* and then skip on quickly to the next sentence.

The memory system appears to be able to indicate to its owner the probabilities of particular words turning up next in the sequence. It is as if the memory system said to him "The next word is *information*," or "The next word is either *information* or *knowledge*."

Reading and Meaning

The discussion to this point has focused on the matter of the decoding of graphic symbols into sounds, but little has been said about how the reader extracts meaningful ideas from the material. One can learn in a single day to read Russian, in the sense that he can learn to look at Russian script and produce the sounds that correspond to that script, but he would not understand a single word of the material that was being read, though a native Russian might listen to the reading and understand it. Decoding the written symbols is a simple matter compared with understanding the full significance of the information they contain. If a person can say the correct words corresponding to the printed words, his problem of understanding is not too different from that of understanding speech. There is, however, an important difference. When one listens to another person talking, one can be fully occupied with what is being said. On the other hand, when a child is reading, he may be so preoccupied with the problem of converting the written symbols into sounds that he does not have time to think much about what the words mean. Adults can have a similar kind of experience when they become so fascinated with the appearance of a speaker that they do not hear what he is saying.

The problem is that one can attend to only just so much at any one time. Another way of saying this in more technical terms is that the human capacity for receiving and handling information is limited. If one is concerned with the information related to the decoding of printed mate-

Reading: A Study in
Perceptual Development

rial into spoken words, then he may not have sufficient information capacity left to handle information related to meaning.

At this point, the reader must be reminded of some of the points made earlier about the development of speech and the understanding of language. In order to understand a spoken communication, a large chunk of the communication has to be retained so that it can be analyzed as a chunk. One does not understand language word by word, for the meaning of a communication depends on the structure it possesses. After a communication has been received, it has to be analyzed for structure, and reading involves such an analysis. This means that, as the child reads, he has to retain in memory groups of words until he has read enough to give them some meaning. Reading for meaning involves a quite complex analysis for structure, in addition to the perceptual analysis involved in recognizing words. It is a marvel that young children can do anything as complex as this.

A Broader View of Perceptual Processes

The discussion of reading presented in the first part of this chapter has been used as the vehicle for introducing the topic of perceptual processes. By the time a student comes to the task of reading, he is already a quite sophisticated person insofar as his perceptual processes are concerned. Let us go back now to earlier ages and consider how perceptual sophistication is slowly acquired.

What kind of information the infant is able to extract from his environment has long been a matter of speculation, because it is very difficult to determine. The reason for this is that the infant has a system that handles complex inputs but has very few outputs that can be used to indicate what information is responded to and what is retained. One can find out what a computer is doing inside its mechanism by noting the data that go in and the data that come out. The difference between what goes in and what comes out reveals what happened inside. Internal perceptual processes are identified in the same way, through the change in information that takes place between the input and output. Thus, in the experiment earlier described in which words were flashed on a screen for very short durations, it can be said that the initial flash produced apparently no identifiable internal process, for the subject reports that he saw nothing. As the same word is repeatedly flashed on the screen, the viewer begins to see parts of letters or even whole letters, which he can sketch or describe. This suggests that there is slow internal analysis of the input into components and that components continue to be identified until the word is recognized. In such an experiment, what is happening in the perceptual process can slowly be identified.

As discussed previously, an adult who gains vision through corneal surgery can see, but he is quite unable to use the visual information provided. Indeed, he finds the visual world difficult to tolerate because of the overwhelming stimulation it provides. Von Senden described patients who were out on a busy street and had to close their eyes because of the overwhelming amount of stimulation the world gave them. Perhaps the baby has a protective mechanism in this respect. The reader will recall that excessive stimulation puts the baby to sleep, whereas it produces excitement in the older child. The tendency for overstimulation to do this to the infant may protect his nervous system from being overloaded with inputs from his sensory systems. The adult does not have this kind of protection. When his sensory system is overloaded, he becomes more and more excited and may reach the point of becoming disorganized, as von Senden's patients did. Ordinarily, the adult is not overwhelmed by complicated and varied visual inputs, because he can attend to just a few inputs or not attend to the scene at all. The person who first gains vision has not yet developed these means of handling complicated visual inputs.

Untrained visual perception has another significant characteristic. The adult who first acquires vision is able to recognize that objects differ in color and can easily learn the names for colors. When he is shown a red square and a blue triangle, he can easily learn that the one color is red and the other is blue, even though it may take him months of practice to recognize a square and a triangle. Presumably, babies can see colors, but, having as yet no language, they cannot give them names. In a search of the literature to find out whether, through classical conditioning, it would be possible to differentially condition an infant to make a response to, say, red light and not to blue light, the author could find no such study. By use of this technique and related techniques, much can still be done to investigate the perceptual processes of very young infants.

The perceptual visual learning of the infant involves, at first, extracting information from its crudely structured visual world. Presumably, this process involves an ever increasing number of characteristics. Seeing an undifferentiated object is perception at its most primitive level. Seeing it as a square is perception at a very sophisticated level. Between these two levels there must be states where some of the attributes are recognized, but not all of them. It is not known at this time just which attributes are recognized first, but it is tempting to speculate that first lines are recognized, and then perhaps angles and corners, and last the number of sides and angles. It also is not known, as yet, what the fundamental attributes of objects are, in terms of which they are rapidly analyzed and identified.

The learning of the basic characteristics of the visual world that differentiate one object from another is a slow task. Von Senden marveled at the fact that a person with new vision could be given training for as long as three months before he could discriminate a square from a triangle, and even then he did it, not at a glance, but by counting the number of corners. The adult, with a well-developed brain, probably has advantages over the baby in learning the fundamental features of the visual environment. The adult has at least some conception of what he has to learn and what he lacks, for he has already mastered an auditory world and a world of touch. The infant has no such conceptions to guide him. Yet, despite these advantages, some of von Senden's patients never did learn to master the visual world, but preferred to live as blind people. They found the task of trying to master the visual world too difficult.

The process involved in the slow extraction of information from the visual world is commonly assumed to take place because it is the very nature of the senses and nervous system to extract information. In this respect, the position taken here follows closely that of Gibson (1969), who expands on the theme that repeated exposure to a particular aspect of the world results in the individual exposed slowly extracting information from it.

Attention

Infants only a few weeks old show a response known as the **orienting response,** which continues to occur throughout life. It was first noted by Pavlov near the turn of the century and has long been of interest to psychologists. It is a component of the complex process of attending and is probably a precursor of the mature **attending response.** Attention has been difficult to discuss on an objective basis because the concept is derived from personal experience. We know that we can attend to first one object and then another in our environment, but we are much less certain about what another person is attending to. In terms of our own experience, we speak about attending to an object when we are taking in information about it. One can look at an object without taking in information about it, but that is not attending. This is the reason why we cannot be certain whether another person is attending to an object or whether his eyes are merely directed toward it. The obvious way out of this difficulty is to find out whether the person viewing the object does or does not derive information from it, but this does not provide an escape from the difficulty, because much of the information derived from objects to which one attends is retained for only a few seconds. For example, I will attend to the puddle in front of the doorway and retain information about the location and size of the puddle just long enough to avoid it. Once I have avoided this obstacle, the matter is completely forgotten. Most of the objects to which one attends during the course of a day provide only the most transitory retention of information. One lesson to be learned by the teacher from this is that attention on the part of the student is no guarantee of learning.

Teachers are often not appreciative of the fact that one cannot tell, by looking at a child, whether he is or is not attending, that is, whether he is or is not taking in information from a particular source.

An experimental procedure exists that can circumvent some of these difficulties, though it has not been explored in classroom settings. There is laboratory instrumentation that will indicate whether a person is attending to an object or merely not thinking of anything in particular. The brain produces different forms of electrical impulses under these conditions, and the impulses can be recorded from the outside of the skull. The record of these impulses is called an **electroencephalogram,** or briefly an **EEG.** When a person directs his eyes toward an object and reports that he is attending to that object, he shows an absence of alpha waves. When he gazes vacantly in front of him, then his EEG shows a typical alpha rhythm that is quite easily picked up with appropriate instruments.

Other physiological accompaniments of the attending response occur. One is the **galvanic skin response** — a sudden change in the electrical resistance across the palm of the hand. When a new object attracts the attention of an individual, he shows a galvanic skin response, and he also shows this response when alerted by a novel or frightening event. The orienting response, which has many bodily components, appears to alert the individual and to prepare him for the intake of information.

The EEG responses and the orienting responses are mentioned because they offer some opportunity for obtaining objective information. It would be of interest to determine the fraction of the time that the typical pupil in the school spends in attending, that is, in taking in information, and the amount of time he spends in vacantly staring.

Attention and the Information in the Display to Which Attention Is Directed

The direction of attention, and the direction of the related sense organs, is toward objects that provide information. The concept of **information** is a technical one and needs some explanation. In common speech, the word generally refers to statements in print or verbal statements that are essentially true, but the behavioral scientist uses it in a very different sense. The scientist would say that a wall painted uniformly white provides almost no information. One could imagine that wall as providing some information under some circumstances. A spy might be told that so long as a particular wall was painted white, it was safe to stay where he was, but if it were painted another color then he should leave the country immediately. The wall would provide information to the spy very much in the sense that the psychologist uses the term *information*. From a technical point of view, information is what makes it possible for the receiver to make a decision. The color of the wall permits our spy to make a decision either to stay or to leave the country, and thus the wall transmits information to him.

Technically, the term *information* as it is used by psychologists means a signal that permits a person who receives it to make a decision or that at least has decision-making potential. Signals that carry information are to be contrasted with noise, in that the former always have some structure but noise is quite unstructured. In order to expand on this point, let us consider auditory noise, an area where the common meaning of noise comes fairly close to the psychologist's conception of noise, and let us contrast music with noise. Music represents a highly structured system of sounds, which can be represented by a musical score. In contrast, noise is a disorganized jumble of sounds with no structure. The everyday conception of noise is that it is unpleasant, but music is agreeable. The psychologist does not include this factor within his definition of noise. As far as the psychologist is concerned, pleasantness has nothing to do with the distinction between message and noise.

In ordinary English, the term *noise* means a sound, but in its technical meaning it can be used to refer to vision, touch, or any other system through which information is communicated. A good example of visual noise occurs when the television station announces "We have temporarily lost the picture, please stand by." On such occasions, the television screen is commonly covered with specks of light against a dark background. The specks have no pattern to them and seem to be distributed at random across the screen. The specks of light are visual noise. Just as a telephone line in which there is a lot of background noise is irritating to the person who is receiving a message through it, so too is a noisy visual signal irritating. People do not like to watch a television show when the picture is noisy even though they have no difficulty in following what is happening. People like to have noise-free communications, even though the communication is well understood despite the presence of the noise.

Where there is some structure or order, there is potential for communicating information. A single line drawn on a white surface has potential for communicating information. The line can be used as a signal because of its length, thickness, blackness or color, or other properties. A line has structure, and because it has structure it has potential for communicating information. A single straight line has limited potential for communicating information because it has limited structure and there are only a few properties about it that can be varied to vary the information transmitted. A slightly more complicated signal would be a curved line, for it could be used to transmit information not only through all the properties of the line that were previously listed but also through the shape of the curve. Consider the two curves in Figure 1. The one is very complicated and *can* transmit a great amount of information, but the other is quite simple and is much more limited in that respect. Curve *A* is reminiscent of a map, which, with its immense complexity of line structure, can communicate a very large quantity of information. Of course, maps also include a great quantity of information printed in words and coded into colors. And maps have very complicated structures in contrast to simple geometric figures.

A simple way of showing that *A* contains more information than *B* is

121
. . . .
Attention and the
Information in the
Display to Which
Attention Is Directed

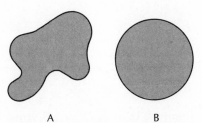

A   B

Figure 1 Diagrams with different amounts of information.

to show each, for about a second, to individuals who have not seen them before. Then ask them to draw what they have seen. Everyone will be able to draw the circle, but no one will be able to reproduce the irregular figure after this brief exposure. One has to take in more information to remember what the irregular figure is like than to remember what the circle is like.

Now it must be quite evident to the reader at this point that, in a technical sense, the amount of information in a drawing has nothing to do with whether the drawing is or is not meaningful. A complex cubist painting can contain a large amount of information, but a picture of a billiard ball may have much less information. This takes us to the next point—that the attention of persons of all ages, from early infancy to old age, is influenced by whether the object attended to has a high or low information content. Consider the two diagrams shown in Figure 2. The one diagram has a much higher information content than the other. The reader should now spend thirty seconds looking at them closely before reading the next paragraph.

Now think back at how you spent your time during the thirty-second period when you were examining the figures. It is highly likely that you spent most of the time occupied in examining B. (Yarbus 1967, has demonstrated this kind of phenomenon). If the two figures had been exposed above the crib of a two-month-old baby, it is also almost certain that the baby would have spent more time fixating B, and A might have been almost neglected (see the study of Thomas, 1965). The generalization to be drawn from this is that objects having a high information content are much more likely to attract attention than are those that are relatively impoverished in terms of the information they contain. However, this generalization needs some qualification. Objects that have a *very* high degree of complexity may not be attended to, probably because objects highly complex in terms of information content may be so complex that the individual is unable to extract information from them and treats them as if they consisted only of noise. One change shown as the infant and child develop is a tendency to choose more and more complex objects to attend to (see Munsinger and Weir, 1967). It is as if the individual has a propensity for attending to the most complex display that he can structure.

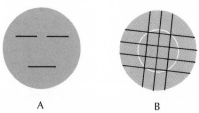

A   B

Figure 2 Diagrams with different attention values.

The Sensory Systems

It seems clear that there is a marked tendency for man, either infant or adult, to direct attention toward the parts of the environment that are quite complex and provide considerable information because of their structure. This leads directly to the next point—that the sensory systems themselves, through which all information flows from the outside to inside the individual, are themselves active scanning and searching systems. The eye is not a passive recipient of information about the world. On the contrary, the eyes of any child busily engaged in any activity are constantly in motion, scanning the various materials before him, as if in a constant search for new pieces of relevant information. The eye, as Gibson (1966) has noted, is not an isolated organ that takes in whatever information happens to come in front of it but is part of a system including muscles and nerves that actively scans and provides information about the environment.

The eye is not unique in this respect. The sense organs are organized into systems, and each system is such that it permits the scanning of the environment to some degree. The human ear is largely nondirectional (though in some animals the external ears can be moved to pick up signals in a particular direction). The ears, unlike the eyes, are permanently set to pick up signals from the entire environment and do not have to engage in scanning it area by area. There seems to be machinery in the nervous system to scan all auditory information coming into the system and to pick out for further attention certain classes of signals. When one's name is mentioned in a crowded room, he picks up the signal immediately and attempts to discern whatever other words are said in connection with it. One never misses the cry of "Fire!" even though deeply absorbed in other matters. Just as the eye picks up relevant pieces of information by scanning the environment, so does the ear do this by scanning internally.

A third complex sensory system is focused on touch but involves much more than touch. This system is called the **haptic system.** It involves many different sense organs in the skin that specialize in particular kinds of sensitivity, such as sensitivity to heat, to cold, to pressure, to stretching, to vibration, and to perhaps even other kinds of contact with the surrounding world. The exact function of each of the various kinds of sense organs has not yet been identified. In addition, the system includes sense organs deep in the joints and muscles that play a crucial role in helping to find out about objects in the outside world. The importance of the sense organs in the deep parts of the body lies in the fact that in exploring an object through touch, as one does in the dark, the shape and size and contours of the object are determined by moving the hand across its surface. The extent of the movement tells one about the size of the object because the sense organs in the joints are there to discern the movement. The haptic sense is highly dependent on movement for its operation, and the muscular system permits scanning and exploration of the environment. Without an effective muscular system, the haptic sensory system would be virtually useless.

The two remaining sensory systems may be mentioned briefly. The **taste–smell system** is a very complicated exploratory system, limited in its exploratory activity by the fact that there must be chemical contact between the system and the source of stimulation. The tongue is a highly mobile organ that can manipulate substances placed on it. One effect of this manipulation of objects by the tongue is to bring the objects into contact with a greater number of taste buds. Very young children achieve the same goal by stuffing their mouths full of food.

Finally, there is the fifth sensory system, centered in an organ associated with the inner ear known as the **semicircular canals.** Any tendency for the head to be suddenly moved, as occurs when a person trips and falls, results in the fluid in the canals moving rapidly in the opposite direction. This stimulates sensitive cells in the canals, which send impulses to the brain where they ultimately produce righting reflexes related to the restoration of balance.

The sensory systems, or the perceptual systems, as they are sometimes called, tell us something about the nature of man. The mechanisms are *not* those of a passive organism with behavior completely controlled by environmental circumstances, for the systems are largely searching systems. This is particularly true of the visual system, which is probably the best developed of all judged in terms of the relative development of the sensory systems in other animals in which the visual system does not play a dominant role.

The high degree of development of the visual system is a feature that man shares with the other primates, and it reflects man's origin in the treetops, where the visual system is of paramount importance. Tree life permits an animal to scan far and wide, and hence visual acuity is of the utmost importance. Also, tree-living animals are fruit eaters and need well-developed color vision if they are to discriminate ripe from unripe fruit at a distance. Tree-living animals are to be contrasted with animals such as wolves that live near the ground, and cannot see very far, and must depend on the other sensory systems for identifying the presence of prey and the approach of danger. A vision-dependent animal is at a disadvantage when on the ground, because he is not necessarily well equipped for sensing things he cannot see. For example, man, compared to the wolf, has a quite undeveloped taste–smell system and is unable to pick up scents either close or far. Man's hearing is also limited by the fact that he cannot direct his ears in a particular direction in order to pick up a faint sound better.

The fact that man has an outstandingly well-developed sense of vision does not mean that he can learn better through vision than through hearing or touch. A human being will generally give priority to information that arrives through the visual system, but available knowledge suggests that he can learn as well through hearing as through vision, and can probably learn as well through the touch or haptic system, although few educational materials are directed toward that system. The remarkable achievements of the blind and deaf Helen Keller bear testimony to what can be learned through the haptic system.

The sensory systems have an intimate connection with the nerve mechanisms involved in the analysis of information. When a scene is scanned by the eyes, there is some kind of rough analysis made of what is there that forms the basis for attending at greater length to some particular part of it. When one looks over the faces in a crowd to find out whether there is a friend among them, the visual mechanism probably does not examine each face in detail. The faces are probably scanned at a crude level, at which gross familiar features might be picked up. For example, suppose that one is an elderly man and knows that any friend in the crowd is likely to be of similar age and sex; then one's scanning of the heads in the crowd may only notice grayness of hair, a feature likely to pick out elderly males. Any person who has this characteristic can then be viewed to determine whether he has other attributes that characterize one's friends.

The visual information is conducted to a part of the brain known as the **occipital area.** This part has been carefully studied in a range of species, including cats and primates. The classic study by Hubel and Wiesel (1959) showed that different layers in the occipital cortex of the cat responded to lines at different angles. Later work by Weiskrantz (1970) suggests that, in primates, the occipital cortex is primarily an analyzer of the position of a visual object and that it also seems to determine the place in the memory filing system where further information related to recognition of the object is stored. The analysis of an object takes place in sequence, with gross features analyzed first and the most trivial items of information last. The best guess is that at each level of analysis several features may be analyzed simultaneously. Objects are only analyzed to the level of detail useful at the time. For this reason, one may hardly notice the appearance of a stranger whom one stops to ask a question. The details of the stranger's face are quite irrelevant to solving the problem of finding one's way.

The information analysis process involves classifying and responding to some features rather than to others. It involves ignoring much of the information present, because the ignored information is trivial for present purposes. The information analysis process results in recognition, but recognition does not require that the person respond to the vast detail presented by the world. We see much, but recognize only a little. Perception is therefore partly a discarding process. The information that impinges on the sensory system is vast in quantity, but the information needed to adjust to a complex world is quite small, and it is that small amount of information that the perceptual process manages to grasp. Since man is a creature built to scan continuously and actively every part of his environment, it is unreasonable to require pupils to keep their eyes glued to the front of the room, as they are required to do in so many classrooms.

Scanning and Learning

The previous paragraphs have emphasized the scanning functions of the perceptual systems. Although scanning functions are inborn, this does not mean that the scanning processes cannot be improved through training, particularly where they involve complex intellectual skills. Let us consider some of the scanning tasks involved in academic work in schools.

The commonest scanning tasks in the classroom are those involved in searching visual material. There is, perhaps, a difference between the scanning of the young child and the searching of the person who peruses a book. The young child who scans the scene in front of him is probably not looking for anything in particular, but his eyes will come to rest on any object that has high interest for him. In scanning a page of a book, the student is generally looking for some particular item of information. The latter might be better described as a **search task,** and we will reserve the term for tasks in which particular items of information are sought. The items of information sought are called **target items.** As an example of the scanning process, in writing this chapter I may want to refer to some research undertaken by somebody named *Thomas.* In order to locate this work, I may search the pages of books where the work is likely to be cited in order to find the titles of the articles written by Thomas. I will go over the pages quickly looking for the name Thomas. I don't read the pages, but will spend perhaps twenty seconds on each page. When the part of the page with the name *Thomas* is encountered, the name seems to stand out from the rest of the print. A point to note is that in conducting this search, all the words on each page are not read. Indeed, one can scan the material and find the name sought without learning anything about the content of the material. There is a difference between reading and scanning. The skills are distinct and should be separately trained.

The basic work on searching behavior has been conducted by Neisser (1964), with some interesting findings. One of these is that it is not economical to search for one piece of information at a time, for, with a little practice, one can search for as many as ten different items simultaneously. Neisser's work indicates that practice is important in developing this skill and that it can be developed to a very high level. He found that persons who work for newspaper scanning agencies may scan newsprint at the rate of a thousand words per minute, looking for as many as a hundred different items at once.

The skill is a very useful one, particularly if one is also trained to use the reference works that have to be scanned for the needed information. Too few children can do this, because they have learned to read and tend to read rather than to scan. The two skills tend to be confused, though they are really very different. Reading involves picking up enough clues to find out what the print has to say. Scanning and searching are much more like setting a filter in one's perceptual system that will pass certain classes of information and no other. A person might be an excellent reader but a poor scanner and searcher. The key to the development of searching skills seems to be to provide practice by sending pupils frequently to reference works from which they must learn to dig out information without actually reading the material. Perhaps pupils need to have explained to them the fact that searching is a different task than reading.

Perception and the Reduction of Information

The quantity of information provided by the environment and available to the person who scans the environment with his perceptual systems is vast. Consider the case of a person who scans a filled football stadium during a game. From his seat he can, if he looks carefully, see the gross features of every person in every seat. He would not be able to identify the shape of the nose of each person, for his eyes do not have sufficient acuity. Nevertheless, our observer could probably identify the sex of each person toward whom he directed his attention and probably the color of their clothing and whether they did or did not wear a hat. Our observer can see in front of him, from his seat, more than half the persons in the stadium, say, sixty-thousand persons. The amount of information that is there in front of him about each of these sixty-thousand people, together with information about their positions in the seating arrangement, is extremely large. Yet our observer, whose eyes see all that has been described here, will actually recognize little of it. If asked what he sees, he would say that he sees a crowd, implying that he sees a collection of individuals without noting the characteristics of each. It is clear that, although the eyes see much, the brain comprehends only the minimum required by circumstances. Perception is hence a process of information reduction. It is a process that results in the reduction of a very complex environment to a simplified system that the nervous system can handle.

Perceptual Constancies

The interpretation of the information provided by the senses is enormously complicated by the fact that the same object must be identified regardless of the position from which it is viewed; the same spoken word must be identified regardless of whether it is spoken loudly or softly, slowly or rapidly, in a shrill or a booming voice, or in a Southern or Midwestern accent. A person recognizes an object or sound to be the same regardless of an infinite number of variations of the conditions under which the information reaches him. The recognition of object identity, regardless of variation in the information it provides the senses, is called the phenomenon of **object constancy.**

Ask a child in the first grade to draw a plate as seen from an oblique view, and he draws a round plate. Indeed, he has to learn to draw in perspective and to understand that he has to draw an ellipse to represent a plate as seen from the side. Many primitive forms of art reveal the same inability to see objects as they are actually presented to the eye. The ancients never solved the problem of drawing objects in perspective, and artists did not discover how to do this until the Middle Ages. Many readers have seen examples of Oriental art in which distant objects are drawn the same size as objects close up. In much Oriental art, a distant object is represented with other distant objects in an area at the top of the picture. Close objects are shown in the lower part of the picture, but they are not drawn much larger in size, if they are drawn larger at all.

Even modern artists do not always make the size of objects proportional to their distance, as they should be if drawn in exact perspective. In a picture by Grandma Moses, human figures on a distant hillside are drawn almost half as large as figures in the immediate foreground. Sometimes the artist may do the reverse and exaggerate the effect of distance. The viewer can still contemplate such pictures without being conscious of the distortions they present. The perceptual process is capable of overlooking extraordinary variations and discrepancies in the way objects appear. An even more extraordinary capability of the perceptual process in arriving at recognition, even though the inputs have been distorted to a high degree, is shown in the case of speech. One can take recorded speech and distort it in various ways, by playing it faster, raising the pitch, changing the wave form through which it is transmitted, and increasing the background of noise. Despite very substantial changes in this respect, listeners still are able to understand the message. The perceptual system has a capability of dealing with markedly distorted inputs without losing the capability of correct recognition.

What are referred to as the constancies in perception are extremely subtle interrelationships among the elements. A word can be recognized because there are subtle interrelationships among the frequencies and sound elements of which the spoken word consists. Even when some of these are distorted, the meaning can still be picked up from those that remain.

The extent to which the constancies are learned and the extent to which man has a built-in ability to identify the constancies and respond to them remains one of the interesting problems still to be solved in the psychology of perception.

The teacher in the elementary grades needs to understand the points made in this section if he is to understand much of the art produced by children. Children tend to draw what they see (a round plate) rather than what is presented to the eye (an elliptical plate, as viewed obliquely). Much of art education involves teaching the person to see what is presented to the eye rather than what his brain tells him is there.

Measuring Readability

An important problem in planning a curriculum is finding reading material suitable in level of difficulty for the pupils involved. The traditional way of doing this has been for the person designing the curriculum to read a variety of materials and to arrive at a judgment concerning the suitability of each item. This has been shown to be a quite unsatisfactory procedure, for adults tend to judge printed materials to be much easier than they really are for children. What is needed is some objective way of measuring the reading difficulty level of the materials involved, a way that does not involve judgment. The long history of attempts to do this has been reviewed by Klare (1963).

Measurement of the reading difficulty of materials generally involves making counts of certain characteristics of the materials. For example, common sense suggests that the average number of words in a sentence might be an important factor in determining reading difficulty and so too might be the average length of the words. Vocabulary is an important element in measuring readability. For this reason, a count is commonly made of the number of words that cannot be considered to be common words. This is done by checking the words against a list of common words. Several such lists are available, some of which are much better for this purpose than others. The various counts made on a passage are then inserted in a formula used to compute the grade level of the passage.

In recent years, considerable improvement in such formulas has been brought about, and modern formulas predict with considerable accuracy the ease or difficulty with which prose can be read. Bormuth (1971) has proposed a formula that seems to be a quite valid measure of readability, involving the number of letters in the passage analyzed, the number of words, the number of minimal punctuation units, and the number of words appearing in a particular list of easy words.

The development of a readability formula requires that one be able to measure directly the difficulty that children have with a passage in order to test the effectiveness of the formula in predicting the difficulty that children actually encounter. One of the best ways of determining directly the difficulty of a passage for children is to print the passage with every fifth word replaced by a blank. The children are then asked to fill in the blanks. If the passage is easy for them, the task is an easy one, but if the passage is difficult the filling in of the blanks poses a hard problem. The number of blanks filled in accurately by the children is a measure of the reading difficulty of the passage. This technique is known as the **cloze technique.** Invented by Taylor (1953), it represents the best method so far developed of measuring, directly, the readability of a passage. It also has the advantage that it can be applied at almost any age level.

Summary

1 Although most of us can read, this does not mean that most of us are experts on the process of reading. A person reads without knowing quite how he does it. A person can perform a complex skill without being able to describe how he does it.

2 In order to read, a person has to be able to discriminate graphic symbols, recognize that letters differ from one another, and understand that groups of letters represent sounds. A child may have difficulty learning to read because his attention has never been drawn to printed letters and he has not learned to discriminate their forms. Children typically learn to discriminate letters between the ages of four and eight. The teacher may have to begin the teaching of reading by showing them that the skill has utility. Letter-recognition training is more effective in producing word recognition than word training is in producing letter recognition. Words may be discriminated and recognized by many different cues.

3 Discriminating words and letters is not reading, which requires a decoding operation. Words are discriminated and read through the use of minimal cues. The task of decoding written English is greatly complicated by the fact that letters do not always correspond to the same sound. Some languages do have phonetic fit, but English does not. There are also no simple rules the child can learn that will tell him how to read particular combinations of letters. Reading materials are designed to present the beginning reader with materials that can be decoded through the application of quite simple rules. In working with such materials, the child has to tease out the perceptual constancies.

4 Numerous studies have been undertaken on methods of teaching beginning reading. A review of these studies shows that children learn to read by all of the methods. There is no clear superiority of one method over another, but perhaps a slight superiority for the method that begins with the teaching of the alphabet. It seems likely that the method best with one child may not be the best with another. Most teachers use a combination of methods. The fact that pupils tend to compensate for poor methods of teaching may minimize differences.

5 Various devices have been developed to help the child to read. These devices provide cues concerning how particular letters should be pronounced. Many attempts have been made to develop a completely phonetic alphabet that would

help children to learn to read. The Initial Teaching Alphabet is one of the more recent and more widely promoted attempts to do this. Children who learn to read with the Initial Teaching Alphabet learn more rapidly than do those who learn with traditional orthography, but when they make the transition to the traditional alphabet, they tend to slip back. Slower children have great difficulty in making the transition. Alternative ways of providing cues and a uniform system for decoding print have also been used.

6 Children from culturally deprived circumstances seem to have difficulty in learning to read largely because they see no utility in the activity. Another problem is that they have not developed the perceptual skills necessary for undertaking the task. Children who have such difficulties should be carefully studied to determine the source of their problems.

7 Studies of the recognition process provide considerable information concerning the nature of some of the basic processes of reading. A child can learn to recognize a letter without learning to name the letter. Letter naming comes after letter recognition. Letters are identified by their specific features. Study of letter recognition is undertaken through the use of a tachistoscope, which can present material for very brief exposures and slow up the recognition process. When the tachistoscope is used for studying word recognition, position and length are found to be the first features noticed. Other cues then emerge in sequence. The perception of a word appears to be facilitated through the existence of some kind of internal representation of the word. Reading a word is not like spelling it out letter by letter. Recognition occurs when a certain minimum number of features have been identified. Words are not recognized by scanning the word from left to right, but the word is held stationary in the field of view. Reading is undertaken fixation by fixation, with each fixation covering one or more words. The sweeping movements between fixations are very rapid. The fast reader takes in more words for each fixation and processes the information faster in his brain. Reading is greatly facilitated by being able to guess, to some extent, what the next word will be.

8 The extraction of meaning is different from decoding. One can decode Spanish, in the sense that he can read the words, but the words may have no meaning for him. A large chunk of the printed information has to be retained before the person can fully extract the meaning of it. Reading for meaning involves not only knowing the words but also analyzing the structure of the words.

9 Perceptual sophistication involves being able to extract an ever more complex array of features from the world presented to the senses.

10 Attention plays a crucial role in the extraction of information from sensory information. Although some of the characteristics of attention are known, the process needs to be further studied.

11 Information is that which permits the making of decisions. Information is to be contrasted with noise. Information has structure, but noise does not. The more complex the structure, the greater the potential for communicating information. The more complicated of two figures is likely to attract attention for the longest time, because it contains more information than the other figure.

12 The sensory systems, or perceptual systems, are active searching systems that scan the environment for useful information. The muscles that move the organs of the body containing the sense organs are essential parts of the scanning system. The sense organs are organized into perceptual systems called the visual system, the auditory system, the touch or haptic system, the taste–smell system, and the balance mechanism of the inner ear. The systems are those of an active organism that goes out and finds out about its environment. The systems vary in the extent to which they are fully developed. The eye of man, like the eye of other primates, is highly developed, and the taste–smell system is much less developed. Man's perceptual systems are typical of those found in advanced tree-living animals. Despite man's superior visual system, he still has great capacity for learning through all of his perceptual systems.

13 The analysis of visual information in the brain takes place in sequence. Gross features, such as size and position, are analyzed first and more subtle details later. Visual information is analyzed only to the level of detail that happens to be needed at the particular time. The information analysis system involves classifying and responding to some features rather than to others.

14 Although the visual system naturally engages in scanning activity, some scanning skills need to be learned. There are special skills involved in quickly scanning the pages of a book, or a landscape in looking for particular forms of life. Efficient scanning can take place at great speed. An interesting finding from research is that one can scan as efficiently for several items at once as for a single item.

15 Perception is always a process that reduces the vast amount

of information presented by the environment to the small amount that can be effectively handled.

16 During childhood, mastery is achieved of the perceptual constancies. There may also be some native basis for the perceptual constancy phenomena.

133
. . . .
Summary

All living creatures move about their environment. Although one may speak of the activity as exploratory behavior, the term is not really an appropriate one in the case of subhuman species. There is no basis for saying that an animal tends to move into new territory that it has not visited recently because it wants to explore the territory. Such an interpretation goes far beyond the known facts. One can say that the behavior obviously has great survival value. For example, an animal that lives on berries would do best to look for berries on a bush it had not visited recently rather than on a bush it had picked clean an hour earlier. A predatory animal is most likely to take game by surprise in places that it has not regularly frequented. If it were to keep to well-trodden paths, then prey would soon learn to move to places that the animal did not frequent. In this way, the hunter and the hunted would be kept apart, the hunter

5

Curiosity, Exploratory Behavior, and Achievement Motivation

would perish from lack of food, and the hunted would proliferate. The tendency of the hunter to keep moving to places not recently visited prevents this from happening and maintains a balance in nature.

Although one thinks of exploratory activity as involving essentially locomotion and movement about the environment, this is a misleading idea. Much of the exploration of the environment takes place through the capability of the perceptual systems to scan the environment. Other creatures than man are able to scan the environment through the auditory sense. The extraordinary ability of the bat to locate objects in the dark has been well demonstrated. These creatures can fly through a room in which many threads have been suspended from the ceiling without touching a single thread. The bat scans for objects and obstructions in the environment by sending out a high-pitched signal that is reflected back by solid objects. The reflected signal indicates to the bat the precise location of the objects. Man's capacity for scanning his auditory environment is very limited, although he does have some capacity in this respect. Like all other primates, man is a visually oriented creature and much of his habitual exploratory activity involves visual exploration. In fact, man's perceptual scanning of his environment is largely limited to visual exploration, much as the exploration of the bat is largely auditory.

Visual exploration of the environment, as has already been indicated, begins within days after birth, when the baby will be able to fixate on a bright spot of light. Cratty (1970) has summarized the activity that occurs in the first few weeks of life—activity that describes much of the infant's early exploration of the world. He points out that the attention of the infant is likely to be attracted by stimuli neither very complex nor very simple, but in an intermediate class. Sources of bright illumination are particularly likely to attract attention. He also finds from the research literature that the human face or facelike objects seem more likely to hold the attention than nonfacelike objects, although there is some conflict of data on this point. Cratty finds evidence that infants tend to fixate on the familiar rather than on the new. Perhaps it might be inferred that the infant avoids fixating on the more complex figures because these are too complex for him to structure and that he may also avoid the new because of the difficulty of perceptually structuring the new.

Cratty points out some interesting findings related to visual exploration and the exploration through grasping activity. The infant given a rich visual environment in the first few months of life seems to delay developing grasping behavior. Indeed, the visual activity seems to reduce the amount of hand and arm activity, but this delay is not necessarily disadvantageous, for as soon as visually stimulated infants start to grasp for objects they rapidly surpass infants raised under visually deprived conditions.

Uzgiris (1967) has attempted to bring together information on the general pattern of motor development related to exploration of the environment, which she organizes in a structure highly reminiscent of Piaget's concepts. The earliest motor response of the hand and arm she notes is

136
· · · · · · · · · · ·
Curiosity, Exploratory
Behavior, and
Achievement Motivation

The curiosity of the scientist finds its roots in . . .

the infant grasping for objects.

what she calls a mouthing response—bringing an object held in the hand to the mouth. By three months of age, there is visual inspection of an object held in the hand. By four or five months, objects are shaken and used to hit other objects. By seven or eight months, objects are thrown or dropped. At the end of the first year, objects are used as a source of social contact, as when an object is shown to an adult. Later, objects become involved in naming activities. Throughout these stages, there is a progressive building of information about objects. Piaget and his associates call this information-building process the development of schemas, but the schema also involves an action system because part of the information built about an object concerns what one can do with the object.

There is no way in which knowledge derived from vision can be transferred to touch. What the infant learns by visual exploration tells him nothing about what objects will be like to touch. The infant has to learn, as von Senden's corneal-graft patients had to learn, that cues provided by vision can be related to what an object will feel like if touched. The infant must also learn to generalize from touch in order to predict what a touched object will look like if seen.

The infant begins by the quite independent operations of inspection by vision and inspection by touch. Vision comes first, perhaps because the grasping of an object requires complex muscular coordination. One can place an object in the hand of a one-month-old infant, but the mere grasping of the object provides almost no information compared to the information available through visual scanning. The infant may grasp the object tightly and may ultimately place it in his mouth, but that is a limited touch experience compared with the experience of the six-month-old child, who grasps at an object first identified through vision and turns the object over and looks at it in different positions and perspectives. The information provided by the hands will thus be related to the information provided by vision. To this information is added that gained through motion of the hand and arm as the infant brings the object to his mouth or bangs it against a surface.

Exploratory Behavior Involving Gross Motor Activity

The type of behavior in which the individual moves about his environment, visiting new parts of it, has long been a source of interest to psychologists. Earlier in the century, E. C. Tolman (1932) pointed out some interesting facts about rats running mazes in which there were a variety of paths that could be taken to the goal box containing food. An animal would find a successful path to the goal, but would then vary the path from trial to trial. Reinforcement theory would lead one to expect that, because the responses involved in traveling one particular path had been reinforced, an animal would continue to pursue the same path indefinitely, but this is not what happens. After a number of trials in which the animal follows the same sequence of responses without variation, a sudden change in path selection is likely to occur. Tolman found another related phenomenon to occur in a wide range of species, including the human. An animal placed in a T-maze, in which a straight alley leads to a T branch at which the animal can turn either right or left, will, on a first trial, turn, say, to the left. Put back in the starting box and allowed to run the maze again, it is likely to turn next time to the right.

The human learner shows a parallel phenomenon first noted by E. L. Thorndike (1927), also nearly half a century ago. Thorndike was conducting experiments in which the experimenter had a list of words, which he said to the subject one by one. The subject had to guess a number, from one to five, after each word. One number was correct for each word and the other numbers were wrong. The task of the subject was to find out which number went with each word. In such an experiment, the subject can only guess when he first starts out. Thorndike noted that when a subject said a particular number for a word, for example, "two," then he was less likely to say that number for the next word. The human subject does not make a different response by taking a different path in this case; rather, he makes a different response by saying a different number. This variation in behavior is sometimes called **alternation behavior.**

The early studies of this phenomenon have been reviewed by Travers et al. (1963) together with some of the explanations of why it occurs. One is tempted to do what some of the earlier research workers did and simply say that there is a basic exploratory tendency to do that which is new and different and to seek out new experiences, but such a position is vague and not particularly useful. Two basic phenomena have been shown to be involved called **reactive inhibition** and **perceptual inhibition.**

Reactive inhibition: Reactive inhibition is easily illustrated. Try writing your name quickly a hundred times in succession. The first twenty times the task moves along smoothly and easily. Then difficulties begin to occur. One blocks in the middle of writing one's name and has to stop before completing the remaining letters. One may even have difficulty in beginning to write his name. The activity is becoming blocked or, in technical language, **inhibited.** Most responses that are repeated a large number of times tend to become inhibited, and this is reactive inhibition. It is particularly evident in the case of complex learned behaviors and is either absent or only very weakly present in the case of activities such as walking that are under control of lower centers in the brain. Much of what is called fatigue and tiredness is of this character. A person who earns a living by undertaking a monotonous and repetitive task may feel too exhausted to do any more of the task at the end of his shift, but he is still able to go home and engage vigorously in other activities. The inhibitions that he has built up in relation to his task or work do not carry over to the chores he does at home. Reactive inhibition is quite specific to the task. Also, it dissipates quickly after the person is taken away from the task. That is why short rest periods are very important when any repetitive task is encountered. The person needs to turn to new activities for the state of inhibition to be dissipated. Teachers should recognize this phenomenon in children asked to undertake a long series of similar exercises in arithmetic. As the children work, they become more and more restless, find excuses for leaving their work, and begin to talk to each other. What is happening is that reactive inhibition is building up that interferes with the smooth performance of the task. In order to prevent this from happening, teachers generally arrange for there to be variety in tasks. If monotonous tasks have to be undertaken, then rest periods have to be systematically introduced. Fortunately, education does not have to involve repetitive tasks, as many educators thought it did during the last century. However, there are tasks even in creative efforts that may produce reactive inhibition. The author has experienced this many times when he has spent hours scanning through literature looking for some particular item of information. The scanning task is a highly repetitive task that can build up reactive inhibition and task-related fatigue.

Reactive inhibition has another interesting effect in the kinds of skills involved in physical education. Substantial evidence shows that when concentrated practice is undertaken in a skill such as the free-throw in basketball, the person's level of performance may, ultimately, either level off or decline. If the person practicing the skill is then given a rest period of a few minutes, his performance immediately after the rest period will be considerably improved. What has happened is that the continuous performance builds up reactive inhibition, which interferes with the skill. The short rest period results in the dissipation of the reactive inhibition, with a resulting improvement in performance. The evidence is so clear on this point that it is easy to understand why the performance of a baseball pitcher can deteriorate over a long game. The coach may go to the mound and thus give the pitcher enough time for the reactive inhibition to dissipate. The coach may not give the pitcher any good advice, but his interruption can perform a valuable function in restoring the level of performance.

Perceptual inhibition: Reactive inhibition is a kind of response inhibition, but it is only a part of the exploratory phenomenon we are now considering. A second aspect involves a tendency to avoid inspecting that which has recently been inspected. Let us say that a creature, human or animal, is placed in an environment in which it can enter two passages—a left-hand one painted white and a right-hand one painted with black and white stripes—and let us say that it enters the white one. It then moves about that passageway in a typical pattern of exploratory behavior. After some minutes, the creature is removed from the passageway, but before it is placed back near the two entrances the passageways are switched. The left-hand one is now black and white and the right-hand one white. Because the creature went to the left on the first trial, the left-going response is likely to be inhibited this time, which will make for a tendency for the animal to move to the right. But this is not what happens. The animal is most likely to move into the passage that is different in appearance from the one he entered before. The commonly accepted interpretation of this behavior is that one *avoids* the perceptual inputs to which one has most recently been exposed. This phenomenon is called perceptual inhibition to imply that it is the input to the perceptual system that produces an avoidance response to a particular place or object.

Perceptual inhibition has an effect on gross behavior, but it also influences the way in which objects are inspected. Yarbus (1967) shows this in his book on eye movements. When a person is shown a new object, he goes about inspecting it and obtaining information about it. When he has inspected one part, he moves his eyes to another part. He would report, perhaps, that "I have seen enough of the one part and want to look at the rest." This is a way of reporting that he is avoiding what he has already seen and is inhibited from inspecting it further. It is another example of perceptual inhibition—a tendency for the perceptual system to avoid that from which information has been derived and a tendency to move toward new sources of information. Perceptual inhibition produces perceptual exploration.

The tendency considered here fits well with the general theoretical position taken in this book that man is an information-seeking and -organizing system. A system that has these properties is not going to spend time engaged in taking in information that it has already taken in. The nature of the system is to seek out and organize new information, and this is what the child typically does. An unchanging perceptual input results in boredom and restlessness.

Perceptual inhibitions, like response inhibitions, tend to dissipate with time. A writer works over a paragraph he has written until he can stand the sight of it no more and puts it away for a time. He realizes that he just has to get away from it, but he also knows that if he puts it aside he will be able to return to it the next day and make additional needed improvements. His immediate avoidance response will wear off, and he can then return to the passage with renewed enthusiasm for improving it. Again, perceptual inhibitions dissipate with time. For this reason, one can continue to enjoy a familiar scene, or a painting on the wall of one's home, or the familiar objects around one. Nevertheless, there are times when one has a need for a thorough change of scene and a vacation in another place.

The phenomenon of exploratory behavior is, in many respects, very similar to a motivational factor or drive. Let us consider briefly the parallels. An animal or young child deprived of food becomes progressively more active. A common psychological interpretation of this would be that food deprivation results in an internal condition, called a **drive,** that energizes behavior. The animal or child then becomes active, and continues to be active until fed. Another way of interpreting the events would be to say that food deprivation produces an imbalance in the internal chemistry of the living creature involved and that the imbalance produces activity that continues until the normal internal chemical balance is restored. This is known as the **homeostatic theory of motivation,** which has long been of influence on psychology. With this brief background, let us return to consideration of exploratory behavior as interpreted according to drive theory.

Fowler (1965) has noted that studies have been conducted in which animals were held in small and barren boxes for considerable periods of time and their exploratory activities compared with those of animals that had greater freedom to move around a richer environment. The studies generally show that the result of life in a barren environment is enhancement, temporarily, of exploratory behavior. Fowler takes the position that when information inputs are highly restricted, as they are in a barren and confining environment, then a drive builds up that produces a tendency to activity, just as deprivation of food builds up a very similar restlessness. The findings discussed by Fowler on laboratory animals parallel common experience very closely. Many have had the experience of sitting in a physician's examination room, waiting for him to appear. The room is barren except for the table, covered with a white sheet of paper, on which one is seated, and perhaps a small cabinet containing a few bottles. As time passes, one becomes more and more restless. One stands up, moves around the confined space, begins to examine the contents of the cabinet, and engages in whatever activity the space may permit. If one has to wait as long as an hour, then the confinement is accompanied by acute discomfort, commonly described as frustration.

A point to note about the performance of the patient under these conditions is that he seeks out whatever information the limited environment may provide. The phenomenon can perhaps be interpreted in another way. Let us stick to the case of the human being in the confined situation. Let us postulate that, in order to obtain a homeostatic balance, the human being requires a continuous input of information, much as an input of food is needed to maintain chemical balance. Continuous inputs in appropriate quantities maintain the individual in a state of quiet, such as occurs when he is watching the daily television news program. Lowered inputs result in the aimless restlessness that characterizes boredom. Up to this point, the parallel between food deprivation and information deprivation is clear, but the two do not fit entirely into the same pattern. When the input of information exceeds what can be handled and assimilated, the result is often a state of confusion or excitement—to stretch a point, the effect of excessive input of information is vaguely analogous to indigestion from excessive intake of food.

Finally, in this connection, the point must be made that some schools attempt to control pupils' attention to the material placed in front of them by removing from the rest of the environment any information that might compete for attention. The traditional American classroom did this, and the classrooms of many modern schools in Europe provide the same barrenness. The practice is of dubious value. What it is is an attempt to make class assignments interesting by making everything else utterly boring. The interest developed in the school materials by this technique is probably about as profound as the interest the patient develops in the wallpaper while waiting in the barren examination room.

142
· · · · · · · · · ·
Curiosity, Exploratory
Behavior, and
Achievement Motivation

The Design of Classrooms
for Exploratory Man

Classrooms have been traditionally designed to reduce, as much as possible, the exploratory behavior of the student. Indeed, exploratory behavior has commonly been regarded by teachers as nuisance behavior that distracts the pupil from his assigned studies. A few teachers, even today, can be observed spending nearly all their time in controlling any behavior on the part of their pupils that deviates from what the teacher has prescribed. Although the older programs of education exercised this control by punishing the student who strayed from his assignments, newer programs achieve the same ends by giving high rewards for completion of the tasks prescribed by the teacher. The kind of classroom designed by psychologists interested in the operant approach arranges rewards for completing assigned work, and these rewards may involve tokens with which opportunities to explore may be purchased. As previously mentioned, a few have even suggested that children be paid for doing the tasks prescribed by the schools. This approach to education fails to take advantage of natural exploratory behavior and replaces internal controls by external controls.

The suggestion that teachers take advantage of exploratory tendencies in behavior, rather than suppress them, does not mean that children have to engage in ceaseless undirected exploration. It does mean that classrooms become places where children do something more than study worksheets. Children should be working on problems, but the work should lead them to investigate various sources of information available to them in the classroom. Exploration must lead to knowing how to explore one's environment. Children should have the opportunity of working on problems that they cannot solve in terms of what they already know but require that they search out information from other sources. There should be reference works immediately available, and children should have direct access to the library. Unfortunately, this is not usually so.

A distinction must be made between encouraging exploratory behavior as a part of the regular schoolwork and providing opportunities to explore when, and only when, regular schoolwork has been satisfactorily completed. The former procedure has long been used in innovative programs. The latter procedure is commonly found in programs run along operant lines, in which children are kept at quite dull tasks by reinforcing them with opportunities to engage in some form of free exploration. This detachment of exploratory activity from the formal school curriculum is absurd and must surely lead the pupil to believe that learning is a drudgery that one has to undertake in order to obtain admission to more interesting procedures. The practice suggests that the teacher does not think much of the interest value of the school program and that children have to be enticed to do the work by introduction of special rewards. The pupil may be expected to share the same view of the formal curriculum.

A final point to be made about exploration activities is that they do not have to be undertaken by the pupil working alone. The author has seen many teachers undertake simple scientific experiments in which the entire class was held in breathless suspense concerning what the outcome of an experiment would be. He has also seen the same experiments presented as dull routines. There is a difference between a teacher who undertakes a simple scientific experiment, telling the children "Now let's see what happens when we . . . ," and the teacher who says "I am going to do an experiment to show you that. . . ." The one teacher sets the stage for showing that certain statements are correct. The other teacher has set the stage for exploration.

Anxiety and Security in Relation to Exploratory Behavior

An additional factor plays a significant role in the development of exploratory behavior. Harlow (1961) and Harlow and Harlow (1965) long ago showed that young primates are more likely to engage in the exploration of novel objects if their mother is present than if they are alone in a bare room. The mother provides a base from which the infant makes sorties out into the environment and initiates contact with what is novel. If an infant with its mother is placed in a room where novel objects are displayed on the floor, one at a time, the infant will observe the novel object from the secure position of clutching the mother and may then make advances toward the object. As the object is approached, the infant shows more and more fear responses and, before it even reaches the object, may retreat again to the security of contact with the mother.

A long series of researches on human infants has been conducted by Ainsworth and her associates on this and related problems. The focus of the Ainsworth studies is the attachment responses of the human infant to his mother and the influence of these attachment responses on the relation of the infant to other objects. The essence of the attachment response is the tendency of the young to remain in proximity to the object of attachment. In the human infant, attachment behaviors involve clinging, approaching, and such signaling behaviors as crying, smiling, and vocalizing. A study by Ainsworth and Bell (1970) explored the relation between attachment behaviors and exploratory behavior in white, family-reared children who were approximately one year old. The study was conducted in the unfamiliar surroundings of a room in a laboratory that was not a part of the ordinary environment of the child. The child was put through a simple series of episodes in the laboratory, and his movements about the floor were recorded by having the floor divided into a series of squares and having an observer record the squares into which the baby moved.

The procedure involved roughly the following routine: The mother, baby, and observer entered the experimental room, and the baby was placed on a particular square on the floor. The mother and observer sat down. A stranger entered the room, conversed with the mother for about a minute, and then approached the baby and offered him a toy. Then the mother left the room. This was followed by a procedure involving the offering of toys. The mother returned to the room, and time was given for the baby to make a spontaneous response to her. Other episodes followed, through which the baby's positive responses to the new toys could be observed and also the extent to which he showed attachment behavior, distress, and spontaneous play.

The results of the study indicated that the presence of the mother tended to encourage exploratory behavior, that is, approach behavior toward the toys offered. The absence of the mother tended to reduce exploratory behavior and to produce distress and what is described as searching behavior. After separation from the mother, there was an increased tendency for the baby to show attachment responses, although such an increase was not found in all cases.

Ainsworth and Bell point out that in the human infant, as in other primates, the presence of a novel object elicits both fear and avoidance on the one hand and exploration and approach on the other. The presence of the mother appears to have the effect of reducing fear responses, and her absence tends to enhance fear responses and reduce approach responses. An interesting point to note is that when the mother left the room and then returned, the return did not immediately make the infant secure again. There was a period of readjustment before exploratory behavior occurred again at full strength.

These studies need to be repeated with older children. One suspects that the exploratory behavior shown by children in kindergarten is greatly influenced by the extent to which a kindergarten teacher is supportive of the children, because such teachers function as mother substitutes. Even at much more advanced levels of education, the teacher may well have an important role in sustaining intellectual explorations. The mature scientist may need some support from others in the scientific community if he is to continue his explorations of the unknown.

What happens when the growing primate is deprived of the normal relationships with its mother is a matter of great interest, particularly in relation to the whole matter of exploratory behavior. Mason (1968) has summarized the well-established evidence related to this problem, which is derived almost entirely from the study of subhuman primates raised in captivity in isolation from their mothers. A similar degree of deprivation could hardly be found in the case of the human being. The most notable behavior of a primate deprived of contact with its mother, and later deprived of normal social contacts with other young, is a repetitive pattern of movements. The animal may sit on the floor rocking itself back and forth and may continue to do this for long periods of time. This repetitive form of behavior is very similar to that found in blind children or in the children called autistic. The hypothesis is that this behavior is characteristic of a creature that has been deprived of making the contacts with the environment that are necessary for natural development. In addition, and of special significance in the present context, is the excessive fearfulness of creatures that have been deprived in this way. One consequence of this fearfulness is a tendency to avoid exploring new objects. Indeed, the animals acquire a very disinterested relationship to the environment. Normal social development seems to have great significance for the development of a useful and adaptive relationship to the environment.

Primates reared in a socially barren environment also display other features, including a later inability to relate to their own species.

The findings discussed appear to have implications for education in that, although the mother is the base for exploring the world in the early years of life, the teacher becomes the base for such explorations once the child enters school. The role of teachers in the lower grades as mother substitutes has long been recognized, and the practice has been to assign women teachers to these grades, although this practice is now changing. Some teachers are successful in providing the young child with a secure base for exploration and encourage the child to find out about the world on his own. Some teachers do not do this and devote much of their energy to controlling the children.

One suspects that the need for encouragement to explore, and the need for a security-giving base, remains in most individuals throughout life. The author has long noted that graduate students are likely to be quite lacking in adventuresomeness either in the research literature they will explore or in the research they will undertake unless they are given much encouragement to engage in adventuresome activities. Most master's theses and doctoral dissertations tend to be quite prosaic documents, because the student was not bold enough to strike out in a new direction and was given little encouragement to do so. All of us need encouragement throughout life to climb out of the rut in which we find ourselves.

146
. . . .
Curiosity, Exploratory
Behavior, and
Achievement Motivation

Curiosity

The everyday words **exploration** and **curiosity** have some meaning in common, and yet they are used quite independently in contemporary psychological literature. Those who conduct research on exploration do not claim to conduct research on curiosity. The term *exploration* is used in reference to both animal and human behavior, but the term *curiosity* is confined largely to discussions of human behavior. Exploration consists of behaviors involving obtaining information either by perceptual scanning or by locomotion. Curiosity involves expressed intentions or desires to find out more about an object or situation. A crowd on the street arouses my curiosity: This means that I am likely to approach the crowd, explore the situation, and spend time investigating it. Curiosity involves an intention to engage in exploratory behavior, if the opportunity presents itself. Berlyne (1965) has viewed curiosity, as defined here, as a motivational condition and considers it to be an exploratory drive state.

Studies of curiosity show that its development in children is closely tied to the kind of behavior that parents manifest. Maw and Maw (1965) studied the relation of parental behavior to the curiosity of children in the junior high school grades. They found evidence to support the contention that children showing a high level of curiosity (as judged in various ways) tended to come from homes where the parents were highly accepting of their children. These parents also encouraged exploratory behavior and were generally "more democratic" in their child-rearing practices than were the parents of children in a low-curiosity group. The parents of these high-curiosity children behaved in very much the way one would have predicted they would behave from the studies reviewed earlier in this chapter.

The high-curiosity children had characteristics that differentiated them from the low-curiosity children. The high-curiosity children were more self-sufficient and self-accepting and freer from hindering anxieties. These are attributes that one would expect rewarding, encouraging, and accepting parents to produce. These children were also better organized in their thought processes, perhaps because they had a closer relationship to the environment because of their information-seeking tendencies. They were more tolerant of ambiguity, more flexible. In addition, they were marked by certain social qualities such as relatively high dependability, maturity, and skill in dealing with others. These social attributes probably reflect the desirable and positive relationships they had with their parents.

A point of some interest in the study is that these characteristics were more successful in differentiating the high-curiosity and low-curiosity boys than these groups of girls. In this area, as in many others, boys are better differentiated than are girls in terms of personality characteristics. The explanation commonly given for this is that the child-rearing practices for girls expose them to a more uniform and protected environment than is provided for boys. Mary has to play in the yard, but John can roam the neighborhood.

A major criticism of the Maw and Maw study is that the measures of curiosity were all derived from judgments—teacher judgments, peer judgments, and judgments that the pupils made about themselves. Judgments show a halo effect. This means that if one judges a person to be good in one respect, then one tends to judge him to be good in all other respects. Thus if a person is judged to be high on intelligence, he is likely to be judged high on curiosity and all other desirable characteristics. This kind of thing probably accounts for a part of the relationships found by Maw and Maw, but it is not the whole story. The findings of the study fit so well with what is known about child-rearing practices and exploratory behavior that they have some credence. Also, a later study by Day (1968) provides evidence that teacher judgments of curiosity are related to the degree of curiosity shown by the children in actual situations. Day found a rank correlation of 0.65 between teacher's judgments of curiosity and curiosity as measured through an experimental technique. The essential nature of the technique was to present pupils with a series of slides showing abstract figures. As each slide was shown, the pupil was asked to indicate on a seven-point rating scale the degree to which he felt interest in the figure. It is really quite surprising that the performance of the pupils on such a simple task should show a substantial relationship to the teacher's judgment of the curiosity level of pupils.

There are some other interesting findings. One is that curiosity shows no relationship to either grades or IQ. This is to be expected, for personal attributes that have their origins in a person's social relationships rarely have much relationship to measured intelligence or achievement.

The trait of curiosity, as measured by Day, does show long-term stability. When the three-thousand pupils tested initially were retested eleven months later, the two measures of curiosity for each pupil were substantially related, with a correlation of 0.48. Also, the pupils showed no significant increase in curiosity scores over the eleven-month period. One wonders what would have happened to the scores if the teachers had made a concentrated effort to encourage curiosity in the pupils.

Many questions about curiosity still remain to be answered. One of these is whether it should be regarded as the virtue it is commonly considered to be. Clearly, curiosity is good, but only up to a point. Most of us would get very little done if we were distracted by every novel object and event that happened to come our way. The productive worker has to exercise much restraint over his curiosity, or he will likely accomplish little.

The Energizing and Directing of Behavior

Much of what has been said in this chapter has had to do with the topic commonly described as **motivation,** concerned with the energizing and directing of behavior. The position taken up to this point is that behavior is naturally energized under ordinary waking conditions and that a human being, from birth, shows much behavior directed toward the outer world. When it is said here that behavior is directed toward the outer world, the implication is that behavior results in the accumulation of information about the outside world. Thus babies in the first few weeks of life fixate with their eyes on any bright source of light and will learn to kick if the kicking results in a changed visual input. The perceptual systems are energized to scan the environment, and attention becomes directed toward certain objects rather than others. Behavior, by its very nature, is energized and directed even at the most primitive levels. Just as the attention of the baby is attracted by a bright source of light, and probably by any other strong signal, so too is the adult's attention controlled by similar conditions in the environment. A loud sound or a bright light attracts the attention of people of all ages, indicating that the energizing and direction of behavior are partly controlled by the inherent nature of the human creature. Other examples of natively endowed mechanisms of motivation are found in the restless activity of the person who is hungry, thirsty, cold, or deprived of any of the essentials of life. The energizing of learning in educational situations cannot take place through exposing pupils to such deprivations, but the kind of motivation related to tendencies to scan and explore the environment is quite basic to most well-designed educational programs.

One of the essential ingredients involved in energizing pupils in the classroom is the provision of materials that permit them to move into ever new fields of exploration, but there are limits to the extent of this source of motivation. For example, children in the first grade may take great delight in learning a few words in a foreign language and may enjoy the baffled expressions of their parents when they use the same words at home. There is no motivational problem in the early stages of foreign language learning, but by high school there is. By then, the acquisition of a new language has lost much of its glamor. The mastering of the foreign vocabulary has bogged down into a routine of rote memorizing, and hours have to be spent on translating the foreign literature at such a slow speed that the value of the material translated, as literature, is lost. How can behavior be energized at this point?

Several answers can be given to this question, but not all are acceptable. The approach in earlier centuries was for the teacher to manipulate a number of factors, a central feature being to have nothing in the classroom to distract the student except the task at hand. If the rest of the environment could be made uninteresting enough, it was thought, then perhaps by contrast the task to be learned would become attractive.

Another procedure is to turn the task into a game. Children do not very readily sit quietly in seats in silent contemplation of their work, but they do like to play games with other children. Some components of many different fields of subject matter can be converted into games that two or more pupils can play. The technique finds support in what we know about humanity, which research tells us is a sociable species. Also, research on primates clearly indicates that play among the primates is not only a natural feature of their behavior but also essential for normal development. Play is naturally energized. The incorporation of the school subject into the play context may help to energize the learning of the subject up to a point, but not necessarily very efficiently. When Myers et al. (1965) studied the use of social situations involving one pupil teaching another pupil, they found that pupils did learn under these conditions, but the learning was slow. When a task is presented for learning in the classroom, and pupils learn in pairs, they do work on the task, but they also engage in a great many other social interactions. Young children will spend time nudging each other, teasing, and horseplay. Learning is energized, but so are many other forms of behavior. Pupils do enjoy this kind of socialized learning situation, but it requires a certain amount of discipline on their part if it is to be effective.

The school subject in which games have been used to the greatest advantage is mathematics. Mathematics games often involve an entire class, and one favorite setting for a game has been experimentation with probability theory. Most games related to probability theory involve gambling, and ethical issues related to the use of such games have often been raised. The usual response of the mathematics teacher is to point out that the children learn one cannot win when the odds are set in the usual way.

A third approach to the motivation problem is to introduce novelty into what is an otherwise inherently tedious task. This is not always so easy. In the teaching of a foreign language, the teacher may have the children prepare and enact short plays. Mathematics teachers attempt to find unusual and intriguing problems. Science teachers invent dramatic demonstrations. The development of such situations taxes the teacher's ingenuity to the limit and often calls for more free time than any teacher can give. Some encouragment to this approach is found in present trends toward giving teachers time during school hours when they can develop such materials, but many schools have only the most limited resources for such activities.

A fourth approach is for the pupil to become motivated in terms of goals that he sets for himself. If a person has a worthwhile goal, then he is willing to forego immediate pleasure and even expose himself to some suffering if what he is doing brings him closer to that goal. Goal setting is quite obviously a very important component of human motivation. The energizing effect related to achieving a particular goal, that is, a particular sought-after state of affairs, is commonly referred to as a **need.** The prime developer of a theory relating goals and needs was Murray et al. (1938), who produced an early and extremely influential theory of the goal systems and need systems of man.

Murray attempted to prepare an inventory of the goals commonly sought after by contemporary man and the needs that were related to them. He recognized the fact that many needs are related to the maintenance of balanced physiological conditions. These needs, related to such conditions as food deprivation, water deprivation, and sex deprivation, he called **viscerogenic needs,** but his position was that these needs are of no great significance in a civilized society. A much more important set of needs are the **psychogenic needs.** Murray's theory made quite explicit what many have long recognized, that individuals differ considerably in the needs they manifest. Not all individuals seek out the same states of affairs. Some strive to find social situations characterized by a supportive warmth toward them, some seek power over other people, and some seek to achieve great excellence in what they do. These are three categories of individuals commonly observed in our society. Murray set out to identify the common major needs that characterize most civilized individuals, but he took the position that not all individuals are characterized by each of these needs. His list of needs includes, in addition to those already mentioned, a need to exhibit oneself, a need to accumulate and collect material possessions, a need to be dominated by others, a need to belong to a group, and a need for approval.

Murray did not deny that there may be highly individualized needs such as the hermit's need to meditate, the masochist's need to have suffering inflicted on himself, or the needs related to the eating of dirt that some children show, or perhaps some even stranger needs. Not only mental hospitals but also every community can provide examples of individuals having rare and unusual needs. Sometimes they are needs that run counter to the values of society, but usually they are not.

Murray's work took more than a decade, after his original volume was published, to reach any kind of fruition. World War II intervened, and basic research on the subject had to be foregone for many years. However, during the war years, Murray did pursue a kind of applied research in work involving the selection and training of men for espionage assignments. In this enterprise were a number of young psychologists who recognized Murray's genius and decided to explore further the work he had begun. The most notable among these young men was David McClelland, who, after the end of the war, was able to take the first steps toward the systematic measurement of the needs that Murray postulated to lie at the very core of human motivation.

Postwar research on the measurement and understanding of human needs was mainly the work of David McClelland in its early stages, but soon it attracted a whole school of psychologists in both America and Europe, who have been the most prolific producers of research. The focus of interest has been the measurement of what are referred to as **achievement need** and **affiliation need,** and the relation of these needs to behavior.

McClelland saw that research on sources of human motivation required the development of techniques for their measurement. Of the more than twenty common needs that Murray had listed, McClelland chose to begin the development of measuring techniques in relation to achievement need. Before discussing measurement techniques, let us consider the nature of this need as Murray had envisaged it. The central idea is that achievement need involves a striving to meet some standard of excellence set by the individual. It is not mere achievement as such. A child who does well in arithmetic because his father has said that he will whip him if he does not is not manifesting achievement need. Such a child is manifesting a pain avoidance response. Achievement need is quite different. Such a need would be manifested by a child who said to himself "I only had 60 on the last test, but I am going to work hard and reach 80 on the next test," or by the child who says to himself "I have to work hard at this mathematics stuff because I want to be a great mathematician." Achievement need may also be manifested in fear of failure, as in the child who says "I couldn't stand myself if I failed tomorrow's test." The essence of achievement need is found in statements that the individual makes about his plans, his future, and his expectancies.

For his purpose of developing a technique for measuring achievement need, McClelland turned to projective techniques that had long been believed to reflect inner structures directing behavior. Direct approaches to the study of human motivation have generally proved themselves to be quite futile. There is little point in asking someone "Are you the kind of person who always tries to achieve some kind of standard of excellence?" Such questions yield virtually no information in the answers they elicit.

People tend to be extraordinarily blind to the conditions that energize their behavior. This is why an indirect approach to human motivations, such as with projective techniques, appeared to provide a key to their measurement.

The essence of a projective technique is that the individual is presented with a highly ambiguous perceptual input and is asked to ascribe some meaning to it. The idea is that the individual exposed to the ambiguous input will not interpret it in an arbitrary way but will reflect in the interpretation his own inner structure. For example, when an individual is asked to view an inkblot and to state what he "sees" in it, he may go about the task either systematically or unsystematically. If he goes about the task systematically, he is likely to begin by looking at the blot as a whole and deciding what it looks like. Then he may take major sections of the blot and interpret them. Finally, he may move down to fine details. The unsystematic interpreter may begin anywhere, perhaps with some minor detail, and end anywhere. Supposedly, the way in which the individual goes about interpreting the blot is a reflection of his intellectual habits. In addition, the belief has long been held, with some evidence to support it, that the motives and drives of the individual are also manifest in the interpretations given to the inkblot. There is some evidence, for example, that hungry individuals are more likely to look for food objects in an inkblot than are individuals who are not hungry. This was the kind of concept that attracted McClelland in his search for a means of measuring achievement need.

McClelland did not use inkblots in his attempt to measure achievement need but preferred visual presentations with a greater degree of meaning. Murray's group of scholars, before World War II, had already developed some materials to be used for the projective measurement of needs in the form of a device that became known as the Thematic Aperception Test. These materials typically showed one or more people engaged in some not readily identifiable activity. They permitted the imaginative viewer to decide for himself what was happening and to "read into the pictures" happenings and events that were really not there at all.

Because McClelland was interested in the measurement of achievement need, he chose pictures likely to trigger interpretations related to that need. One of the pictures he used showed a boy, perhaps of high-school age, sitting at what might be a desk. It cannot quite be seen what the young man is doing. The person in whom achievement need is to be measured is asked to look at the picture and discuss the events leading up to the scene depicted. Then he is to say what is happening in the scene. Finally, he is to tell what he thinks is going to happen next. Usually, four or more pictures constitute the series, and the stories told by those who view the pictures may be quite long and detailed, and often are.

The pictures have to be very carefully selected for this kind of use. Pictures that obviously present some person who is struggling to achieve a standard of excellence are not generally used. Such pictures, called high-cue pictures, are not generally suitable for measuring achievement need. On the other hand, pictures that provide no cues whatsoever are also useless. What are needed are what are called medium-cue pictures, in which there are slight suggestions that the individual is striving to achieve some degree of excellence on the task at hand.

The research on achievement need, up to about 1967, has been summarized in a book by Heckhausen (1967). Although each individual study may not contribute much to knowledge of the field, the overall body of knowledge built by the hundreds of studies in the area is of considerable importance to education. A first point of importance to note is that the measure of achievement motivation depends on whether the person's achievement need is or is not aroused at the time when the measurement is made. Let us consider what this means. Suppose that we are concerned with a high-school boy who has high achievement motivation, and we expose him to the picture test. Suppose also that we bring him into the test situation and tell him that this is a task on which one can neither do well nor poorly, for we are measuring some quite obscure aspect of personality that has little reference to his particular life. Under such conditions, there is nothing in the test to challenge him and nothing to arouse his need for achievement. He would probably make few statements about the pictures that had any reference to achieving a standard of excellence or to the person in the picture striving to either achieve success or avoid failure. Under such conditions, the record derived from the test situation would indicate the pupil to be low in achievement motivation. This would be a correct description in that there would have been nothing in the test situation that had aroused the pupil's achievement need. The pupil would be manifesting low achievement need.

However, this same pupil on other occasions may manifest high achievement need. Let him work on the task of preparing an exhibit for the state science fair, a task that challenges him to an enormous extent. Then his achievement need will be aroused and energize his behavior to a high degree. In the kind of test situation described, one can also arouse his achievement need. One can bring him into the situation and tell him that the test he is to take has considerable significance in predicting his success in life. Such a statement is sufficient to arouse achievement need in most persons. When this is done, the pupil with high achievement need will get a high score on the achievement need test.

These findings have implications for teaching. One major implication is that even though a teacher may have pupils with high achievement needs, the needs will not be manifested in behavior unless they are aroused. An important task of the teacher is to provide challenging materials that will arouse the pupil's need to strive to achieve a standard of excellence. Unless the teacher does this, a pupil with the capability of manifesting high achievement need may die intellectually from boredom.

A point to note is that not all achievement in school is energized by achievement need. Even if pupils have developed little with respect to achievement need, they may still be high achievers. A pupil may do well in school to please his parents, to be accepted by other pupils whose friendship he values, or because he is afraid of some punishment if he does not do well. In the case of girls, achievement is often motivated by a need for social recognition, a very significant need for women. Achievement may be motivated from many different sources.

Now let us return to a consideration of the measurement of achievement motivation and what that measure predicts. The information one generally wants to derive from such a measure is the degree to which a person will show achievement motivation when challenged, and to do this the test has to be given under a condition of arousal. As one would expect, achievement motivation measured under aroused conditions can be used to make many interesting predictions, but measured under relaxed conditions it predicts almost nothing.

A point of considerable interest is that the arousal effect is much more pronounced with boys than with girls. Indeed, there is evidence that the motivational structure of the male in our society is very different from that of the female. As mentioned, this may be due to the different approaches parents take in rearing boys and in rearing girls. There may be an innate factor, but child-rearing practices appear to be crucial.

Achievement motivation is not distributed equally through all classes and subcultures within the United States, and there are probably differences in its distribution across different nations and different times in history. Heckhausen (1967) summarizes the findings in this respect, pointing out that evidence from many different sources indicates that achievement motivation is particularly pronounced in the more educated classes and among those in the higher occupational levels. He also points out that the American culture is very mobile and those who are moving upward socially tend to be people in whom a high level of achievement motivation is found. Growing up in a closely knit family seems to be a condition particularly favorable for its development. Many studies have been undertaken to find out whether religious background has an effect on the development of this motive, but they have failed to identify any particular trend. Different religious groups show very large differences in the percentage of their members included in *Who's Who*, suggesting that there might be corresponding differences in achievement motivation, but such differences have not been found. The evidence suggests that there are many different motives that may be at work in making a person a success in the American scene.

The fact that achievement motivation is tied to certain social and cultural conditions suggests that it is a learned form of motivation and hence can be brought under control. Although it seems to be a positive and desirable trait, one does not quite know what the social repercussions would be if steps were taken to raise it in our civilizations. It may well be that a culture needs to have some of this characteristic in its members, but too wide a distribution might make for a very difficult society in which to live.

Now let us consider some of the predictions that can be made from measures of achievement motivation. One of the most interesting of these is related to what is known as **level of aspiration.** This is a concept originally introduced into psychology by the late Kurt Lewin, who stressed the importance that goals play in determining behavior. Lewin pointed out that individuals could set goals that were very easily achieved or goals that were extremely difficult to attain. Although the concept would appear to be a highly significant one for understanding human behavior, it did not lead to any very useful or interesting findings until it was studied in relation to achievement motivation. The early studies turned up such surprising but unhelpful results as that a person's level of aspiration was unrelated to his intelligence or his success in reaching the goal.

Studies of achievement motivation have come up with some very interesting and perhaps unexpected results in relation to level of aspiration. The trend of the findings is that persons who score high on measures of achievement motivation and who are failure oriented tend to choose goals either very hard to achieve or very easy to achieve. They do not choose goals that represent realistic levels of aspiration in terms of their abilities. A realistic goal is defined here as one that offers challenge but is not of such a level of difficulty that it probably cannot be reached. The person high in achievement motivation does this because he cannot stand personal failure. He may select a very difficult goal because it would represent a great achievement in meeting a standard of excellence. If he fails to achieve the goal, then he has the alibi that failure was not his fault at all but a result of the extreme difficulty of the task. On the other hand, he may choose a goal that is very easy to reach, in order to be sure of success.

The success-oriented person with high achievement motivation is much more realistic in the goals he sets, tending to choose goals only moderately difficult to achieve. Success orientation is far more realistic than is failure orientation. The failure-oriented person has substantial internal conflict that he has to resolve in achieving or not achieving a goal. His choice elicits a conflict between a desire for success and a fear of failure. The success-oriented person, in contrast, finds no conflict between his expectation of success and his need for success.

Every teacher has encountered children who set goals for themselves either too high or too low. Such children need help and guidance in setting realistic goals, and they need to learn through experience that there is much advantage in achieving goals that are more in the middle range. At this time, nobody knows whether the habits of the failure-oriented person in this respect can be changed through guidance, but they probably can be.

A matter puzzling to those who first have contact with the literature of achievement motivation is that there is no very simple, straightforward, direct relationship between measured achievement motivation and achievement in such tasks as school learning or learning in laboratory situations. Let us illustrate this point through a simple laboratory experiment that has been undertaken a number of times. Suppose that high-school students are brought to the laboratory and given an achievement motivation test under directions that produce arousal of achievement need. At the end of the test, they are told that their help is needed in undertaking a dull and trivial task involving the cancellation of all the *es* in a page of type, because the experimenter wants to find out which of the *es* tend to be missed under these conditions. The students then perform this task for, say, three minutes. Now under these conditions one would almost certainly find no relationship between the measure of achievement motivation and the measure derived from how many *es* were cancelled. The reason for the lack of relationship is that the cancellation task was one that did not arouse the individual to achieve some standard of excellence.

Now suppose that the same experiment was undertaken once more, but with a very important variation. This time the students are told that the cancellation task, although it appears to be very simple, is nevertheless highly predictive of the kind of success they may hope to achieve in life. This time cues will have been provided that arouse achievement need in those in whom it can be aroused. The result is that performance on the simple cancellation task is now correlated with the measure of achievement need. At the end of the experiment, the students are of course told the nature of the experiment so that they do not leave the room and disseminate false information.

This kind of experiment explains why measures of achievement need have sometimes been found to predict grades in academic courses but sometimes not. The crucial factor appears to be whether the courses do, or do not, challenge the student to do his best. Teachers know well that not all courses are a challenge to the student, and many students with a high need for achievement may do poorly in a course that they regard as a stupid requirement. One would expect that in a well-designed educational program, in which each course challenged the students, there would be a substantial relationship between measured achievement need and grades.

Since achievement motivation represents a characteristic considered desirable, and one, among others, that contributes to achievement, teachers are interested in how it develops. Teachers who inquire about this problem generally have at the back of their minds the thought that perhaps there may be some way through which achievement motivation can be enhanced in the pupils in their classes. At the present time, it must be admitted that much more is known about the conditions under which achievement motivation develops than how to control it in children of school age. Heckhausen has carried out a series of studies of the problem of its development and has summarized them in his book. His studies show that children three and one-half to four and one-half years old show marked emotional responses to success and failure. The younger children in this group approach new tasks with no indications that they may fail, a finding that has been interpreted a little too freely to mean that these children expect success. On the other hand, children of four and one-half years and older are likely to be selective in the tasks that they are willing to undertake and will not try those they do not think they can succeed at.

Heckhausen takes the position that the early behaviors involving responses to success and failure represent the early stages of development of achievement motivation. Distinct striving to achieve a standard of excellence has perhaps been formed by the time the child enters elementary school and perhaps by the age of ten has reached the form it will take through the individual's adult life. The general trend of the evidence is that early experiences, before the child enters school, are important for the development of achievement motivation. This does not mean that the teacher cannot develop achievement motivation in a child in whom it has not been developed in the preschool years. It means only that the typical pattern of development is one in which the foundation for the attribute is laid in the early years.

The conditions that produce achievement motivation are now understood in general terms, but the details still have to be worked out. There is just about complete agreement that the crucial factors involve the child's relationship with his parents during the preschool years. Heckhausen has summarized a very large number of researches that indicate that a warm supportive role on the part of the mother is important. There is also some evidence suggesting that encouraging the child to engage in independent achievement-oriented activity is of considerable importance. Merely leaving a child alone so that he can assert his independence is not enough to develop achievement motivation, but the child has to be encouraged to engage in constructive and purposeful activities with the helpful support of his parents as it is needed. Parents who are overanxious to have their children achieve may fail to develop in them achievement motivation, because the pushing of the child into ever new tasks may be viewed by the child as rejection. When children and parents are able to do things together, very favorable circumstances are provided for the development of achievement motivation.

The roles of the two parents in this respect are somewhat different in the American culture. The mother of the highly achievement-motivated child has functioned as the teacher of the child and has provided him with close guidance in the activities in which he chooses to engage. The mother is a direct reinforcer of his successes and a helper where he fails. She may punish him for wrong behaviors, but the relationship is still one of warm support. Parents who push their child ahead may not be successful in developing achievement motivation in him because they have a cold and intellectual relationship with the child and may perhaps see him as a means of achieving what they themselves would like to accomplish.

The father's rather different role in the development of achievement motivation is—at least in the American culture—to provide a model for his children to imitate. There is some evidence that the model of a successful father is of particular importance to the daughter in the development of achievement need.

A point that requires special stress is that the mere giving of independence to a child is useless unless it involves the child in assuming responsibility for some activity and some goal. The children of the poor typically find themselves at home alone and with complete independence at an early age, but this does nothing for them and may develop in them insecurity and a poor adjustment to their environment. As was clearly shown in the research on the development of exploratory behavior, the parent provides a base from which the world is explored, and without that base very little exploratory activity is ever likely to take place. The development of exploratory tendencies follows very much the same pattern as the development of achievement motivation.

Just as the children of the poor are likely to manifest a rather low level of achievement motivation, though of course there are many exceptions, so too are there other groups whose children grow up with a similar deficiency in this respect. Indians on reservations present this pattern of development. However, it is not just poor minorities who show this pattern. Studies have been made of upper-class South Americans who show a pattern of low achievement motivation. The reason for this appears to be that the upper-class South American is brought up with the idea that he has inherent status because of his circumstances of birth. His role in life is to behave in a way that maintains his status, and that way of life does not involve a striving to achieve a standard of excellence on tasks involving knowledge and skill.

The teacher would like to know whether achievement motivation can be developed through the school. This is a very important question, but the answer to it cannot be given at this time. Certainly, the teacher can do much to provide a secure base from which the world can be explored, and the teacher can urge the pupil to set up goals for himself to be achieved through independent activity. One does not know whether the conditions favorable to the development of achievement motivation have to occur at a particular age level, such as before the age of six or even younger, for them to build motivation into the growing individual. This is the well-known issue of whether there are critical ages at which particular aspects of development have to take place. Many psychologists have long taken the position that there are, and they also maintain that if the critical age is passed without the significant conditions for development having been provided, then these conditions cannot be provided later.

Emphasis must also be placed on the fact that even if the school can do little to develop achievement motivation, there are other categories of motivation that may play a part in producing adequate school achievement. At the elementary-school level, children may work hard because the teacher has arranged that the pupils who succeed may be given some special social status such as that of leading a group in some activity or chairing a meeting. Also, much can be done to give parents a greater role in the education of their children, and children may achieve just to please their parents. This kind of motivation often cannot be used because

158
. . . .
Curiosity, Exploratory
Behavior, and
Achievement Motivation

parents may know little, and care less, about how their children are doing in school.

Incentives and Reinforcers as Energizers

The previous section emphasized that teachers may be able to energize behavior by providing situations that challenge those in whom achievement motivation can be aroused. By providing such challenge, the teacher may be able to raise the energy level of the pupil, if the pupil can be so aroused. The difficulty with the suggestion is that the technique fails to touch large groups of students, particularly those from underprivileged areas in whom achievement motivation has not developed. Other means of energizing behavior have to be used on such groups; some of the research on reinforcement and incentives suggests ways of doing this.

It will be recalled that reinforcers of behavior have the capability of keeping particular aspects of behavior occurring in specified situations. Children rewarded in some way for saying "please" continue to say it on appropriate occasions. In a sense, the reward energizes the production of the response "please." Many psychologists would say that the **incentive** for saying "please" in the particular situation is the reward provided. Those who interpret behavior in this way would view the reward as an event the anticipation of which energized behavior, and incentives are events that energize behavior. The teacher has opportunity to provide and control some incentives in the classroom. Let us turn to research on the various forms of incentives that the teacher may control and see what this research says about the various categories of incentives involved.

An excellent summary of research on incentives has been provided by Lipe and Jung (1971). An interesting feature of this review is that it points out the large number of studies in which incentives have been used to control gross activities such as staying seated in the classroom, avoiding disruptive behavior, and spending time with the eyes on the work materials. Much less of the research is concerned with more specific aspects of learning. One is unlikely to find a study concerned with the effect of incentives on learning long division, even though one may find studies of the effect of incentives on the amount of time spent studying mathematics materials. Most of those who do research in this area seem interested only in the gross control of pupil behavior rather than in specific aspects of cognitive learning. The assumption is that if the efforts of the pupil can be directed toward the curriculum materials, then learning will occur. This is not a very good assumption to make. Let us consider what is known about the various classes of incentives that have been used in experimental studies.

Material incentives: A great number of studies have used concrete objects as incentives. These include snacks, candy, trinkets, crayons, money, gum, and articles of clothing. Most of the studies using such rewards have involved underprivileged and underachieving children.

It seems reasonable to assume that these objects have high value for many of these children who have so little. The findings of such research are equivocal. Sometimes the rewards have been effective in facilitating the achievement of the desired goals, but sometimes they have resulted in a depressed performance. Two studies included in the group (Marshall, 1969; Spence, 1966) in which rewards produced a depression in learning suggest that the depression may be caused by distraction from the learning task by the introduction of highly prized rewards. Such distractions may produce a high level of excitement, which may also disrupt learning. There is also the possibility that high excitement after mastering a task may disrupt the consolidation of the learning in the nervous system. Another problem related to the use of material rewards that has to be considered in planning to use them in the classroom is the fact, demonstrated in much research, that if certain phases of work are so rewarded and other phases are not, then the learner puts all his energy into the phases that are rewarded, and the nonreward tasks tend to be neglected. Although many operant psychologists write as though the value of material incentives was unquestioned, the data suggest that their use must be considered as controversial and experimental. The data also show that it is easy to make naive assumptions about what behavior is being energized or reinforced. A study by Risley (1968) illustrates this point. In it, children were given a snack when they reported that they had spent time playing with paints. What was found was that the children increased the frequency with which they reported playing with paints, but the time spent with paints did not change. It may be much easier to increase the time a child spends gazing at his book than to increase the amount of time spent learning.

Social incentives: The commonest social incentives are those of the teacher praising, reprimanding, or ignoring the pupil. Approval by peers and related group pressures have also been used. An earlier review of incentives by Kennedy and Willcutt (1964) came to the conclusion that praise generally raises the level of performance in the classroom. The data are not clear on this point, for, as Wallen and Travers (1963) have pointed out, classes where there is much positive praise tend to be classes in which pupils have considerable freedom, and these classes tend to have pleasant teachers. Research workers have not been able to sort out the effects of these various factors.

Praise may be either contingent on performing in particular ways or noncontingent. In the one case, praise is given only when the pupil performs a specific act, such as looking at the work in front of him. In the other case, the teacher provides such praise as "You are certainly doing well today," or "I am glad that so many of you have worked so hard this morning." Operant psychologists have generally advocated only the use of contingent praise, as is evident from such books on classroom management as those by Buckley and Walker (1971) and Homme (1971). Despite the fact that contingent praise is advocated, some evidence is provided in the Lipe and Jung (1971) article that noncontingent praise is effective.

The behavior of these children is highly energized but probably has little goal direction.

The behavior of these children is both highly energized and highly directed.

This finding is of some consolation to teachers, for it is much easier to administer noncontingent praise than contingent praise.

Student goal setting as an incentive: Many have long advocated that students be permitted to set for themselves goals to be achieved and then be held responsible for achieving them. A systematic way of doing this was widely practiced half a century ago in a classroom management procedure known as the Morrison Contract Plan. This procedure has been reinvented over the years on a number of occasions and today appears in the form known as **performance contract plans.** Much has been written in recent years about performance contracting between teachers and students, but relatively little research has been done to study and evaluate the procedure. The one novel element introduced into the new performance contracts, in contrast with the older contract plans, is that the newer plans generally provide some kind of bonus for completing the contract on time. The bonus may consist of permitting the child to engage in some high-interest activity, the implication being that the goal set and the work related to it did not have very high interest value. Plans also vary in the extent to which the pupil chooses goals for himself or merely decides when a goal set by the teacher can be achieved. The incentive value of the procedure probably depends on the extent to which the goal is one chosen by the teacher or one chosen by the pupil.

Knowledge of results as an incentive: Many laboratory experiments have shown that, on dull monotonous tasks, feedback—telling the individual how well he is doing—does have a motivating effect. Indeed, one can keep a person for long stretches of time performing the uninteresting task of trying to draw a line two inches long from memory if he is told how well he is doing after he draws each line. The task then becomes something of a challenge. Lipe and Jung suggest that the same phenomenon may occur in schools and cite several articles suggesting that knowledge of results may have incentive value. One can understand that a child given fifty addition problems might keep going if he were told after each problem whether he was right or wrong. The more usual way of providing feedback would be for the teacher to correct the entire set of fifty problems at once, but the completion of fifty problems might seem to the pupil to be such a remote goal that it has little incentive value. Of course, many teachers would say that pupils should not be assigned such tasks at all, because the tasks are inherently uninteresting and may antagonize the pupil toward all of education.

The large number of studies reviewed by Lipe and Jung suggest that incentive systems may be used effectively for relating the pupil to his tasks but that, once the pupil–work relationship has been established, the incentives may have little function. Most incentive systems appear to have been developed within school programs in which the work to be done by the pupil is not particularly attractive to him. Indeed, operant psychologists commonly assume that schoolwork is not intrinsically attractive and, for this reason, offer the children opportunities to engage in more attractive activities once their work is completed. This is a Victorian conception of education, for there are school programs in which the work is attractive and in which the children would prefer to do the work rather than anything else. The author can remember visiting a school in the East End of London and watching the children when the bell sounded at the close of the day. Not a child stopped what he was doing. The teacher moved among the pupils and suggested that they bring their work to a close. Finally, after fifteen minutes of effort to terminate the work, the teacher said "I am sorry, but I am going to have to send you home now, even if you want to stay." The pupils reluctantly cooperated and put away their work. Events at the close of the day were no different in the other twenty classrooms in the school. If anyone had suggested that an incentive system be introduced into such a school, he would have been looked at in amazement. Engaging in the schoolwork was a sufficient incentive. When the author encounters a school that proudly displays its incentive system, he begins to wonder whether adequate thought has been given to the program. All too often, incentive systems are used as a substitute for a well-designed program. The excuse sometimes given is that "these children come from poor homes and have no appreciation for the importance of academic work." This is no excuse. The school visited in the East End of London was in one of the poorest districts in that city. Nevertheless, the school was characterized by the qualities described in Chapter 1 and by other qualities. The children worked on problems of interest to them under the supervision of a faculty that encouraged and respected student ideas and utilized these ideas in every way. The program was flexible and variable. Teachers did not feel bound by a rigid routine but were able to change their plans to take advantage of a point raised by the students. Although the atmosphere was business-like, student–teacher relations were cordial and relaxed. Because there was little emphasis on competitive grades, pupils were free to help one another. Teachers were viewed as friends rather than as the symbols of law and order.

Generalized Drive

Up to this point, motivation has been discussed largely in terms of the effect of particular events in energizing behavior. Challenging situations arouse achievement motivation, the presence of other people arouses the need to affiliate with them, numerous objects used as incentives have the property of activating behavior, and novel objects may arouse exploratory behavior, though such behavior may occur in the absence of such objects. The study of these sources of motivation tends to obscure the fact that living creatures, by their very nature, are active and, by their very nature, come into contact with the environment and interact with it. Behavior, during a large fraction of the life span, is active and energized, and the energizing of behavior comes from within. Chapter 2 of this book pointed out that the baby shows states varying from highly energized behavior to deep sleep. Woodworth (1958) has pointed out that this energizing of behavior results not only in physical activity but also in direct action on the environment. A kitten is not just active, but it plays with any loose object that happens to be around. The infant doesn't just wave his arms and legs but grasps at objects. The kindergarten child doesn't just show an exuberance of energy but concentrates on experimenting with the wonderful things in the world around him. Behavior is not just energized but is directed toward the environment. This broad-base energizing of behavior is referred to as **generalized drive.**

The idea of a generalized drive has been investigated from many different angles. Neurophysiologists have been successful in identifying parts of the brain that have to do with the energizing of behavior. One part, the reticular activating system, serves the function of bombarding the higher levels of the brain with impulses that keep it in a state of excitement. The reticular activating system is itself activated by any inputs to the sensory system. The reticular activating system is least active when there are no inputs to the sensory systems, as when a person lies on his bed quietly with his eyes closed in sleep. When the reticular activating system is active, the individual is said to be in a state of **arousal,** in which there is a high level of generalized drive. Thus there is now some physiological basis for the idea of a generalized drive. Another part of the nervous system, known as the limbic system, also has related arousal functions.

Attempts have been made to develop psychological interpretations of generalized drive. Hull's (1943) original concept of a generalized drive was that it was a sum of all the components of drive operating at a particular time. Thus generalized drive might have a hunger component, an exploratory component, and other components that added together to form an overall generalized drive. In more recent times, a major component of generalized drive has been considered to be emotionality, particularly that aspect of emotionality related to anxiety. With this in mind, attempts have been made to develop devices that will measure anxiety. One of the earliest of these was the **Taylor Manifest Anxiety Scale.** This device was a set of questions to which "yes" or "no" answers were given. The questions pertained particularly to physical manifestations of general anxiety such as sweating of the palms of the hands, digestive disturbances due to tension, and sleeplessness caused by worry. Early research showed that the measure derived from this inventory of anxieties was like a measure of motivation or drive. Much research has been done with this device, a substantial part of which has been summarized by Cofer and Appley (1964). In many ways, the measure provided by the Manifest Anxiety Scale does predict, in simple laboratory situations, in the way that a measure of motivation should predict. In the case of simple laboratory tasks, high scores on the anxiety scale are related to good performance on simple learning tasks. When the tasks become complex, then high anxiety scores are related to poor performance. The latter effect occurs, it is presumed, because high anxiety tends to produce quite confused responses when tasks are difficult. In the case of academic learning, simple relationships between anxiety and school performance have not been found, perhaps because what is a simple task for one child is a complex task for another. Extensive research has been done in the latter case, using a device called the **Children's Manifest Anxiety Scale.**

165
. . . .
Generalized Drive

Summary

1 Living creatures move about their environment, avoiding the particular locations they have most recently visited. This is one aspect of exploratory behavior, an aspect clearly advantageous in foraging for food. Another aspect of exploratory behavior is found in the normal scanning of the environment by the perceptual systems. Visual exploration and manual exploration are related in the infant in that opportunities for visual exploration reduce the extent to which manual exploration will take place.

2 Inspection by vision and inspection by touch develop independently. The information derived through the two systems has to be related by experience. Man has great skill in exploration through his hands because of how they are built.

3 Living creatures show variability in their behavior. Two major mechanisms seem to be involved. Reactive inhibition is a tendency for any response made to build up an inhibition of that response. The strain produced by repetitive work is a result of the building up of reactive inhibition. Reactive inhibition results in variability in behavior. When repetitive tasks have to be undertaken, reactive inhibition leads to a decrement in performance commonly attributed to fatigue. Reactive inhibition is quickly dissipated when the individual turns to some entirely different activity.

4 Perceptual inhibition also builds up when attention is continuously directed toward the same scene. One does not like to hear the same bar of music played over and over again. One likes to make changes in the home by redecorating from time to time or by introducing new objects or new colors. Perceptual inhibitions, like reactive inhibitions, dissipate rapidly when new circumstances are provided. One may become tired of the familiar scene in the living room, but, even after a short vacation, it is good to see again. Thus one continues to enjoy familiar scenes, familiar stories, and other familiar experiences.

5 Exploratory behavior can be viewed as being behavior based on a drive that energizes behavior. A person deprived of opportunities for engaging in exploration shows a heightened tendency to explore. The tendency can also be viewed as reflecting a need to have a continuous input of new information. This fact should be kept in mind in developing programs for schools. Children have a need for a continuous input of

new information. Classrooms should be rich in interesting displays, which should be changed frequently. Proposals that children should be permitted to engage in exploratory behavior as a reward for undertaking dull tasks are nothing short of absurd. There is no reason why all school tasks should not be inherently interesting. Teachers should raise questions that set the stage for exploration.

6 The development of exploratory behavior, as a positive asset, is closely related to conditions of security in infancy. The mother plays an important role in providing a base of security from which the child can explore the world. The absence of the mother tends to reduce exploratory behavior, that is, approach behavior toward unfamiliar objects. Such approach behavior toward the unfamiliar builds up anxiety, but the presence of the mother tends to reduce the level of anxiety. An initial response to unfamiliar objects is fear, and the development of exploratory behavior requires that this fear be either eliminated or controlled. The absence of the mother during infancy has other important consequences. In studies of primates, maternal deprivation resulted in repetitive behavior similar to that manifested by autistic children. The deprived primates also grew up to be adults unable to relate adequately to other adults in the primate community.

7 Curiosity refers to expressed intentions or desires to find out more about an object or situation. One can also think of it as an exploratory drive state. The development of curiosity is highly related to the behavior of the parents, and accepting parents provide a particularly favorable condition for the development of this characteristic. High-curiosity children, in contrast to low-curiosity children, are more self-sufficient, more self-accepting, and less anxious. They are also more tolerant of ambiguity and more mature in dealing with others. Boys are better differentiated in this respect than are girls. Teachers seem to be able to identify curiosity successfully. Curiosity shows little relationship to grades and IQ. Curiosity seems to show some stability in children from year to year.

8 Motivation has two aspects. One is the energizing of behavior, and the other is the direction of behavior. Behavior is naturally energized in that the infant and child are built to interact vigorously with a rich environment. A rich environment in the classroom will have the same effect and will result in energized behavior on the part of the pupil. Play is naturally energized and may form the basis for socialized learning in the classroom.

9 Behavior in the classroom may also be motivated by the use

of novelty. In addition, if goals are set by the pupils themselves, then the goals themselves may have energizing properties. The energizing effect related to the achievement of a particular goal is called a need. Murray has developed a highly influential theory of needs, classifying them as viscerogenic and psychogenic. Although the viscerogenic needs are quite uniform from person to person, the psychogenic needs show great variation. Different individuals are motivated by different needs. The main outcome of the work of Murray has been the development of extensive research on achievement need. The early measures of achievement need were developed by McClelland. The essence of achievement need is that it involves the striving to achieve a standard of excellence. McClelland measured this need through a picture interpretation technique known as a projective technique. Individuals read into pictures their own needs, provided the pictures are ambiguous and straightforward interpretations are not possible. The achievement need manifested by an individual through such a test depends on whether his need is or is not aroused. The more useful measure of achievement need is provided when it is measured under aroused conditions. A point to note is that a class may consist of pupils with high potential achievement need, but the need may never be aroused by the curriculum.

10 All achievement in school is not energized by achievement need. Indeed, it may well be that the majority of pupils in many schools are energized much more by need for approval or other needs than by need for achievement.

11 Achievement need is not distributed uniformly through the various social and cultural groups. It is particularly characteristic of the more educated classes and of the middle class. It is characteristic of those in society who are moving up the social and economic ladder. Growing up in a closely knit middle-class family seems to be a very favorable condition for its development.

12 There is some evidence that the person high on achievement motivation who is also failure oriented tends to choose goals either very hard to achieve or very easy. The success-oriented person with high achievement motivation tends to choose goals that are moderately difficult to achieve and is realistic in what he can accomplish.

13 Measures of achievement motivation predict performance on tasks that are seen as some kind of challenge. Thus these measures may or may not predict academic performance, depending on whether the courses involved are or are not a

challenge to the student. In a program that challenges students, one would expect achievement to be related to achievement motivation. Achievement would also be related to other characteristics of the student including aptitude and previous experience.

14 More is known about how achievement motivation develops in the family environment than how to develop it in school. Evidence of achievement motivation is apparent by about the age of four, when children begin to show that they know when they have succeeded and when they have failed. By the age of ten, achievement motivation has developed in its adult form. A crucial factor in the development of achievement motivation is encouragement on the part of the parents for the child to undertake meaningful independent activity. Merely pushing the child ahead does not develop achievement motivation. Also, independence on the part of the child is not enough unless it is accompanied by some worthwhile goal.

15 Although some students may be energized by challenges provided by schoolwork, events described as reinforcers also can be interpreted as having incentive value. Much is known about the use of incentives for controlling the gross activities of the student but little about their value in controlling behavior more closely related to academic learning. Research related to the use of material incentives has not provided clear results concerning where they can be used to advantage. It is known that if some tasks are rewarded in a program, then the nonrewarded tasks tend to be neglected. Children also learn how to manipulate the incentive system. Praise seems to raise the energy level of pupils, and this effect takes place regardless of whether the praise is contingent or noncontingent on particular activities on the part of the pupils. Various contract plans have long been used to provide the incentives that come through setting goals. Knowledge of results also has incentive value. Individuals will keep active at dull, monotonous tasks provided they are given information about how they are doing.

16 Psychologists have long had the concept of a generalized drive. The central idea is that behavior is naturally energized and that living creatures naturally interact with their environments. Generalized drive level is also called arousal level. Attempts have been made to find additional meaning for generalized drive, and some psychologists have considered it to represent a state of anxiety. Measures of anxiety drive have been developed both for adults and for children.

· · · · · · · · · · ·

Summary

A child is in school for only about nine-hundred hours per year, about 10 per cent of the total time. The remaining 90 per cent of the time is spent in sleeping, eating, physical activities, pastimes, washing, doing home-work, discussing, and so forth. The 10 per cent of the time spent in school is, for most children, the only time devoted to the systematic acquisition of knowledge, and even though it is a small percentage of life it is an extraordinarily important part of it. The time spent in school can also be more, or less, efficiently used. Teachers and curriculum experts have long recognized the importance of teaching children ideas that have wide application rather than narrow skills of very limited use. A skill such as is involved in arithmetic has applications in thousands of daily situations that the adult encounters, but skill in spelling has only the most limited use for most people, whose writing rarely involves anything more than

6

Transfer of
Training

writing to a friend. Although some skills such as spelling have to be taught, an important consideration in deciding what to teach is whether the skill acquired in school can be transferred to many other situations outside of the classroom. Learning a skill that will transfer to many problems outside of school is always an efficient use of the student's time. Before considering the matter of what skills have the maximum transfer value to problems in daily life, the point must be emphasized that this is only one of many reasons for including a particular topic or subject in the curriculum. Other subjects or topics may be included because they are fun or because they provide the child with a worthwhile experience. Students in school may spend time in listening to music, because it is worthwhile. Listening to music may not provide children with a skill that can be used in solving life's problems, but it may bring delight.

Over the centuries, educators have had many different theories concerning the subjects that should be included in the curriculum in order to build in students the skills that can have the broadest possible impact on their lives. The emphasis has long been on the development of thinking skills, because it can be argued that the person who can think logically and effectively is the person most capable of handling the great variety of problems that life will almost certainly bring him. Although educators over the past century would have agreed that the development of thinking skills is one of the most worthwhile of educational objectives, they would not have agreed on how that objective could best be achieved. The classic theory held throughout the last century, and to some extent in this one, was that the way to develop thinking skills was to give the child difficult and abstract problems to solve. Because the hardest subjects taught in school were Latin and mathematics, it followed that students should be given ample doses of these subjects to make them effective problem solvers. The fact that these were the subjects in which so many of the pupils failed was considered to be a further argument for emphasizing them in the curriculum, for this simply showed that they were the tough enterprises needed to train the mind. This approach to education involved what was known as the **doctrine of formal discipline.** It has proven itself to be a doctrine difficult to dislodge, and relics of it can still be seen in some corners of education.

The doctrine of formal discipline came under attack from scientists early in this century, through two different kinds of studies. In one type, it was shown that those exposed to difficult subjects, such as Latin, were not particularly more able to succeed with other high-school subjects. A second type of experiment showed that training on one particular problem had virtually no effect on the student's ability to solve other types of problems, except insofar as the two sets of problems contained similar elements. Studies of the latter type also showed that training tended to be quite specific to the class of problem on which the person was trained and that one could not depend on there being sufficient overlap of common elements in two sets of problems to conjecture that training on one set would produce improved performance on the other. The results of such studies were generalized to mean that it might be worthwhile to teach

Latin as an end in itself and for the values to be discovered in the literature of the language, but there was little point in teaching Latin because of any general beneficial outcomes.

The early studies of the effect of training in one area of skill on performance in another area of skill not only had great impact on the design of curricula but also helped to define the problem of **transfer.** Research has shown that practice on a particular task may have effects on subsequent tasks that are learned, and it may also have an effect on the retention of other tasks that have been previously learned. When the effect is on the future learning of tasks, then it is said to be a **proactive effect.** When it is on the retention of previously learned tasks, then it is said to be a **retroactive effect.** The effect may also be facilitative or interfering. When the learning of a task facilitates the learning or retention of another task, then the transfer is said to be **positive transfer.** When the effect interferes with the retention or learning of another task, it is said to be **negative transfer.**

Much of the curriculum of the elementary school is built around skills that are considered to have high transfer value to a great variety of real-life situations. Their transfer value derives largely from the fact that they share common elements with problems encountered outside the school. Arithmetic is an example of one such curriculum area. In the teaching of arithmetic, the instructor is likely to provide problems similar to those encountered in real life, but he cannot possibly include examples of every real-life problem that the pupil will ever have to solve. He hopes that the skills acquired through his guidance will be applicable to a much wider range of problems than he can cover in class time. He assumes that transfer of training will occur. The assumption is not always sound, for it has long been demonstrated that even slight differences in the format of a problem may disrupt the skill that has been acquired. Over half a century ago, Thorndike demonstrated that if children were taught algebra using the symbols x and y, then they would have some difficulty in solving problems that used the symbols p and q.

The development of mathematical skills is generally carried far outside of the area in which there is potential application. Many kinds of problems presented in arithmetic workbooks and algebra workbooks refer to real situations, but real situations that the student is unlikely to encounter. Whether practice on unlikely-to-be-encountered real situations develops skills that can be transferred to other problems actually encountered is a matter for speculation. There is certainly ample evidence that extensive practice on problems having substantial variation is a condition favorable to transfer to new situations. This has been demonstrated in a series of studies of the formation of what are called **learning sets.**

Negative and Positive Transfer of Training

In thinking about educational problems, one commonly thinks of transfer in a positive sense, that is, in terms of the extent to which the learning of one task facilitates the learning of another. All transfer is not of this kind, for there is also negative transfer to consider. Examples of negative transfer are quite hard to find in education, suggesting that it is a much less important matter than positive transfer in terms of its impact. One can find examples of negative transfer in daily life, and some of them are quite dramatic. Consider the case of a person who is raised in Germany and who has German as his native language. At the age of eighteen, he migrates to America and there makes every effort to acquire the English language with an American accent. He manages to master the grammar flawlessly, and acquires a vocabulary of which any American could be proud, but the accent he cannot master. The fact that he has learned German as his original native language makes it virtually impossible for him to learn to speak English with an American accent. Even after forty years of life in America, he still speaks English with a German accent. The reason for his inability to acquire the accent he would like to acquire is complex. It is not just that his native language was German and that the vocabulary of sounds he can put together to pronounce a word is that of the German language. There is also a real possibility that the speaking of German during childhood may have tended to shape the mouth and soft tissues related to speech in a certain way so that they could not be easily reshaped to facilitate speech with an American accent. The habits of the tongue related to speech may also be so firmly established once the mother tongue has been learned that new habits cannot be acquired. The inability of the foreigner to acquire the accent of his adopted land is a very dramatic example of negative transfer.

Nearer to the problems of the school are cases of negative transfer such as that of the pupil who, through a misunderstanding, spends his homework time performing a task incorrectly. A child is given the task of adding fractions and spends his time adding together the numerators and adding together the denominators. The next day the teacher corrects him and shows him how the task should be done. In such a case, the wrong procedure may interfere with learning the right procedure because the wrong procedure looks right and probably makes sense in terms of the pupil's experience with simple addition. The teacher can overcome this negative transfer by showing the pupil why his incorrect procedure is wrong and why the correct procedure makes sense. Incorrect procedures, practiced for a short time, generally can be expected to have only a brief negative transfer effect.

Some Simple Forms of Transfer

The nervous system is equipped to perform certain forms of transfer from the very beginning. Examples of such phenomena in infants have already been considered in Chapter 2 of this book, but let us consider here an illustration from the world of a child a little older. Such a child learns that he had better stop doing what he is doing when his parent, or anyone else, says "no." Once he has learned this fundamental fact of life, he will also manifest the class of behavior known as "stopping what he is doing," whenever a person makes a sound that even remotely resembles the sound of the word "no." He will show this behavior when somebody says "nnn" but does not finish the word. He will also perform the same behavior when any short vocal sound is made, as when the parent simply makes a staccato "er-er." What has happened is that what the child has learned to do to the sound of "no" is generalized to other sounds that resemble the original sound in some way. The phenomenon is called **stimulus generalization.** It is a basic phenomenon that results from the very nature of the nervous system. A person or animal does not have to learn to generalize his responses in this kind of way; it is inherent.

Stimulus generalization is a simple form of transfer that is of immense significance in the lives of all of us. Without it, much of our behavior would appear to be stupid. For example, a person learning to drive soon learns to appreciate the fact that the appropriate response to a flashing red light is to stop and then to proceed when it is safe. After he has learned to do this at a particular crossing, he does not have to learn to do this with larger red lights and smaller red lights, or with lights that are not as bright as or are brighter than the original one. Once he has learned the response to the original light, he performs it to a wide range of lights.

There is, nevertheless, a limit to the extent to which generalization will take place. A red traffic signal with a burned-out bulb will not produce the stop response even though it gives a faint flashing by swinging in the daylight. At times, the automobile driver may make the stop response only hesitatingly because the light is dirty and he has a hard time telling whether it is or is not operating. The response generalizes to only a limited range of situations. The individual behaves as if he categorized situations into those in the category of flashing red lights and those not.

A somewhat related problem has been described by Reese (1968) as the generalization of stimulus relations. A person hears a melody played several times on a particular record. From that time on, he can recognize the melody regardless of whether it is played in the same key, in a different key, or with the same or different instruments. He will even recognize the melody if it is whistled or hummed. He himself may also hum the melody in one key today and in another key tomorrow.

A similar phenomenon exists in numerous other areas, in which a complex pattern is identified in some way and the pattern can then be identified when it is varied. A child learns the nature of a parallelogram from a drawing made by the teacher on the board. The child will, from that point on, recognize parallelograms that are larger or smaller, drawn in different colors and with different internal angles. This process is also greatly aided by the fact that the teacher is able to define the properties of parallelograms, but even if the teacher did not do this the child would show some capacity for identifying the pattern of relationships shown by the parallelogram when they appeared in another form. Patterns can be identified despite wide variation in the form in which they appear.

The generalization of patterns occurs regardless of whether the patterns are visual, auditory, or derived from the sense of touch and movement. Such generalization takes place not only in the case of human learning but also occurs, at simpler levels, in animals. School learning would be virtually of no consequence were it not for this kind of transfer, but it is not entirely an unmixed blessing. Some errors of performance may be attributed to this same trend in behavior. A child learning to read may have just learned to decipher the word *man*. He is then likely to read other words presenting a similar visual pattern as though they were the word *man*, particularly words of similar length and with the same or similar first letters. Such words would include *mat, net, met,* and *was*.

Specific and Nonspecific Factors in Transfer

Research workers have long taken the position that there are both specific and nonspecific factors in transfer, but in actual fact it is sometimes difficult to say what is specific and what is general. Consider, for example, the task faced by a child who is beginning to learn German. The child immediately discovers that many German words are very similar to English words and, in fact, so similar that they can be immediately recognized. In his first lesson, he is likely to encounter such words as *Mann, Haus,* and *ist*, which the designer of the text or workbook has introduced deliberately so that the child can have the immediate illusion of being able to read German. This is a case of **specific transfer.** The specific words previously learned in English are almost identical with the specific words to be learned in German.

The child also has to learn that German has a grammatical structure that determines the order of words and the rules by which meaning is extracted from a sentence. He already has a general conception of the nature of grammar, because he has learned to talk about verbs, gender, predicates, and so forth. In this case, he is transferring his knowledge of general rules of language structure to his understanding and learning of the structure of a new language. Such transfer would be referred to as **nonspecific transfer.**

Of course, this example makes division of transfer into specific and nonspecific seem much more easy than it really is. Consider the instance when the child encounters the German word *Ding*. The child may recognize that this word means *thing* because of its general similarity to that word. The child also has learned the rule that the letter *d* in German is often equivalent to the English letter combination *th*. This rule might be considered to be a nonspecific basis for transfer. However, the rule is so specific that it also might be classified as a case of specific transfer. There is a continuous gradation between cases of specific and nonspecific transfer.

Specific transfer is more readily and more accurately identified than nonspecific transfer. Indeed, the history of education reflects numerous

Specific Transfer

Nonspecific Transfer

examples of educators expecting nonspecific transfer that did not really exist. The theory of formal discipline was a case of fruitless anticipation of nonspecific transfer. Contemporary educational theory also presents numerous examples of anticipations of nonspecific transfer that may well be demonstrated later to be nonexistent. Among areas where nonspecific transfer has long been anticipated is that of critical thinking. The belief has been held that children can be taught to think critically with a diversity of materials and that critical thinking learned with one set of materials will transfer to other materials. Enthusiasm for teaching to develop critical thinking is perhaps not as great today as it was in the 1930s, when this goal was strongly emphasized by the Progressive Education Movement. Despite the great interest that has been shown in this goal for nearly half a century, there is still little definitive research designed to determine whether such nonspecific transfer does or does not take place. Those who endorse this goal naturally believe that such transfer does occur, but common observation provides much evidence to the contrary. For example, a well-known scientist, the epitome of careful criticism when it comes to undertaking research in his own field, may be extraordinarily uncritical in his thinking about political matters. Indeed, one can find famous scientists who have given their active support to all kinds of ill-conceived political movements, although scientists are becoming much more politically sophisticated today than they were formerly. This is not to say that scientists are any more politically naive than the rest of us but only indicates that people who are trained to be fine thinkers in their own fields may be gullible in others. The evidence does not seem to support the notion that training in critical thinking transfers from the area in which it is taught to other areas.

Learning Sets — A Case of Nonspecific Transfer

A very interesting case of transfer, mentioned briefly before, with important implications for education is found in the phenomenon known as learning sets, a term originally coined by Harry Harlow (1959). The original demonstrations of this phenomenon were undertaken with monkeys, which were taught relatively simple choice discrimination problems, but the work has been repeated with young children. A monkey was presented with the problem of discovering under which one of two dishes there was a raisin. The dishes were different in one particular feature, such as shape, color, or size. In the first problem, the dishes differed in, say, one being small and the other large. After eight successive problems, the monkey would have come near to the solution of the problem. Next, the monkey was given a new series of eight problems, but this time the raisin was under the larger of the two dishes. Then he was given a third problem with the raisin under the red dish and not the green dish. So the process was continued with hundreds of different problems. In the early series of problems, the animal has great difficulty in mastering the discrimination, but after it has had experience with numerous different problems it becomes highly adept at solving these problems and can solve a new one of this class in two or three trials. This does not mean that it has become more proficient at solving all kinds of problems, for the skill learned is applicable only to problems within a certain category. A similar kind of phenomenon has also been demonstrated with preschool children. These children do learn skill in solving a whole class of problems after extensive practice, but they learn with considerably more speed than the experimental monkeys.

Ellis (1969), who has reviewed research in this area, points out that the main concept behind the work of Harlow was the idea that most studies of learning involve only a very short learning period, generally less than an hour. The phenomenon of the development of a learning set could not be demonstrated in such a short period of practice. Indeed, there are probably many learning phenomena that become evident only when prolonged training is used.

Although the development of a learning set that results in the transfer of what has been learned to the solution of new problems has been well demonstrated experimentally, the nature of the phenomenon is far from clear. Harlow originally thought that it was simply a matter of learning to eliminate errors. For example, a monkey might have a tendency to choose the left-hand dish, or the one closest to it, and experience with the problem taught it to avoid such response tendencies. Undoubtedly, the elimination of such error tendencies is a part of what is learned, but only a part. The learner also acquires knowledge about the kind of attributes of the dishes to inspect and learns to try using cues in solving the problem. The learner may also acquire understanding that whatever is the cue that makes a dish right or wrong in one series may be a different cue from the crucial one in the next series. Perhaps study of the development of learning sets also shows that one can train a learner to be flexible—that is, to quickly abandon an attempted solution that does not work. Ellis points out that perceptual learning may be involved, in that the learner acquires skill in scanning the object presented for the presence of characteristics that can be used for solving the problem.

Ellis also points out that one of the more systematic attempts to make an analysis of the phenomenon of learning sets has taken place in the area of verbal learning, mainly through the efforts of Leo Postman and his students. The situations studied differ from those involved in the Harlow researches in that they focus on relatively brief amounts of training time. In the typical study, the effect of learning one series of verbal paired associates on the learning of a subsequent verbal task is studied. The two tasks may be very similar or very different, and they may differ with respect to particular features. By making the list differ in particular features, one can see how this influences the amount of transfer. The two tasks may require similar or different learning methods, and they may involve similar or different materials to be learned.

The research on verbal learning with human subjects indicates that learning sets are generally a combination of specific and general factors. Quite regardless of whether the two verbal tasks are or are not entirely different, there is a marked tendency for the person to do better on the second list than on the first. A part of this effect is due to the need for a learner to warm up to any learning situation. A part of it is sometimes due to quite specific elements that are common to the two tasks, as when both tasks call for the learner to make the association between the words *cloud–tear*. There is, in addition, some transfer of the learning strategies acquired through the learning of the one task to the learning of the second task. An example of this would be the case of a person confronted with the task of learning to associate pairs of words who finds ways of linking up the two words. A person asked to associate the words *wind* and *greeting* may say to himself "*wind–hail–greeting.*" Through discovering ways in which words that are not readily tied together may be tied together, the person acquires a strategy for associating words, and a task that was initially a difficult one becomes quite easy. Much of what is transferred through the acquisition of learning sets involves the acquisition of strategies. The acquisition of such strategies is commonly called learning how to learn.

Many areas of study in the elementary school involve a similar acquisition of learning strategies. In learning long division, the pupil works a number of problems and acquires the general strategy that will permit him to divide any number into any other number. One cannot give him all the problems to solve that he will ever encounter, but, in a well-planned program, he will be given problems that cover a wide range of difficulties. For example, he will be given problems in which the divisors are larger as well as smaller than the first two digits of the numbers to be divided. If his practice in long division were limited to problems involving a two-digit divisor and a three-digit number to be divided, then he might develop very limited strategies. As a general rule, one can say that the more extensive the practice with varied problems, the broader are the strategies developed. The elementary-school child does not have to acquire the general rules to be applied entirely through the slow experience of solving problems but can be told what they are. The younger child may have to learn, as other primates learn, through slow experience in solving numerous problems. Explanation is a short cut, but in order to be effective it has to come at the right time. A general rule to follow is that some experience with a class of problems is desirable before general strategies are discussed. Strategies can be discussed at too early a stage for them to be understood. A few long-division problems can be solved profitably by rule-of-thumb procedures before the broad strategies involved are considered.

Much the same applies in the teaching of reading. Children will learn to read such words as *man*, *ran*, *can*, and *pan* before the teacher points out that all have the same ending. The children then acquire a rule for saying the *an* ending of the word and then apply the rule to some new situations. Phonetics is complicated by the fact that very often there are many different rules that can be applied to decoding a particular group of letters, and the child has no basis for knowing which rules to apply in a particular situation. The child knows, for example, how to pronounce the two groups of words *near, fear, rear* and *bear, pear, wear*, but what does he say when he encounters the word *gear?* He has to learn that strategies are good only up to a point, and that beyond that point custom prevails.

Unwarranted Extensions of the Idea That Practice in Solving Varied Problems Develops Transferable Strategies

An important point to note is that in the examples of transfer of training previously discussed, much more than practice was involved. Practice may develop learning strategies, but it may not. An important role of the teacher is that of pointing out to the pupil what the strategies are. If practice does not result in the development of strategies that can be applied to the solution of new problems, then practice serves no purpose. All too often, pupils have been given practice in solving problems by rule of thumb without developing strategies that will help them to solve new problems in the same category. When this happens, the pupil ends up incapable of applying what he has learned to new situations.

Some aspects of some modern curricula seem to be based on the assumption that mere practice will produce a highly generalizable skill. A good example of this is found in attempts to develop creativity in pupils. The mere practice of creative skills is assumed to develop highly transferable skills.

The Guilford system for classifying components of the intellect has been suggestive of the general area in which components of creative behavior are to be sought, and most of those interested in this area have concentrated on the area of what has been termed behavior. One component of behavior in this area is referred to as fluency of ideas, and this is an area in which it is quite easy to develop exercises. An example of such an exercise is to ask children to list as many things as they can think of that they can do with a piece of broken glass. Their lists include using it as a cutting instrument, using it to dig up a weed in the garden, or adapting it as a scraper to remove paint. One can easily think of many exercises of that kind. There is no doubt that children show some improvement in performing these tasks as they work on them, but the question is whether practice on such tasks provides some general improvement in performing other tasks that fall into the category of creativity. For example, would daily practice on such tasks produce some improvement in one's ability to invent a new and better way of doing the laundry or a new and better way of cooking the family dinner roast? Although there have been numerous studies of these and related problems, the effect of practice cannot be clearly seen in the research results. The main problem in

181
· · · · · · · · · ·
Unwarranted Extensions
of the Idea That
Practice in Solving
Varied Problems
Develops Transferable
Strategies

drawing any conclusions from these studies is that the majority of them include some gross flaw in experimental design—flaws that have only slowly become identified as the research has progressed. A flaw in experimental design that was not recognized until recently stems from the fact that one thing learned by people performing fluency tasks is that they are expected to perform them rapidly. When they first start working on such tasks, they pursue them at a leisurely pace and enjoy the mental activity involved. Soon they find out that in order to do well they have to work quickly. When tests of fluency are given before and after training, any improvement shown on these tests comes from the fact that the training teaches them to work quickly (see the research by Gerlach et al., 1964).

The writings on creativity most familiar to teachers are those of Torrance (1965), who has reported some classroom experiments on the rewarding of aspects of creative behavior. Although these experiments are superficially convincing, just what learning they demonstrate is hard to say. Suppose a child is rewarded in some way every time he expresses an original idea or makes any kind of novel contribution, and suppose that he tends to increase the number of original ideas and novel contributions as the reward system is used. Does this really mean that he has been taught to be creative by this procedure? Probably not! A much more likely explanation of the change in his behavior is that he has learned what the teacher wants and is shrewd enough to give it to him. Every child has some capacity for producing novel ideas, and the mere fact that the capacity to do this is exercised does not necessarily mean that the capacity is improved. The child learns where the rewards lie but may not learn anything about how to be creative. A point to note is that the technique proposed by Torrance is virtually that of operant conditioning, though he makes no reference to Skinner in his entire book. Those who read the book and similar books should also be cautioned that colorful anecdotes do not provide the evidence needed to set up a program to help children to become more creative. A much more substantial basis for such programs is needed.

A recent volume by Shouksmith (1970) provides a sophisticated effort to describe the kind of environment in which creativity can develop. He takes the position that the creative thinker has to develop internal standards by which he can judge the worth of a new idea and that new ideas themselves must flow from a vastly deep and broad range of knowledge. Thus the child seeking to develop these and other essential qualities related to creativity probably needs to be placed in a demanding environment and not in one that is nonpressurized, in which ideas flow easily and glibly. Development of creativity requires that the child must learn to bring together diverse materials with flexibility while exercising meticulous care that they fit together in a fine composite and not in a crude conglomerate. The would-be creative individual must learn that creative work places great demands on him and calls for high standards.

What has been said here does not mean that creativity is some sort of gift with which a person may be endowed and that if he does not have such endowment it is something in which he cannot be trained. What is much more likely is that the training conditions that ultimately produce a creative person have to involve a very complex constellation of circumstances. Most creative acts that involve invention call for a very rich background of knowledge. The writing of poetry calls for many skills and talents, but a mastery of a sufficient vocabulary is essential for the successful pursuit of the art. An architect cannot expect to be creative until he has mastered not only the materials and media of his profession but also the drawing skills through which his ideas can become realities. Sheer intellectual factors are clearly not enough to produce creative performance. The history of creative accomplishment shows that those who pursue it are able to struggle with the problems involved over long and exhausting periods of time. The task of being creative is far more than that suggested by educational programs that involve little more than training individuals to think up clever ideas in quantity. (See the review of this problem by Dellas and Gaier, 1970.)

Language as a Highly Transferable Skill

The one identifiable skill that provides nonspecific transfer to a great range of situations is the use of language. Many lines of evidence point to the truth of this statement. In the first place, psychologists have observed for over half a century that any attempt to develop a measure of what may be termed general intelligence leads to the development of tests that are largely verbal. A person who has skill in the use of words and a facility for such tasks as constructing verbal analogies, or who is skillful at much simpler tasks such as defining words, is likely also to be skillful at solving a wide range of problems. It is suggested that skill in the use of words lies at the very core of human intelligence. This is not to say that such measures can appraise the inborn potential that a person has for exhibiting intelligent behavior but only that those who have the greatest verbal skill also tend to show the greatest degree of intelligent behavior. This finding is to be contrasted with the fact that measures of memory show little capacity for predicting the extent to which a person can behave intelligently and even little potential for predicting success in academic subjects in school. Of course, some capacity for exhibiting intelligent behavior can be manifested by those who have no capacity for verbal behavior. For example, primates such as the chimpanzee may solve problems of various kinds, and a few children who have been raised with absolutely no opportunity for learning language show some limited capacity for problem solving, but their capacity in this respect is far less than that of children who have acquired language in the ordinary way.

A second line of supportive evidence comes from numerous studies during the last half century showing that children who have limited opportunities to learn language generally have great difficulty in other aspects of learning. Such children get relatively low scores on intelligence tests, indicating that they are not functioning effectively in the intellectual field.

Ghetto children fall into this class, but studies have shown that these children improve in verbal and academic skills merely by being placed in schools with children from more affluent homes (see Weinberg, 1970). Similar reports have come from Israel, where many of the early settlers, who themselves had had little education, raised children in impoverished environments that provided poor opportunities for intellectual development. Such children came to school without knowing the names of what most would call common articles, because these articles were not present in their homes. They had never heard of such items as forks, or spoons, or clocks. The children had most limited vocabularies because they were not familiar with the objects represented by common nouns. The Israelis not only studied this problem but took steps to remedy the situation. The essential remedy proposed is quite familiar on the contemporary American scene, for it involved the development of preschool programs designed primarily to remedy the linguistic deficiencies of these children. The programs were very much like the Head Start programs developed twenty-five years later in America to handle the language deficiencies and other deficiencies of American ghetto children raised under conditions of intellectual deprivation similar to those of the Israeli poor.

At the present time, the results of such programs must be regarded as inconclusive. One can say that they are planned on the basis of sound scientific knowledge about the effects of language deficiencies on intellectual functioning. There is a real question whether the deficiencies generated by many years of deprivation can be overcome in programs that involve six-hundred hours of special training. Six-hundred hours in school during a year may be a poor substitute for the four-thousand hours or more of intellectual stimulation that a child may receive during the same year from a home that provides every opportunity for intellectual development. For this reason, some have suggested that the only substitute for a good home environment is an all-day school that will provide an equally stimulating environment for children for an equal amount of time—perhaps twelve hours a day or more. The development of skilled use of language may require an enormous number of hours of contact with spoken language.

This leads to the question of why language is so crucial for intelligent performance. The answer is intimately connected with the nature of human memory as well as with the fact that operations can be performed with language that cannot be performed otherwise. First, the point must be made that language permits one to communicate information about the environment that cannot be well communicated by other means. For example, suppose a child three or four years old finds a seed inside an apple and asks what it is. No simple demonstration can show him that the seed has the capability of developing into a tree. At least, such a demonstration would take far too long to satisfy the child's curiosity or to provide him with the information he needs. Verbal explanation has to be the means through which he learns that seeds can grow into trees. Perhaps this can be followed by demonstrating the process of germination

184
• • • • • • • • • •
Transfer of Training

with some quick-growing plant, such as a radish. Much information has to be obtained through immediate verbal explanation, although in a school situation this sort of experimental verification or demonstration may be possible. If the child has not acquired skill in understanding language, he has difficulty in acquiring the information that can virtually shorten the period of growth of a tree into the time taken to say a few sentences.

Another source indicating the importance of language as a skill that opens the door to the acquisition of knowledge and to thought and problem solving is found in the case of totally deaf children (see Myklebust, 1964). These children have great difficulty in acquiring mastery of language. For them, written language is more difficult to learn than it is for ordinary children, and the acquisition of spoken language is an extraordinary feat of skill. Sign language is, at the best, a crude form of communication. Its crudeness is evident in the fact that in sign language all forms of the verb *to be* are represented by a single sign that does not differentiate between past, present, and future and makes no distinction between singular and plural. Such a grossly simplified language cannot make very precise statements. The best one can say for it is that it is perhaps better than no language at all. The limitations of sign language, as well as the fact that it is understood only by some deaf people, have led many to advocate that all deaf children be given training in lip reading and in actual vocal language, even though the latter is enormously difficult for most totally deaf children to learn. If they have even a little hearing, spoken language can be much more easily acquired, but the speech of the totally deaf often is extremely difficult for others to comprehend. Although substantial research supports the idea that deaf children have intellectual inadequacies resulting from their limited knowledge of language, Furth (1971) has assembled evidence that such an interpretation may be oversimplified. Deaf children have often been misjudged mentally backward merely because they have difficulty in expressing themselves. Furth's position is supported by research indicating that on some problems the deaf perform as well as the hearing.

A further reason for the importance of language as a generally transferable skill lies in its significance in problem solving. A person who has command of language gains in the very first stages of problem solving because he can state the problem with precision. Lower animals are unable to organize their problem-solving behavior by stating what the problem is. Indeed, often a human being's main difficulty in solving a problem stems from his inability to state clearly what his problem is. For example, a teacher may know there is something wrong with the way he manages his classroom, but the statement "something wrong" is too vague to be helpful. If the principal tells him, after extensive observation, that his main problem lies in talking too fast and hurrying on from one topic to another before the children have time to grasp what he has said, then he has something quite specific to work on and can begin to experiment with answers to the problem. There is only a vague "something wrong" with the situation until the precise nature of what is wrong can be specified, and the exact specifications require the use of correspondingly precise language. Recent writers, such as Inhelder and Piaget (1958), take the position that logical and precise thinking requires skillful use of words as a necessary condition, although thinking requires more than the use of words.

One has to view with some skepticism those who claim that there are individuals who have a good sense for solving practical problems that is entirely different from that needed for solving verbal problems. To be sure, there are practical areas where experience with the actual problems of the field is of the greatest importance in solving the new problems that present themselves, but this does not mean that verbal behavior does not play a significant role in the solution of these problems. An auto mechanic may say to himself, or even say aloud, "The problem is not in the ignition, because I can see that the wire to the spark plug gives a spark. Perhaps the cylinders are not getting any gas. Let's take a look at the carburetor." Language behavior is of the greatest importance in solving the most practical of problems. The mechanic who runs into a problem may even go to another mechanic to talk about the difficulties he has encountered. The good mechanic can state a possible solution to the problem before he tries it out and can tell an observer why it seems to be a good solution. Only the most incompetent of mechanics cannot say what he thinks might be wrong or why he is trying the solution he is trying. The incompetent mechanic is likely to proceed by first changing one component and then another, until the equipment works. He is ineffective because this procedure is likely to be slow and may not even result in a solution. It is also a costly procedure for the person whose car is being fixed. The point that is being emphasized here is that there is no means of handling complex problems except through the mediation of language. If the person solving the problem has little mastery of language, he is limited in the approach he can make to the solution of the problem.

Transfer of Principles

A verbal device that has long been known to provide important transfer properties is the statement of a principle or a generalization that has been demonstrated to be true. Consider, for example, the case of a child who has learned the geometrical principle that the sum of the lengths of two sides of a triangle is always greater than the length of the third. In geometry, this is called a theorem, but it can be described equally well as a principle or generalization. The child who learns this generalization can solve many problems. If he looks at a map, he can tell that one way of going from one village to another is shorter than an alternative route involving, so to speak, two sides of a triangle. He will also know that, in running a wire across the basement, the shortest route will be the direct route across. The wire may be less conspicuous if it is laid in another way, but it will have to be longer. The principle is such a simple one that it is completely obvious to most adults, who automatically apply it to numerous everyday situations, but the child has to learn the principle before he can enjoy applying it to the situations he encounters.

Principles and generalizations are statements of the general form "If this class of situation exists, then that particular consequence follows." In the case of the simple illustration discussed, the class of situation includes all those that involve joining two points by a straight line. In that class of situations, it follows that the straight line is shorter than any other system of lines that might be used to join the two points. In deciding whether the principle can or cannot be applied, the student must decide whether the situation to which he wants to make application does or does not fall into this particular category of situations. Generalizations that are learned may be true, partially false, or false. Regardless of their veracity, they are likely to be utilized in interpreting and in responding to a great range of situations.

Much as concepts are simplifying ideas that permit a person to respond to a rather complex environment as though it were quite simple, so too are generalizations simplifying devices. A generalization always involves a statement including several concepts, but it still assumes simple orderliness in the environment. Consider, for example, physics as it was developed by Isaac Newton. In his famous *Principia*, Newton was able to reduce the complexity of what his predecessors saw as an overwhelmingly intricate universe by showing that a few quite simple principles could account for much of that apparent complexity. The positions and motions of the planets in the solar system could be accounted for in terms of the force of universal gravitation balanced by the centrifugal force exerted by the planets as they rotated around the sun. His explanation was simple and straightforward and much easier to comprehend than the almost incomprehensible explanations given by his predecessors, who had believed in all kinds of mystical forces holding the system together. The principles of Newtonian physics provide a simplified view of the nature of matter and the nature of the universe, and the simplicity and orderliness make it possible for man to think with precision about the world in which he lives. Scientific concepts are generally clearer, simpler, and more precise than the concepts that precede them. The modern concept that the brain is mainly an information analysis, storage, and retrieval system reduces the enormously complex mass of about 11 billion cells to terms that can be easily comprehended. This concept of the brain as an information-processing system is also simpler than the concept of the brain as the producer of animal spirits, a view commonly held up until the middle of the last century. Scientific principles provide an orderly and simplified view of the universe.

A long history of research has been concerned with the problem of the extent to which the learning of principles provides knowledge that is highly transferable to the solution of a wide range of problems. One of the earliest and most classic of these experiments was undertaken in the laboratory of C. H. Judd at the University of Chicago near the beginning of this century. By present standards, the design and reporting of Judd's experiment were sloppy and unpublishable, but almost all of his conclusions have been verified and have stood the test of time. In the experiment, pupils were given training on the task of shooting darts at a target placed under water. Now most adults know that an object on the bottom of a pond does not appear to be where it actually is, for the intervening water and water surface distort the apparent position. The principle of physics involved is the principle of refraction — a principle that can be easily explained to most pupils in junior high school. Some of the pupils in the Judd experiment had explained to them, before they threw darts at the object, the nature of the principle of refraction and how this influenced the apparent position of an object on the bottom of a pool. Other pupils did not have the opportunity to learn the principle before throwing the darts. Judd (1908) reported no data in his account of the experiment but only the general findings. He found that on the first series of trials of hitting the target that the two groups did about equally well, but when they were all confronted with a second problem in which the position and depth of the underwater target were altered, the group that had learned the principle of refraction showed a superior performance to that of the other group. Similar results were reported by Overing and Travers (1966, 1967) in studies that introduced other variations into the same experimental situation. The question arises of why the group that had learned the principle of refraction did not show superiority on the first test of hitting the underwater object — a finding that has been consistently reported.

The reason for the lack of difference on the first problem but substantial difference on the second problem is probably that even those who know the principle of refraction still have to learn something about the practical situation and what it involves before they can apply the principle. A knowledge of refraction does not tell a person how much below the submerged target he must aim in order to hit it. However, if he has learned the principle, then with just a little practice, as in the first trial, he becomes good at applying it. The data bring out rather nicely that the academic learning of a principle does not provide one with real skill in applying it until one has had the opportunity of trying to apply it. This is why classes in physics have very limited value unless they are accompanied by laboratory sessions in which the principles are applied. For much the same reason, one does not learn to cook by reading a recipe book. The recipe book and the lecture on culinary practice are a fine beginning but not of much use until the prospective cook has entered the kitchen and made many mistakes, which are significant learning experiences.

In later studies, Overing and Travers made some refinements in procedure. Shooting at a target with darts is fraught with error. Indeed, it is hard to understand how Judd ever managed to derive such verifiable results as he did when his subjects threw the darts at the object. Most pupils might have difficulty in hitting the basin of water in which the target was placed, let alone the target. In the Overing and Travers procedure, the children aimed a gun at the target, but they never fired an actual shot. What they did was to report the place on the surface of the water at which they were shooting. A lucite grid floated on the water, and on the grid numbered lines were marked off; the child, on each so-called shot, merely had to report the number of the line at which he was shooting. The children could have been just asked to tell the experimenter which line they would shoot at if they had a gun, but the children liked the activity of aiming the gun, even though it was never fired and even though many of the children obviously did not know how a gun should be aimed. Through this procedure, much of the error in the original experimental situation was eliminated.

In addition to cleaning up the experimental situation itself, Overing and Travers introduced a number of variations that throw some light on the conditions that influence transfer. First, they tried various methods of teaching the children the principle of refraction. Some children learned by observing the actual refraction of a beam of light as it entered and left the water. Another group learned the principle through the use of very simple diagrams. A third group was given a verbal explanation only and a fourth group was given the information with diagrams, but the instruction was preceded by an account of a hunter faced with the problem of shooting a crocodile from the bank of a river. Thus the various educational conditions varied from the concrete to the abstract, and they also varied from those that tied in the new information with familiar concepts to those that provided no tie-in.

The data provided evidence that the best transfer of teaching the principle of refraction was found when the teaching involved a realistic demonstration of the refraction of light. When similar teaching was undertaken, but accompanied only by diagrams, less effective results were obtained. However, when the teaching and diagrams were preceded by a story about the problem of shooting an underwater crocodile from the bank of the river, the results were almost as good as those achieved by means of teaching with the realistic demonstration. This really is an example of one of the very old principles of teaching derived from experience and common sense, which tells the teacher to be sure to link up new knowledge with old. Perhaps, in addition, the data suggest that knowledge presented to children in terms of words and symbols such as in diagrams should be linked up with real-life situations if the knowledge is to be usable.

Some other problems were investigated in this study. One of these was the old problem of whether a person who can verbalize a principle can apply it better than one who cannot. In terms of the ideas presented here, it would be expected that the ability to verbalize a principle would be an important consideration, and the evidence from the study provided mild support for the position. Presumably, the more precisely a person can state a principle, the more likely he is to be able to apply it. But principles can sometimes be understood at a crude intuitive level, and even though the person may have difficulty in stating them, he may be able to apply them. Many good mechanics can comprehend that a particular mechanism will not work, but they are not able to say in words why it will not work. The intuitive understanding of a principle may be expected to have limitations that the precise knowledge of the principle, shown by the ability to state it, does not have.

In their second study, Overing and Travers (1967) demonstrated that even though the pupils learned to apply the principle of refraction in a particular situation, changing irrelevant features of the situation was somewhat disruptive of the ability to apply the principle. This finding suggests that an important condition for learning to apply a principle in many and varied situations is practice in varied conditions. This is very much like the development of learning sets, in which the key to effective transfer has been found to reside in providing extensive practice with variations in the characteristics of the materials involved. There is some evidence that whatever is learned can be recalled best under conditions the same as those of the original learning. Of course, what one wants, as a teacher, is to produce learning that will be of value to the pupil under new conditions. Irrelevant cues influence what can be recalled.

Finally, the point must be made that if a principle can be learned that can be applied to the solution of a great range of problems, then very efficient learning has been accomplished. Such learning is to be contrasted with the acquisition of a rule that will help only in solving a single specific problem. One wants to plan the curriculum in such a way that what is learned has a maximum effect on behavior in a maximum number of situations. Education having only narrow outcomes is generally inefficient, though sometimes it has to be resorted to. For example, it is good for children to learn that home-canned vegetables should be cooked for fifteen minutes before use to prevent the possibility of botulism poisoning. This information has limited applicability, but it is nevertheless valuable; efficiency—as defined here—must be sacrificed because of the importance of the item to be learned.

Specific Transfer

The discussion up to this point has focused on nonspecific or general transfer. In a sense, a principle or generalization is a specific entity, but the transfer involved is to a broad class of situations. In specific transfer, one is referring to a situation in which the skill originally acquired has some identifiable elements that also appear in the situations to which the learning is transferred. Study of specific transfer has been undertaken through the use of quite simple tasks in which there are clearly defined stimulus elements and clearly defined response elements. Transfer is from one task to another task that may have similar stimulus elements or similar response elements or both.

Consider a case in which training is undertaken on a task, which we will call task 1, and in which components of the skill thus learned have to be undertaken in task 2. A common case would be learning to type on one machine and then typing on another machine. Let us suppose that one machine is an American electric typewriter and the other is a foreign nonelectric portable made for the American market. The two tasks involve similar stimulus elements in that both machines have the same keys with the same letters printed on them in the same location. The stimulus elements, up to this point, are the same in both the typewriter used for learning and the typewriter used later. The response elements in the two situations are somewhat different in that the learner has only to touch the keys on the electric machine used for acquisition of the skill, but the operation of the nonelectric portable requires him to strike the keys. If the person just uses the responses learned on the electric machine with the nonelectric machine, the keys will never strike the paper. There is another feature about the two machines that has a marked effect on the transfer of the skill from one to the other: the margin release and backspacing keys are in opposite positions on the two machines. In such a case, what is learned on the original typewriter is a response the opposite of that called for by the second machine.

Now one could carry out investigations of the extent to which learning on one typewriter was transferred to working on a second machine, but the typewriter is not a very good device for conducting research. Psychologists have developed laboratory techniques for the study of this problem that may seem quite remote from such practical activities as learning to type. To the outsider, these laboratory tasks seem to have little superficial resemblance to what one wants to find out in the matter of transfer, but they have been highly productive.

Such laboratory studies have brought out a great many matters related to the problem of transfer that earlier psychologists had failed to note. These studies have brought out that in transfer studies two tasks can resemble or differ from one another in two ways—they can provide the learner with different or similar stimuli, or they can require the learner to perform different or similar responses. Of course, if task 1 and task 2 are identical, then the person who performs both tasks one after the other is undertaking two learning trials with the same task. This is the situation that produces maximum transfer. When one repeatedly performs a task in order to master it, learning can occur only if what is learned on one trial is transferred to the next trial. In this way, learning is cumulative.

Now what happens when the two tasks are related in different ways? For example, what happens when the two tasks provide similar stimuli but call for opposite responses? The two typewriters in which the margin release and backspacing keys are reversed provide tasks close to the latter condition. Under such conditions, there is a maximum of negative transfer; that is, the learning of the one task interferes to a maximum degree with the learning of the other task. Negative transfer produced by very specific features of two tasks does not usually have any very permanent effect. If I sell my old typewriter and buy a new one with the margin release and backspacer in reverse positions, I have trouble for a day or two, but then I settle down to the new machine. If I had to change back and forth from one machine to the other, then the interference effect would be quite devastating.

One can draw a graph showing how the way in which two tasks resemble each other or differ from each other influences transfer of training, and Osgood (1949) has done this in an interesting article.

The effects that have been discussed are not confined to the acquisition of motor skills but are also found in verbal areas. For example, a student who has learned French has learned to pronounce correctly the word *que* (pronounced *ker* as in *marker*). The student then starts learning Spanish, in which the same word *que* is pronounced differently (*kay*). Here, the stimuli are the same, but the responses to be learned are different. The result is some **proactive** negative transfer and interference with learning.

It should also be noted that not only can tasks originally learned interfere with new learning but what is newly learned can interfere with or facilitate the retention of what was previously learned. Once the student has learned the Spanish pronunciation of *que*, he may have difficulty pronouncing *que* correctly when he re-encounters it in French. This is known as the **retroactive effect** of transfer. Though not much research has been done on this effect, Anderson and Myrow (1971) have demonstrated that the reading of a paragraph can interfere with the retention of a previously studied paragraph.

In the design of simulators for training purposes, every attempt is made to ensure that the stimuli provided by the simulator and the responses called for by the simulator are as near as possible to those that will be encountered on the actual equipment. By designing training equipment in this way, maximum transfer can be expected to take place from the simulator to the real situation. An example of such a simulator is found in driver education, for which simulators have been developed where a person sits before a screen that looks like a road seen through a windshield and operates controls similar to those on a car. By operating the controls correctly, he can have the illusion of keeping a car on the road. Considerable difficulty has been experienced in designing the controls so that they have the same "feel" as those in a car; the controls tend to be rather different from those on a real car. Nevertheless, there seem to be considerable advantages in providing boys and girls with simulator training, which can be given at far less expense and much less hazard than in a real car.

The same kind of principles apply in designing training situations involving much less sophisticated equipment. Consider a course in business English in which students learn to handle correspondence. It is much better to give the students an actual letter to answer than to tell them *about* a letter they should answer. The stimuli should be as nearly the same as they can be to the situation students are being trained to handle. The response they make should be as close as possible to the response they will have to make in the real situation.

A Review of the Implications of Research on Transfer for Teaching

Throughout this chapter an attempt has been made to bring out the implications of research on transfer for teaching, and in this final section we shall try to bring all the loose ends together. Other attempts at this have been made, including a short book by Ellis (1965). Let us consider first some broad rules that emerge in the case where teaching is undertaken in anticipation that there will be nonspecific transfer.

1. *Don't just hope for nonspecific transfer.* The history of education is filled with illustrations of curricula established in the hope that they would provide broadly transferable skills. The teaching of Latin and mathematics in the last century was undertaken in the hope that these would develop widely applicable thinking skills, but they failed to do so.

2. *Expect broad nonspecific transfer when one can identify quite specifically what the strategies or skills are that can be transferred to new situations.* A mechanic taught to troubleshoot gasoline engines by following a systematic and orderly procedure, who understands why an orderly and systematic procedure is efficient, might be expected to be systematic and orderly in troubleshooting other types of mechanical equipment if he knows enough to follow such a procedure. One can never be sure that there will be this kind of transfer, but it is reasonable to expect that there will be.

3. *In development of broad strategies and skills, practice with a wide range of tasks is necessary.* The problems should provide varying circumstances under which the strategy or the skill is applied. Too often, a strategy for solving a class of problems is practiced with only one problem, and the student does not learn much about the *class* of problems he is learning to solve.

4. *Transfer is most likely to take place if a high level of mastery is originally achieved.* A child who can haltingly solve a simple problem of addition of two fractions is unlikely to be able to apply the skill he has learned to new problems that look a little different from the one he has solved. A high level of mastery is important for effective transfer of training to occur.

5. *If transfer is to be in terms of a strategy, then be sure the student known exactly what that strategy is.* The student of auto mechanics who has learned to *systematically* troubleshoot a car may not recognize that being systematic is an important feature of the procedure unless it is pointed out to him. A social studies teacher may help the student to analyze a newspaper editorial for poor logic but may fail to point out the procedure involved in this analysis so that the procedure can be applied by the student to other reading material. Too much is often learned as a rule of thumb specific to the particular situation, and too little is learned as a general problem-solving strategy.

6. *Because principles have great capacity for transference to the solution to other problems, stress should be placed on the learning of principles.* Too often, stress is placed on facts related to a principle rather than on the principle itself. The student may remember that Archimedes jumped out of his bath shouting "Eureka! Eureka!" but may forget just what Archimedes had discovered. Good teaching requires that emphasis be placed on that which is important.

7. *When a principle or strategy is learned, make sure that the student can verbalize, that is, state in words, the principle or strategy involved.* Because principles and strategies can be understood in a vague way, intuitively, or in a much more precise way, verbally, teachers should make sure that pupils can talk with precision about the principles and strategies they have learned.

8. *Training to handle specific problems should be undertaken in situations in which both the stimuli and the responses are closely similar to those involved in the situation for which training is given.* This is the essential rule for designing simulators for training.

194
. . . .
Transfer of Training

Summary

1 Time spent in school can be most efficiently used if the curriculum emphasizes transferable skills. There has long been dispute concerning what are the most transferable skills, but research has provided some answers in recent times. Subjects such as Latin certainly have little transfer value. The mere giving of difficult and abstract problems does little to train thinking skills. This procedure constituted the doctrine of formal discipline, which was overthrown through research early in the present century. These early studies of transfer tended to show that whatever transfer occurred was likely to be quite specific. Studies of transfer early in the century had great impact on problems of curriculum design, perhaps more impact than any other studies ever undertaken.

2 The modern elementary curriculum is built around skills believed to have extensive transfer value. In the curriculum, an attempt is made to give the pupil extensive practice on problems that show variation.

3 Positive transfer is that which facilitates the learning of a new task or the retention of a previously learned task. Negative transfer is that which interferes with the learning of a new task or with the retention of a previously learned task. Thus transfer may have a backward effect, a retroactive effect, or a forward effect, a proactive effect. Most negative transfer effects are quite transitory.

4 A very simple form of transfer is found in what is known as stimulus generalization. Without stimulus generalization, learning would be completely specific to the situation in which learning took place and behavior would be extraordinarily stupid. There is a limit to which stimulus generalization will take place. A similar phenomenon is that known as the generalization of stimulus relations. This kind of generalization occurs through all of the perceptual systems and throughout higher forms of life.

5 There are both specific and nonspecific factors in transfer. The words common to two languages represent specific elements transferred from the learning of one language to the learning of the other. The common broad rules of grammar represent the basis of nonspecific transfer. Strategies of problem solving that can be transferred in solving a wide range of new problems are also examples of nonspecific transfer. Nonspecific transfer is probably not as broad as it is commonly expected to be. One probably cannot learn rules

for critical thinking that can be easily applied in any situation. Teachers have long hoped that creativity training might teach strategies that would be transferred to new situations, but little is known about whether such transfer actually takes place. A good rule to follow in education is never to expect transfer unless one can demonstrate that it actually takes place.

6 A well-studied case of transfer is found in the development of learning sets. The development of sets results from solving very large numbers of problems, and the skill developed represents strategies useful in solving new problems within the same general category. Learning sets are the result of very extended periods of learning, in contrast with laboratory studies that involve, with few exceptions, learning of very short duration. The learning involved in the development of sets involves both specific and nonspecific factors. Harlow's work on the development of learning sets in monkeys has been repeated with young children, with essentially the same results. However, children of elementary-school age can learn problem-solving strategies by having them explained to them and do not have to solve very large numbers of problems in order to master the strategy. Explanation is a short-cut method of arriving at knowledge that otherwise must be acquired by extended experience.

7 An important point to note is that mere practice in solving problems may not necessarily develop adequate strategies but may just be practice with a rule of thumb. In some educational experiments, the result of the training procedure has not been development of some transferable skill, as the experimenter has supposed, but rather improved test-taking skills.

8 Perhaps the skill that provides the strongest foundation for nonspecific transfer is language. Deficiencies in opportunities to acquire a native language result in all kinds of intellectual deficiencies. For this reason, programs of compensatory education have stressed language development as their central task. The importance of language as a transferrable skill has to do with the fact that much of memory is probably a memory for language and facts stated in language. Speech provides a particularly precise way of recording and remembering events. The behavior of deaf children provides further indications of the importance of language in intellectual development, for these children have many difficulties in solving certain types of problem. Research on problem solving also provides evidence of the importance of language

in finding solutions. Abstract problem solving is inevitably a linguistic skill, but problem solving at a more concrete and primitive level may be nonverbal.

9 One of the most important verbal devices, with high potential for transfer to new situations, is a principle. The learning of principles is a very efficient form of learning. Research has shown that knowledge of a principle may be the basis for transfer; the Judd experiment is one of the most famous experiments in the history of educational research. There is some evidence that, in the case of children in the upper elementary grades, a principle of physics can be most usefully learned in a realistic setting. Some tie between the principle and reality seems to be important if the pupil is to be able to transfer what he has learned to new situations. There is also some mild support for the view that a person who can verbalize a principle is most likely to be able to apply it to a new problem.

10 Specific transfer is helpful when one has to adapt to new pieces of equipment similar to those with which one is familiar. There is much specific transfer in mastering the driving of a new car or the operation of a new sewing machine. Simulators are designed to provide the maximum amount of specific transfer.

I. APPRAISING PUPIL ACHIEVEMENT

Teachers have to keep track of the learning that is taking place in each pupil. If they do not do this fairly systematically, they are likely to find that much of the learning that they think is taking place actually is not. The problem of appraising student development is an extremely difficult one, and many of its most important aspects have not yet been solved.

Some of the learning that takes place in school is toward objectives set by the school, the district, or the state. These objectives involve the mastery of the skills that most citizens have to acquire in order to survive in their particular culture. For this reason, some effort is made to teach a child to read, to calculate and to solve simple mathematical problems,

Appraising and Predicting Pupil Achievement

and to write simple communications. For the same reason, children are taught the geography of their state and country and some information about the present and past condition of the human species. In addition, most curriculum designers make an effort to teach children some knowledge and skills that go beyond the matter of helping them to adapt to a complex civilization and may help them to improve the civilization. Thus children in some schools are helped to become critical thinkers with the idea in mind that if they can think about their world critically and intelligently, then they may be able to change it in a desirable direction. Just what the skills are that may have this impact still remains to be discovered, and there are numerous curriculum recipes suggested. The fact is that one can probably do no more than speculate about the skills that will produce cultural change. Only the more recent schools in the history of civilization have been permitted to have goals related to the changing of the culture they serve; the sole purpose of most schools of the past was to preserve knowledge and provide the individual with the skills to survive.

Now children not only learn to some degree what is supposedly required of them in schools, but they also may learn much that is not required of them yet may become of great significance to their entire lives. Charles Martin Hall, a student at Oberlin College who spent his spare time in the chemistry laboratory, succeeded, where others had failed, in making metallic aluminum, although the making of metallic aluminum was not a part of the set curriculum. A child who, with the encouragement of the teacher, explores through his reading some area of knowledge may be on the way to developing a life-long interest. Schools and curricula differ considerably in the degree to which they keep the child's nose to some administratively established grindstone or permit the child to engage in explorations. Miller (1969, 1970), for example, found that children of preschool age who had been through the DARCEE program tended to show more exploratory and achievement-motivated behavior than those who had come through the Bereiter–Engleman program. The DARCEE program is one that exercises a low degree of control over the activities of the children, and the Bereiter–Engleman program exercises a high degree of control.

The history of education is a story of conflict between those who would like to exercise a high degree of control over the behavior and learning of children in school and those who would give the children considerable autonomy in this respect. This is what the great reform movement in education, beginning with Horace Mann, was about. The most vigorous attempt to change education from a highly regimented activity to one in which pupil initiative was encouraged was found in the Progressive Education Movement that developed after the end of World War I. This movement was worldwide, though it developed under different names in different countries. Wherever it occurred, it stressed the need for an educational program in which children could exercise initiative in setting goals for themselves. In the program advocated by this reform movement, the school was to be a place where children might learn to do all of the important things that adults do, including making decisions for themselves. The argument is highly persuasive that, if children are to grow up to be something more than sheep to be herded by an establishment or by a bureaucracy, they must learn to be decision makers early in life. The Progressive Education Movement argued strongly that children should be encouraged to make real and significant decisions in school. Many regimented programs delegate to the children the task of making trivial decisions, but the reform movement in education wanted to encourage children to make the kinds of decisions that might change the course of their lives. In such a program, the goals are highly individualized, in contrast with the more traditional educational programs in which all children are expected to work toward a uniform set of goals. Those who promoted the idea of individualized goals of education generally recognized that particularly high skills would be required of the teacher. Opponents of such reforms argued that most teachers could not be expected to have the skill that such individualized programs required.

The contemporary scene shows some schools in which there is great freedom for the pupils to set and accomplish their goals and also schools that provide a rigid and controlled educational experience. Both types of schools claim to show the impact of modern psychology of learning, and both do, because a science of learning can be used to help achieve many different kinds of goals through many different means. Both claim to encourage self-initiated behavior on the part of the pupil, but they mean very different things by this. In one school, when the pupil finishes arithmetic unit number 117, he has it scored by a teacher's aide. If he achieves a sufficiently good score, he will then go pick up the worksheet corresponding to arithmetic unit number 118. In this program, the behavior of the pupil who goes to pick up the next worksheet is said to be self-initiated in that he is not told to do so. The behavior would be much more adequately described as being system initiated, because it is the instructional system that makes it a virtual requirement for the pupil to go pick up the next unit. It is self-initiated in much the same sense that a soldier whose boots wear out turns in the old pair and obtains a new pair from supply. The soldier has no other choice than to do what he does within the system in which he works, and the pupil has no other alternative than to go pick up the next unit of work. Any virtue that self-initiation of behavior may have can only be in instances in which there is choice of alternatives. The pupil and the soldier have no choice of alternatives, and any self-initiation of activity involved is trivial. In an entirely different type of school, a pupil might have just completed a unit involving the study of the solar system and then tell the teacher that he would like to find out more about the possibility of life on other planets. The teacher encourages him to do so and enlists the help of the librarian in finding suitable material for the pupil to read. The teacher then works out a study plan with the pupil and encourages him to prepare a report that he can present to the others in the class. Such a pupil not only has the exhilarating experience of studying a problem of interest to himself, but he gains experience in finding out things for himself. The experience may also be sufficiently rewarding that he will begin to form a habit of exploring things for himself. In such a case, the self-initiated behavior of the pupil is not merely a product of the system forcing him into doing what he does. This kind of self-initiated activity would appear to be of the kind that makes for a vigorous society.

Many forces in our society have tended to promote educational programs designed so that all pupils work toward the same identical goals, though there may be some latitude in the rate at which they attain these common goals. One reason is that such programs are very easy to administer from the points of view of both the teacher and the principal. The ease with which such programs are managed results from the fact that they tend to be tied more and more to sets of packaged materials. The teacher has the role of handing out the packages of instructional materials, administering the tests, keeping the records, and so forth. Such packaged programs have been advocated by many interests. One of the most influential has been the businesses collectively referred to as the education industry, but it is not just profit-making concerns alone that have been interested in promoting and developing the self-contained packaged material. The product is claimed to have much the same advantages as the cake mix has for the unskilled cook. If the cook will do exactly what the printed instructions tell him to do, then the result will be exactly that described. Perhaps the educational package cannot be viewed as having the same reliability as the packaged cake mix, but the intention of the manufacturer is roughly the same. The emergence of completely packaged curricula is an innovation that carries with it the notion that the products of education should be uniform, much as the products of a factory are expected to be uniform. The conception of education on which such packaging is based is that the school should be operated with the same kind of efficiency as found in a factory.

Those who prefer some degree of individualization of objectives would not quarrel with the notion that education should be efficient. They would say that some aspects of the curriculum are directed toward common objectives and that these objectives should be achieved with some degree of efficiency. They would also say that it is sometimes important to sacrifice efficiency in order to permit the pupil to explore some avenue unrelated to the main current of the work in progress.

Appraisal of Progress Toward Preset Goals

Much of the systematic appraisal of pupil progress, and in most cases all of it, involves the determination of the extent to which preset goals, that is, fixed objectives for all pupils, are reached. On the surface, this seems an easy matter, but in actual fact it is not. Indeed, the author can say from his own personal experience with many different educational programs and studies of pupil progress in them that he has rarely seen data that provided clear evidence that the objectives were or were not reached. The results are generally ambiguous, and there is no simple formula for removing the ambiguities involved. There are formulas and procedures that can be applied to help make the measurement of pupil progress more systematic and freer from ambiguities, but these still do not permit one to obtain clear evidence of the extent to which pupil progress meets specifications. A central problem involves the specification of the objectives of instruction. Let us turn to that problem and see some of the difficulties involved.

Specifications of Objectives

Thought concerning how objectives should be defined emerged in the context of evaluation studies during the 1930s. At that time, a young man, Ralph Tyler, at Ohio State University was struggling with the problems of conducting evaluation studies in a group of progressive schools. He saw clearly that the chief weakness of earlier evaluation studies was that they attempted to determine the extent to which vaguely defined objectives were achieved, which led nowhere. Of what avail was it to attempt to determine whether the children in such schools were achieving the goal of developing critical thinking if one could not specify what was meant by critical thinking? In a classic article on the subject, Tyler (1934) took the position that objectives should be defined in terms of specific behaviors. He pointed out that it was not enough just to say that an educational program was designed to develop critical thinking, and he proposed that the objective of critical thinking be defined in terms of quite specific activities on the part of the pupil that would demonstrate this ability.

The project in which Tyler was involved, known as the **Eight Year Study,** was particularly concerned with the development of thinking skills through education. Tyler partitioned off four of these skills:

1. The ability to interpret data.
2. The ability to apply principles of science.
3. The ability to apply principles of logic.
4. The understanding of the nature of proof.

His next step was to break down these broad categories of behavior into narrower categories. He divided the first of these into the following two subcategories:

1. The ability to perceive relationships in data.
2. The ability to recognize the limitations of data.

These subcategories were then broken down further. For example, the first of these was broken down into

1. The ability to make comparisons.
2. The ability to identify the common elements in data.

3. The ability to read data.
4. The ability to make simple computations from data.
5. The ability to understand symbols used and methods of representation.

The last group were the specific behaviors that Tyler believed represented the elements in terms of which objectives should be defined. One could, of course, be even more specific by listing actual test situations that could be used to measure the extent to which the objective was achieved, and the test situations would then provide a definition of the nature of the objective. The procedure leaves to the judgment of the test maker just how specific one has to be in defining objectives.

The procedure for defining objectives later was applied by Tyler (1950) to problems of curriculum development, and the procedure has had an intimate relationship to much of the recent educational technology in the development of packaged curricula. Several more recent books and articles have expanded on the Tyler theme, including those of Mager (1962), Popham (1969), Gronlund (1970), McAshan (1970), Baker and Schutz (1971), and Baker (1972). The procedure has also influenced large curriculum projects. For example, the American Association for the Advancement of Science Commission on Science Education (1965) has attempted to define scientific competencies in terms of such processes as

1. Observing likenesses and differences in single objects.
2. Observing likenesses and differences in sets of objects.
3. Observing and classifying in terms of concepts larger–smaller, higher–lower, etc.
4. Ordering objects within categories.
5. Correctly categorizing objects.
6. Observing and classifying objects in terms of derived characteristics.

These are just a few of the "specifics" used for defining the objectives of science teaching as set up by the Association.

A point to note is that these are really not specific behaviors at all, but categories of behavior. Consider the last of the objectives listed. Surely classifying seeds may be a rather different process from classifying postage stamps or classifying chemicals. Even after one has defined objectives in such terms, different curriculum builders may still conceive of them differently, devise different curricula to achieve them, and evaluate pupil progress with different test. The remedy for this would seem to be to make objectives even more specific, as some do. In such a case, the last of the objectives listed would specify just what was to be classified and include such statements as "classifies seeds and flowers in terms of derived characteristics."

The kinds of analyses of objectives that we have considered up to this point have been concerned with what are sometimes called **process objectives.** The way in which they are defined takes little account of the subject matter through which they are achieved. Baker (1972) points out that many who have worked in recent years on the problem of defining objectives have come to believe that this omission has to be remedied. As a result, there has been a renewed emphasis on including in any set of specifications of objectives a set of statements attempting to define the subject matter involved.

The specification of the subject matter through which objectives are to be achieved appears to be a simple matter, but to do it with any degree of precision is not usually easy. If one's objective is to teach children to add together two single digits, then one can list all the combinations of two digits and thus specify the objective completely and comprehensively. On the other hand, if the objective is that of studying foreign policy of the United States since 1918, one could fill a volume listing everything that he might want to include and the volume might still not include every event. Most people attempting to specify such an objective would not attempt to list every fact, issue, controversy, significant personage, speech, or document, but would be likely to give illustrations of the nature of the course content. What such a person would be doing is providing a **sample** of the content, but such a sample, like a sample of fruit from an orchard, can be misleading unless it is very carefully selected. The fact is that, in most subject matter areas, attempts to define goals generally lack precision.

A program of education confined to the achievement of fixed and well-defined goals would almost certainly be narrow and dull. It would not permit the teacher to exploit the many interesting incidents that arise during the course of the school day. For instance, such a curriculum would find no place for the discussion of an editorial, brought in by a child, related to a crisis in the local community. It would provide little opportunity for children to develop their own ideas or pursue work toward goals that they themselves had found. The latter is possible only in an educational system that also has broad goals such as "the development of each individual pupil along lines that he, the pupil, has chosen for himself." Such a goal is not formulated in the precise terms favored by those who insist that every objective should be precisely developed. There is a place for broadly stated overall goals of education that provide general goals for all participants in the educational program. In this author's opinion, the overall encompassing goal of American education is to fulfill the dream of society expressed in the Declaration of Independence and the Constitution. The teacher must have freedom in interpreting such goals and how they are to be achieved and must take advantage of unplanned incidents that open up opportunities for discussion and sometimes for action, such as the incident involving a pupil who brought in an editorial.

The Concept of Mastery Learning

The view of most teachers and principals of the last century was that the objectives of education could be achieved in all who were fortunate enough to be exposed to schooling. Failure on the part of the pupil was moral failure, a lack of effort on his part. The advent of the mental measurement movement in the first quarter of this century persuaded teachers that pupils differ in their ability to learn and that a particular objective cannot be achieved to the same degree in all pupils. The practice of grading on the curve became firmly established, supposedly having the support of research workers in the field of individual differences.

In the last century, Maria Montessori had claimed that her dull slum children could, through education, become capable of competing with the children of the privileged, but her claims were rejected by all but a few. Then, late in this century, international studies began to appear indicating that the children in some countries showed very low failure rates, even in subjects such as mathematics that were believed to be beyond the ability of many children. The international study of Husén (1967) is an example of such an enterprise. The evidence that accumulated slowly became almost overwhelming that most school failure had nothing to do with any genetic inferiority of the children involved. Failure could be a product of many circumstances in the environment over which some control could be gained.

So impressive has been the evidence that failure in school is largely unnecessary that some have suggested that the common objectives of elementary and secondary schools can be achieved by most children. Skinner (1959) long ago suggested that proper educational planning and teaching modeled according to the principles of operant conditioning would do this. Mager (1962) followed through on this idea and proposed that educators should aim at achieving 90 per cent of the objectives in 90 per cent of the children. This is a statement that sounds quite precise but is actually extremely vague. Later, Bloom (1971) proposed that about 90 per cent of children could be expected to master most school subjects, conceding that about 10 per cent might have problems preventing them from accomplishing what the other children accomplished. Bloom also made another point of great importance—that children do differ in the time they require to achieve particular goals. One child might take twice as long as another to achieve a particular objective, but he could get there just the same. In the lock-step system of education in which each child is given the same time to achieve each objective, many will fail simply because they are not allowed enough time to accomplish the tasks and goals set. The implication is that some children could skip through twelve grades of schooling in perhaps four or six years, but others might take fourteen.

A difficult problem is the matter of what constitutes mastery. Suppose the objective is to be able to add together single-digit numbers. One proposal (see Glaser and Cox, 1968) has been that, at the time when the objective is set, some statement be made concerning the performance that can be said to constitute achievement of the objective. The statement might be that pupils should be able to solve such problems with 95 or 98 per cent accuracy. Presumably, some objectives should be achieved with a higher level of performance than others. A surgeon should know how to remove an appendix with 100 per cent correctness. The same level of performance is hardly required in spelling, where an error does not have disastrous consequences and some degree of error is generally considered to be excusable. The level of mastery set is a matter of judgment based on reflective thinking concerning the social consequences of the actions involved. One must point out that only under exceptional circumstances can one determine exactly what 90 per cent mastery or any other percentage means. What is 90 per cent mastery of the content of a textbook on American history? Does it involve mastery of 90 per cent of the subtle innuendos of the story of history as it is written? Does it involve remembering 90 per cent of the facts, and, if so, what are the facts? The historian may freely admit that he does not know exactly what the facts are. The concept of 90 per cent mastery is nearer to being a catch phrase than a clear standard to be achieved.

The problem is, in fact, still more complicated. If a child shows 100 per cent mastery of a task at the end of the school semester, it does not mean that he has mastered the task for life. This is shown by the fact that most adult illiterates once learned to read to some degree, but lack of use of the skill produced a slow deterioration until no useful skill remains. Unfortunately, not much is known at this time about how to produce lasting skills, except to suggest that it involves review at intervals. A school program should provide opportunities for repeated review of the skills that are vital in adult life.

Classification of Objectives

Educators have long looked for a classification of objectives. Because the goals or objectives of education involve what the person will do in his entire life, a classification of objectives would involve a classification of all human activity. No such classification has yet been evolved by scientists and is not likely to be for a long time. For this reason, educators have tried to settle for a classification involving a much less extensive range of events. An old classification made use of the categories of thinking, feeling, and action. Another used the categories of cognitions (activities related to knowing), feelings, and motivations. A more recent attempt, described previously, has been to begin with broad categories and then break down these categories into smaller components. The major categories that have emerged in this system are those of cognition, affective behavior (positive and negative feelings), motor components, and perception. The categories are makeshift, and, far from being comprehensive, they represent a patchwork derived from several different psychological conceptions of behavior. The best-developed set of categories within this system has been developed in the cognitive domain. The main subcategories are those described by Bloom (1964) as knowledge, comprehension, application, analysis, synthesis, and evaluation. These form a useful system for classifying test items and have some value in keeping track of the content of tests. One can classify items in a test in such terms and obtain an idea of whether the test is broad or narrow in scope. This is a useful kind of activity to undertake in that so many tests, particularly teacher-made tests, are very narrow in scope and often concentrate on the retention of facts. Checking a test against these categories can keep one on guard and help one to keep in mind a broad range of activities.

The difficulty with all such classification systems is that they have been evolved before the scientific knowledge necessary for a useful classification system has been produced. Most scientific disciplines have had a history of prescientific classification systems. Such prescientific systems have generally been of limited value, have become quickly entrenched, and have often prevented a useful system of categories from being evolved. An example of a useless classification system that persisted for centuries was that developed by the alchemists and early chemists, who classified compounds into such categories as flowery, oily, and corrosive. This classification was based on superficial characteristics of the compounds that had little to do with their chemical properties. Occasionally, the alchemists did manage to hit on a useful category, as they did in the identification of carbonates. Despite such occasional successes in establishing useful categories, the system they developed was no more useful than that of the Greeks, who had attempted to think of all substances as consisting of air, water, earth, and fire. The system of the alchemists persisted for hundreds of years and was given up less than two-hundred years ago. It became a virtual block to the discovery of a scientific basis for the classification of chemical substances, and new classifications attempted by the early chemists were vigorously resisted. The development of a sound basis for classifying elements and chemical compounds had to await the emergence of systematic experimentation with chemicals and the discovery of the laws related to their combination. The periodic table of chemical elements could not be developed until the atomic weights of many elements had been established. The emergence of such categories of compounds as acids, alkalis, salts, sulfides, and sulfates was based on a very large body of information about how elements combine.

At the present time, the behavioral sciences are not very near to producing a scientific basis for a comprehensive classification of behavior. Perhaps the scientific enterprise that comes nearest to providing a basis for classifying objectives related to thinking behavior is the work of Piaget, who has listed numerous intellectual operations that, for him, constitute the core of intelligence. Mention has already been made of the operation known as conservation, but Piaget provides a long list of other operations. Although these operations are closely linked to that department of philosophy known as logic, they have been derived from experimentation with children and adolescents and are not philosophical in derivation. As behavior becomes better understood through experimentation, a basis will emerge for a scientific classification of educational objectives—that is, a scientific classification of behavior.

Krathwohl et al. (1964) have developed a classification of objectives in the affective area (feelings, likes, dislikes, attitudes). The criticism that has been made of the Bloom categories applies equally to the Krathwohl categories.

Appraising Progress Toward the Achievement of Fixed Objectives

The statement is commonly made that any program should have means built into it for determination of the extent to which the goals of the program are being achieved. Cohen (1970) has pointed out that many federally sponsored educational programs are supposed to meet such a requirement but that this has often resulted in the most superficial appraisal, involving little more than the judgment of those involved. Although the Federal plan was to appraise each program in order to determine which ones should be developed further, the difficulties of appraising the extent to which an educational program has been effective were vastly underestimated.

Appraisal in terms of follow-up: It has often been said that, under ideal conditions, the effectiveness of educational programs should be judged in terms of the performance of the individual, in real-life situations, after he leaves school. Insofar as school is preparation for life, the effectiveness of schooling should be judged in terms of the extent to which it provides such preparation. Tests and examinations may indicate the extent to which the pupil has mastered particular aspects of the educational program, but they lack much in telling us whether the school can produce a person who can meet life's problems with competency. The argument is plausible, even persuasive, but the many attempts to evaluate schooling in terms of adult performance have shown up the many difficulties the procedure encounters. Consider, for example, the commonly professed goal that the school should prepare the individual to take advantage of the many cultural facilities offered by his community. One can quite easily find out how many go to concerts, listen to concerts on the radio in their homes, borrow books from the library, buy books, and so forth, but such data tell little about the effects of schooling. There are times when a large section of the public may not be able to afford seats at concerts, has no money for books, is too busy moonlighting to listen to music on the radio, and so forth. Such data may tell one more about prevailing economic conditions than about the habits acquired in school. Furthermore, the cultural activity may also reflect the habits and ways of life that the student acquired in his home, and it is difficult to distinguish the effects of schooling from the effects of family life. In addition, behavior that one might expect to occur as a result of the intensive efforts of the school to produce cultural development may be masked by other social conditions. In a period of rapid social change, individuals may be engaged to such a degree in activist movements that they have little time for conventional cultural activities. Others, who are part of an affluent society, may be so busy all weekend playing with their recreational vehicles that they have no time for reading or music or the other arts.

Now consider another case in which one might attempt to study the effectiveness of schooling. Most school systems devote some attention to the matter of health and diet. One should be able to determine the effectiveness of that program through the study of the health and dietary practices of those who have gone through the school system. The effect of what is taught in school may manifest itself in only a very weak form, because the effect of schooling has to compete with the effect of commercials that advise the individual to consume large quantities of "junk" foods. A one-semester course in health or biology can be expected to have only a small effect compared with the effect of a lifetime bombardment of television commercials imploring the viewer to buy relatively worthless forms of starch or poor-quality protein found in gelatin. One cannot expect that the school program will be able to override all the competing elements in society.

Follow-up studies designed to explore school-related behavior in real-life situations generally provide quite disappointing results. What such follow-up studies give is an overall appraisal of the total effects of all the influences designed to produce learning in our society, and many of these competing influences draw the individual in different directions. At the time of writing, the same television station will provide educational materials produced by the American Cancer Society on the hazards of smoking and also commercials for manufacturers of tobacco products designed to develop an addiction to tobacco. These two sets of influences are opposite, and it is doubtful whether studies could be made that would separate out and measure the relative influence of these two forces in our society.

Although follow-up studies designed to evaluate the effects of schooling generally yield little useful information, there are a few cases in which they can be fully justified, for instance, in driver training. Such studies have produced substantial evidence that school driver training does produce better drivers than the home-brand of driver training. There are excellent criteria of the extent to which a driver is proficient, and nearly all members of society have to drive. One might run into difficulties in evaluating driver education if good public transportation systems were evolved and most people drove cars only rarely (a situation analogous to teaching people to enjoy reading and then having them live in a society where there were alternatives to reading).

An interesting case of the follow-up technique is found in the numerous studies of compensatory education. Programs developed for underprivileged children who have difficulties in school because of the limited opportunities for learning provided by their home environment.

The obvious way to evaluate the effectiveness of such programs is to follow the children into the school that they enter after the program of compensatory education comes to an end. Such children have been followed through the lower elementary grades, but the data that have come out of such a follow-up are difficult to interpret. The findings are typically negative. The children who have been exposed to compensatory education show little, if any, advantage over those that have not been thus exposed. The difficulty with such studies is that short periods of compensatory education can hardly be expected to compensate fully for years of deprivation, and the tests and devices used to conduct the appraisal are inevitably quite crude. Most of the tests, rating scales, and other means of collecting data on such children are probably not sufficiently sensitive to show what compensatory education has accomplished. It is like trying to show slight changes in the temperature of the body with a thermometer calibrated in twenty-degree intervals.

Appraisal in simulated situations: There are real, and often insuperable, difficulties involved in obtaining information about how the individual performs in life situations. An investigator could probably never find out how well a physician performs in the secluded examination rooms of his private practice. One is equally unable to check on the plumber. The private lives of individuals are hidden to an even greater degree from the scientist's eye. Sometimes it is possible to study the behavior of those who have been trained or educated in some way, not in real-life situations, but in situations that simulate closely those of the natural world. If one cannot observe the behavior of the pupil in the real world, then perhaps one can stage for him some of the problems that life presents. Such staged situations are referred to as **simulated situations,** and they can approximate closely the situations that he has been prepared to handle.

Simulated situations for appraising pupil progress can be found at all levels of education. An elementary-school teacher may find out whether the children can apply the mathematics they have learned to such problems as determining the best buy in the supermarket. The testing situation may involve showing the children a set of cans of different sizes, and contents and determining whether they can arrive at a correct decision. The appraisal of their achievement may be informal and involve no more than a class discussion of the problem, or it may involve a formal testing situation. Aspects of achievement in the language arts may be evaluated by having the children undertake such activities as preparing a letter on some school issue to be sent to the local newspaper. Pupil's speaking ability may be appraised by having them make speeches. The outcomes of health education can sometimes be evaluated in a real situation by observing what food choices the children make in designing a meal, and one can also have testing situations in which children have to state what food choices they would make when confronted with a particular variety of foods. Most education in the lower grades is designed to provide knowledge and skills useful in a great variety of situations, but all too often the teacher makes little attempt to discover whether the children can make any applications at all of what they have learned.

The more specialized education becomes, at higher levels, the more readily it lends itself to the development of simulated test situations. The teacher of business English has little difficulty in concocting practical situations in which the students can demonstrate the extent to which they can apply, in a simulated real-life situation, the skills they have supposedly been taught. The student trained in radio and television technology can be given troubleshooting problems to solve on equipment that has been deliberately made to malfunction. The medical student can be given recordings of human hearts to listen to, and a determination can be made of his skill in diagnosing heart ailments from heart sounds.

At all levels of education, there are some possibilities of making such simulated real-life test situations. An evaluation of education and an appraisal of the pupil's ability to come to grips with the realities of the world can be undertaken through such situations. All too often the tests given in school determine only whether a child can perform the skills exactly in the way in which he has learned them, but learning to pass such a school test is different from learning to pass the test of life. Many children learn skills in school in such a way that they can apply them only to school situations. Testing for the ability to transfer knowledge and skill to life situations is an essential feature of useful evaluation of the pupil.

Appraisal through the observation of pupils: Some teachers are very skilled in obtaining data on the progress of their pupils through information about how the children behave in school-related situations. Some aspects of the success of the language arts program in the school can be obtained by finding out what books children borrow from the library of their own free will. If the program of language development in the school is successful, one might expect pupils to become individuals who read on their own and who borrow library books to develop knowledge about matters of interest to them or for the enjoyment of reading literature. The extent to which children are absent from school is a strong indicator of the extent to which life in school has been made pleasant, for it is known that differences in absentee rates in different schools reflect far more what happens in the school than they reflect differences in actual sickness rates. The effectiveness of the school program in the area of ecology is seen, to some extent, in the degree to which the schoolgrounds are cluttered with rubbish, the extent to which pupils participate in drives to control pollution, and the extent to which the spare-time activities of the pupils involve the preservation or destruction of wildlife. If the social studies program is designed to help the pupil become a concerned participant in local or national affairs, then it is relevant to determine whether he does or does not read a newspaper and what he reads in the paper. The role that the individual wants to play in the larger society is also seen in the role that he plays in the classroom.

Such methods of appraising pupil development have potential for providing highly important data on the extent to which the goals of the program are being achieved. The main difficulty in the use of these methods of appraisal is that they are time consuming. Many teachers claim they do not have the time, but sometimes administrative arrangements can be made to make the application of these methods possible. For example, the author is familiar with a school in which two first-grade classes are combined under the direction of two teachers. At certain times in the year, one of the teachers leaves the classroom and goes to visit in the homes of the children for the purpose of finding out something about their out-of-school behavior. The teacher can then find out, for instance, whether the uncommunicative child who is slowly beginning to communicate with other children shows a similar progress in out-of-school hours. Such contacts of parents and teachers can be extremely important in keeping the school program from becoming a meaningless routine, unrelated to life in the community. Another approach is that developed in North Dakota, in which parents participate in classroom activity and a close link is developed between the teacher, the parent, and the school program.

Appraisal in terms of teacher-made tests: Although one may exhort teachers to make observations on pupils, the fact remains that most teachers rely largely on classroom tests to determine the progress that pupils are making. Classroom tests appear to be an easy and quick way of collecting information. For this reason, a consideration of evaluation techniques has to include some discussion of paper-and-pencil tests. Books on this topic written twenty-five years ago offer much the same advice as those written today, but the advice given is useful and some of it will be summarized here. Readily available and readable books on this topic include those by Ebel (1965), Lindeman (1967), and Gronlund (1970). Several new books on the construction of classroom examinations are in the process of publication, but they are unlikely to show any new departures.

Classroom tests typically measure the aspects of behavior that can be translated into words or are essentially word skills. Many of the important skills taught in schools are word skills. The teacher of English is interested in developing the ability of students to communicate both orally and in writing. Such a teacher may appraise the ability of pupils in the latter respect by asking each to write a letter applying for a particular job and outlining the qualifications they may have for it. The test measures an actual sample of the behavior that the teaching is designed to develop. However, sometimes an examination may be designed to measure a skill that is not ordinarily considered a word skill but can be translated into words. For example, a chemistry teacher might ask his students to design an experiment to show whether a particular sample of orange juice contains vitamin C. The chemistry teacher could, of course, ask the students to conduct the experiment in the laboratory, but this might involve providing many sets of equipment, and perhaps more than were available. Most of the skills involved can be translated into words, but not all. A student might be able to give a flawless description of the experiment and yet be too clumsy to actually carry out the routine he can meticulously describe on paper. Nevertheless, the chemistry teacher may justify the written test by saying that if a student cannot describe how he would carry out the experiment, he almost certainly would not be able to undertake the task in the laboratory.

One can easily think of some cases in which a verbal, written test could not possibly measure the skill that had been taught. One may teach generosity and kindness, but no one would attempt to measure these attributes through a paper-and-pencil test. Nobody would attempt to measure the ability to play a musical instrument by giving a written test. One could, perhaps, devise a test that would indicate the person's familiarity with a particular musical instrument, but performance on the test has only a remote relationship to performance on the musical instrument itself. Although one can add many items to this list of skills that cannot be convincingly measured by means of a verbal test, one can also make a strong case for the position that most of the knowledge, skills, and perhaps even appreciations taught in schools can be measured adequately with paper and pencil. Let us consider some of the characteristics that should be found in an adequately constructed test.

Pupils voice many complaints about the tests given in school, and these inadequacies can be viewed, from a technical standpoint, as involving a lack of what are referred to as **validity** and **reliability.** Let us consider these two concepts from the point of view of constructing classroom examinations.

Suppose that a teacher had given a course in twentieth-century American history and followed a syllabus put out by the state education department. For the final examination, the teacher asked the pupils to list six Supreme Court decisions of the present century that had had impact and to explain what that impact was. Because the course had barely touched on Supreme Court decisions, having been focused on foreign policy, the students had a right to complain that the examination lacked relevancy for measuring the outcomes of the course. The educational psychologist would prefer to say that the examination lacked validity, for a core concept in validity is relevancy. Valid examinations are highly relevant measurements of the outcomes of the particular course in which they are used for appraising pupil achievement.

A second implicit concept is that a valid test should include a representative sample of the achievement expected in the course. In the case of the course in twentieth-century American history, the valid achievement test should include problems representing each important area included. It is not enough that the test cover particular areas included in the course; the test must also present problems measuring the ability of the pupil to perform each of the skills supposedly developed.

Although it seems logical to say that examinations should have validity in terms of the stated objectives of the course, one may well ask what should be done when the course itself does not closely correspond to the objectives. For example, suppose that a college teacher designed a course in statistics for graduate students of education and prepared a valid examination that would measure the extent to which the outcomes were achieved. This same college teacher then had the task of teaching the course. After a few meetings with the students, he found that they had far less background in mathematics than typical graduate students of education, and so he had to modify the course. Should he give them the examination based on the original set of objectives and show them their inadequacies in terms of the stated goals? Of course he should not. He should recognize that his modification of the course involved a modification of the objectives. The items in the test should match the new objectives if the test is to measure achievement in relation to realistic goals.

Reliability, the other test characteristic related to validity, may be discussed with respect to our teacher of twentiety-century American history. Suppose that he viewed the course as involving six main areas and prepared an examination covering one very specific point in each of the areas. Some students might complain that, although they had studied, the six points covered in the examination just happened to be points to which they had not given any special attention. The students might argue that, because of the nature of the test, luck played an important part in the scores they obtained. They point out that if the teacher had asked questions related to six other relevant points, they might have obtained excellent scores. The questions asked were valid enough, but the test lacked reliability. A test is always a sampling of the knowledge and skill that the student has supposedly acquired, but the sample should be large enough so that a fair appraisal can be made of the student's accomplishments. If two tests are given, each one of which provides an adequate sample, the performance of the student on one test should be very similar to his performance on the other. In such a case, the tests would be said to have satisfactory reliability.

Let us consider some of the down-to-earth ways in which teacher-made examinations are deficient in these respects. Essay examinations are often deficient in that the teacher thinks of some "clever" questions, which generally detract from the validity of the tests. Essay questions may also sometimes lack validity becuase the writing of the essay calls for skills that have nothing to do with the content of the course. An examination in history is quite often a moderately good test of skill in English composition, but a valid test of English composition is unlikely to be a valid test of knowledge of American history. A good test of the wrong subject is likely to be demoralizing to the student. Another reason for poor validity of a test is inappropriateness of the item form. Suppose a teacher gives a course in modern American history and the main objective is an understanding of the development of American democracy. At the end of the course, the teacher gives an examination consisting of matching items, in which events are to be matched with their dates. Matching test items are simply not appropriate for measuring the kind of understanding that the teacher hoped to develop. Essay tests are particularly useful for measuring the student's ability to organize his thoughts and his ability to

215
. . . .
Appraising Progress
Toward the
Achievement of Fixed
Objectives

present arguments for and against particular positions. Multiple-choice questions have excellent properties for measuring knowledge of facts, the ability to interpret data, and the ability to distinguish between relevant and irrelevant data and correct and incorrect statements, among other common objectives.

Lack of reliability of classroom tests derives from two main sources. The test itself may have inherent properties that make for low reliability, and the scoring procedures may be unreliable. Scoring procedures are particularly the problem in essay examinations. Two scorers, quite obviously, show much less agreement in scoring a set of essay papers than they do in scoring two objective examinations. Indeed, if the same person were to score and rescore the same set of essay examinations measuring writing skills, one would expect only very moderate agreement between the two sets of scores: Quite commonly, a paper given an *A* on one scoring would receive only a *C* on a second scoring and vice versa. The scoring procedure for teacher-made essay examinations typically has poor reliability. Unfortunately, scoring procedures are particularly unreliable for such worthwhile features as the style of writing, the degree of organization, the thoughtfulness of the material, and originality. Scoring procedures are relatively reliable for such features as the amount and correctness of the information given and the number of spelling errors and simple grammatical mistakes. It has sometimes been said that the greater the triviality of the outcome, the greater the reliability of scoring.

Objective examinations do not have the same problem with reliability of scoring procedures. In fact, objective examinations are called objective because judgment does not enter into the scoring procedure; two persons scoring a set of such examinations would agree almost perfectly on the scores to be assigned. Therefore, scoring procedures have high reliability in the case of objective examinations. A major source of unreliability in objective tests arises from the fact that, with a short test, the pupil may obtain a high score through lucky guessing. If a teacher gives a sixteen-item true–false test, pure guessing will produce an average score of 8, and pure guessing will sometimes produce a score as high as 12 or more. The chances are actually about one in twenty that sheer guessing will produce at least as high a score. The remedy for this source of unreliability is to provide quite long objective examinations, but most teachers do not do this. The reason, of course, is that a good examination, with potential for being thoroughly reliable, might involve the use of seventy-five items and several full days of work on the part of the teacher. The fact is that most teacher-made objective tests have very poor reliability because they are far too short.

One way of overcoming this difficulty is for groups of teachers to develop pools of items. This can be done within a department of a high school, and perhaps within a particular grade of an elementary school. This kind of operation has been referred to by some European writers as **item banking** (see Wood and Skurnik, 1969). Such pools of items may be informal assemblies of test questions produced by an interchange among teachers of their examination materials or may involve sophisticated and centralized files also containing information on how difficult or easy each item has been found to be. In schools run along the lines of the Individually Prescribed Instruction program, this problem is solved by incorporating short tests with each unit of subject matter. The tests may be nothing more than the exercises through which the unit is mastered, or the tests may be separate from the unit of work. Many teaching kits also provide similar built-in procedures for evaluation. For example, some of the kits developed by Science Research Associates for the teaching of reading include tests of comprehension in order to measure the extent to which the pupil has understood what he has read.

Standardized tests and national testing programs: Attempts are made in most school systems to obtain some evidence concerning the progress made by pupils through the use of standardized tests. The use of such tests is based on the assumption that there are certain goals that children should achieve by a certain age and that the degree of achievement of these goals can be effectively measured by standardized instruments. Even if there is such unity of purpose among teachers, school administrators, and parents, there probably should not be. Consider the case of reading—an area where one would think there is considerable agreement on what should be achieved and by what age. What should the child have achieved in this respect by the end of the third grade? Some would say that the most important goal achieved by that time would be the ability to read simple material accurately. Others would have quite a different opinion, taking the position that by the end of the third grade the child should have discovered that reading is an exciting and worthwhile experience through which he can obtain information he needs and also enjoyment. The two sets of goals are not necessarily compatible. A child who has learned to read simple materials with precision may be much less enthused with reading than the child who has stumbled through materials that fascinate him and who has not been drilled with the kinds of simple materials likely to appear on a standardized test. The teacher who works to develop a fascination for reading may take the position that speed and accuracy will come as the child becomes more and more engrossed in reading what he wants to read. Traditionally, the stress has been on accuracy rather than on developing enthusiasm, but this may well be the wrong approach. The fact is that not enough is known about the whole problem of developing reading skills to say who is right. It would be unfortunate if the makers of standardized tests forced teachers into developing the skills that the test makers had arbitrarily decided to be the most important.

Much greater controversy exists in such areas as social studies, in which there are many different views about the content to be covered and the particular age level at which particular objectives should be achieved. When, for example, should the concept of democracy be introduced? At what age should children learn that there are forms of government other than our own? When should children begin to understand

217
. . . .
Appraising Progress
Toward the
Achievement of Fixed
Objectives

the diverse origins of Americans? At what age are children mature enough to understand that just as a person is fallible, so too is the government of their country sometimes wrong in the decisions it makes? Are elementary-school children too young to begin to understand that governments have to make important moral decisions about such issues as whether the poor should be helped, whether the oppressed should be freed, and who should be free to say what? Issues such as these are of vastly more consequence than those involved in deciding which details of history shall be taught at each age.

Standardized tests tend to avoid the crucial issues related to curriculum design and to concentrate on the areas about which there is agreement. In the social studies area, they tend to include test questions related to simple facts of history that have played an important role in the building of the American tradition, and they avoid the social problems and issues that form the crux of controversy and dissent on the contemporary scene. Nevertheless, they will continue to be given for a number of reasons. One is that school boards and principals like to have data that appear to provide evidence that the school system is doing as well as any other school system. The possibility that the evidence may not show anything much at all does not seem to bother those who make the decisions to use standardized tests.

If a teacher is competent, the administration of standardized tests is not going to tell him much about each pupil that he did not know in the first place. He already knows much about Jimmy, who came to him from the previous grade three years behind most of the other children in reading skills. He has worked with Jimmy over the past year and knows that a little progress has been made, but not enough to remove the gap between him and the other children. He also knows that Doris and John come from homes that provide no intellectual encouragement whatsoever, and his task has been to show these children that intellectual pursuits can be rewarding. He has tried to interest them in hobbies and find related reading materials for them. Then there is June, who has been diagnosed as having brain injury. She is never in her seat long enough to learn anything, but she is now under the care of a physician who seems to be helping her to some extent. June should be in a special class for such children, but the school system has no facilities of this kind. The teacher just does his best under the circumstances, but the best he can do is far from what could be done if a special classroom were available. Then there is Bill. His problem is that he is enormously overconcerned with obtaining good grades. He is bright and competent as a student and performs far above his age group, but good grades come before anything else in his life. Even when a game is introduced as a technique for learning a particular skill, Bill cannot enjoy the game, for he is far too intent on winning.

The point is that the teacher should know a great deal about the pupils in his class and far more than he can find out from a standardized battery of tests. The tests may be useful to the principal or school board

218
· · · · · · · · · · ·
Appraising and
Predicting Pupil
Achievement

in helping them to believe that the school system is as good as others, but they have little value to the competent classroom teacher.

Finally, the point must be made that standardized test batteries are often enthusiastically endorsed for the wrong reasons. Such tests represent popular activities in schools. The pupils who take them have an easy day. The pupils know that chances are the results of the tests will never be used, so they experience little anxiety and spend the day working on quite interesting problems. Teachers are generally pleased to know that a standardized achievement battery is to be given, for this gets the pupils off their backs and they have time, while administering the battery, to catch up with reading pupil assignments. A day that involves the administration of an achievement battery is a peaceful day for all. Perhaps only the principal has anxiety when he wonders whether the pupils in his school will do as well as pupils in comparable schools in other school districts. Some weeks or months later, when the scores on the tests come back, they may be scanned by the principal and superintendent. Then they are likely to be sent to the guidance office, where they rest in peace because help is not available to have them added to the records of the individual pupil. If the overall scores are examined by somebody in the school system, they are likely to reflect certain familiar facts. Scores will be relatively low in schools that serve the underprivileged and also low in rural areas, as contrasted with suburbia. Pupils in the Rocky Mountain states will show a tendency to be relatively low in the language area and relatively high in the scientific areas. Schools that belong in the progressive education tradition will tend to have high scores in the social sciences and the humanities. It is very unlikely that the results from the typical standardized battery will come up with any new and startling facts that the staff of the school do not already know. At the best, they can assure the school board that the educational system of the school district is not falling to pieces.

Incentive Value of Examinations

One of the few saving graces of the examinations to which pupils are typically exposed is that they provide some incentive to the pupil. Textbooks on educational psychology of past decades have reviewed the evidence for this, and the reader interested in the original studies is referred to textbooks published at midcentury. The evidence shows that pupils working under conditions in which they can expect an examination learn more than pupils working in a no-examination condition. There is no intent here of reviewing these studies in detail, but our purpose is to consider this finding and whether it means that teachers should follow the lock-step system of education and the examination system that it incorporates.

It is hard to believe that the examination, in and of itself, is the source of superior achievement. Indeed, there is ample evidence that examinations do not add to the information of the pupil, and the wrong alternatives that are presented on multiple choice tests do not add to the store of incorrect information that the pupil may possess. The examination has other and quite complex effects on behavior. One of these is that it sets a deadline for the pupil—a deadline by which certain materials have to be mastered. Most of us require that our work be paced by deadlines. Otherwise, important tasks are put off until some vague future date, and little is accomplished. If the pupil does not meet his deadline, then there are unpleasant consequences to be faced involving a poor grade. The effect of the examination is avoidance learning. The pupil has learned to avoid the unpleasant consequences of poor performance on the examination by studying to meet the deadline that the examination imposes on him.

When an examination is given to an entire class, the same deadline for mastering the same content is set for all pupils. This reflects one of the evils of the uniform examination system. It assumes that all pupils can work in lock-step fashion, which they certainly cannot do efficiently. The uniform examination should be reserved for the few situations in which pupils are sufficiently uniform in their present learning capabilities to master the material in the time set.

The spur to learning provided by the typical examination system can probably be produced by other means. The individualized examination, which today comes packaged with many learning kits, is an improvement over the nonindividualized uniform examination system. One suspects that a teacher who assigns a pupil to work on such a kit should also set a time limit and tell the child that he will have to take the test that goes with the kit when that time limit is reached. Teachers generally do not do so, failing to recognize the importance of setting a deadline. Many teachers take the position that the individualized kit disposes of any need to set deadlines and that pupils working with such materials should work "at their own pace." There is really no such thing as a pupil working at his own pace. Both children and adults work at the pace that convention and the requirements of the situation demand. One works at what is believed to be an acceptable pace. A faster pace may result in rejection by one's associates. The typical pace of work represents custom, but a custom that can be changed. The teacher has to see that children work at a reasonably efficient rate; the dawdling child, like the dawdling adult, simply has not set an appropriate deadline that he must reach. Children can be encouraged to set deadlines for themselves and then see whether they can beat their own deadlines. A deadline-free work situation, for either children or adults, is an inefficient work situation.

The use of examinations can also control learning behavior in another way that may have some significance. Pupils who undertake an assignment often have no incentive for retaining what they have learned over a long period and will not review the material unless required to do so. An examination given at the end of a semester requires the student to review material he has learned earlier in the semester and that he has partially forgotten. The effect of the examination is to require the student to undertake additional learning sessions or learning trials with the material. Such additional sessions are important for the permanent learning of material. Material studied only long enough so that it can be remembered for a quiz given shortly thereafter is likely to be retained quite temporarily.

Studies by Nuttin and Greenwald (1968) have shown that one of the most important conditions for relatively permanent learning is expectation of future usage. Learning for tomorrow's quiz is learning oriented to retaining the material only for a very short period of time. Learning for tomorrow's quiz, plus learning for an examination to be given some months later, comes nearer to learning for future usage.

Thus it can be seen that decisions related to the matter of giving examinations involve the weighing of many factors that often cancel out one another. Examinations tied to lock-step systems of education tend to maintain and perpetuate the systems. On the other hand, examinations may help the student to set goals and deadlines. Perhaps the compromise is to have individualized examinations, but the work involved in such a system might be far beyond that which the classroom teacher can undertake. Here again, one can see that an increase in the amount of help available in the classroom would permit the teacher to undertake more efficient practices.

Diagnostic Tests

Those who construct tests have long hoped that it might be possible to develop devices that would pinpoint the source of a student's difficulties in various areas. For example, a student is slow at reading. Surely, a set of tests could be developed that would indicate the particular aspect or aspects of the skill in which he performs inadequately and that hold down his entire performance. Attacks on this particular problem are numerous, as is evident from a perusal of the *Sixth Mental Measurements Yearbook* (Buros, 1965). Also evident is the fact that there is absolutely no agreement on what the components of the reading act are, for the various tests that claim to provide a diagnosis of the source of a reading difficulty do not agree on what the variables are. The tests listed in the *Yearbook* refer to such varied components of the reading task as phonetic discrimination, matching letters to vowel sounds, interpreting phonetic symbols, structural analysis, letter and form memory, vocabulary, misread endings of words, oral reading skill, syllabication, eye–hand coordination, story comprehension, vowel confusions, word recognition, rate of silent reading, and potential level of comprehension. No two tests seem to measure the same components of reading, reflecting the disagreement that exists among the experts concerning the basic components of the reading task. If one took the time to measure all of these characteristics in a group of children, one would have the greatest difficulty in making much sense out of the data. Indeed, one would probably find himself swamped with massive data that would be very difficult to interpret.

Some reading experts would even say that more could be found out by merely asking the child to read aloud a passage. Nevertheless, the experts in the field of reading may be able to use effectively the diagnostic tests and procedures with which they have had substantial experience.

The problem of developing diagnostic tests in reading is probably as difficult a task as one could undertake in education. Ultimately, a truly diagnostic test will be developed, but it will take far more basic research on perception than has been undertaken at this time. Present attempts to develop diagnostic tests in the reading area are overambitious and should be considered to be strictly experimental ventures.

In some areas of achievement, there is much less controversy concerning the components of the skill to be taught that are essential. Mathematical skill at the fifth-grade level will require that the student have mastered such components as addition, subtraction, division, and multiplication of single- and multiple-digit numbers. Fourth-grade problems will typically require that the student have mastered also the various operations that can be performed with fractions. Though it is rarely done, all of these components of mathematics can be tested, because the field of elementary mathematics is logically structured and one can indicate with certainty the elements that have to be mastered to solve successfully a particular problem. On the other hand, in fields of knowledge that are not logically structured, one often has difficulty in identifying the underlying skills for which a diagnostic test might be made. Once again, the problem is that it is not known what are the prerequisite skills for performing at a particular level of proficiency.

In order to obtain reliable scores on the component skills that constitute a diagnostic battery of tests, the components have to be quite long. This means that an effective diagnostic test has to be a very long test indeed, and so diagnostic testing is time consuming and often not too practical. A few schools with experimental programs have attempted to administer batteries of such tests at the beginning of the school year in order to determine both present levels of skill and the weaknesses that need to be remedied. In one such case familiar to the author, a whole month was occupied in such testing. At the end of that month, even those developing the program were extremely skeptical about whether the amount of time could be justified. It might well have been that the time would have been far better spent on instruction, even though such instruction would not have been based on a thorough knowledge of the pupils' standing and difficulties.

There are always many different ways in which a pupil's time may be occupied. Teachers and curriculum developers have to make some guess concerning the activities that will have the greatest payoff.

National Assessment

Some mention must be made about the project known as **National Assessment,** although many would say that it is much too early to provide any fair evaluation of this enterprise. The project arose during the

1960s, an era of great expansion of Federal support for educational projects. Many Congressmen began to wonder whether the money spent on these programs was being wisely invested, and, as new appropriation bills were passed, a tendency developed to write into the bills provisions that evaluations had to be undertaken to provide evidence of the effectiveness or ineffectiveness of the programs. A group associated within the Carnegie Foundation became interested in the problem of monitoring the overall improvement in education that was expected to occur as a result of the increased expenditures. This group proposed that there be developed a program that would provide evidence of the general progress of education and was able to persuade the Federal government to invest many millions of dollars in it.

The program encountered considerable opposition from those connected with schools, largely because similar programs at the state level had long been recognized as having been disastrous to education, because they had the effect of standardizing education. Under the influence of such programs, teachers would drill the children in their classes in the kinds of problems that the children would have to face on the standardized tests given at the end of the year. In some programs, such as that in California in the 1920s, the teachers were actually paid in terms of the increment in test scores achieved by the children on the state-wide testing program. Such a plan corrupted education even more than it was corrupted by a state-wide testing program that was used only for pupil evaluation and school evaluation. Problems raised by related plans have been well described by Callahan (1962). A book by Rusk (1933) entitled *A History of Infant Education* describes how the principals of schools in Great Britain nearly a hundred years ago were paid in terms of the achievement of pupils, with the result that the pupils with the greatest potential for achievement received the most attention. Such items of educational history made educators very wary of embracing the concept of National Assessment. Added to these criticisms are other criticisms from those who would like to see less of a big brother looking over their shoulders. Such an enterprise, sponsored and financed largely, but not entirely, by the Federal government, would do much to extend the controlling power of the Federal government to education. Nevertheless, despite widespread criticism of this kind, the project has tended to move ahead and has not lacked funds. The sponsors and supporters have tried to answer these criticisms by saying that only very scattered children would be given the tests so that no teacher could ever be evaluated in terms of the results. Also, no child would ever take the entire battery of tests, and there would be no way of knowing which child was going to be tested with what part of the battery, so there would be little incentive for coaching the children on the tests.

A much more serious question is whether the approach used in National Assessment can ever provide evidence concerning progress or lack of progress in education. For example, one might test a cross section of nine-year-old children with reading tests today, and undertake the same kind of testing with nine-year-olds ten years from now. It is quite possible that the average scores of the two groups might not be significantly different and show no significant effects of various programs designed to improve reading. The effects of such programs might not be shown in the results because the programs concentrated on helping perhaps only 5 per cent of the pupils. The improvement in these pupils would be swamped by the other 95 per cent who had not received special help. The problem of showing the effect of a special program designed to help the slow reader is a much more difficult problem than the designers of National Assessment have planned to cope with.

Just what National Assessment can find out that is not already known is difficult to envisage. The data from the project will show that lower socioeconomic groups do less well than the prosperous and that the school districts that spend more money have higher-scoring pupils than those that spend less. The data will also show differences between North and South and between cities and rural areas. All these differences are well established. Whether National Assessment can produce any notably new findings in return for the millions of dollars spent is an open question. Most who view the project from the outside do not expect any great return.

II. PREDICTING PUPIL ACHIEVEMENT

Potential for learning is a term that embraces several concepts. First, there is the concept that individuals are born with a certain potential for learning that may be greater or less than the potential of other individuals. Potential, in this context, refers to an innate capacity to learn. The social context of this concept is that children are born with great individual differences in this respect and that, for each person, there is a limit to the achievement that can be expected of him. In its most naive form, the concept is that some children are born as *A* students, others as *B*s, and some as *F*s. This was a popular concept among both psychologists and teachers early in the century. At that time, it displaced the earlier concept that most children were born with approximately equal potential to learn and that failure to learn when opportunity was provided was a kind of moral failure that had to be punished. One may note that the latter doctrine is still widely held in some countries in which children may be whipped if they do not learn their assigned lessons. The whipping is supposed to tell them that they are responsible for their own learning and that failure is a result of the fact that they did not decide to exert enough effort. The theory is that the whipping will teach them to try as much as is necessary to master the subject matter. The punishment is for moral failure and not for a failure to achieve as such.

The notion that scholastic failure is moral failure was one of the concepts that Binet attacked in his classic studies of human intelligence.

Binet held that there were great innate differences in human capacity to learn and set about the task of developing a device for measuring these differences. The measuring instrument still had a distinctly moral flavor with respect to its use, for it was developed to differentiate between those who could not master the work assigned to them in school because they lacked the innate capacity to do so and those who were indolent. Those lacking the necessary capacity to learn were to be assigned to special classes, and the indolent were to be treated more sternly.

Binet made the basic assumption that there were certain tasks that all children had equal opportunity to master, and these were used in the design of his famous intelligence scale. Those who could not solve the problems at a particular age level, in relation to their own age, were considered to be innately inferior intellectually. Such was the theory on which Binet worked. His scale included a great range of functions related to intelligent behavior. Some of the problems in his scale referred to quite practical activities, such as finding a lost ball in a circular field, but many were verbal in nature. The latter tasks included a test of vocabulary.

In terms of what is known at present about the effect of environmental conditions on the development of intelligence, it can be said with some confidence that many of the tasks called for abilities that develop well only under favorable environmental conditions. We know, for example, that the vocabulary test developed by Binet appears to measure the extent to which the child has been exposed to a highly verbal world such as in the middle-class home. Children who come from underprivileged environments do not develop the same vocabulary as middle-class children, and such children do poorly on vocabulary tests. They also do poorly on all other tasks that involve the manipulation of words. Many tasks that do not appear to be verbal tasks on the surface, such as problem solving, are in many respects verbal tasks, and the child with limited verbal skills will have difficulty in handling them.

The fact is that there are no tasks that all children have had equally favorable backgrounds for handling. Also, one cannot find problems on which children from a disadvantaged environment do as well as children from a favorable environment, although some educators have held the implausible theory that there are tasks at which the child from the disadvantaged environment does better than the child from a good environment. Man's superior problem-solving skill has much to do with his ability to state problems in terms of words and to use his language skills in searching for a solution. The disadvantaged child lacks the very skills that are necessary for effective problem solving.

Binet's intelligence test, subsequent revisions and translations of the famous test, and related devices do not measure native potential as they were supposed to do, but this does not mean that they are wholly useless as devices. Because they cannot measure inborn capacity to act intelligently, they cannot discriminate between those who had inborn intellectual deficiencies and those who were not functioning well in school for other reasons. A low score on such a test *may* be attributable to innate limitations, but it can also be a result of damage to the brain at birth or the effects of an intellectually impoverished environment. A low score does indicate that the individual is not functioning very adequately, but the next stop is to attempt to pinpoint the reason for this. If the low level of intellectual function is believed *not* to be innate, this does not mean that there is any easy way of overcoming the deficiency. If the child has lived under intellectually impoverished conditions for ten years, the resulting limitations on his intelligence are not going to be remedied by placing him for a few months in a rich environment or by providing him with an enriched school program for a year or more. The deficiency is likely to be so deep that it can be overcome only through years of effort, to compensate for the years of deprivation.

The main sources of information on this point come from two sources. One of these is the effect of differences in the environment on identical twins, children who inherit identical genetic structures. In a classic study by Newman et al. (1937), an attempt was made to find sets of identical twins who had been raised apart. Now, identical twins were much more rare at that time than they are today, since fertility drugs have increased greatly the frequency of identical twin births. These investigators did manage to locate twenty-nine pairs. The members of some pairs had been raised in very similar environments, but in the case of a few, one twin had been raised under very favorable conditions for intellectual development and the other under very unfavorable conditions. Such a difference would be comparable to that between a child raised on an isolated farm by uneducated parents and a child raised by parents who had college degrees. The difference in environment produced a difference in intelligence of about twenty-six points on the Binet type of IQ scale. Because an even greater discrepancy can be found, for instance, between the living conditions of the well-to-do educated white and the poor uneducated migrant farm-worker, one can estimate that such differences in environment might produce as great a difference as thirty points on the IQ scale of the Binet type test.

Although we have discussed at length in previous paragraphs the effect of cultural conditions on intelligence-test scores, one should not overlook the new and overwhelming mass of data showing that poor nutrition of the pregnant woman, coupled with poor nutrition of the infant after birth, can have quite disastrous effects on the development of its nervous system. Green et al. (1973) present evidence that poor nutrition of the pregnant woman produces a smaller brain in her child, with a fluid space between the skull and the brain. They also provide startling evidence that even quite specific deficiencies in vitamins may have dramatic effects on the developing intellect. Thus these deprived children grow with inadequate nervous systems, which places them at a disadvantage in a competitive society. What is not known at this time is the extent to which such damage can be reversed by providing improved nutrition or whether the improved nutrition can have impact only on the next generation.

Such differences as have been found in studies of the effect of the environment account for much of the differences in measured intelligence among different groups such as white, black, and Latin. Typical differences among such groups are on the order of ten points — small compared with the differences that can be produced by favorable and unfavorable social positions in the culture. To some extent, equality of educational opportunity may help to eliminate those differences, but education is probably not enough in terms of a 180-day school year of four to six hours per day.

This does not mean that, given genuine equal opportunities for all children, all individual differences among children would disappear. Even among dogs, some are brighter than others. Also, there are obvious individual differences in beauty, size, and other physical attributes that cannot be largely accounted for by differences in environmental conditions. Equality of opportunity would probably reduce greatly the intellectual differences found, but there would still be some differences. These would probably not be tied to social class, skin color, and income of the parents as they are at the present time, but they would be there.

Until social conditions were greatly changed, equality of intellectual opportunity would not eliminate certain other potentially controllable sources of individual differences due to poor nutrition, prenatal conditions, accidents at birth producing brain damage, and some intellectual defects produced by malfunctions of the glandular and metabolic systems. These constitute a major source of mental handicaps, and many could be prevented if greater attention were devoted to the problems involved.

Some psychologists have hoped that tests might be developed that would permit the prediction of adult level of intelligence from performance in infancy. Many attempts have been made to develop such devices, but they have generally failed. The reason for this is quite obvious from what has been said. Let us suppose that such an intelligence test has been given to a child at the age of two, and it is used to predict performance on another intelligence test at the age of ten. Between the ages of two and ten, the environment may be much more or less favorable than it was in the first two years. The eight years that intervene between the two testings may be much more influential in determining his intellectual level at the age of ten than were the first two years of his life. The result is little relationship between performance at age two and performance at age ten (see Bloom, 1964).

One must thus regard an intelligence-test measurement as one providing an indication of the present level of intellectual functioning of the individual, which reflects a combination of factors. The inherited characteristics play a part, but so too does the nature of the experiences to which the individual has been subjected. With respect to the latter, the score reflects the cumulative effects of what has happened to the individual during his entire lifetime. For this reason, the score in relation to that of other children of the same age is not going to be rapidly changed by a good school environment or by placing the child in a stimulating foster home. Such changes will slowly have effects on scores of intelligence tests. A guess, based on the little evidence available, would be that there might be an increase in perhaps one or two IQ points a year. This may seem small, but over a period of ten years it might raise an individual from the state where he probably could not enter college to where he could complete college with quite respectable grades. There are not likely to be any magic programs that can produce such large changes in short order. The intellect is slow to build, and what counts in the building is the nature of the program to which the child is exposed over the years.

Finally, this author would take the position that there is virtue in giving intelligence tests in schools to provide some indication of the *present* level of intellectual functioning of the children, but, when such tests are given, teachers must clearly understand that the scores represent functioning level at that time. Teachers must understand that a part of their task is to provide stimulation and training of those who have lower scores, so that the level of intellectual functioning of these pupils can be slowly raised.

Separate Aptitudes or a Single Sovereign Intelligence

Fifty years ago, before the effect of experience on the development of intelligence was fully recognized, psychologists argued among themselves about whether the intellect could be regarded as consisting of a single unitary trait called intelligence or whether it had a set of quite independent components. Those who believed that the latter was a correct view of the nature of the intellect often took the position that everybody had strong and weak components in his intellectual makeup and that the function of educational guidance was to identify the strong components so that these could be used to greatest advantage. The speculative psychology of the last century, called **faculty psychology,** had long taken the position that the intellect could be regarded as consisting of a number of departments such as imagination, analytical ability, and memory, and each one of these could be either strong or weak. Faculty psychology also took the position that each of these faculties could be trained through proper practice. The problem faced in faculty psychology and by later students of individual differences really has two aspects—the extent to which the intellect can be regarded as consisting of separate and independent components and the extent to which each of the components, if there are such, can be regarded as representing some innate capacity. Complete solutions to both of these problems have never yet been found, though great progress has been made in the development of techniques through which such problems can be studied.

Great progress in the development of an attack on this area occurred in the period between the world wars. The main problem attacked was whether the vast proliferation of tests of various aspects of the intellect could be reduced to a battery involving only a few tests, each of which measured a separate and distinct component of the intellect. The technique that evolved for the study of this problem was **factor analysis,** a sophisticated mathematical technique that provided some hope of discovering what the basic components of the intellect might be. The evidence from factor analysis indicated that there might indeed be many quite distinct components of the intellect, and that these could perhaps be separately measured. On this basis, general intelligence could be regarded as an average performance over several components of the intellect. Factor analysis never provided the clear solutions to problems that the developers of it hoped it would. Indeed, different systems of factor analysis yielded rather different results depending on the assumptions made and the operations performed on the data.

Particularly notable were the contributions of L. L. Thurstone, who spent a lifetime working on the analysis of the intellect. Thurstone believed that the abilities measured by his tests were largely innate components of the intellect. What Thurstone did not know was that most tests designed not to give much advantage to the culturally privileged actually did. Most tests that psychologists believed in the 1930s to represent measures unaffected by special training were not of this nature at all. Thurstone typically used quite abstract materials in the design of his test, with the anticipation that performance on these tests would not be influenced by any special training the person might have had with special kinds of concrete materials. Such tests actually give advantage to children who have had training in the handling of abstract materials. Thurstone eventually developed a battery of tests for children aged eleven to seventeen that he believed measured what he called the **primary mental abilities.** These tests measured six factors — verbal meaning, word fluency, reasoning, memory, number, and space. Thurstone had hopes that the primary mental abilities he believed he had discovered would eventually be demonstrated to be innate components of the intellect, and perhaps even linked to certain genes.

Thurstone's expectations were never fulfilled. Indeed, the work of those that followed him moved in the opposite direction. Rather than a search for components of the intellect that were more and more independent of training and experience, the trend became that of developing measures highly related to experience. The reason for this was the finding that such tests had the best predictive powers.

The later trend in aptitude testing, which came into being during World War II, was associated with the production of tests that emphasized experience and proficiency in particular areas, and the attempt to build items based on experiences that all persons are supposed to have was abandoned. The major classification battery of the armed services of that period included a general verbal test, a test of mechanical knowledge, and a test of electrical knowledge. The latter two tests were used because of their value in predicting success in training men for mechanical or electrical occupational areas. The mechanical and electrical information tests are clearly tied to specific kinds of experience and represent the competence already acquired in such areas. They probably also reflect interest factors. A person not interested in mechanical things is very unlikely to acquire much mechanical information. These tests are based on the theory that the best predictor of future learning is the extent to which the individual has been successful in learning in the corresponding area in the past. Intelligent performance in, say, the mechanical area is a matter of experience, though there is also the possibility that those who expose themselves to mechanical experiences are those who have the aptitude of deriving knowledge from them.

Most aptitude batteries in existence today designed to predict success in training and educational programs are basically tests of broad achievement. They measure specialized knowledge, but the kind that is picked up outside of formal training by those who have the inclination to pick it up. Some batteries of tests include tests of skill in the use of the English language, skill in computation, and skill in reasoning with quantities. Tests of mechanical knowledge and mechanical reasoning are also commonly included. Absent are the kinds of tests that deal with the manipulation of abstract forms or word puzzles, largely because such tests have not shown themselves to be as satisfactory predictors as those tied to more concrete matters. The tests are far different from the kinds that Thurstone sought to use in his investigations.

Despite this practically oriented turn of events, there have remained some theoretically oriented psychologists who have continued to search for fundamental categories of behavior that might be measured by tests. Prominent among these has been Guilford (1967), who has spent his life searching for such a set of categories. The outcome of his research has been a three-way classification of human abilities, a classification that some have compared with the chemist's classification of elements in the periodic table. Whether Guilford's classification of elements in human performance will have the same fundamental status as the periodic table remains to be seen.

Guilford's three dimensions are what he calls **content, operations,** and **products.** Let us explain these categories by considering a specific example. Suppose that a child is given the following problem printed on a sheet of paper: "What city is the capital of France?" The child looks at the problem and answers "Paris." Now one can classify the situation in three ways. One can classify the content of the problem, the operations that the pupil has to perform internally to solve it, and the pupil's product or solution. These are the three dimensions of classification used by Guilford. In the case of our particular problem, its category on the content dimension is semantic, meaning that it is a verbal problem involving the meaning of a sentence. The operation necessary for solving the problem is called cognition, in that it involves the process of knowing. The product is a particular unit — the city Paris.

Guilford provides four categories of content, called figural, symbolic, semantic, and behavioral. These roughly correspond to problems involving figures and diagrams, symbols as in algebra, verbal statements as in our illustrative problem, and problems presented by the behavior of other individuals.

The operations performed in solving problems fall into five categories, called evaluation, convergent production, divergent production, memory, and cognition. A problem in which a child is asked whether there is more water in the tall slim jar than in the short wide one calls for evaluation for its solution. Convergent production and divergent production are broad categories of behavior involved in the solution of problems. They may involve deduction, analysis, synthesis, and many other operations. The essential difference between convergent operation and divergent operation is that the former arrives at a single unique solution that is the only one that will solve the problem. Divergent thinking involves the solution of problems for which many different solutions may exist, and these solutions may lie in many different directions. An example of the latter is development of a new way of frying foods. Solutions might involve the development of new liquids in which to fry, new methods of coating the object to be fried, or perhaps even processes that did not involve immersion but involved spraying the object to be cooked, and so forth.

The outputs of the person confronted with a problem may be classified as units, classes, relations, systems, transformations, or implications. The answer to the question "What is the cost of two oranges priced at five cents each?" is in terms of units, namely cents. The answer to the question "What is the name given to high flat country?" ("A plain") represents a class. An answer that would be classified as a relation would be the answer to the question "Where is Paris located in relation to Rome?" The question "How is the power of the engine of a truck transmitted to the wheels?" calls for an answer that refers to the transmission *system*. The question "What happens to zinc when it is placed in hydrochloric acid?" calls for an answer classified as a transformation, for the person answering the question has to figure out what the zinc is transformed into. The category of implications is self-explanatory.

This classification system means that problems can be of any four kinds of content. Five different sets of internal processes exist for solving the problems, and there may be six different kinds of outputs. Of course, the nature of the problem determines the kind of internal operation needed for solving it and the kind of outcome that can be expected.

Just what will be the use of this kind of classification is hard to say at this time. Some curriculum workers have seen it as an inventory of all of the abilities that can be developed through instruction. However, this does not mean that because man has certain potential abilities they should be developed. Life is probably too short for the development of all of the abilities that might be developed.

Individual Differences and the Organization of Learning

Two kinds of action can be taken to arrange learning so that individual differences may be taken into account. One of these is the practice of grouping children so that those ready to learn particular skills or to acquire particular items of knowledge are grouped together, known as **homogeneous grouping.** Homogeneous grouping may be within a class, or students of different ability levels may be separated into different classes. The alternative is to let each child work at his own pace, and when this is done it is generally referred to as an **individualized program of instruction.** Let us consider each one of these quite briefly.

The practice of homogeneous grouping has long been advocated and looked to as a means of handling individual differences, and research workers have been intrigued with the problem of determining what such grouping accomplishes. Hundreds of studies of this problem have been undertaken, but let us consider the most comprehensive and perhaps the last major effort of this kind, a study undertaken by Borg (1964). The Borg study is a comparison of performance between a school district that adopted the practice of homogeneous grouping and a district in which teachers were encouraged to take into account individual differences and were advised to enrich the programs of the abler pupils with special materials and special experiences. The latter is what teachers often do when faced with a group of unselected pupils. They help the backward and extend the horizons of the more advanced. The study is then not a comparison of classrooms designed to take into account individual differences and classrooms not so designed. It is a study comparing two methods of taking individual differences into account.

The curricula in the two districts were very similar. Achievement was measured by means of a published test that was judged to represent a fair measure of the extent to which the objectives of the school curriculum were achieved. The study was also extended into an attempt to determine the degree to which the two procedures had effects on the personality development of the pupils. It lasted for several years to explore the possibility that one form of grouping might have long-term effects that would not show up in a shorter study.

In terms of the achievement of the pupils in the two educational conditions, no systematic differences favoring the one or the other could be found. Because the homogeneous grouping method of handling individual differences is commonly believed to be better for handling the slow pupil, Borg compared the two procedures also for the slow pupils. Again he found no consistent tendency for one method to be better than the other. The recommendation of the report is that the choice of one or the other method of organizing schools should depend on considerations other than that of achievement.

The Borg study fits well with the findings of the numerous smaller studies that have been undertaken. These smaller studies sometimes show an advantage for homogeneous grouping and sometimes show an advantage for the comparison classes—whatever they happen to be. The general trend of these studies is to show that there are no consistent differences in the achievement and development of pupils who are homogeneously grouped and pupils who are grouped together in unselected classes. Indeed, there seem to be disadvantages to almost any system that is adopted.

The California Test of Personality was given to pupils in both systems. The only consistent finding was that pupils in the homogeneous grouping system showed more "Anti-social Tendencies" than did pupils in the other system. This trend was a fairly clear one through both the elementary and the secondary levels. Other inventories administered gave no indication of any consistent pattern of differences. The same negative findings were also reported in the case of projective tests. A point to note is that these various devices showed *no* trend for one system rather than the other to dispel feelings of inferiority on the part of the slow pupils.

The results of the Borg study are a little difficult to fully interpret. One of the difficulties is that one does not know the extent to which the teachers in unselected classes took steps to recognize individual differences and provide appropriate assignments. If the school system was typical, then one would expect that teachers took quite minimal steps to individualize instruction so that different pupils would be working on different assignments. This minimal recognition of individual differences is far less than it has to be, for one can observe classes in schools in which there is a high degree of individualization. To organize learning in such a way requires great skill on the part of the teacher and a head for planning and organizing. One of the great difficulties encountered by teachers who do individualize instruction to a high degree is keeping track of where each pupil is in the overall curriculum. In schools in which there is a paraprofessional, the task of keeping records may be assigned to that person. If the teacher has to do everything by herself, then individualization calls for record keeping that places a severe demand on her time.

At the time of writing, considerable experimentation is in progress on the use of computers for maintaining student records. Quite simple systems have been devised by which the teacher can type into the computer information related to the tasks that the pupil has been undertaking and his success at them. The information can be retrieved on the computer either through the data being printed out on a screen or through data being typed out on a teletype. Experience with such devices still has to show that they save teachers' time and provide records that are at least as usable as those provided by other means. In addition, the cost factor will also have to be determined, and it will have to be shown that the computer system costs less than the services of the paraprofessional.

In the present experimental systems, the computers are often located at a great distance from the school, but this has no significance. For example, a computer in Iowa serves experimental programs in Seattle as well as other schools in different parts of the country.

The centralized system of records is greatly facilitated if a curriculum is used that has been reduced to a set of packages. Packaged materials can be identified by number and include testing devices that will show the relative standing of the pupil on the particular unit involved. When such materials are used, all that has to be recorded in the computer is the pupil's number, the number of each unit that has been completed, and the performance of the pupil on the test that accompanies the kit. But although the computer fits well into a packaged system of education, many who have pondered the problems of education would doubt whether a really good education is to be found in such a system.

234
• • • • • • • • • •
Appraising and
Predicting Pupil
Achievement

Summary

1 Some of the learning taking place in schools is toward fixed objectives, set in terms of the requirements of the culture. Some of the learning is toward goals that the faculty and the school administration did not anticipate. The one aspect of education requires considerable control over the behavior of the pupil, but the other calls for considerable freedom on the part of both pupils and teachers. The Progressive Education Movement, between the two world wars, was a particularly important sponsor of the latter type of program. An evaluation of the virtues of each type of program has to take into account the extent to which each can provide opportunities for self-initiated behavior. Many forces in our society have encouraged the development of school programs in which an attempt is made to achieve the same goals in all pupils. In particular, the so-called education industry has encouraged the development of this type of education. Uniform, packaged curricula developed for such programs are easily manufactured by the industry.

2 Considerable effort is expended in most educational systems to find out the extent to which preset goals are achieved. A central problem in such an undertaking is the specification of objectives. The idea has long been voiced that objectives should be defined in terms of specific behaviors. The procedure has been influential throughout both education and educational research, but there is always some ambiguity involved in it concerning just what is a specific behavior. One cannot generally list all the specific behaviors that could represent outcomes of learning, so only a sample of these behaviors can be specified. This raises unanswered questions concerning how the sample is to be chosen so that it will be representative. Unless a sample is carefully selected, it can provide a distorted idea of what it is supposed to represent.

3 Teachers also need goals stated in more general terms as a guide to behavior. There is a use for goals stated at all different levels of generality. Such statements of objectives are guides to what happens in the classroom, but they are only guides and should not be in complete control of classroom events.

4 The development of means through which the success of teaching is determined generally requires that the goals to be achieved should be specified. The development of packaged

materials for the classroom also requires that objectives be well specified.

5 Education has long been conducted along lines such that some children succeeded and some failed. The practice of grading on the curve made the assumption that children would differ in the extent to which they achieved the objectives of instruction. Substantial research now suggests that typical school objectives can be achieved in most children. Some children may take longer than other children to achieve a particular objective, but most children can achieve it. This is the concept of mastery learning. Although the concept of mastery learning seems clear, it is not as precise as it seems to be. The advocates of mastery learning suggest that 90 per cent of the children should achieve 90 per cent mastery on all objectives, but just what is meant by 90 per cent mastery? A score of 90 per cent on one test may have very different significance from 90 per cent on another test. The concept of 90 per cent mastery is little more than a catch phrase. In addition, 90 per cent mastery today does not mean that the child will have 90 per cent mastery tomorrow. Learning is not that permanent. Repeated review appears to be necessary to produce lasting learning, and efficient education is that which produces lasting learning.

6 Attempts have been made to classify objectives, much as botanists have attempted to develop classifications of plants. The classifications that have emerged have provided a useful way of classifying test items. Unfortunately, these classifications have not been based on a scientific theory of how ideas are ordered or should be ordered, but rather have been intuitively derived. Systems of classification based on intuition have not had much success in the history of science. At the present time, the behavioral sciences have not provided the foundation necessary for developing a scientific classification system of objectives and of behavior.

7 An educational program should have built into it a means of determining the extent to which it is successful. The success of an educational program should be determined, as far as is feasible, through a study of the behavior of its graduates in real-life situations. Did the program really make a difference to them in their day-to-day lives? This is a crucial question that should be answered. However, there are serious difficulties involved in evaluating programs in this kind of way, and the results of such evaluations are often difficult to interpret. Follow-up studies have typically been used to evaluate compensatory education. The difficulty with such studies

is that the effect of compensatory education becomes quickly diluted with the other influences that have impact on the child.

8 Teachers may obtain some evidence of the extent to which some goals are achieved by observing the behavior of children in school situations or by obtaining information concerning how the pupils behave outside of school. In order for the teacher to do this effectively, in many areas, appropriate organization on the part of the school is necessary.

9 Most teachers rely on tests they have made in order to keep track of what their pupils are learning. The ease with which such tests are given tends to make the teacher rely on them and to ignore other and more difficult ways of evaluating pupil progress based on observation.

10 Inadequacies in classroom tests all involve issues related to the reliability or validity of the tests. A valid achievement test is one in which the test problems are relevant to measuring the outcomes of the course. An examination must also test a sufficient sample of the skills and knowledges involved so that the scores of the pupils are closely comparable to those that would be obtained from another sufficient sample. Essay tests tend to be unreliable because they cannot be scored reliably. Objective tests are likely to be unreliable, when made by teachers, because they are too short, and guessing plays an important factor in determining a student's score. Because objective tests are tedious to write, teachers do well to pool their test items.

11 Standardized tests have had the unfortunate history of exercising control over the curriculum. Such tests also tend to restrict themselves to outcomes that are widely endorsed, but these may represent a quite narrow range of outcomes. The school administration does like to have the data provided by standardized tests to justify the school program, even though such tests cannot really provide a strong justification. Such tests are unlikely to tell the teacher much that he does not already know. A competent teacher should know much more about the pupils than a standardized test can provide.

12 There can be no doubt that examinations have incentive value and improve learning. The examination sets a deadline for the procrastinating pupil and provides aversive conditions if he does not meet the deadline. Nevertheless, the uniform class examination carries with it bad features, including the fact that it requires all pupils to work at the same rate. The individualized examination has merit, but it should also involve the setting of an individual deadline for the individual

pupil. Unfortunately, the pace of learning is set more by the customs that have evolved in the group of students than by the rates at which students can learn. Examinations also provide incentives for retaining material learned. Intent to remember is an important factor in transferring information to long-term memory. Expectation of future usage is an important factor in retention.

13 Attempts have long been made to develop diagnostic tests that will indicate the particular weaknesses in a pupil's knowledge and skills. A major problem in the development of such tests is that there is usually no agreement concerning how the skill or area of knowledge should be divided up. Mathematics represents one of the few areas in which one can make a set of diagnostic tests on the basis of a set of well-established categories. In order for a diagnostic test to be effective, the parts have to provide reliable measures, and for them to do this they have to be quite long. In fact, a battery may have to be so long that one may doubt whether the giving of it justifies the time involved.

14 Interest has been rearoused in recent years about the possibility of assessing the state of education by giving national tests. Education has had a long history of attempting to do this at the state and local levels. In the past century, many teachers were paid in terms of how well their students performed on standardized tests. In England, the entire system was dominated by this practice for most of the last half of the previous century. The payment-by-results system proved to be not only demoralizing to teachers but also damaging to the development of the curriculum. There are real questions that might be asked about whether National Assessment can yield information useful for guiding the future of education.

15 Psychologists have long been interested in measuring potential for learning. Attempts to measure potential have often been based on the idea that measures of potential are measures of innate abilities. Tests of IQ were originally developed in the hope that they would measure innate ability to learn. Research has now established that scores on such tests are highly influenced by the conditions under which a child is raised. Although attempts have been made to develop test items that even underprivileged children should be able to handle, these items are still greatly influenced by environmental circumstances. A low score on such a test may reflect limited innate capacity, but it may also reflect a disadvantaged background. A low score indicates that the person is not functioning very adequately in the intellectual realm but

says nothing about the causes of the condition. Intellectual inadequacies resulting from poor environmental conditions cannot be quickly remedied but require prolonged exposure to an improved environment. Some intellectual inadequacies can be attributed to poor nutrition either before birth or during the early years of life.

16 Attempts have been made to break down general intelligence into a set of distinct components. Faculty psychology was a speculative early attempt to do this. Later research based on factor analysis indicated that there might be several distinct components of general intelligence. Thurstone developed what he described as a set of primary mental abilities. Thurstone hoped that these would represent distinct inheritable components of intelligence, but his hopes were not fulfilled. Indeed, the components of intelligence that it has been most profitable to measure have been those that are clearly tied to specific training and experience. Most modern batteries of aptitude tests might well be described as tests of achievement. Guilford has attempted to provide a complete inventory of all the components of intellect. The classification has been influential in directing the attention of educators to aspects of intellect such as those involved in convergent and divergent thinking.

17 Attempts to group pupils in terms of their learning aptitudes have not been particularly successful in improving learning. If such a system of grouping is used, it should be introduced for reasons other than that of promoting academic achievement.

239
. . . .
Summary

Most learning studies have to do with the various conditions under which a response will be acquired, retained, made more frequent, or become inhibited. Research on memory is primarily concerned with the internal processes that have to do with the storage of information and the later retrieval of that information. The immediate purpose of such research is the building of a model of human memory, some kind of representation of what the mechanisms are like. Until a decade ago, one would have been hard pressed to locate a book or article that focused on that problem, but today there is a substantial scientific literature devoted to the topic. The reader is referred to the book by Adams (1967), which provides an excellent source of references up to the time when it was published. Later works by Norman (1969) and Howe (1970) provide rather less technical accounts of the problems that research workers are study-

Memory

ing and the findings. Topics related to memory, such as the nature and function of imagery, are now also receiving attention that they have not received for half a century and are generating important research programs. These are topics that will be considered in this chapter.

Most studies of learning are concerned with how various conditions in the world of the learner facilitate or interfere with the subsequent retention of whatever is learned. The learner takes in information and may be able to reproduce it later with more or less precision. The study of memory is the study of the processes that intervene between the taking in of information and the subsequent reproduction of that information. These are all internal processes and, because they reside inside the learner, are often very difficult to study. Scientists have had a long and successful history of making accurate inferences about hidden processes. For example, scientists knew a great deal about atoms long before they had the apparatus to obtain precise information about atomic structures. The physicist J. J. Thomson was able to study electrons before there was any direct evidence that electrons were real particles. The psychologist is able to make inferences about the nature of memory even though he cannot look right inside the brain and see what happens to the individual nerve cells through which information is stored. The psychologist, like the physicist, has learned to make inferences from laboratory data carefully collected for that purpose.

Most of education is planned on the basis of a very simple theory of memory, which might be stated by saying that individuals are able to "remember" what they have been exposed to. In accordance with this theory, the teacher provides demonstrations of how to perform particular mathematical operations and anticipates that children will absorb the essence of the demonstration. Children are also exposed to examples of good literary style in anticipation that they will absorb enough about good style to be able to write clearly and correctly. Every teacher also knows that the theory of memory and the system of instruction based on it do not always work out very well. Some children do not remember much about what they have been exposed to. There is obviously much more to the matter of memory than the simple theory implies. Indeed, modern theory of memory has a lot to say about the conditions under which information will be remembered and the length of time that the information will be remembered. Before taking up such matters, let us consider the important educational problem of what information should be committed to memory in a well-designed curriculum.

Children at all levels of education spend a great amount of time learning by heart all kinds of materials. Now there can be no doubt that some information of great utility has to be learned thoroughly and permanently early in life, because it has very general utility. A child has to be able to learn and to use thousands of words, for the forgetting of the name of a common object would be awkward, if not embarrassing, as the aphasic finds when he acquires this difficulty. Although there can be no question that some information has to be permanently stored inside the individual, his storage of useful information is not confined to what he can put inside of himself. Reference books and libraries of knowledge exist so that the individual can have access to a much wider range of knowledge than he can possibly store within himself. In order to use the library, he has to have some information stored inside of him that will lead him to the right place in the library. He has to know, for example, that in order to obtain information about the size of wire to use in replacing a wire in his house, he should go to a book on practical electricity or home construction and not to a dictionary or encyclopedia.

How much information and what kind of information should be stored in the brain are difficult to determine. Educators have proposed a number of quite different solutions to this problem.

One solution proposes that the learner be required to commit to memory as much information as he possibly can. This was the solution offered by many educators in the last century, when countless hours were spent by each child in committing to memory a vast number of details about the world. This solution really was a leftover from the Dark Ages, when students did not have books of their own and the knowledge they had available was the knowledge stored in their brains. In the early days of education, the professor had access to books or manuscripts, and these he often read to his class and required the students to memorize large sections of them. Most of the students would not later have ready access to the books or manuscripts, and the material memorized represented the only lasting contact they would have with knowledge contained in these documents. The practice of memorizing large quantities of information was perpetuated long past the time in history when, for reason of lack of books, it could be justified. In modern times it has been justified by other rationalizations that are probably quite irrelevant, namely, that a broad base of memorized information provides the individual with the key to all other sources of knowledge.

A second approach to the problem is to provide the student with a smattering of knowledge in a great range of areas, giving special attention to what are considered to be the key concepts involved. Within this program, the person who learns what the teacher believes to be the most significant events of history has a framework from which he can explore the details or the background related to those events. A little knowledge of chemistry and physiology, provided it involves the key terms and principles, gives the individual access to a great range of technical literature to which he can refer in working on a problem. This solution to the problem of what to memorize has a certain amount of merit to it. A knowledge of key terms and concepts is a store of information much like a library card catalogue, for it helps one to locate books in which additional related information can be found. To be useful it has to be well organized, just as a real library catalogue has to be.

Controversy centers around the question of what the key facts are that should be memorized. The controversy is clearly seen in the work of the **Biological Sciences Curriculum Study.** This study set out with the object of developing a thoroughly modern textbook on biology for high schools. The experts brought together to plan a textbook of general biology could not agree on what it should contain. The experts finally agreed on plans for three different textbooks that approached biology from very different viewpoints, and three textbooks were written. The books do, inevitably, overlap to some degree in content, but there is also a great amount of nonoverlapping content. There may be some agreement on what the key concepts are in each of the three approaches, but they are too numerous to be included within a single course. A study of just one of the texts probably does not provide a sufficient base from which one can go on to explore all other aspects of biology in the reference literature in the library.

This second approach has merit, but it does not completely solve the problem of equipping the pupil with the information that will give him access to all other information in other books.

The third approach, which may be coupled with the second approach, is that of requiring the pupil to use reference sources. In the use of such an approach, the teacher may adopt the policy of never answering directly the questions asked by the pupil. The teacher's role is that of helping the pupil find the correct resource in which he can locate the information. Such procedures do give children access to large amounts of information stored in libraries but do not necessarily develop the habit of searching for information whenever it is needed. This third approach is sufficiently widely used in schools that many standardized batteries of achievement tests have sections appraising the pupil's skill in using and locating sources of information. The main drawback to the approach is that it may not provide a very efficient way of acquiring knowledge. A child may spend substantial amounts of time looking for a particular item of information when the teacher could give him the information without delay. Of course, he has also learned other things while looking for the information, for he has learned where to find it.

Short-Term Memory Systems

The day is filled with incidents, most of which will not be remembered by tomorrow. If one were to remember all of the trivia he encountered during a day, he would be a vast information source cluttered with inconsequential items. I stare at the crowd on the subway or bus, noticing briefly the woman with the red hat, the tired factory worker, the sickly child, the advertisement on the wall, and so forth. Tomorrow these will not even be ghosts in my memory system. They will have no more place there than if they had never happened. The human being does have a short-term memory system that enables him to take note of the ongoing flow of events, sort out the events that have some significance for him, take appropriate action, and then forget the whole affair. I am standing on the bus; I see somebody about to rise from his seat and leave the bus, so I move over to the seat and sit down. The chances are I will have forgotten the entire incident by the next day. These are the kinds of trivia that one may remember for a short time, but readily forget. Some of the information from such incidents may be recorded in a more permanent memory system. For example, somebody may ask me "How often do you manage to find a seat on the bus when you are coming back from work?" I think for a minute and then answer that I find a seat about as often as not. What has been recorded in permanent memory is information about the probability that the particular event of finding a seat will occur. The circumstances under which a seat was obtained on any particular day fade from the memory system.

We all take for granted that we have a short-term memory system that will dispose of trivial memories, but we expect the child to remember everything. "Didn't I tell you yesterday, Mike, not to run in the halls!" Tomorrow Mike will once more hear the same admonition. The event is just one of the daily trivia that his memory system disposes of before the next day. Children, as well as adults, have memory systems that hold much information for only a short period of time. Information is transferred from the short-term to the long-term memory system only under certain exceptional circumstances that will be discussed later.

Short-term memory exists as a system to handle the daily exigencies of living that require the retention of information for only a short time and to prevent cluttering of the long-term memory system. Indeed, the capacity of the long-term system might not be large enough to handle all of the details of life that one encounters in a single week. Some have suggested that the long-term memory system may not even have the capacity of recording and retaining all of the information that confronts us when we see a single scene.

Let us consider short-term memory further. It is not only an important function in itself, serving us well in daily life, but it also provides a key to understanding some of the characteristics of the long-term memory system.

First, let us note that the short-term memory is selective in what it retains. It does not gather up all the details related to the trivia it retains for a short period. As I leave the bus, I may recall the fact that I occupied a seat vacated by a lady who left at an earlier stop, but I may not remember the color of her hat, how tall she was, or whether she was young or old. These and many other details were not recorded. Now I had seen all of these details at the time the lady stood up and vacated the seat, but I remember only the fact that the seat was vacated by a lady. Sperling (1960), who conducted classic experiments on a laboratory version of this kind of problem, wrote that one sees much but retains little. A child in a classroom sees much but retains little. One of the problems of the teacher is to see that he retains the important features of what he is exposed to and not the trivial features. This is sometimes quite difficult to do.

In one of Sperling's experiments, he flashed on a screen nine letters or numbers arranged in a three by three square. After such a brief exposure, his subjects could generally repeat back four or five of the letters or numbers, and these might come from any part of the display. If they were told, in advance, to concentrate on a particular row, then they could easily take note of that row and repeat back the letters or numbers in it. Such a finding is not very important, for they could just read the letters in the row and call them back to the experimenter. What was surprising was that, if a signal was given concerning which row was to be read as long as a second after the termination of the flash then a subject could still read back the designated row. But how could he be reading the row of letters when they were no longer there? One assumes that what he was reading was some lingering internal image of the letters. This lingering internal representation of the letters is referred to as a **trace** or **buffer.** One assumes that the trace is a detailed internal representation of the stimulus that lasts up to about one and a half or two seconds. At the end of that time, it will have faded into oblivion.

Psychologists have long supposed that such a trace exists. In conditioning experiments, it has been shown that a dog can become conditioned to salivate at the sound of a bell even if the food is delayed for several seconds after the bell. The assumption is made that the food becomes associated with the lingering trace of the bell.

The trace is rich in information, but what is pulled from the trace for further retention is just a small amount of information. In the case of the numbers and letters presented in the type of experiment undertaken by Sperling, just four or five digits or letters are pulled from the trace. This same number of elements, just four or five, is pulled even when sixteen or twenty or more elements are presented in the first place. This is a sophisticated way of saying that we see much but recognize little.

The elements pulled from the trace are then retained in the short-term memory system. Although we know that the trace fades in two seconds or less, we know much less about the way in which information is lost from the short-term memory system. Most psychological experiments on memory undertaken in the laboratory require the retention of information for short periods of time rarely in excess of thirty minutes. Presumably, some information is retained in the short-term memory system for longer periods, but the course of this retention and loss has not been plotted. One can require a subject in an experiment to learn a set of twelve nonsense syllables by a procedure in which he reads the list, then tries to recall the syllables, and then he reads the list again, and so forth. After about twelve trials, he will be able to write out or say all the nonsense syllables. If one then lets him read a magazine for fifteen minutes, he may, at the end of the reading period, be able to recall perhaps half of the syllables. If the reading period had been an hour, then only two or three might be recalled. The information would be slowly disappearing from short-term memory. Next day, he might not remember any of the syllables. However, some of the information about the syllables would still be there in a latent form. One can demonstrate this fact by asking the person to relearn the series. One would probably find that, after only two repetitions of the list of syllables, the subject would be able to recall the entire list once more. The information has been lost from what can be readily and immediately recalled, and has been transferred to the long-term memory system. In the latter system, a residue remains that still can continue to influence behavior. The syllables have had a longer life in the memory system than did the memory of the transitory encounter with the lady in the bus. If the exposure to the syllables had involved only a single reading, then the number immediately recalled might have been no more than three or four, and the retention of these syllables might also have been extremely transitory. Much of what happens in school is not too different from a transitory encounter. Small wonder it is that the information involved often reaches no further than the short-term memory system of the pupil.

There has to be some mechanism that eradicates the trace. If there were not an erasure mechanism, the perception of one scene would be likely to interfere with the perception of the next scene to which one turns one's head. It is likely that when one's attention is turned to a new scene the attention process automatically eradicates the trace left by what one was attending to previously. Without such an erasure mechanism, a delay of about two seconds would be required between attending to one scene and attending to the next so that the trace of the first could fade. The erasure process is probably not quite instantaneous, and this may well be the reason why there seems to be some time lost when one shifts attention from one source of information to another. Various estimates have been made of the time lost in shifting attention, a kind of time out from the game of perceiving; it is found to be about a third of a second.

The trace is what is called a **holding mechanism.** That is to say, it holds information for a short time and thereby prevents information from becoming lost and unusable. In the case of hearing, the trace has a function not quite so obvious as in visual perception. If one is listening to a sentence, he generally has to listen to the entire sentence before he can tease the meaning out of it. If there were no holding mechanism involved in hearing, then one would not be able to understand much of language. If a sentence is very long, components of the sentence have to be transferred to short-term memory, where they are temporarily held while the rest of the sentence is being analyzed. Sometimes, in reading a long sentence, one has to go back over it several times. This is because elements of it have been lost from the short-term memory system. Because of this kind of difficulty, most speakers and writers tend to avoid using very long sentences. This is particularly important in the case of speech, because it is often inopportune to have the speaker repeat what he has just said. In the case of written materials, longer sentences are permissible because there is opportunity for rereading.

Most of those who have written about teaching the native language to children have noted that the younger the child, the shorter is the sentence that he can handle. This appears to be a result of the fact that children have a smaller capacity than adults for holding information in temporary storage.

Many common tasks can be identified in which one is responding to the trace rather than to the actual stimulus. The secretary who is taking shorthand is generally writing down what was said a second or two before, not what is being said at the actual time she writes. What the secretary writes down is the information in the trace. The Morse code receiver has to wait until the end of each group of dots and dashes before he can decide what letter to write, because a dash–dot means one thing and a dash–dot–dot another. He waits until the complete letter is in the trace, and then he writes down the letter.

The trace system can hold very large amounts of information for a very short time. In contrast, the short-term memory system is believed to be a rather small-capacity system. Most of the experiments undertaken on short-term memory in laboratories involve quite small amounts of information such as ten nonsense syllables or ten pairs of words. Longer lists become extremely difficult or tedious to learn. A list of twenty nonsense syllables may require four or five times as many repetitions to learn as a ten-syllable list that is quite easily mastered.

The durability of information in the short-term memory system is a matter of debate. In the experiments on what is here called short-term memory, the assumption is commonly made that one is dealing with memory for material lasting perhaps as long as thirty minutes but not much longer. Graphs can be drawn showing exactly how information decays in the trace system, but a graph cannot be produced that would be widely accepted to show how information is lost from the short-term memory system. The typical curve of forgetting, which shows a rapid decline immediately after learning and a much slower decline thereafter, probably reflects the rate at which the short-term memory loses information. The amount that remains, after hours or days, probably represents a small residual that is transferred to the long-term memory system. The life of information in the short-term memory system remains a matter of speculation to be resolved through experimentation.

Filtering of Information

Broadbent (1971) has long proposed that between the trace or buffer and the short-term memory there is something analogous to a filter. That is, according to this analogy, only a small amount of information in the trace enters the short-term memory system because this is all that the filter permits to pass. The analogy can be further extended to propose that the filter can be set to pass only certain items of information. Thus, when one is searching for mislaid car keys, the filter would be set for seeing the car keys. One simply does not notice the hundreds of objects he encounters during the search, but as soon as the car keys come into the field of vision they are immediately seen. In the same way, in looking for a particular topic in a textbook, one may scan thousands of words without noticing any of them in any detail, but as soon as the key word related to the topic appears, one knows immediately that he has found what he wants. Broadbent states that the filter can be set for receiving one channel of communication rather than another. In a crowded room filled with the buzz of conversation, one may listen to only one voice and virtually exclude all other voices. This is commonly called selective attention, but such a name does little to describe what is taking place.

The filter may also be set to give priority to certain classes of information that have great significance for the individual. One can hear one's name being mentioned even amid the din of many simultaneous voices. The exclamation "Fire!" is almost certain to attract attention, even though spoken relatively softly. The filter also passes any unusual communication, as when an impolite word is said in overpolite company.

The filter analogy does a good job of describing some of the common perceptual phenomena such as selective attention, but there are others that do not fit the filter concept too well. In the case of vision, we do appear to scan the visual world and take first one sample and then another of the trace. In viewing a work of art for the first time, we may be immediately struck by the mountains included in it, if the filter is set to pass anything that has to do with mountains because we like mountains. We do go on to inspect other parts of the picture, inspecting successively the figure in the foreground, the trees, the sky, and the dwelling. However, we also behave at other times as though we kept on obtaining successive samples of information until we had enough information to enable us to handle the situation presented. Information does not always have to go through a filtering mechanism.

Why There Seem to Be Two Major Memory Systems

Many lines of evidence suggest that there are two distinct systems of memory rather than one. Perhaps the most impressive source of evidence comes from the study of patients who have had injury to the brain through tumor, accident, or necessary surgery. Adams (1967) and later Broadbent (1970) have summarized the evidence, which comes mainly from medical literature.

In these cases, patients have shown an inability to enter new information into their long-term memory system. Such patients do not generally show much difficulty in remembering what they had learned before the damage took place. A person may thus remember how to find his way around the neighborhood with which he has long had familiarity, but he may find it virtually impossible to master the geography of a new neighborhood. In addition, such a person can retain new information for a short period of time. In one case, the patient had to move to a new street but, ten months after the move, he had not been able to learn the new address and was lost if he ventured more than a block from the house. His difficulties became particularly evident in locating the place where common objects were stored in the house. When told where to find an object, he was able to remember the information long enough to locate the object, but if he had to find the same object an hour later, he would have to ask once more where to find it. Because he was unable to remember any new information for more than a short while, he could read the same story again and again, enjoying it as though it were the first time he had ever read it.

The neurological data suggest the existence of a short-term memory system, a long-term memory system, and a mechanism for transferring information from the one to the other. The reader interested in learning more about the details of this phenomenon is referred to an experimental study by Wickelgren (1968). The patient showed all of the characteristics of those who have been discussed, but Wickelgren was able to obtain some quite precise data that strongly suggested the existence of two memory systems rather than one.

A second important source of evidence summarized by both Adams and Broadbent is that confusions in memory are different for short-term memory than for long-term memory. In short-term memory, errors of recall are likely to involve similar-sounding words, whereas errors of long-term memory involve confusions of meaning. A person sees a series of words flashed on the screen, and these he rapidly reads. One of the words is *tree*, but when he comes to recall it immediately after the words have been presented, he says that the word was "something like *free*." This represents what is called auditory confusion. In long-term memory, a typical error would be to recall the word *tree* as *wood*. This is a confusion of meaning or a semantic confusion. In recalling information from the long-term memory system, one can often recall a word in the same general memory category but not the exact word.

Another source of evidence is found in a study by Kleinsmith and Kaplan (1963), which has been repeated and verified a number of times. These research workers exposed their subjects to a paired-associate learning task, requiring them to learn to say the second word of each pair of words when the first was given. The experiment showed that the conditions favorable for long-term memory are not necessarily the conditions that favor short-term memory. The data seemed to show that when information is easily recalled from short-term memory, it is not information readily transferred to long-term memory.

There is a related line of evidence explored in a series of studies summarized by Lewis and Bartz (1970), who also conducted a study of their own. The essential feature of these studies is the demonstration that items of a list of words that are most readily recalled immediately after learning are often the items that are the most difficult to recall after a period of time has elapsed. The data show that, after a list of words is read, the last words are the easiest ones to recall but they are the ones least learned, as is evident from later tests. Similar findings have been reported by Craik (1970).

The last cited study has some implications for teachers, who often mistake immediate recall for permanent learning. A teacher goes over a set of facts and then tests the pupils to find out what they have retained. If they show immediate memory for the facts, he is likely to assume that the children have learned the material. But what he is testing is immediate recall, and immediate recall is a very poor criterion of how much learning has taken place.

Other evidence could be cited here to indicate that there are two basic memory systems and not a single one, but enough has been said. The importance of the theory of a dual-process memory system for the teacher is that it reveals that information is not necessarily and automatically transferred from the short-term memory system to the long-term system. Indeed, the short-term memory system is essentially a system that discards most of the information that enters into it. The short-term memory system performs many important functions in handling information needed for only a short time, but it is not the seat of learning.

Short-term memory is sometimes referred to as **primary memory** or as the **primitive memory system.** In a sense, the latter term describes it rather well, for the system appears to be unaffected by age and education or level of ability. Walen (1970) has shown that adults and fifth-grade children have about the same capacity for holding information in short-term memory. Also, data from intelligence tests including both tasks involving short-term memory and tasks involving reasoning show that the children classified as dull on the basis of IQ do just about as well on short-term memory tasks as those classified as bright on the same basis. The short-term memory system is a primitive mechanism for holding information for short periods of time. It involves recognition of the information, but reasoning and other forms of thinking activities are not a part of the system, although one may think about the information in the short-term memory system.

Walen's study has some other findings that are quite difficult to interpret. The children took longer than the adults to reach a particular criterion of learning. This is entirely within expectation in that rate of learning is generally believed to increase until the early twenties. However, when the adults and children learned the material to the same degree and were tested after seven days, the children showed the greatest degree of retention. It is not known whether children have inherently better memories or whether they have had fewer factors in their lives that might disrupt the remembered material. Children also have a way of rehearsing what they have learned in experiments as a kind of game among themselves. It is very doubtful that children have better memories than adults, although this belief is widely held among the public.

Transfer to Long-Term Memory

A crucial problem in education is how information is transferred from short-term memory to long-term memory and how to facilitate that transfer. Although one can provide some rule-of-thumb methods for facilitation, virtually nothing is known about the mechanism involved. Let us begin with the long-discussed method of memorization known as **rehearsal.**

Rehearsal: A person who has to memorize material may approach the problem in many different ways. One way is to read and reread the material. Another is to spend part of the time in reading the material and a part of the time in rehearsing it internally. The essence of rehearsal is that it involves responses similar to those that take place when the material is being read, but the responses are made in the absence of the printed material. In a classic experiment by Gates (1917), it was shown that much more was learned if the substantial part of the time was devoted to rehearsal and minimal amount of time to the actual reading of the material. The results of Gates' experiment have never been seriously questioned. The traditional explanation of the results has been that rehearsal permits the individual to practice the response he wants to perfect, namely, the ability to recite the material without the aid of the source or prompts. However, it now seems clear that rehearsal and the holding of information in short-term memory perform other functions significant for the transfer of information to the long-term memory system. Some of the factors involved have been brought to light by the work of Tulving, but much more needs to be discovered about this very significant phenomenon.

Tulving (1967) showed a list of twenty-two nouns, at a rate of one per second, to his subjects for sixteen trials. After each trial, the subjects were given forty-four seconds in which to recall orally all the words they could remember from the list. At the end of the forty-four seconds, one group then proceeded to the next reading of the list of words. A second group was instructed at the end of the forty-four second interval to attempt, once again, to recall orally all the words they could remember. Thus one group performed a second recall task while the other group was reading the list. One interesting finding was that the group that performed twice as many readings of the list as the other group showed about the same amount of learning as the group that made twice as many efforts to recall. Reading the list once produces just about as much learning as attempting to recall the list once. The difference in the learning for the two groups was small, but the group that spent the greater amount of time in recall activity had a slight edge over the other group. This difference is not as dramatic as in the original Gates study, but it is there, once again stressing the importance of the activity of the learner if the information is to be transferred to the long-term memory system. Tulving turned up some other interesting findings. One is that, on two successive attempts to recall the words, the same words may not be recalled. A word that a person is unable to recall may not be lost from his memory system, but he may not be able to retrieve it at a particular moment. Given an additional attempt to recall, less than a minute later, he may be able to remember the word. Such data suggest that rehearsal may be effective because it gives the person practice in retrieving information. Perhaps the information gets into the long-term memory system quite early in the process of undertaking a learning task, but the information cannot be readily retrieved. Rehearsal improves retrieval. What has been said here is quite speculative, but the discussion has been introduced so that the reader will be on guard against adopting any simplistic view of rehearsal, such as the one suggesting that rehearsal is merely a matter of practicing the response to be performed.

Another point to note is that rehearsal also involves placing the information, once again, into the short-term memory system. Putting it in and out of the short-term memory system seems to result in some advantage in making the information retrievable. In a sense, all retrieval of information involves obtaining the information from the long-term system and placing it in a register much like that of the short-term memory register.

Organization: Over two centuries ago, the great German philosopher and pedagogue Johann Frederick Herbart took the position that an important condition for memorizing material is **organization.** He proposed that the human memory was an organized bank of information and that information had to fit into that organization if it was to be retained. Although this opinion has long been a cornerstone of education, only in the last decade has there been any concerted attempt to investigate its validity.

There is substantial evidence that information received in short-term memory, if it lacks organization, tends to be organized before it is transferred to long-term memory. Bower et al. (1969) have reviewed studies showing that when individuals learn lists of words they do not typically repeat back the words in the same order in which they have been received. If the words represent a mixed group of common nouns, there is a tendency for the person recalling the list to group the words in terms of categories. If the words *paper*, *ink*, and *print* appeared in different parts of the list, then, on recall, the individual would be likely to list these words together. Such grouping of words on recall is helped if the individual is able to write out his responses. The grouping together of words in related categories is a common feature of the memorization process. If individuals gain by organizing what they have to remember, then it would seem very likely, and consistent with common experience, that material organized prior to presentation should be more readily memorized than material not so organized. Puff (1970) has reviewed studies showing that words organized in groups are more readily learned than when they are not thus clustered in advance. Puff has also undertaken a study of his own.

Now let us return to the well-established fact that organized information is generally, but not always, more easily learned than is poorly organized or disorganized material. An explanation for this phenomenon has not been well established, but some reasonable guesses can be made. One is that the learning of words in a category involves learning a name for that category. The words *hat*, *socks*, *suit*, and *shirt* are grouped into the category *clothing*. By remembering the name of the category, one then knows where to look in the memory system. There is certainly some support for the position that a search of the memory system, without any clues concerning where to look, is an almost hopeless task. It is like looking for a book in a large library when one does not know the section in which to look. Another result of grouping words is that one makes use of associations already learned. One already has associations between such words as *hat, socks, suit,* and *shirt,* and he has to strengthen these associations only a little for the words to hang together as a group and then to be easily recalled as a group. If words are unassociated in the first place, then the building of associations between them may be a very tedious and time-consuming task.

Thus it is quite evident that the curriculum designer, textbook writer, and teacher have a responsibility to organize material before it is presented to the learner. This is easier said than done; educators have long recognized that the organization of subject matter is a critical task, but no sure way of developing good subject matter organization has yet been developed. Those originally concerned with this problem were the teachers in the monastic schools of the Middle Ages. In these schools, the catechisms that were developed supposedly reflected the best order for learning in which subject matter could be arranged. In more recent times, those interested in operant conditioning have revived interest in this ancient art, largely because B. F. Skinner has stressed the importance of acquiring complex skills piecemeal but in an order facilitative of learning. Programmed learning, the modern version of the medieval catechism, is one of the products of this new preoccupation with the problem of ordering subject matter. In such instructional devices, the order selected is generally derived intuitively by the person preparing the materials. There may or may not be some kind of tryout of the materials thus ordered. When there is a tryout, then there is some opportunity for identifying the items of information that come too early or too late in the sequence, but most programmed materials have only intuition to support the order in which materials are placed.

The procedure commonly adopted is that proposed by Gagné (1970). His suggestion is that the first step in organizing subject matter is to establish the final objective to be achieved. The next step is to note the immediate prerequisite skill or skills that have to be acquired for the attainment of the final objective. Then each one of these prerequisite skills is analyzed in terms of skills that are prerequisites for them in turn. Thus the procedure is pushed further and further back. This form of analysis is quite easy in elementary mathematics. One can, for example, look at the process of multiplying together two two-digit numbers and see that one prerequisite skill is that of multiplying together single-digit numbers. Another prerequisite is addition. A prerequisite for addition is being able to count, and a prerequisite for counting is being able to arrange objects in serial order. Much less easy to establish are the prerequistes for developing the concept of democracy, or the concept of good style in writing, or the concept of mass in physics, or the concept of a vacuum. Most areas do not consist of subject matter that can be easily ordered into a particular sequence. This is why textbooks on almost any school subject show great differences in the order in which ideas are presented.

For example, most educators agree that children should learn something about the geography of the country in which they live and of the world to which they belong, but there is little agreement concerning which facts are the crucial and important ones and how these facts should be organized. Logic is obviously not the basis on which subject matter in such an area should be organized. One can make some argument for beginning with the local community and the surrounding region and working out to more and more remote areas, but there are probably as many ways of organizing the subject matter as there are courses of study available. Certainly nobody has yet shown that one way of ordering this kind of subject matter is better than other ways of doing so in terms of ease of learning. Perhaps it may not make much difference which method of organization is used, provided the student sees and understands the structure.

A special case of the effect of an organizing factor on the retention of information is found in the use of what are referred to as **advance organizers,** a term originally invented by Ausubel and described in detail by Ausubel and Robinson (1969). The essential notion of an advance organizer is that, prior to being presented with a particular subject matter, the pupil should be given ideas around which he can build the new knowledge. The advance organizer is a set of ideas that performs two functions. First, these ideas link up the new knowledge with what the student has already acquired. Second, the advance organizer may help the student to bring order into the new material. A teacher telling children about X-rays might begin by pointing out examples of energy that can be seen but cannot be sensed by the skin and of energy that can be sensed by the skin, such as heat, and cannot be seen. The idea that energy can be directly experienced only when one is equipped with an appropriate sense organ might represent a concept around which the idea of an invisible X-ray can be developed. The principle of the organizer is really a very old one. It is found in the writings of Johann Frederick Herbart, who took as one of the cornerstones of good teaching the notion that the teacher had always to take the pupil from the familiar to the unfamiliar. Herbart also viewed the memory system as an organized system of knowledge. Indeed, he went so far as to take the position that information could not be retained in memory if it did not already fit into the structure of previously acquired knowledge.

Ausubel and Robinson have reviewed research on the effectiveness of using or not using advance organizers, but the results of studies are perhaps not as striking as might be expected. They do suggest that advance organizers may be effective mainly with students of lower ability. This finding is hardly surprising, because low-ability students tend to be characterized by an inability to organize new information. A major difficulty encountered by these students is that they do not seem capable of organizing material for themselves, an important activity related to memorizing.

The research on advance organizers still leaves much to be discovered. One difficulty in undertaking such research is that the children given advance organizers are devoting more time to learning unless the control group is also given some additional learning time. It is also difficult to separate the effect of the advance organizer from that of the warm-up provided. Indeed, in the various studies on this topic, the main effect of the advance organizer may well be that it provides a warm-up, that is, gets the pupils into the mood for learning what they are to learn.

Expectancy of subsequent utility: Textbooks on psychology have, for nearly a hundred years, stressed the importance of a factor described as intent to learn as an essential condition for transferring information from the short-term memory system to the long-term system. Certainly, common experience tells us that we do not learn information that we do not have to learn. We rapidly forget the names of strangers we will never meet again. We never learn our way around a strange city if we are always driven around it by a friend. But anecdotes are different from scientific evidence, and it is always easy to find incidents and stories that support a particular view. The laboratory study of what has been called an intent factor has been difficult to undertake because the term itself is vague. How can one ever be sure that a person has or does not have intent to learn a particular set of materials?

Intent can be viewed in another way that makes it much more amenable to experimental study than the vague way in which it is commonly used. An essential feature of a situation in which there is intent to learn is that the learner expects to use what he is learning in some way. The way in which the information is to be used may be quite trivial, as when a person in a laboratory is given a list of words to learn. He expects that he will be tested on whether he does or does not know the syllables, at the end of a period of time. In a sense, the person expects to use the results of his learning, and the fact is that most subjects of laboratory experiments would be embarrassed if they could not remember any of the syllables they had been asked to learn. A situation in which there would be no intent to learn and no expectation of future usage would be one in which a person was asked to read a set of nonsense syllables to another person who was asked to try to remember them. The person reading the syllables would almost certainly not attempt to memorize the list. He would not expect to be tested on the list and would be very surprised if he were.

Thus one common component of intent to learn is expectation that the information will later be called for or used. Nuttin and Greenwald (1968) have experimented with the effect that this condition has on learning. For the purposes of their research, they refer to tasks that are one-time tasks, which a person performs never expecting to use again the information acquired, as **closed tasks.** These are to be contrasted with **open tasks,** which are tasks a person performs with the expectation that the information acquired will be used at a later date when the same task or a related task is given again. In the Nuttin and Greenwald studies, information about the correctness or incorrectness of responses was given on both tasks. When subjects were later tested, it was found that those who had performed the original tasks as closed tasks retained little information about which responses were right or wrong. Those who had viewed the original tasks as open tasks retained substantial information. These findings have been confirmed through research by Longstreth (1970).

The studies of Nuttin and Greenwald once again bring out the fact that transfer from short-term to long-term memory is a highly selective matter. Utility appears to be a consideration involved in determining whether there is or is not to be this transfer. Although only recently have psychologists begun to study this problem, educators have long insisted that if learning is to be effective the pupil must see that what he is doing has utility. A very essential element in the Progressive Education Movement of the 1930s was its stress on the importance of showing the pupil the significance and utility of the learning tasks that he undertook. Without such a program, pupils were not assigned tasks that they could not see meeting either their present or future needs.

Information should be converted into the most storable form: Experimental studies have been done that show that some information is more storable than other information. If information can be converted into a storable form, then retention can be improved. Stefan (1970), for example, taught subjects to convert three-digit numbers into pronounceable syllables according to a system. After they had mastered the system, they were given numbers to remember. These numbers they then converted into syllables. Thus the number 157 would be converted into the syllable *jos*, because they had learned that the number 1, appearing in the first place, was a *j*; the number 5, appearing in the second place, was an *o*; and the number 7, in the third place, was an *s*. The number 631260 would be coded as two groups of three and come out as *dan bur*. Stefan showed that the coded numbers could be remembered much more easily than could the original groups of digits. Theory might suggest that the syllables could be remembered three times as easily as the numbers, but the advantage was not quite as great as that. The reason for expecting that the system might facilitate memory threefold was that, through the coding system, *one* single syllable had to be remembered instead of the three-unit collection of digits. Theorists have long suggested that one can remember chunks of information with equal ease, regardless of whether they are small chunks, as is the case with the single digits, or larger chunks, such as are provided by syllables. The proposal is that whatever is put into memory is a chunk, that is, a piece of information having a certain unity. The theory was that if one could remember three chunks after a single exposure, then the chunks could either be three digits or three syllables.

It should be noted that the gain produced by such recoding devices is not as great as it may seem. The subjects in the Stefan experiment had to spend substantial time in mastering the coding system. They had to practice the system until they could immediately convert the digits to letter sounds. The time in mastering such a system might be worthwhile if they were to spend much time in the future remembering numbers. Otherwise, the time lost in learning the system would not be at least balanced by the time saved in the application of the system. What was studied in the Stefan experiment is similar to a phenomenon that learners have long recognized—that the reduction of complex information to a simple code word helps retention. Mnemonic systems are of this character, but they also do more than just code the information. They provide cues for its recall.

The coding of information to make it easier to remember also occurs through the use of language. If one looks at a neighbor's antique car and says to oneself "That is just like a Model T Ford," then it is very easy to remember exactly what that car is like. It is also easy to describe the car to another neighbor. By making the remark to oneself, one has tagged certain information he possesses about Model T cars to indicate that this information applies to the car belonging to the neighbor, and in this way the three words or symbols "Model T Ford" acquire the capability of carrying also all the information that one has about that particular model.

Because the mnemonic device is one of the best-known memory aids, let us consider an example and see how it operates. Suppose a teacher discussing problems on communication takes the position that there are four factors determining the influence a speaker can have on his audience (our example is hypothetical and should not be taken too seriously). The teacher tells his students that an influential speaker has to have status, education, knowledge, and a message of significance. He points out that the first letters of these four terms form the word *seks* and that if the students remember this word they will have no trouble in recalling the four factors. The students find this word easy to remember and generally have little difficult in remembering the four factors they have been told produce influence. Once a student recalled the mnemonic device, he will say to himself "Now what is there about a speaker that begins with *s* that makes him a source of influence?" There are not many answers he can give to this question. He might first think of the word *sex*, but this does not fit very well into the context. The word *stature* has greater possibilities, but the student may not remember having heard that word in connection with the class. Eventually, he hits on the word *status*, which seems to him to fit well. What the mnemonic device has done is to provide him with a cue concerning the class of words that are to be sought. The first word has to begin with *s*, and this limits the search. The task is then like that of knowing a certain document is in a certain folder. This piece of knowledge tells us where to look and we no longer have to search through the entire filing cabinet. Mnemonic devices tell a person where to look in his memory system. Norman (1969) has said that a mnemonic device is really a kind of plan that organizes one's search of the memory system. It could also be regarded as a kind of strategy. Individuals have all kinds of plans and strategies that permit them to search their memories with efficiency.

Mediating Processes and Remembering

Remembering is not a passive process. When one has to memorize a speech, a list of chemical compounds, or words in a foreign tongue, he works at the process involved. Sometimes we work so hard that we may be exhausted by the task of committing some information to memory. We know that we do not memorize material very effectively by going through the motions of reading it passively. Internal processes involved in memorizing play a crucial role in the task. Scientists are only just beginning to understand something about what these processes are.

The internal processes related to memorizing are referred to as **mediating processes,** a technical term that covers almost all internal processes influencing behavior. The word *mediating* is derived from the fact that these processes can be considered to mediate between stimuli and responses. A person is confronted with some kind of situation, but before he can make an appropriate response he has to view the situation and interpret it, consider alternative responses, and be busily engaged in internal activities. These internal activities are the mediating responses. Some mediating responses are commonly called thinking responses, but the word *thinking* implies that the person is aware of the internal processes involved. The term *mediating response* is neutral in this respect, carrying with it no implications of whether the processes can or cannot be accurately reported and described by the person in whom they are occurring.

Some mediating processes are essentially verbal, and these are the ones about which information can be most directly obtained. A person working a crossword puzzle comes across a five-letter word with the clue "Form of energy," and he can report the words that come to mind while he is searching for the correct word. The words represent important components of the mediating processes involved.

Kjeldergaard (1968) has provided an excellent review of what is known about mediating processes in associative learning. The review is very technical and difficult to understand, unless one is thoroughly steeped in the research in the area, so let us begin with a simple example of mediation derived from common experience. A common associative task involved in schools is learning the vocabulary of a foreign language. Although many teachers of foreign languages would take the position that the new language should not be learned by developing ties between English words and words in the new language, pupils commonly do work on the development of such ties. Those pupils who learn the English equivalent of foreign words generally use what are referred to as **verbal mediators.** Suppose that a child is learning French words and he comes to the word *livre,* meaning *book.* He may say to himself something like this: "A book has leaves so that is why it is called *un livre*." This internal talk is a mediating process. By doing this, the learner has found a link between the word *book* and the word *livre*. There is no doubt that effective learners do this, and the evidence is ample that this kind of process has a facilitating effect on learning. One of the effective strategies of the good learner is that he is clever in developing such mediating processes. Teachers should help pupils do this.

There are now many studies showing that those who engage in developing such chains of associations are better learners than those who do not, and most of the studies undertaken to demonstrate this phenomenon have depended on the learner reporting the way in which he hooked up the elements to be associated. More recent research has been able to demonstrate that learners do not have to be aware of these kinds of processes for them to operate and be effective (see Hall, 1971). The way this is done is to undertake an experiment that goes through the following steps:

1. The subjects learn a list of paired associates; that is, they learn to say the second word in a list whenever the first is presented. For the purposes of illustration, one such pair of words might be the pair *tree–barrel*. The associations are learned, and the subjects are dismissed at the end of the experiment.

2. The same subjects are later asked to participate in another experiment. It is also a paired-associate learning task. Among the items to be learned is the association between *barrel* and *wine*.

3. In a later and third experiment, the subjects learn an association between *tree* and *wine*. The data show that those who have learned the previous associations of *tree–barrel* and *barrel–wine* learn more easily the association *tree–wine*. (The experiment would, of course, involve a control group that did not learn the *tree–barrel* and *barrel–wine* associations.)

Now in such experiments the final association is, presumably, facilitated through the person having already learned a mediating link in the form of *tree–barrel–wine*. When the participants in such experiments have been questioned, they have generally failed to note the presence of such a mediating link. Such links operate whether the person is or is not aware of their existence, and they have a facilitating effect on learning.

Although the effectiveness of verbal mediators has been well established, knowledge is not available on the issue of whether use of such mediators can be learned. Those who use verbal mediators may be superior intellects who have developed this capability for themselves. Those who do not use them may lack the capability of using this tool for memorizing materials. The deliberate use of such mediators may require an inventiveness that many individuals do not have. If this is true, then instruction might still be improved for such individuals by pointing out to them the mediators they might use.

Verbal mediators always involve chains of words. Because the mediator is used as a part of a chain, it is commonly said that the mediator involves a sequential type of activity, for the items and the mediators are memorized in a sequence. There are other kinds of mediators that do not involve a sequential type of activity. These are mediators related to what are called **images.**

During the last half century, the attention of psychologists was directed toward the study of observable behavior largely because they believed that a science of behavior had to be founded on direct observation. Also, studies that attempted to investigate internal processes had not been successful. In recent times, there has been a return to the study of internal processes, including the study of verbal mediators, and somewhat greater success is expected because of the existence of greatly improved experimental techniques. One cannot escape from the fact that aspects of the environment are represented in memory, for if there were no such representations a living creature would never learn to cope with the environment. Also, individuals commonly report that they can close their eyes and inspect some kind of internal representation of what they have seen. This internal representation, commonly described as an indistinct and faint representation of a previous experience, is what is called an image. There may also be internal representations of printed and spoken words that represent a **coded** form of information and a coded internal representation of the world. Images of objects, or of sounds, represent uncoded internal representations of the real world, and these uncoded internal representations appear to play a role as mediators in learning.

The newly revived study of imagery has a growing literature to its credit, including a book by Richardson (1969) and review articles by Paivio and Csapo (1969), Paivio (1969, 1970), and Palermo (1970). This new form of research related to imagery has demonstrated that just as words may be involved in mediating processes, so too may images serve as mediating elements in learning. When trying to remember that the chief agricultural crop of Turkey is cereal, I may imagine a picture of a turkey eating from a bowl of cereal. Those who produce such images in learning such associations generally learn better than those who do not. Studies by Robinson and London (1971) show this and so too does some striking research by Anderson and Hidde (1971). Paivio also demonstrated the phenomenon. Despite the strong supportive evidence for this statement, one should be hesitant in concluding that imagery produces learning. It may be a by-product of effective learning. Also, there is no evidence available at this time whether training individuals to use imagery in such a context results in more effective learning.

Verbal mediators function as a link in a chain, but imagery of concrete events occurs simultaneously with the words that they hook up. They seem to represent a tie between the symbolic world of words and the world of concrete phenomena. The retention of useful coded information that can be applied to problems in the real world would appear to have that kind of linkage.

Finally, the point must be emphasized that images represent a very crude form of stored information. They provide little precise information except in the case of a rare form of imagery known as eidetic imagery, commonly referred to as photographic memory. Man's extraordinary capacity for storing very large quantities of information, in comparison with other primates, must be largely attributed to his ability to retain information in a verbal form. The very basis of the human memory system is a verbal memory core.

Some caution in suggesting that imagery is advantageous in learning comes from Richardson's (1969) suggestion, based on data, that children up to about the age of seven use imagery in the process of memorizing but that if such children persist in this use of imagery they may perhaps find themselves at a disadvantage in school learning. Richardson suggests that, around the age of the early elementary grades, children learn to use words both in their mediating processes and in their way of storing information. Words are presumably under better control and are more precise than the primitive imagery elements. Nevertheless, imagery may be better than no mediating processes at all.

Time Taken to Transfer Information to Long-Term Storage

The evidence seems quite clear that the transfer of information to long-term memory is not instantaneous but quite a slow process. Evidence for this comes indirectly and from an unusual source. A person who receives a concussion, that is a severe jolting of the brain, is unlikely to remember the events that preceded the accident. He will typically remember what happened thirty minutes before the accident, and occasionally events that took place twenty minutes before the accident, but events closer to the accident he cannot recall at all. A football player carried off the field after a head-on collision with another player may not even recall the touchdown he scored just fifteen minutes before the accident.

Now it is clear in such cases that the total memory is not deranged. The jolt is selective in what it does. The player on a college team does not forget all he has learned in classes that semester. The effect is on the information that has entered the short-term memory system and that would ordinarily be transferred to the long-term memory system just before the accident. Players can talk about games long after they have ended, and much of the information about the general strategy of the game is remembered on a long-term basis. The injured player does not transfer to long-term memory the information that was in the short-term memory system just prior to the accident. Presumably, there is some kind of disruption of the transfer process. But the disruption is for information acquired during the twenty to thirty minutes preceding the accident. The implication is that the process of transfer of information takes from twenty to thirty minutes.

Another point to note is that the player's touchdown scored twenty minutes before the accident is lost to memory. This touchdown was followed by all kinds of other events that the player might have later related about the game. The implication is that one item is being transferred to permanent memory while other events are taking place that might also, later, be transferred. The process of memorizing goes on after the event to be memorized has passed and after the person becomes preoccupied with other matters. During this time of consolidation, the information to be stored is particularly liable to disruption.

The evidence is quite clear that severe physical impact is disruptive of information to be remembered, but the effect is not confined to severe physical impact alone. It can be shown experimentally that other activities will disrupt the memorization process, particularly if they provide information similar to the information to be remembered. Children of school age often show intuitive understanding of this fact when they learn material by heart just before going to bed because they know that there is advantage to be gained by using the moments before sleep for learning purposes.

This leads us to a related problem, namely, whether one should spend a single, long, concentrated effort learning a batch of information, or whether one should engage in a series of short learning periods interspersed with other activities. This problem has generally been called by psychologists the massed versus distributed practice problem. **Massed learning** means a single, long, concentrated learning session. **Distributed learning** means short learning sessions distributed over a longer time. It is one of the oldest problems ever studied experimentally and one that has yielded consistent experimental results over the last hundred years. The findings are very consistent and lead to the firm conclusion that distributed practice is more effective than massed practice. Now let us relate this finding to the discussion of the fact that it takes up to thirty minutes to consolidate information in long-term memory.

The advantage of distributed practice appears to lie in the fact that a short learning session not resulting in complete mastery of the material continues to produce learning after the session comes to an end. Memorization processes continue for another twenty or thirty minutes. A period of five minutes devoted to learning initiates internal learning activity that goes on for a total of perhaps thirty minutes. If a person arranges to learn a skill through five daily periods of five minutes, then he is able to engage in learning the material for a total amount of time of about five times thirty minutes. If the five-minute learning sessions were consolidated into a single twenty-five minute session, then he would be learning for only the twenty-five minutes of formal learning plus about twenty-five minutes of consolidation time. This is the main reason why distributed learning is so very much superior to massed learning.

In all activities in which detailed information has to be consigned to permanent memory, pupils should be urged to use distributed learning sessions. They do not usually want to do this because such distributed practice leaves them with the feeling that they are making very slow progress. However, teachers should explain to children, even in the lower grades, that there are advantages in distributed practice and that the technique of learning requires some patience and planning. Work in the classroom should be so arranged that the children gain experience in the use of distributed practice. Teachers should avoid the practice so commonly observed of requiring children to master a block of material at a particular session. It is easier for the teacher if work is organized in this kind of way, but, over the long haul, it does not make it easier for the pupil. What it does is to encourage poor study habits.

Finally, mention must be made of the fact that only a rather limited amount of information can enter the short-term memory at any one time. This in turn limits the amount of information that can enter the long-term system, assuming that information can enter the long-term system only by way of the short-term system. The limited capacity of the short-term system to handle information has certain implications for what the teacher does. One can very easily tell children so much in a short time that they become unable to handle the information. An adult can have a similar experience when he hears a lecturer give a speech about a technical matter and finds he is unable to follow what is said because too many ideas arrive too quickly. Most speech, about simple matters, does not do this, because it carries only very small amounts of information. However, the teacher explaining a matter to a young pupil may be supplying him with very large amounts of information that arrive very quickly. In the laboratory, experimenters can easily demonstrate the **overloading phenomenon.** Some years ago, the author was involved in an experiment in which nonsense syllables were presented at a rate of one every half second. A list of ten syllables was presented. At the end of the presentation, the subject was asked to write out all the syllables he remembered. Then he was shown the syllables again, asked to write out those he remembered, and so on for ten trials. Some of the college students who were exposed to these learning conditions were unable to write down a single syllable, even after ten trials. The experimenter was surprised that such subjects were not able to remember at least the first syllable or the last, but they could not. They gave the appearance of utter bewilderment at the rate at which the syllables were presented, although most of them could read syllables at that rate. Indeed, most college students read at a rate of four to six words per second. The subjects who could not recall a single syllable were completely swamped by the rate of presentation of the nonsense material.

When a teacher presents information for the first time, the rate of presentation should be slow. Most information has to be presented more than once, and on subsequent presentations the rate can be increased. This is what the experienced reader does himself. He comes to a difficult passage and reads it through very slowly. Next time he reviews the passage, he will go through it at a faster pace.

A final point that needs to be made is that when material has to be presented several times there are advantages in having a delay between presentations. This gives the individual time to process the information he has received. A statement takes time to soak in. Teachers must provide that time.

The Total-Time Hypothesis

Many teachers have asked themselves whether more is learned when more tasks are crammed into a given time than when fewer tasks are presented. The question is whether one can hurry up learning by setting time limits and other devices to speed up the pupil's activity. To some degree, one can produce gains in this way with some pupils. Many pupils, working alone, may dawdle along at a snail's pace that is quite ineffective. Other pupils, working in pairs, may become involved in activities and games other than the assigned task and may hence work very inefficiently. Teachers can easily see when such adjustments in rate of work need to be made. The question is not so easily answered when one asks whether a student would do better to read a page at, say, 250 words per minute, or at a much slower rate of, say, 125 words per minute. If the student learns as much by reading it once at 250 words per minute as he does when he reads it once at 125 words per minute, then he can save half of his time for other learning by reading at the more rapid rate. It should be pointed out that the faster of these two rates of reading is not a particularly fast rate for a high-school student, provided the material is clearly written and is nontechnical.

There is some evidence that time is a critical factor in learning. Reading a passage slowly produces about as much learning as reading the passage twice at double the pace. The amount of learning taking place is critically related to the total time involved. Hall (1971), who has summarized the data behind what is called the **total-time hypothesis,** concludes that it applies within wide limits. The total-time hypothesis states that the amount of learning taking place depends primarily on the amount of time assigned to learning. Another way of saying this is that one can learn only so much in a given time, and no more. However, if material is presented very fast or very slowly, then the total-time hypothesis may not apply. In the case of the example considered, if the reading were undertaken at such a pace that the person ended up confused, then he might not learn at all from exposure to the material. Also, if the rate were very slow, he might not learn much during the time spent on reading because the material would be so boring.

What the data suggest is that the particular manner in which material is presented to be learned may not be as vital a matter as the time allowed for learning. It should also be noted that the total-time hypothesis assumes that the time assigned to learning is actually used for learning. A pupil may learn more by one teaching method than by another because the one method keeps him at the learning task but the other method lets him dawdle and daydream. Most studies that have compared the effectiveness of one teaching method with that of another have come up with negligible differences. This lack of a difference between teaching methods may be due to the overriding importance of time as a factor in learning.

If the total-time hypothesis is correct, as it seems to be, then one would not expect much improvement from some procedures that have been invented to save students' time. For example, some have suggested that speeded-up speech, referred to as time-compressed speech, might be a good way to pump more information into a person in less time. The total-time hypothesis suggests that nothing is to be gained by speeding up what one wants to tell the pupil. Sticht (1971), who reviewed studies of this problem, found little evidence that the speeding up of information communicated through speech improved the amount a person could learn in a given time. There appears to be just so much that a person can learn in a given amount of time.

What has been said in the previous paragraphs does not mean that the dawdling pupil is learning efficiently. The total-time hypothesis applies only when the learner is receiving information at a rate that does not bore him and does not apply when information is being received by the learner at either a very fast or very slow pace.

What Is Learned?

On the surface, the question "What is learned?" appears to be easy to answer, but it is a very complex matter. Many psychological problems, as they are commonly stated by psychologists, are of this character. A similar problem is encountered when we reward a child with a smile of approval for behaving in some way that we consider to be good. On the surface, it would seem that we are quite simply rewarding his good behavior, but what is happening is much more complex. We shall consider this matter of what is rewarded or reinforced in a later chapter, but for now let us return to the matter of what is learned. Let us begin by considering a very simple learning task such as learning to repeat a set of ten words in order. Such lists of words represent a quite common learning task. Students of chemistry learn the names of groups of elements, biologists learn the names of the twelve cranial nerves, and astronomers learn the names of the nine planets.

When a subject in the laboratory learns to repeat back a list of ten words presented to him one at a time on a screen, he is likely to say that he is "learning the words." The fact is that he is not learning the words at all, for he knows these words. They are all familiar to him and he encounters them nearly every day of his life. Then what is he learning? What he seems to be learning is that, of all the words he knows, certain ones appear on the screen and he is to repeat back these words at the end of each trial. What he has to do to perform the task is to tag certain words stored in his memory system as those to be repeated back at the end of the trial. In a similar way, when the pupil learns the names of the planets in order of increasing orbit, he is not learning the names of the planets at all, for the names are all familiar to him. What he is learning is to assign numbers to the planets. The "tags," in this case, are numbers or cues that indicate the order in which the planets are to be recited or written down. Much of learning consists in tagging information that is already in storage. Sometimes the tagging involves indicating that the information can be used for a particular purpose. A pupil may know, for example, that Archimedes' principle explains why some objects float in water and some sink. Then, one day, he is told that the same principle can be applied to gases. From then on, he uses the information incorporated in the principle to help explain why a hydrogen-filled balloon floats up in the air. The principle is, as it were, tagged for certain uses. But the concept of the tagging of information is an analogy, and only an analogy. There is nothing presently identifiable in the nervous system that corresponds either to a piece of information or a tag attached to it, but it is a convenient way of thinking about learning. It also makes the distinction between learning the original piece of information and learning to use the particular piece of information in some special way.

The student who learns botanical names for ten different forms of plant life is confronted with a somewhat different task than the student who learns the relative positions of familiar planets. He has never heard the names of such groupings of plants as basidiomycetes, bryophytes, angiosperms, and so forth. As he acquires some familiarity with these names, he also has to learn what they signify. This is altogether a much more difficult task than tagging with additional information names that are already stored in memory. Indeed, it may be many times more difficult. Placing entirely new material in memory is a much harder task than adding meaning to information already stored.

Common language is misleading when the teacher makes such statements as "Johnny would do well if he could learn to sit at his desk and work." Johnny knows perfectly well how to sit at his desk; he also knows how to work. The problem is not to teach Johnny to sit down and work but to arrange conditions so that Johnny will want to sit down and work or will choose to sit down and work. The problem is essentially one commonly described as motivational. Much of the research undertaken in the area of reinforcement and rewards has to do with arranging conditions so that responses already in the repertoire of the individual will actually take place or will take place with greater frequency. The manipulation of rewards, punishments, and reinforcements has to do with the matter of arranging for already-learned behavior to take place on appropriate occasions.

Storage of items in memory probably takes place in terms of the attributes of the items. The evidence for this is quite indirect, but a great many facts point in the same direction. One piece of evidence of considerable interest is that derived from what is known as the **tip-of-the-tongue phenomenon,** which has been investigated by Brown and McNeill (1966). The essence of this phenomenon is that when one has a word on the tip of the tongue but cannot recall it, he is still able to recall certain attributes or characteristics of the word. The essential feature of the technique used by Brown and McNeill was to read to subjects definitions of rare words. After each definition, a subject indicated if he knew what the word was. Many of those who said they knew the word were not able to say it, but they could give some of its characteristics. These subjects indicated that the word was on the tip of their tongues but it would take a little time for them to recall it. They were then questioned on what they knew about the word—whether they knew the initial letter, or how many syllables long it was, or what it sounded like. A very significant finding in the study was that these subjects were able to report quite accurately some of the characteristics of the word even though they could not recall the word. It was as if they were able to retrieve some attributes of the word but could not recall a sufficient number of the attributes to produce the complete word. The subjects showed some accuracy in guessing the number of syllables in the word they could not bring to mind. They were also able to guess, with better than chance accuracy, the first letter of the word. They also showed some ability to guess the suffix of the missing word and were able to select other words that sounded like the word they sought. These kinds of data suggest that what is stored, in the case of a word, is a set of features of the word rather than the word itself.

Underwood (1969) has collected evidence indicating that verbal information is stored in terms of attributes rather than in terms of word units. We may think in terms of words and phrases, but how we think does not necessarily indicate how the information used in our thoughts is actually stored. Underwood's position is very much like that of those engaged in research on perception, who view the process of recognizing an object as a process involving a comparison of the attributes of the object to be recognized with an inventory of attributes stored within the individual engaged in the recognition process. If this is so, and it seems quite a tenable position at the present time, then it becomes evident that memory and perception are two processes intimately connected and inseparable. One can recognize insofar as he has stored in his memory system elements corresponding to those found in the object recognized. If there are no such common elements, then recognition is virtually impossible. The development of perceptual processes involves the incorporation in the memory system of elements abstracted from whatever is presented to the senses.

There are examples from daily life showing how information is stored piecemeal. Sometimes, while writing a chapter, I decide I want to make reference to a book I know I possess. I may know that the book covers the topic of conditioning, but I cannot remember the author or title. Nevertheless, some items of information about the book can be recalled. I remember that it has a red cover and that it is a thick book, perhaps two inches from cover to cover. These attributes of the book have been stored separately from the name and title. At least, it seems likely that if all of the information had been stored together, as a block, I would have either retained or lost the entire block. But I lose information piecemeal. One piece of information can either drop out of the system or cease to be available. The attributes seem to be stored as distinct and separate pieces.

Memory appears to be a system that stores little components of information, and these small items of information are probably stored on an all-or-none basis. By this is meant that the component of information is either stored or it isn't stored and there is no way in which the component can be stored in a weak form. When an incident is remembered vaguely, it is likely to mean that the person remembers certain components, perhaps trivial components, quite clearly but does not remember or cannot recall enough of the components to reconstruct what happened. This is like the example of being able to remember the general nature of a book I own and the fact that it has a red cover but not being able to remember the title or author. I remember enough components to make me think that the book contains information I need and enough clues to find it, but my memory of the book is somewhat vague.

At one time, some believed that as large a component as a syllable was learned on an all-or-none basis, but the components of a particular memory that are stored are probably much smaller than that. If I have been learning syllables in a laboratory experiment, I may remember that the syllables were all three letters long, thus indicating that I can remember a component of them.

The psychological concept that information is stored in little components fits well with some of the concepts derived from neurophysiology concerning the storage of information in the nervous system. Despite the extensive research undertaken on this problem, scientists have not discovered how information is stored in the nervous system nor where storage takes place. The most commonly held theory is that storage takes place in the microscopic areas of tissue where the fibers protruding from one nerve cell come into proximity with the protruding fibers from another nerve cell. The cells do not join, but are separated by very small amounts of tissue. These areas of separation are called **synapses.** It has been established that chemical reactions may take place in the synapses that may block the transmission of a nerve impulse from one fiber to the other, and other chemical reactions may take place that will facilitate the transmission of an impulse. The synapse is very much like a small switch that can be turned on or off. The view is widely held that the synapse is the place where information is stored through the switch being turned on or off. This is very much like the way information is stored in a computer. Computers are filled with electronic off–on switches used to store information. If such a switch is set in the off position, then it might signify a zero. If set in the on position, then it might signify the number 1. A combination of such switches can, in this way, signify a larger number. Combinations of switches can also be used to represent letters of the alphabet and combinations of letters to represent words. Thus very small pieces of information can be stored, but they can then be combined to represent complex pieces of information. It may be assumed that the storage of information in the nervous system involves the storage of information in terms of a set of components, but one can only speculate what those components could be.

Some of those studying the chemistry of the nervous system have suggested that information may be stored at an even more microscopic level than the synapse, that the information is stored in terms of the modification of particular molecules. Both the chemical theory and the synapse theory of information storage may be correct in that information may be stored in molecules in the synapses, but then there is still an issue of whether more than one piece of information can be stored at a particular synapse.

The storage system, if information is stored at the synapses, has a very substantial capacity, probably larger than that of any computer in existence at this time. Although it is known there are about eleven-billion nerve cells in the nervous system and an even larger number of synapses, it is not known at this time how many of these are involved in the storage of information. The nervous system has many other functions besides storing information. The nervous system also engages in the analysis of information and the matching of incoming information with information already stored. Probably only a small fraction of the total number of nerve cells in the entire system is involved in the actual storage of information.

The amount of information that can be stored does not seem to be limited so much by the number of synapses or components available for storage as it is limited by the time it takes to place information in permanent storage. The reader has already had brought to his attention the fact that the placement of information in permanent storage is quite a slow matter. Every learner who tries to master a new language is fully aware of this fact. The time taken to place information in storage may well be such that a typical individual cannot, during a lifetime, use up all of the storage capacity provided by his nervous system.

There do not appear to be in the human brain particular locations where sizable chunks of information are stored. There are specific locations where such functions take place as the analysis of visual information, the comprehension of auditory speech, and the control of the muscular components involved in speech. However, these areas are quite distinct from those involved in the storage of all the information that one takes in from day to day. It can be said with some certainty that information has a diffuse form of storage, because damage to a particular location in the brain does not knock out particular items of information. This is to be contrasted with the computer, in which damage to a particular place in the storage system will destroy a particular item of information. It may well be that different components of the same chunk of information are stored in different places. If this were so, then the destruction of some of those components might still leave one with a sufficient number of components to recall the general nature of the item. I may forget the color of the binding of a book and the author, but I still know about the general nature of the book by remembering the title.

Finally, there is an accumulating amount of evidence suggesting that information is probably not just stored in the higher centers of the brain. It is quite probable that all levels of the nervous system are involved in both the analysis of information and the storage of information. There is certainly abundant evidence that all levels are involved in the analysis of information, but the suggestion that all levels are involved in the storage is much more speculative because of the difficulty of obtaining direct evidence to substantiate it. Some evidence exists, but it is not overwhelming in quantity.

From components to complete memories: The examples discussed in the previous section are special cases in which recall is incomplete and only components of the original information can be recalled. Most recall is not of this character, for one typically recalls complete incidents and complete words and complete units of experience. This leads to the question of how the components stored in the memory system are recombined. A first point to note in this connection is that this theory of memory takes the position that recall is an active reconstruction of the original experience. The process is not like pulling from an album a photograph that shows the original incident. It is more like choosing a cast of actors who together can reconstruct the original scene. The director, the person doing the remembering, decides the details of how the scene is to be enacted, but he may not be completely concerned with historical accuracy. Norman (1969) has reviewed this problem and has pointed out that it was not until about fifty years ago that psychologists came to recognize the significance of the fact that recall is often quite inaccurate. This fact has been known to lawyers for a long time, for they have seen witnesses in court honestly believe that certain events happened even though they could not possibly have happened. This phenomenon could take place under either one of two conditions. One condition that would produce the effect would be if the person retrieving the information managed to retrieve the wrong items of information. This probably does happen occasionally. My wife asks me whom I met downtown yesterday. I say I met Jones, but it wasn't Jones at all. Jones was the man I met on the previous day. Time errors of this kind are common. A much more important source of error is incorrect assembly of the information that constituted the original experience. What probably happens is that I find I am unable to retrieve certain elements that constitute the totality of what I want to recall. What I am likely to do is to fill in the missing items with the information that seems to fit best. I do not do this deliberately, but my brain is so constituted that it inevitably performs this activity.

Psychologists have developed various techniques for studying this phenomenon. One technique is to read a story to the person whose memory system is being studied. Then, after some interval has passed, the individual is required to tell the story as he remembers it. The version of the story reproduced differs in important respects from the original. It is shorter and more compact than the original and often more coherent. If the stories are from classical literature, then the reproductions tend to modernize the language. Those who participate in such an experiment cannot generally tell whether elements in their version have been invented in order to fill in the details that have escaped memory. In the early studies of this phenomenon, experimenters reported that memories of stories underwent slow modification with the passage of time, but this does not seem to be the case. The important point to note from this line of research is that recall is considered to be an inventive, reconstructive process.

In terms of the theory of memory based on a concept of the storage of elements, recall cannot be other than a reconstruction process. One generally recalls total events, not a collection of unorganized elements laid down in memory.

Psychologists have taken the position that there are organizing elements in the memory system. These elements coordinate and bring together the stored elements in order to generate meaningful recollections. Henry Head, a neurologist, was the first to call such an organizing element a schema. The term has caught on and has been widely used—for example, Piaget's references to the schemas of early infancy. Piaget believes these schemas to be innate organizers of primitive experiences related to feeding, defecation, and other basic biological functions. They represent foci around which new knowledge is acquired. Piaget is inclined to take the view that the primitive schemas form the core of organized experience.

Piaget's concept of a schema is different, in many respects, from the concept as it is used by other psychologists. For Piaget, schemas also include action systems. Experience is not only recorded as so much information, but there is also recorded with it certain systems of action that are related to, and an integral part of, the memory system. He and some other psychologists have taken the position that much of the storage system of the human brain involves the storage of action tendencies. Those who take such a position would view the memory of an auto mechanic as being a large store of actions to be taken to correct defects and actions related to conducting tests that will locate the source of malfunctions.

Most of those who consider the memory system to consist of elements of stored information and schemas view them as being organizing systems acquired through experience. Just how such organizing systems are acquired is not clear at this time, but an alternative to the rather vague notion of the schema is offered by Norman (1969). He proposes that what one learns is a set of complex rules for combining the elements that are stored so that earlier experience can be reconstructed. The word *rule* should not be taken literally. He does not mean that written into the tissue of the brain are sets of rules such as the rules followed when a motor vehicle is driven. The rules may be implicit kinds of rules. For example, a computer follows certain rules in adding two numbers together. The rules are not stored in some special place in the computer, but they are inherent in the operation of the computer. Computers are so designed that when they are given the two numbers 2 and 3 and are told to add them, they come out with the inevitable answer. The human being learns, as he deals with the environment, to take to bits the experience he has and store the components separately. Perhaps the brain is such that when it breaks down experience into components for storage, it also stores the rules involved for the recombining of the components into their original form.

Memory is an inventive and reconstructive activity in much of life, but it does not always have to be of this character. It is inventive and reconstructive because the information is not fully learned in so many instances. Nobody who listens to a story plans to remember every detail. Indeed, the hearer is likely to remember only enough to keep track of the main theme. He forgets the precise wording used and many of the details. He will forget the metaphor, and perhaps forget the existence of some of the minor characters. He remembers the general theme, some of the attributes of the main characters, and perhaps some of the features of the general style of the story. One can hardly be surprised that, when he retells the story later, he has to fill in the details from his imagination. This does not mean that all memorizing and recall are of this character. Anyone who has watched a Shakespearean play and followed it with the text knows that the accomplished actor can render his part almost letter perfect. His performance is that of a person who has taken in large quantities of verbal information, has recorded the information with precision, and is then capable of accurately reproducing the original material in all of its detail. This recall process is not then a reconstruction process in terms of the person supplying, by invention, missing details. The brain has an enormous capability of storing, and reproducing accurately, highly detailed *verbal* information.

Now, although the brain can record and reproduce accurately very large quantities of verbal information, this does not necessarily mean that time in school should be devoted to the mastery of detail. The joker in the situation is that mastery of the details of verbal material requires an immense amount of time. The transfer of information to the long-term memory system is a very tedious and time-consuming matter. The human learner generally *sets for himself* the task of learning a minimum of detail. Some have even suggested that the living creature learns, on a permanent basis, only the minimum needed for adjustment to his environment.

Retrieval

Ample evidence has already been provided in this chapter to show that most problems of forgetting are problems of retrieval. That is to say, the information is stored but cannot be obtained from the memory system. This suggests that the mechanism for placing information into memory is different from the mechanism that reaches into the system and makes it available for use. Remembering mechanisms and retrieval mechanisms are different mechanisms. Studies of memory defects also point in the same direction. The problem with the aged who suffer difficulties with their memories appears to be a result of the deterioration of the retrieval mechanism and not a problem of placing information in memory.

The older person is probably quite as capable as the younger person of placing information in his memory system. His problem arises from the fact that he cannot draw the information out of storage.

At this time, there is no very good representation of the human retrieval system. One can build many complicated devices for storing and retrieving information, but most of those available work at a rather slow rate. The typical computer system, in searching for a particular piece of information stored on a tape, requires that all the information on the magnetic tape be examined by the computer, item by item, until it is found. The process is greatly shortened if the information is classified into categories. Then, if one knows that an item belongs in a particular category, that particular category can be searched. This is the principle involved in searching a library for a particular item of information. One does not start by working through the entire card catalogue. What one typically does is to go to the cards indexing the materials that fall into that particular category. This restricts the area to be searched. Indeed, without such a restriction, the process of searching a library would be an impossible task to perform. The more cues that are provided, the easier one can retrieve information from his brain (see Tulving and Osler, 1968).

The essence of effective retrieval of information from the human memory system is to start with some piece of information indicating what category of stored information to search. The student who is reviewing work before an examination is likely to go to his notes. The notes tell him which category to go to in his memory system for all of the information he has about the topic to be reviewed. His notes tell him, for example, that one of the topics to be covered is metabolism. So he begins to think over the knowledge he has about metabolism. What he is doing is rehearsing the material, an activity that can be expected to have two consequences. One consequence is that the material becomes consolidated in memory. Another consequence is that the material becomes more easily retrieved. One cannot really separate out these two effects in experiments, but it seems likely that merely obtaining information out of the memory system may improve the retrieval of that particular piece of information.

There is also a third consequence of the review process—it permits the student to identify gaps in his knowledge. A search of his memory system, in the particular example, may tell him that he can recall absolutely no knowledge about the metabolism of fats. He may have that knowledge stored, but it may be stored in a form that does not permit him to retrieve it at the present time. What he then has to do is to return to his books.

Some psychologists would describe the notes used by the student as a set of **cues.** A cue is generally interpreted as being a stimulus that has the property of triggering a particular response or class of responses. The author, who prefers to use an information-processing model of learning, takes the position that a cue is a "category to be searched."

There is a little evidence to show that retrieval can take place more easily in the situation in which the original learning took place than in other locations (see Bugelski, 1956). If one learns to work out a square root in a classroom, then he is more likely to be able to work out that square root in that classroom than in other locations. This is, in many ways, an unfortunate feature of human learning, suggesting that when one learns to work out a square root in a classroom, this information is stored in the category of "things learned in the classroom." Once it is stored in such a category, then it is most readily retrieved in situations leading to a search of that category. The situation most likely to result in the search of that category is the situation in which the original learning took place.

Failure to retrieve information may occur for many different reasons. One of these is that the information may be held in long-term memory in such a disorganized and chaotic fashion that a search of the memory system may not be easily undertaken. Talland (1965), who has devoted a great amount of effort to the study of disturbances of the memory system, points out that the efficient retrieval of information from a system can occur only when the system is well organized. If one wants to search for a document in a set of file drawers, the problem of finding the document is easy if the material is systematically arranged in the file drawers. The system tells the searcher where to go to locate the particular document. On the other hand, when the file system is completely chaotic, the task of locating a document may be so time consuming and overwhelming that it may seem impossible. Many of us have desks where there is so little organization that the location of a piece of paper in the pile may involve going all through the material. Talland suggests that the analogy is useful for describing many memory problems. Some memory problems in seriously disturbed individuals may well be due to the chaotic nature of the material in the memory system. All of us probably suffer from this problem to some degree. We may have difficulty in retrieving a piece of information because it was filed under some unusual category, or we may be looking in the wrong category. My wife says "What is the name of that first turning off Milham Road, named after a flower?" I try to recall the name of the road and, eventually, run through the names of common flowers, but all to no avail. I cannot remember the name because I am looking in the wrong category. My wife has mentioned that it is named after a flower, but it is really named after a tree. The wrong cue leads to a search of the wrong category.

Teaching and Memory Training

The emphasis in this chapter has been on the importance of enabling the student to acquire knowledge in an orderly way so that he may become the possessor of a well-ordered mind. Not only can knowledge be more readily acquired in this way, but the knowledge thus acquired is more readily retrieved than if it is stored in a chaotic system. The organizing function of teachers in this respect has long been recognized, but too many teachers have failed to recognize its true significance. There is some evidence that teachers who are well organized in their behavior produce rather greater achievement in their pupils than teachers who are less orderly. The lesson is familiar, but it still has to be taken to heart.

A second important lesson learned is that the human being is equipped with a short-term memory system. Information that enters this system does not necessarily become permanently recorded in memory. Teachers complain that information enters one ear of each pupil and leaves by the other ear. This is what naturally happens. Information does not reach the long-term memory system unless special provision is made for it to do so. An important responsibility of teachers is to arrange conditions so that information is transferred to permanent storage. One of the important conditions that the teacher can control is that of showing that the information being learned does have genuine future utility. The human learner is so designed that he is most likely to remember what is potentially useful. This finding has important implications for the curriculum designer, who often has in mind remote utility that the pupil (or even the teacher) never recognizes.

Finally, brief consideration must be given to the matter of whether the memory can be trained. In every large city, there are individuals and institutions claiming to provide memory training. At one time, a chain of Pelman Institutes around the world offered memory training. Just what success can such enterprises be expected to have?

A first point to note is that courses designed to improve memory are all designed around the problem of producing better learning. Most psychologists would agree that this is a reasonable approach. If one is very poor at recognizing faces, the problem is probably that he has never learned to take careful note of the characteristics of faces that differentiate one person from another. A first step in learning to remember faces would be to draw attention to the critical differentiating characteristics of faces. What needs to be trained is discrimination learning, and not memory. This is what most memory training courses do.

Memory training schemes also tend to stress the application of what is known about associative learning. Even though one can remember faces, he may not be able to remember correct names. If one forgets names but remembers faces and is left in the bewildering position of saying to himself "I know him, but what on earth is his name?" he can remedy this situation by learning techniques of associating names with faces. Most of those who have this problem never take the trouble to learn a person's name when introduced. If they take the trouble to study carefully the face of the person to whom they are being introduced, and then say his name to themselves several times, their chances of remembering his name are improved. This is a teachable learning strategy. It results in the person appearing to remember better, but what it does is to help place name–face associations in memory. The person who needs this help does not have a poor memory but lacks techniques for placing material in the memory system.

Most courses designed to "train memory" provide useful tips on how to learn better, and those who take the courses may benefit from them. Insofar as students learn to learn more effectively, they have the illusion of improving their memories.

Memory

Summary

1 During the last decade, a substantial body of knowledge has been developed concerning the nature of memory. The memory system cannot be observed directly, but much can be found out about it indirectly. There is no simple system for prescribing what a child should learn by heart. Some programs of education have been built on the assumption that the child should learn by heart as much as possible. Others take the position that the child should master key terms and concepts and have facility in their use, but there is controversy concerning what those key terms and concepts are. A third approach views education as a process of learning to use reference materials and other external sources of information.

2 Much information needed for a very short time is held temporarily in short-term memory. The short-term memory prevents the long-term system from being overloaded with trivia that have no later utility. The short-term system is, nevertheless, selective in what it retains, as is evident from the Sperling experiment, which shows that one sees much but retains little. There is also a memory system of even shorter duration known as the buffer system or the trace system. It is a large-capacity system that holds information for a just a few seconds or less. The trace is rich in information, but what is pulled from it for retention in short-term memory is just a very small amount of information. Information that enters the short-term system does not necessarily enter the long-term system. A pupil exposed to information in school does not necessarily place it in long-term storage. When attention is switched to a new source, the trace is erased and does not interfere with new information provided.

3 The trace is a holding mechanism. The trace has special functions in the comprehension of speech, because it must hold components long enough so that they can be understood. The short-term memory has to hold sentence-length units until they are analyzed and comprehended. Young children have a smaller-capacity short-term system than adults; hence, they have difficulty in understanding long sentences.

4 Filter theory holds that the information that enters the short-term memory system is filtered from the trace. The filter can be set to pass particular classes of information. It is always set to pass certain kinds of information that have great significance for the individual. The filter analogy, and it is an analogy, provides a rather useful description of some aspects of the selective nature of perception and memory. The human being also behaves as though he systematically sampled events in the surrounding world.

5 Many different sources of evidence indicate that there are both a short-term and a separate long-term system of memory. Patients with brain damage have been identified who show no damage to short-term memory but are unable to transfer new information to the long-term system. Such cases are not caused by damage to the long-term system but by damage to the mechanism that transfers information from one system to the other. A second source of evidence is that confusions in memory are rather different for the two systems. Some conditions that interfere with memory in the short-term system do not seem to have the same disruptive effect on the long-term system, and vice versa. In addition, conditions favorable for short-term memory may not be favorable for long-term memory, and the reverse is also true. Items in a list that are most easily recalled in short-term memory may not be those that are most easily recalled at a later date. This is an important finding, because teachers often test retention in terms of an immediate memory for facts.

6 Short-term memory is sometimes referred to as primary memory. The ability of the system to function is quite independent of age and education. There is some evidence that retention *may* be better in children than in adults over a substantial period of time, but the facts need to be verified and explored.

7 A crucial problem is how information is transferred to long-term memory and how this can be facilitated. Rehearsal has long been shown to be an important factor. The Tulving type of experiment provides some information concerning why rehearsal is important. The evidence is that rehearsal and recall involve organizing processes that are necessary for transfer of information to the long-term system. Information thus becomes organized in a form compatible with the organization of the long-term memory system, and only then can information be effectively placed in storage. There is also the possibility that placing the information several times in the short-term memory system gives some advantages with respect to retaining the information over long periods of time.

8 Because the long-term memory system is an organized information system and an important condition for adding information to the store is that it be organized, teachers can help pupils learn by providing them with information in an organ-

ized form. Even if information is presented without organization, it will be organized to some degree before it is transferred to the long-term memory system. When material is organized, there are previously learned associations between components that facilitate the task of learning. One of the merits of programmed learning is that it emphasizes the importance of organized subject matter. Various procedures have been suggested for organizing subject matter. One is to begin with the final stage of knowledge to be acquired, then to identify the prerequisites, and then the prerequisites of the prerequisites. There is very little evidence that one procedure for ordering subject matter is better than another. An essential factor in the ordering of subject matter is the way that the body of knowledge itself has grown and become organized. Some psychologists have proposed that pupils should be assisted in organizing knowledge to be acquired by being given advance organizers around which the ideas to be acquired can be clustered.

9 A very important factor in determining whether information will be transferred to long-term memory is whether the individual expects the information to be of later use. When the learner knows that the information is trivial and will not be called for later, the information remains in the short-term memory system, where it is rapidly lost. Tasks involving expectation of future usage of information are called open tasks.

10 Information can sometimes be more easily learned if it is coded into a new form, such as with mnemonic devices. One of the ways in which mnemonic devices work is through telling a person where to look in his memory system for the information he wishes to retrieve.

11 Mediating processes play an important role in remembering. Some of the mediating processes are organizing and thinking processes, and some are verbal and involve the development of word links between the items to be retained. A person may not be aware of the links that he forms in the memory system for these links to be effective in influencing subsequent behavior. It is not known whether it is profitable to attempt to teach children how to use such mediators.

12 Imagery appears also to provide a system of effective mediators that facilitates transfer of information to long-term memory. Images appear to function as mediators much as words do. In addition, images appear simultaneously with the elements to be memorized and have functions other than that of just linking together the elements to be memorized. Some

evidence suggests that verbal mediators may represent a more mature level of functioning than do images.

13 A certain amount of time is occupied in transferring information to permanent storage, estimated to be about thirty minutes. In other words, the processes involved in transfer continue after the individual stops formal learning and turns to other activities. During this thirty-minute period, the processes of transfer may be disrupted by mechanical injury or by psychological processes that disrupt the information being transferred. The relatively long time involved in making the transfer explains why learning takes place most effectively if it is followed by a very different activity that will not interfere with the learning that has been undertaken. Distributed practice takes advantage of the fact that learning continues after study has stopped. A long series of investigations over nearly a century have shown that distributed practice is superior to massed practice. Teachers should explain to children the advantages of distributed practice and urge them to plan their studies so that massed learning does not take place just before deadlines. Teachers should also remember that few ideas are learned by being presented once. When a teacher plans to go over work on more than one occasion, the occasions should be well separated.

14 Evidence has accumulated that, for any given pupil, only a given amount of learning can take place in a given time. This is known as the total-time hypothesis. If this hypothesis is correct, it accounts for the fact that various experimental attempts to speed up learning have not been particularly successful. Any gains produced by new methods tend to be quite small, and most gains can be accounted for by the fact that the novel method induced the student to spend more time learning than he would have by the previously used method.

15 When a pupil is said to be "learning" a list of words, he is not actually learning the words, for they are all familiar to him. What he is learning is to tag the items in his memory system as those that he is to recall. This is a different task from learning ten words of a foreign language when he does not know the words and has never heard them before. Items are probably stored in memory in terms of their attributes. Experiments with the tip-of-the tongue phenomenon illustrate the kind of attributes that may be stored about particular words. In trying to recall an unusual words, one may be able to recall many of the features of the word, such as length or the first letter, without being able to recall the word itself. Many examples from daily life illustrate how information is

stored piecemeal. One remembers particular characteristics of events without remembering the entire event.

16 Perception and memory are intimately related. One recognizes an object by identifying its particular features, and one remembers an object, and what it is like, by recalling the critical features and thus reconstructing the object. Perception is intimately connected with placing information in memory, and retrieval involves taking that same information out of the memory system. How the component pieces of information are stored is a matter of conjecture. Many scientists conjecture that the synapses in the nervous system are the locations where information is retained. The synapses function like on–off switches, but complicated information can be stored in systems of on–off switches, as it is in a computer. Another proposal is that information is stored in the nervous system at an even more microscopic level, in the structure of molecules. In any case, the storage system has a very substantial capacity. Only a part of the nervous system is involved in the storage of information. Much of the nervous system is involved in other functions such as analyzing incoming information and transmitting information from one location to another. There do not appear to be in the nervous system particular locations where large chunks of information are stored.

17 A person typically recalls complete incidents and not just features of the incidents. This raises the question of how the features stored in memory are recombined. Recall is to some degree a reconstruction process, and it is in the process of reconstruction that errors of recall are largely introduced. The recall process generally involves incomplete information, and information has to be created to fill in the gaps left by memory. Another source of error may be that incorrect features are recalled during the reconstruction process. In order for recall to be a reconstruction process, there must be stored in memory rules involved in making reconstructions. The rules for combining elements into meaningful memories may be the same as what other psychologists call schemas.

18 Most problems of forgetting are problems of retrieval. The information is there stored in memory, but it eludes the searching process. When a person searches his memory, he obviously does not search the entire system, for this would be a long and tedious task. What he appears to do is to go to a category of information in the system. The cues presented by the situation confronting one indicate the category of memory to be searched. The search of one's memory is much like searching for a book in a library. The more cues one has concerning where to search in the memory system, the more likely he is to find what he wants. An orderly memory is a necessary condition for effective retrieval.

19 Memory training seems to involve three factors. One is teaching a person to organize information that he wants to remember. A second factor is teaching him to take the trouble to learn what he wants to learn. People don't learn the names of other people largely because they do not bother to. A third factor is teaching the person to respond to the cues necessary for later recognition and recall.

282

• • • • • • • • • •

Memory

In this chapter, consideration must be given to the loss of information from the memory systems. This is not an easy matter to investigate, because direct determination of what information is held in the memory system at any time is impossible. As mentioned previously, when a person is unable to recall information already learned, the trouble commonly lies in the retrieval system rather than in the memory system itself. There are great difficulties involved in disentangling failures of recall due to actual memory failures and those produced by inadequacies in retrieval.

Although one is inclined to think of the loss of what he has learned as being a result of an inevitable defect in his constitution, there are many situations in which such a loss is an advantage. Throughout the growing period, the child learns ways of behaving that he later has to discard and

Forgetting:
Behavior Elimination
and Information Loss

replace with more mature habits. He needs to forget his old habits as he learns new ones, but that is not always easy. The baby words he uses and has learned must become displaced by the words of the adult world. Many of the demands he directs toward his mother when he is little have to be replaced by demands made on himself. Old habits have to be discarded, that is, inhibited or forgotten, and then be replaced by more mature habits. If the old habits are not "forgotten" but persist to an age when they are no longer appropriate, then they may present a serious behavior problem. Indeed, the clinical psychologist spends much time with patients who need help in discarding childish ways of behaving that have persisted far beyond the age when they are acceptable. The clinical psychologist is often impressed with the extraordinary persistence of these habits, and he wishes that the memory system did not store them so faithfully for later use.

Just as behavior covers a range of phenomena, so too do forgetting and retention cover a range. In school learning, one is largely concerned with problems of retention and forgetting of verbal information, but one also remembers or forgets motor skills such as dancing and bowling and emotional responses such as fear of dogs or even fear of people. This last represents what has been appropriately called gut learning in that it involves visceral responses to situations often described as anxiety responses. The clinician is particularly concerned with these quite basic responses, because, when they are inappropriate and severe, they can play havoc with a person's life. Much of what has been learned about the elimination of these responses has been derived from studies of very basic learning in laboratory animals. So let us begin the study of forgetting phenomena with a brief discussion of classical conditioning, for it is through the study of classical conditioning that useful knowledge has been derived concerning ways to control unwanted anxieties.

Consider the typical classical conditioning experiment. Animals can learn to produce a flow of saliva at the sound of a bell by being exposed to the sequence bell–food. When they are then exposed to the bell alone, without the food, the salivation declines. Eventually, the bell is sounded but it produces no increased flow of saliva. The conditioned response to the bell has been **extinguished.** In common language, it might be said that the response has been forgotten, but this is likely to be misleading. What has happened to the response? It can easily be demonstrated that the internal mechanism of the response has not been eliminated, for a single pairing of the bell and the food will bring it back to full strength again. This is known as the phenomenon of spontaneous recovery. The response has been inhibited, and the underlying mechanism has entered into a dormant condition.

Various techniques have been developed for extinguishing classically conditioned responses, that is, producing a forgetting of the response from occurring when the conditioned stimulus is presented. An animal learns to raise its foot when a bell sounds, for the sounding of the bell has been followed by an electric shock on several previous occasions. The response can be extinguished by holding the foot on the plate when the bell sounds. The conditioned response, the raising of the foot to the sound of the bell, is not allowed to occur in the presence of the conditioned stimulus, the bell. A technique analogous to this has been used with psychological patients, called the desensitization technique (developed by Wolpe, 1958). In the application of this technique for eliminating anxiety responses, the patient first identifies many of the conditions and events that produce anxiety. These are arranged in order from those that produce the least anxiety to those that produce the most. In the next step, the patient is asked to relax completely and is then asked to think of the least anxiety-producing of these situations. Now complete relaxation is incompatible with anxiety, so the situation involves an anxiety-producing stimulus but the prevention of the anxiety response from occurring. After some practice in this situation, the individual is able to think of the anxiety-producing event without manifesting anxiety. Then the patient is taken to the next anxiety-producing situation, also under a condition of extreme relaxation. Ultimately, the patient is able to think of what were originally highly anxiety-producing situations without the accompanying responses of anxiety. There is now considerable evidence that the technique is effective in lowering the anxiety level of neurotic individuals and that the technique does improve their general adjustment to life (see Rachman, 1967).

Just as a classically conditioned response may be extinguished through arranging for it to occur in the absence of food, so too may operants become extinguished through their occurrence in the absence of a reinforcer. A child who finds that a candy machine occasionally produces a chocolate bar when the lever is pushed will develop the operant of pulling the lever whenever he passes the machine. However, if the machine is repaired, he will continue to pull the lever for a time. His tendency to do this will slowly decline, until he is likely to pass the machine without touching it. The response tendency is not completely eliminated, as is evident from the fact that the youngster will still continue to give the lever an occasional pull. Laboratory experiments suggest that the response tendency in such a case is not eliminated but is **inhibited** or **blocked.** This is evident from the fact that the response will return at full strength if it is just once reinforced by the delivery of a candy bar.

Because most bad habits that one would like to eliminate can be described as operants that have been well reinforced, the obvious way of eliminating these habits is to arrange for them to occur in the absence of the reinforcer or other reinforcers. This is easier said than done. How can one arrange for a person to smoke a cigarette without the various reinforcers that result from smoking? One attempt to do this is to remove the nicotine from the cigarette, but the results are not very successful. Although it is true that the presence of nicotine in the smoke has reinforcing properties similar to those found in all addictions, there are other much more subtle reinforcers operating. The smoker enjoys the entire ritual of pulling a cigarette from the pack, lighting it up, blowing the smoke across the room, and drawing the warm (polluted!) air into his lungs.

There are many aspects of the smoking routine that almost certainly have reinforcing properties that ensure that the habit will remain at a high level of strength. It is virtually impossible to arrange for smoking to take place in the absence of reinforcers. The habit has built-in characteristics that ensure a continued profit for the tobacco companies. For the same reason, all addictions are difficult to cure. They all represent highly reinforced habits, though reinforcement alone does not account for the enormous strength of the needs developed in the case of hard drugs, or even in the case of alcohol.

There are no doubt some habits that can be broken through the withdrawal of reinforcers. In some cases, at least, habitual tantrums in a child can be reduced if they are ignored. As every parent knows, there is a tendency to show attention to the child having a tantrum. Sometimes this attention is shown in mild reprimands and admonishments, which may be entirely nonpunishing to the child and even rewarding. Not long ago, the belief was also held that crying in infancy would be increased if the crying baby was picked up, but this does not seem to be the case. For the young infant, the stimulation provided has a calming effect and sleep is likely to result. The effect of handling on a young infant is quite different from the effect on an older child, and it may well not have the reinforcing properties it was originally supposed to have had.

B. F. Skinner and his followers have claimed that teachers often unwittingly reinforce bad habits in pupils and thus strengthen the habits rather than eliminate them. The case that always seems to be cited is of a teacher who dismisses an unruly class and thus reinforces the unruly behavior he would like to eliminate. Such claims about the behavior of teachers seem to be derived from hearsay. The author has spent hundreds of hours in classrooms, observing and recording the behavior of both teachers and pupils, and cannot remember a case in which such unwitting reinforcement of bad behavior occurred. Teachers may sometimes reinforce behavior of dubious value, as when a child is praised simply because he did not say a word during class, but the reinforcement of bad behavior is probably very rare indeed. What one might call bad habits of students take place and persist for reasons other than teacher reinforcement.

The discussion up to this point has dealt with cases in which learned habits are inhibited. This is a very different matter from erasing information from memory. The Wolpe technique prevents the anxiety response from occurring in the presence of the memory with which it was originally tied. The anxiety component of the response becomes inhibited or blocked. The extinction of classically conditioned responses or operants also represents inhibition of responses, and there is no reason for believing that the tendency to make the extinguished response is reduced in strength. The suppression of gross motor responses appears to be a matter of inhibiting them rather than eliminating them. However, there are other aspects of memory in which different processes appear to be operating in the matter of forgetting, and it is to these that we must now turn.

286
. . . .
Forgetting:
Behavior Elimination
and Information Loss

The Retention and Forgetting of Verbal Information and Cognitive Skills

Up to this point, no consideration has been given to the retention and forgetting of academic information of the kind acquired in schools. The motor skills and emotional responses considered represent an important aspect of life, but what has been said about the acquisition, retention, and inhibition of these aspects of behavior does not necessarily throw light on the retention, inhibition, and forgetting of other acquisitions. A few psychologists have taken the position that all inhibition and forgetting phenomena are essentially the same as those involved in the extinction of classically conditioned responses or the extinction of operants. However, virtually no major book on memory published in the last five years takes this position. Indeed, these books provide a much more complete and detailed account of forgetting and retention than the extinction view provides.

Much of the investigation of retention and verbal forgetting has revolved around two concepts—**decay** and **interference.** The decay theory of forgetting is in many ways the popular view of how information is lost from the memory system. The decay concept of forgetting is that memories fade much like the pattern on the drapes fades as it is exposed to the sun. Information placed in the memory system does appear to fade in this kind of way, but appearance can often be deceptive. One important task of research has been to determine the extent to which decay theory does actually describe the way information is lost from the memory system.

A second general theory of forgetting is that it is a result of different items of information interfering with one another in the memory system. Here again, everyday experience gives some support to this kind of theory. If I do business with three clients named Smolenski, Solinski, and Snelerski, I am very likely to have difficulty in remembering which one I sold particular items to. I am also likely to confuse their names, calling Smolenski by the name of Solinski or Snelerski. The retention of information about one of these characters tends to be confused with information about another. Indeed, the confusion may be so great that, a year later, I may not remember any of their names but only that I had three clients whose names I could never remember correctly.

Decay theory and interference theory have been the starting points for most of the research on memory of the last decade. The research problem has been to determine the extent to which forgetting can be accounted for in terms of each one of these two theories. Let us consider each aspect of memory separately.

The trace or buffer: The evidence is overwhelming that the trace decays rapidly and that all the information in the trace is lost in less than three seconds. Auditory and visual traces seem to have about the same decay rates. In addition, there is probably a very rapid decay process, amounting to immediate erasure, that takes place when a person turns his attention from one kind of input to another.

287
. . . .
The Retention and
Forgetting of Verbal
Information and
Cognitive Skills

Short-term memory: Let us consider the retention of information such as is involved in remembering a telephone number for a short interval of time while waiting for the phone to be free. Of course, psychologists do not do experiments with telephone numbers, but they select the materials very carefully so that they will be of just the right difficulty and meet other specifications. In a study by Peterson and Peterson (1959), the task for their short-term memory experiment was that of remembering groups of three consonants such as *KBL*. In the technique used in this particular experiment, the experimenter spoke three consonants and then a number such as 500. The subject repeated the number and counted backward in threes from that number saying, for example, "500, 497, 494, ..." When a light went on, the subject had to recall the group of three consonants. The purpose of asking the subject to count backward was to prevent him from rehearsing the group of three consonants during the interval between presentation and recall. Information can be held in short-term memory indefinitely if it is rehearsed. While waiting for the telephone line to clear, we repeat to ourselves the number that is to be called. This helps us to retain the number until we can dial it.

Peterson and Peterson were able to vary the interval between the original presentation of the group of three consonants and the recall over an eighteen-second interval. The results of their study are presented in Figure 3. The graph shows that the loss of information is rapid, and little remains after an eighteen-second interval. More information probably remains than is evident in the figure. Given more time to think about what they remembered, the subjects might have recalled more of the groups of letters.

It is possible that the repeating of numbers in the waiting interval

288
• • • • • • • • •
Forgetting:
Behavior Elimination
and Information Loss

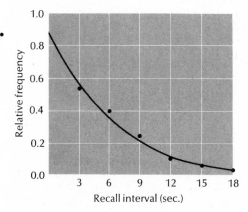

Figure 3 Correct recalls as a function of recall interval. (After L. R. Peterson and M. J. Peterson, Short-term retention of individual verbal items. *J. of Exper. Psych.*, **58**, 1959, pp. 193–198. Copyright 1959 by the Americal Psychological Association, and reproduced by permission.)

might have disrupted the information to be retained as well as serving the purpose of preventing rehearsal. The experimenter has to choose between allowing the subject opportunity to rehearse or introducing some activity that prevents rehearsal but also may influence the outcomes of the experiment.

The reader should also note that the loss of information from memory is rapid at first but slows down as time passes by. As we shall see, the curve is rather typical of forgetting under many different conditions.

In the course of everyday activities, information probably does not decay so rapidly, and we may be able to hold information in short-term memory for much longer periods involving many minutes. To do this, it is probably necessary to repeat the information under the breath or silently talk about the information. A student dreamily listening to a lecture, with little intention to remember what he hears, may well show the same decay of the information in short-term memory that the Peterson and Peterson study showed. On the other hand, the pupil actively discussing some information provided by the teacher may be continuously placing the information back into the short-term memory system and also transferring the information to the long-term system. It does seem fairly clear that information that decays in short-term memory in about eighteen seconds probably has little chance of being transferred to the long-term system.

In the case of short-term memory, decay is not the only factor producing forgetting. There is now very substantial evidence, assembled by Broadbent (1970), that one piece of information in short-term memory can disrupt another. Give a person a telephone number to dial and before he can dial it read him another number, and the chances are that his memory of the original telephone number will be disrupted. If the procedure is varied so that the subject is first read a telephone number and then a set of letters, the disruption is much less. Similarity is an important factor in producing disruption. In the case of the example discussed, the effect is known as **retroactive inhibition.** This simply means that something works backward (retroactively) to block (inhibit) something else. Retroactive inhibition is quite clearly one of the ways that information in short-term memory is disrupted and lost.

The rate at which information is lost from short-term memory depends also on the extent to which it has been learned. Figure 4, from data of Hellyer (1962), shows the retentions of the same kind of material, but the curves are given for eight, four, two, and one presentations of the three-letter groups of consonants. The loss in short-term memory is much less rapid if the verbal information is presented several times.

What we have been considering is information retained for just a short time—what teachers call the in-one-ear-and-out-the-other phenomenon. The information stays just long enough to be repeated back, but even after the repetition the life of the information in storage is a matter of seconds rather than minutes. Although the data have been derived from studies of verbal behavior, very similar retention curves could have

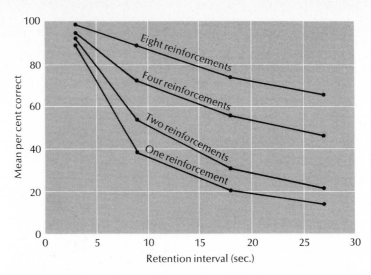

Figure 4 Short-term retention for a verbal response. (After data given by S. Hellyer, Supplementary report: Frequency of stimulus presentation and short-term decrement in recall, *J. of Exper. Psych.*, **64,** 1962, p. 650. Copyright 1962 by the American Psychological Association, and reproduced by permission.)

been presented for the short-term retention of motor skills of comparable difficulty.

Retention in long-term memory: Now let us turn our attention to the retention and loss of material stored in the long-term system. First, let us consider some facts. A graph from Cain and Willey (1939), shown in Figure 5, demonstrates the usual curve of retention. The reader cannot help noting the striking resemblance between this graph covering a span of seven days and the previous graphs, which covered a span of only seconds. Later, we will see that the two kinds of graph depend on different processes.

The long-term retention generally declines rapidly, particularly during the first day, and then a much less rapid loss of information occurs. The loss shown by the typical so-called curve of forgetting exaggerates the actual loss. This can be shown by asking the subject, at the end of a period of time, to relearn the material. It is generally found that, although as many as twenty repetitions were required to learn the material originally, a single repetition may change recall from 25 per cent correct to 100 per cent correct. The curve represents what appears to be retained under certain conditions. Under other conditions, a different curve might be produced. For example, if the amount of retention over a long period of time were measured by asking the person to choose from a number of alternatives the items he had learned, he would appear to have retained more than if he were just asked to recall the items. Recall provides few cues, but recognition tasks provide many. The latter tasks are, in a way, tasks that prompt the individual. The more an individual is

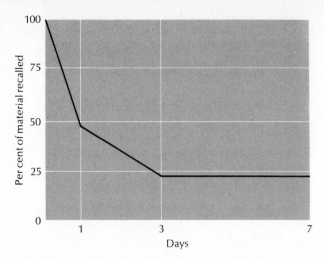

Figure 5 Curve of retention for nonsense syllables. (After L. F. Cain and R. de V. Willey, the effect of spaced learning on the curve of retention. *J. of Exper. Psych.*, **25**, 1939, pp. 209–214. Copyright 1939 by the American Psychological Association, and reproduced by permission.)

prompted, the more he appears to be able to remember. Thus it can be seen that different procedures for measuring memory provide different pictures of what is retained and what has been lost. The relearning method is the most sensitive method of all of showing that some information has been retained. Prompts and cues have the property of priming the retrieval system. Perhaps they function by indicating to the retrieval system where to look for the information that is to be retrieved.

The measurement of the pupil's retention of information related to what he has learned in school is commonly undertaken in situations that make it as difficult as possible for him to retrieve whatever information he may have stored in his memory. Essay tests provide a situation of this character. Probably a better situation for measuring the information that a pupil potentially has at his fingertips is one in which he has access to books and materials that have been used in instruction. The adult has to rely on the information he can retrieve from books and other materials rather than on the skeleton of material that he has stored within himself, and the teacher may well emphasize the measurement of how the pupil can use the information he has memorized to obtain information stored outside of himself.

There is absolutely no evidence that forgetting in long-term memory is produced by decay. On the other hand, there is substantial evidence that much of the loss of information in the system is due to the interfering effect that one item of information has on another. Hundreds of laboratory experiments demonstrate this influence. Indeed, the demonstration is so convincing that one may well suspect that when a new piece of information is placed in long-term memory, the effect is to disrupt some of the

291

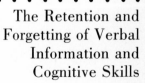

The Retention and Forgetting of Verbal Information and Cognitive Skills

other information already placed there. This is the retroactive effect already referred to in this chapter. The effect works forward as well as backward; that is, what I learn today may interfere with something that I attempt to learn tomorrow or it may interfere with the retention of that information. This is the **proactive effect.**

The proactive effect on forgetting may be much more important than the retroactive effect. Underwood (1957) has pointed out that when one encounters a learning task, some interference with retention is produced by perhaps a large part of what one has learned in the past. For example, I sit down to begin learning a new language and begin to work on placing in memory the essentials of the new language. However, what I place in memory immediately begins to be disrupted by the knowledge I have of other languages, for the knowledge I have of other languages is somewhat inconsistent with the knowledge to be acquired. Underwood estimated that the forgetting to be expected from this effect during the first twenty-four hours after learning would be about 25 per cent. Underwood took the position that proactive effects might produce much more forgetting than retroactive effects.

The retroactive and the proactive effects have an important consequence. Because the adding of information to long-term memory tends to reduce the information already stored there, and because it interferes with the later storage of information, there is a limit to what one can store in the memory system.

One way to prevent deterioration of information is periodical review, a procedure essential for maintaining a store of information in good condition in the memory system. Such review, in schools, is generally unplanned and unsystematic. In some areas, such as history, there is a tendency for successive courses to be over-repetitive. In others, particularly in the science areas, there may be little review at all. Perhaps one of the advantages of the French school-leaving examination, the baccalaureate, is that it forces a continuous review of what has been learned. The main disadvantage is the immense strain it places on the student when he realizes that on this examination depends his entire future.

Because one has to live with a memory system from which there is a continuous loss through the process of interference, an important practical matter is how to reduce the loss.

Maximizing retention in long-term memory: It has already been stated that additional trials with the material to be learned reduce the loss from the short-term memory. The same is true for the long-term system. Additional periods of learning result in greater stability of the information stored. Learning material beyond the point where it can be recited back with only a short delay is referred to as **overlearning.** The effect of overlearning is to improve the retention of the information. Overlearning may be undertaken to the point where there is virtually no loss of the information stored in memory over a period of months or even years. The best-studied examples of such overlearning are found in the case of motor skills. A person learns to iceskate, perhaps as a child, and engages in the activity every winter for many years. Then he moves to a warm climate where there are no opportunities to iceskate, but after many years, on a winter trip to the North again, he takes to the ice. The skill is then found to have deteriorated little over the intervening years. The skill had been overlearned, with hundreds of hours of practice, and had reached the point where it would be retained for life. Overlearning seems to give information stored in memory some immunity to interference and disruption from other information.

Generations of schoolchildren have known that one of the best ways to prepare for recitation is to read through the materials to be remembered just before going to sleep. When this procedure is followed, then material appears to be easily learned. Jenkins and Dallenbach (1924) long ago studied this problem and found laboratory evidence to show that the phenomenon is a genuine one. Data from Jenkins and Dallenbach are shown in Figure 6. There is a marked difference in retention between those who slept after learning and those who stayed awake.

The effectiveness of sleep in improving retention can be attributed to

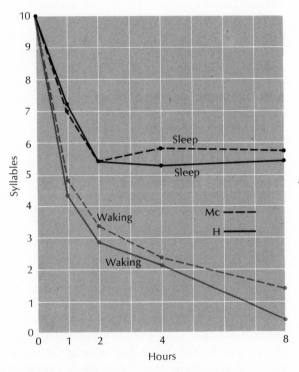

293
· · · · · · · · · · · · · ·
The Retention and
Forgetting of Verbal
Information and
Cognitive Skills

Figure 6 Average number of syllables reproduced by each of two subjects, identified as H and Mc, after the various time intervals of sleep and waking. (After J. G. Jenkins and K. M. Dallenback, Obliviscence during sleep and waking. *Amer. J. of Psych.*, **35**, 1924, pp. 605–612. Reproduced by permission.)

two causes. Sleep may well facilitate the transfer of information to long-term memory, but this is a conjecture. A much more plausible explanation is that during sleep there are no new encounters with the environment to interfere with the retention of information already stored.

Probably no condition is more important for long-time retention than provision for regular review. Regular review is different from overlearning. To some extent, regular review takes place over the typical kindergarten through twelfth-grade school program. What is learned in one grade is covered again in another. There is also a hidden kind of review. Every time a child works a problem in long division, he has opportunity to rehearse and review the skills related to multiplication and subtraction. The more advanced skills give practice in other skills at a more elementary level. The amount of review undertaken of some of the more basic skills is enormous during thirteen years of school, and probably so much so that they remain with the individual for life.

Semester examinations also have the function of requiring the learner to review what he has learned. The positive effects of examinations in promoting retention are probably due to this review factor. Oddly enough, those who have come to education from the field of operant conditioning have generally followed a practice of giving daily examinations as an incentive to study and have failed to recognize the importance of examining over larger chunks of material so that the individual is required to review what he has already learned. Indeed, many classroom practices seem to be based on the dubious assumption that what is learned once is learned for life. The idea of mastery learning is this kind of an idea.

Language represents a highly overlearned activity. Probably few skills are ever practiced for so many thousands of hours as are the skills related to speaking and listening. A person who speaks several languages fluently will retain them over the years. Such an individual does find, when he is going to have to speak a language he has not spoken for a time, that he requires a warm-up period. Sometimes he will read a newspaper or a book in the language he is to speak for a warm-up, which probably warms up the retrieval system.

One suspects that children could well learn to arrange for themselves the systematic review of the aspects of subject matter that they can profit from retaining in detail. Facts about learning that are useful should not be the monopoly of the teacher but should form the basis of the pupil's own strategy of how he plans his own learning. Such matters are generally called study habits and form the subject matter of courses in high school and colleges. But perhaps they should be systematically introduced in the elementary school, beginning at least as low as first grade. The techniques of good study should also not be regarded as something to be studied only by the failing student, as at the present time, but as an essential part of every child's education.

Forgetting:
Behavior Elimination
and Information Loss

Meaningfulness and Retention

One of the oldest clichés of educational literature is that meaningful material is more easily learned than is meaningless material. Suppose one asks an English-speaking seven-year-old who knows no German to learn the first two lines of the *Lorelei* by having the lines said to him:

> *Ich weiss nicht was soll es bedeuten*
> *Das ich so traurig bin.*

The English-speaking child must begin by developing perceptual recognition of the words, which, as said by the experimenter, consist only of a jumble of sounds. The child must first discriminate the component sounds of the jumble. The experimenter may help the child by speaking each of the words distinctly so that he can begin to identify components. The child who speaks English does not have the word elements stored in his memory, so his next task is to store them. This is a difficult thing to do. Just try to memorize a set of meaningless words, such as *drethca dla serhylt blin dzeabcol* and see how difficult it is. After the child has memorized the words, he then has to go through the final stage of learning—learning the order in which the words are to be recited. The learning of the set of twelve meaningless words is a very difficult task and consumes considerable time.

Now contrast the task as analyzed in the case of meaningless material with the task of learning two such lines as

> *Now listen my children and you shall hear*
> *Of the midnight ride of Paul Revere.*

The English-speaking child who learns these lines can already discriminate the words and has the words all stored in his memory system, except perhaps for the word *Revere*. Instead of having to learn all the words, as in the case of the child learning the German lines, he has to learn only one word. His main learning task is in learning the order of the words. This is a simple task compared with the long learning sequence that has to take place before the child can master two lines of German.

Our analysis here of the difference between learning meaningless material and learning meaningful material brings out the fact that meaningless material involves far more learning components. It involves far more learning. The meaningful task is easy because most of the learning involved in memorizing it has already been undertaken before the person ever began the task. All learning is probably equally easy, or difficult, but some tasks call for more learning than do other tasks. If most of the components of learning have already been undertaken at some prior time, then the task is an easy one to learn.

Learning in infancy appears to be so slow because it involves many learning components that facilitate learning later in life. An infant has to learn to discriminate the component sounds of words before he can begin to show any comprehension of language, and such a task is a difficult one. Listen to a recording of an Oriental language and see how long it takes you, experienced in the use of language, to begin to differentiate the basic sound components. The task, at first, will seem to be one of immense difficulty, and it is. Yet you have enormous advantages over the infant in that you know what you are looking for in listening to the sound.

Because meaningful material is much more easily learned than meaningless, it is also the material that is most likely to be overlearned. A child given relatively meaningless material to learn is likely to use so much time in learning it just to the point where he can regurgitate it that he is not likely to have either the time or inclination to overlearn it in the way he probably should. For this reason, meaningless material, even if mastered originally, is not likely to be retained very long.

Intention to Forget and Forgetting

A question commonly asked is whether one can deliberately forget. The assumption is often made that one can, for a person who has been slighted is told "Just forget about it." The advice is easily given, but not readily followed. The facts indicate that once information is placed in the long-term memory, it will stay there until it is disrupted by other information in the system. There is absolutely no evidence that one can erase information in long-term memory merely by deciding to do so. The memory is not like a sheet of paper with erasable marks on it. Indeed, our access to our long-term memory is very indirect, and only through the retrieval system.

A person can fail to retrieve information when he is highly motivated not to do so. The classic case is forgetting a dental appointment. One does not want to remember the appointment and one does not. The same forgetfulness may occur when one cannot remember the names of persons he does not like or incidents from the past that caused him anxiety or grief. Freud developed the term *repression* to cover such cases of apparent forgetfulness. His idea was that anxiety prevented the information from coming to the surface. Today it is known that the effect of anxiety, in this respect, is on the retrieval system.

There is another sense in which one can actually forget material. Bjork (1970) showed that when subjects were asked to learn lists of pairs of words, and some pairs were marked to indicate that the material did not have to be remembered, then the subjects read the marked words but did not learn them. What happened was that the information entered the short-term memory but was never transferred to the long-term system. This is a case in which there was perception of the words and reading of the words, but without intent to learn, and the result was no permanent learning. One can deliberately forget information from the short-term memory system.

The inability to erase information in the long-term memory system accounts for the difficulty the clinical psychologist has in disposing of past experiences that continue to trouble the patient. The clinician is unable to erase these experiences, but he can detach from them the anxiety that is the main source of trouble to the patient or he can find ways of blocking the anxiety.

297
. . . .
Intention to Forget
and Forgetting

Summary

1 Loss of information from memory is difficult to investigate because of the problem of distinguishing between true loss and inability to retrieve. Inhibition is another factor that may be confused with loss of information. One can retain or forget not only verbal information but also motor skills, visceral responses, and emotional responses.

2 Study of the control of emotional responses has been undertaken by the techniques of classical conditioning and has shown that such responses can be extinguished and also recover spontaneously, as will any other classically conditioned response. Practical techniques have been developed for extinguishing unwanted emotional responses. One of these is the desensitization technique, which involves thinking about the emotion-producing situation without manifesting the unwanted emotional response. Extinction is made to occur by providing the stimulus that ordinarily produces the response and then preventing the response from occurring by having the individual relax as completely as possible. Such a condition of relaxation is incompatible with emotional responses related to anxiety.

3 Many bad habits cannot be extinguished by a simple extinction procedure, because there are reinforcements related to the habit that cannot be eliminated. For example, a candy-eating habit is reinforced by the sweetness and flavoring of the candy. Sometimes, inappropriate behavior in the classroom can be extinguished by being neglected, but teachers often cannot control the reinforcements that maintain such behavior.

4 The loss of information from the nervous system, as time passes, cannot be understood in terms of the process of extinction alone.

5 Two concepts, interference and decay, have dominated research in the area. The evidence is overwhelming that the trace undergoes rapid decay. In the short-term memory system, there is decay of information but it can be put back in the system, as when one repeats a telephone number to himself. Loss of information from the short-term memory system is also produced by one piece of information interfering with the retention of another piece of information. Several presentations of information produce a slower rate of loss in the short-term system than does a single presentation. In the long-term system, loss of information seems to be due entirely to the interference factor. Long-term retention generally shows a rapid decline at first, followed by a reduced rate of decline.

However, different procedures for measuring loss of information from the long-term system give rather different results. The greater the number of cues provided for recall, the greater is the amount of information retrieved. This is one reason why an essay test may provide fewer opportunities for the pupil to display what he knows than an objective type of test.

6 Interference effects are of two kinds, proactive and the retroactive. Although the retroactive effect has been the most closely studied, the proactive effect may be greater. What one learns may be interfered with by much of what he has previously acquired. The proactive and retroactive effects together limit the amount of information that can be permanently stored in the memory system.

7 In order to maximize retention, acquisition should not be followed by tasks that might interfere with the learning undertaken. Overlearning is an important factor in preventing loss. Regular review is also of great importance.

8 Meaningfulness appears to facilitate learning because meaningful material is already partly learned. Learning in infancy appears to be slow because it is not facilitated by component learnings that have already taken place.

9 There has not yet been any demonstration that one can deliberately erase information from the memory system. One can decide not to learn certain material presented to him, but that is different from deliberate forgetting.

299

. . . .

Summary

Chapter 2, on development, discussed the fact that some events following a response tend to increase the frequency of the response. These events are commonly described collectively as **reinforcers** and constitute a very broad category of events. Give a child a cookie for remaining quiet while a visitor is present, and this increases the chances that quiet behavior will occur next time a visitor arrives on the scene. The cookie functions as a reinforcer of that particular form of behavior. Tell a child that you are happy to see the craftsmanship he is exercising in his hobby, and he is likely to show that same fine craftsmanship on future occasions. The praise functions as a reinforcer. A child looks at the clock and eventually says "The clock says it is half past ten." You say "That's right." The latter statement is likely to reinforce the behavior of the child that led up to his announcement of the time and strengthen the processes in-

10

Information Feedback, Rewards and Punishments, and the Guidance of Learning

volved. In saying "That's right," you are providing the child with information about the correctness of his conclusions. Some psychologists classify this event in the broad category known as reinforcers. This author's position is that the term *reinforcer* is too broad a category to be very useful because it groups together events in terms of their consequence of increasing the strength of a response. Classifying events just in terms of their consequences has had a long history of futility. Let us consider a classic example of this.

The early chemists classified some compounds as corrosives. Such a classification was misleading because it placed acids and alkalis in the same category. Both will eat away metals, dissolve fats, and burn the skin, but they function in this respect by entirely different means. Only later, when the mechanism of corrosion was understood, did chemists begin to understand that two entirely different classes of compounds were involved and not a single class. The error of the early chemists was to classify compounds in terms of their consequences. A similar error has been made by psychologists in classifying as reinforcers all events that increase the probability that the behavior they follow will take place, so that reinforcers include food, praise, the giving of information, opportunity to view a moving display such as is provided by a television screen or a movie, a light being turned on or off, a nod of the head, and a vast array of other events. To classify all of these in the broad category of reinforcers is of very doubtful utility.

In this chapter, discussion will be focused on various aspects of reinforcing events. First, let us consider the information provided by reinforcing events. This kind of information is sometimes called **feedback** and sometimes **knowledge of results.** It will become evident, later in the chapter, that there is considerable difference between telling a child he is right after he has completed working a problem and giving him a piece of candy. To equate these two kinds of events is not far from being silly. Yet there are many psychologists who treat the two kinds of events as essentially similar, mainly because they fall within the broad category of reinforcers.

Time When Information Is Given

Information related to the performance of many tasks may be given equally usefully before the task is undertaken or after the task is completed. Let us first consider laboratory studies. There are well-known studies by Annett (1961), in which a large number of dots were flashed on a screen and the subjects' task was to estimate how many dots were there. Subjects learn to improve on this task, but improvement is dependent on obtaining some information that will guide their initial guessing. The information can be given either in advance of the presentation or after the presentation has been flashed on the screen and the subject has made his guess. In the first case, the experimenter will make some such announcement as "The number of dots that will be flashed on the screen is 48." The dots are then flashed on the screen. In the second case, the dots are flashed and then the experimenter makes an announcement of the form "There were 63 dots." Learning to guess the number of dots is about equally effective in these two procedures, but on other tasks the same generalization may not hold. Anderson et al. (1971) found on a verbal task that information was better given after responding.

Annett's experiment brings out an important point. If one had been dealing with a reinforcement system, then the reinforcement would have to follow the action of the subject that was to be recorded. It is fairly common knowledge that for a reward system to be effective it must follow and not precede the action to be rewarded. For this reason, people are paid after performing the activities for which they are to be compensated. Hardly ever is a person paid in advance for his performance. If one does offer a child a cookie for being good, the cookie had better arrive after the performance and not before. In contrast, people do modify their behavior and learn regardless of whether information is given before or after the performance of certain classes of tasks. In many tasks, the person is told in advance just what is the criterion of an effective performance. A foreigner being introduced to bowling would have to be told just how he could tell that he was doing well or poorly in performing with the ball.

Feedback in Nonverbal Tasks

Let us first consider the function that feedback plays in tasks involving gross muscular movements of the limbs and then later move on to a discussion of feedback in verbal tasks. The school has an interest in the development of some motor skills, notably in the physical education field and in such activities as typing and the operation of business machines.

Let us consider a skill such as typing, which has been analyzed by West (1969) in considerable detail. Our discussion here will be based to some extent on the analysis provided by West, but it will also draw heavily on later knowledge of the acquisition of motor skills summarized by Posner and Keele (1973). A readable discussion of the subject can also be found in Fitts and Posner (1967).

Let us consider the case of a child sitting at a typewriter, prepared to type three-letter words flashed on a screen. Let us say that the letters are printed on the keys and the child can see the keys. Before each word is to appear, there is a warning beep. Then, two seconds later, the word appears, and the pupil makes an effort to type it as quickly as possible. The initial response of the pupil to the screen has to be one of attention, that is, a condition propitious for the reception of information. This reception process must involve the learning of whatever information happens to be in the trace system at the time. The process of attention itself is complex in that it involves more than the mere orientation of the eyes toward the screen. The eyes might look at the screen but not see the syllable presented. In other words, there are central processes that are of critical importance in the attention phase of the performance of such a task.

Some would even say that the central processes are the really significant processes. It should be noted that it is possible to attend to a visual signal even though the eyes are not centered on the source. One can attend to a signal in peripheral vision, as one does while watching somebody out of the corner of his eye.

The signal then appears on the screen and takes the form of the word *the*. Let us assume that it is correctly read, though there is evidence that most errors of typing are errors of reading rather than errors of striking the wrong keys. The reading of the word to be typed is then followed by a search of the keyboard for the correct letters. While this search is being undertaken, the child prepares himself to strike each key as it is found. This process has been described as the development of a **motor set.** A motor set is to be contrasted with a **sensory set,** which occurs while the child waits for the word to be flashed on the screen. In the case of the sensory set, the individual is prepared to take in and analyze information. In the case of the motor set, the individual is readied to act. A person readied to act can act more rapidly than a person who has not been so alerted. Evidence indicates that the alerting process saves about half a second. Skills can be performed rapidly only when the individual is properly and continuously alerted to perform each step in proper sequence.

The child finds each key and strikes each key in sequence. When he finds a key and begins to move to strike it, he cannot correct the movement. All of us have the experience of hitting a wrong key, knowing beforehand that we are going to make an error but not being able to stop ourselves in time. The observation is an important one, and it has been the focus of much experimental inquiry. What it means is that the nervous system is able to assemble a program for performing an act and to set that program into action, but it takes another quarter to half a second to assemble a new program of behavior that will stop or replace the original one. Action in the performance of a skill involves the internal assembly of a program of movements to be performed and then the initiation of the program, which takes place quite automatically until it is completed and stopped. An act to be performed through such a program may be quite short or it may involve a long and complicated sequence, as it does when an accomplished bowler throws a ball down the alley (see Posner and Keele, 1973).

In the case of a novice learning to type, the motor program produced by his brain is quite short and involves the typing of single letters. In actual fact, he comes to the learning situation already equipped with such programs, for he long ago learned to press bell buttons and perform other similar motor activities. As he progresses, the motor programs emitted become longer. An experienced typist types the entire word *the* as a unit. He will type this word in perhaps as short a time as half a second. The speed with which this motor program of movements is emitted by the typist is such that once he begins to type the word, he cannot stop himself even though he sees that he is about to strike the wrong key. The time required to stop the program is about as long as the program itself.

304
. . . .
Information Feedback,
Rewards and
Punishments, and the
Guidance of Learning

Indeed, the expert typist may find that a whole group of words has run off before he can bring the activity to a halt.

Now the entire procedure involved when the child haltingly types the word *the* is intimately controlled by the use of information. Holding (1965) has pointed out that information is related to the performance and acquisition of skill in such a task in three ways. First, there is the kind of information that precedes the undertaking of the task—knowing what it is about, what one is expected to do, how one's work at the task is to be evaluated, and so forth. Second, there is the information that is used while the task is in progress—the initial perception of the word to be typed, the perceptual information needed to guide the fingers to the keys, and also the result of striking particular letters. Third, there is the information indicating that the task has been correctly performed. This involves an inspection of the word as it is typed on the page. Some of the information that guides the task and the information indicating final success at the task are called information feedbacks. The information that guides action is called **concurrent feedback,** and the final product provides **terminal feedback.** The latter serves several purposes. It may indicate what part of the original performance needs to be redone and corrected. It may serve the purpose of correcting the internal program so that an error in the program is corrected. An example of the latter is provided by an incident that occurred in the typing of the manuscript of this book. The author noticed that he was persistently writing the word *the* as *hte*. Something had gone wrong with the internal program that resulted in the typing of the word.

The concurrent feedback of the learner is useful in the early stages of learning, but it may interfere at later stages with the actual performance of the skill. A typist who had to look at each letter as it was printed on the paper would never acquire any great speed but would remain at the level of the hunt-and-peck beginner. As soon as the initial stages of learning the skill have been mastered, the student is encouraged to do without concurrent feedback. He is then urged to look at the copy to be typed and not at the machine.

The acquisition of the skill also involves the elimination from use of other cues that play an important part in the early stages of learning. The beginner may attend carefully to the letters on the keys, but speed cannot be achieved so long as he does this. The earlier methods of teaching typing tried to solve this problem by providing the student with a typewriter that did not have any letters printed on the keys. Although such a procedure prevented the student from developing a dependency on cues that he could not use later, the procedure also introduced enormous frustration into the learning task. Present recommended procedures involve the use of a typewriter on which the keys are all labeled.

Improvement in the performance of a skill can take place through two different means. One method is to devise new ways of performance as the skill develops. The role of the teacher in doing this is of crucial importance. The student of typing will not typically learn for himself to avoid looking at the keys as he performs his tasks. He needs to be urged to do this by the teacher and given encouragement in so doing. The student is likely to find that his early attempts to practice a touch system bring him the greatest discouragement, for they lead to a substantial increase in the number of errors and a slowing down in the pace at which he works. Improvement in the performance of many skills requires that there be some outside source of information that will show the way to improved perceptual and motor patterns.

A second way of improving the performance of a skill that is being acquired is to improve the internal program or programs involved in its execution. This can be done in many ways. The obvious procedure is to practice the skill again and again, slowly eliminating all surplus movements. Another is discussed by Posner and Keele (1973) and also by Nixon and Locke (1973). These authors point out that there is a growing body of literature indicating that motor skills can be improved through what is called mental practice, referring to an internal attempt to rehearse the skill without having the equipment involved present and without going through the entire sequence of movements involved. The place of mental practice in the learning of many motor skills is familiar to most people in modern civilization. I can remember when I was about to learn to drive a car that I would rehearse in my mind the activities involved in working the clutch pedal, changing gears, pulling away from the curb, pressing a foot on the brake, and the other components of the skill. I knew how to perform all of these component skills before I ever sat in the driver's seat. What I had done was to establish internal programs for performing these components, and the actual process of learning to drive involved only the refinement of these programs.

The concept of a program that guides the performance of a motor skill is derived from the field of computers. Such devices commonly have designed into their structure the detailed directions for performing a commonly needed set of operations. For example, many computers have built-in sequences of directions that can be used in the computation of a square root. The sequence of directions is called a program or a subroutine for calculating square roots. The program is set into action by a simple command, and once the command is given, the square root of the number with which the computer is working is then calculated. Many such programs are permanently stored in the memory banks of most computers, and when such a program has been activated its full routine will be completed before the computer moves on to perform other operations.

The parallel between a computer program and a program that controls the performance of a skill is clear. The program in the nervous system consists of sequences of commands to the muscles that are run off in their proper order, much as when the commands in the elements in the computer program emit a series of directions of mathematical operations to be performed. The part of the brain that appears to be the main source of assembly and storage of the muscle control programs is the cerebellum. The cerebellum functions in many ways as a computer, taking information into the system and assembling it into a set of operations that control the performance of the skill.

Programs of motor performance resemble computer programs in other respects. Both, generally, run off to completion and cannot be stopped in the middle. A point of difference is that the computer program runs off in a few thousands or millionths of a second, but the muscle control program may occupy as much time as a few seconds. The computer operates more rapidly than the human being, even though the human being can operate at incredible speeds in information-processing tasks.

Learning by Observation: A Substitute for Learning by Doing

Up to this point, we have discussed learning through performing and then receiving back information concerning how one is doing. Much of the task of mastering typewriting is of this character. One strikes the keys as best he can and then receives feedback on how he has done. Not all learning is of this character, but much important learning occurs without attempting to perform the skill that is to be learned.

The human being appears to have the capacity of observing a complex motor activity, then developing some kind of internal representation of what he has seen, and then assembling a motor program that will produce an output corresponding to the performance, but this can occur only under certain conditions. One does not learn to hit a golf ball in this way, for the simple reason that the entire act is not only complex but occurs so swiftly that one cannot assimilate the information involved. There is an additional problem in observing such a complex act in that one does not quite know what to observe. The typical observer watches the golf ball, but this tells him nothing about how to hit it. The club is also likely to attract attention because of its central instrumental role. What one needs to watch are the arms, legs, hips, and trunk of the golfer. There may also be some difficulty in converting these observations into an internal motor program in that these have to be observed from the front and at a different position, in relation to the ball, from the position in which the movements are to be made. There is some evidence that the position from which a skill is observed makes some difference in whether it can or cannot be easily reproduced. Another factor is observability of the components of the skill. Teaching the pronunciation of a foreign language is difficult partly because the learner cannot observe the position of the tongue and other crucial features in the motor components of the task. Learning to pronounce a foreign language is also difficult because the learner may not be able to discriminate between correct and incorrect pronunciation. His pronunciation may sound entirely correct to him and entirely incorrect to his teacher. When this happens, the teacher may have the greatest difficulty in explaining to the pupil what is wrong. The teacher may attempt to exaggerate how the pupil pronounces words, but the pupil may still not understand what is wrong. He may even say that the exaggerated wrong pronunciation still sounds like the correct version. Under such conditions, the teacher may have to be resigned to having a pupil who speaks the language understandably rather than correctly. Nevertheless, despite this limitation of learning by observation, many skills can be acquired through seeing a skilled performance of them.

The human learner has a capacity to observe another person, take in information from what he observes, and then use what he has learned to guide his own performance. This kind of a capacity to learn by observing is not very evident in animals, and because much of learning theory is based on animal studies, psychologists have commonly failed to recognize the immense capacity of the human being to profit from what he sees another do. There are some notable examples of animals learning from other members of their species. Some birds do appear to learn the song appropriate to their species by being exposed to the song of the adult bird. Birds will modify their song by being raised in the presence of birds that sing different "dialects" (see Nottebohm, 1970). Birds deprived of exposure to the song of the adult during their first summer never learn to sing.

There are other examples (see Scott, 1969) of animals acquiring skills from other members of their species, though the mechanism may not always be one of simple imitation. Japanese rhesus monkeys given a mixture of sand and grain slowly learn to separate out the grain by putting the mixture in water. Other monkeys have then rapidly learned the trick from those who first learned it, but learning may not have been by observation. A monkey that picked up some grain and sand and did not know how to separate them might follow another monkey who knew the trick to the water. Monkeys naturally follow one another. Once in the water, the uninitiated monkey would be likely to spill some of the mixture and learning would ensue.

Learning by observation is clearly rare in animals, though it does take place. The human species has an extraordinary capacity in this respect, and much of our learning is of this character. Educators have long stressed learning by doing, perhaps partly because we have not learned as much as is needed about the conditions under which effective learning by observation takes place. Much of the problem of producing important learning by observation is ensuring that the would-be learner attends to the components of the situation that can teach him. A demonstration of how to sew a seam is not going to produce much learning if the learner is only interested in the color of the fabric or is fascinated by the sewing machine itself. Whenever demonstrations are arranged from which students are to learn, the teacher is likely to have to indicate to the students just what is to be watched.

Learning by observation can be considered to be learning that often takes place independently of the rewards or reinforcements available. Sometimes observational learning takes place as a side activity, quite unrelated to the central task in which the person is engaged. Thus a person searching for information in a book may pick up information about the color of the book, the size and peculiarities of the type, the width of the margin, and so forth. One walks down the corridor to go to the library and can later remember seeing a girl in a red dress and a janitor cleaning the floor. Such learning is called incidental learning. An interesting feature of incidental learning is that the more highly motivated the person is to work on a central task, the less he is likely to pick up incidental information (McLaughlin, 1965).

Delay in Feedback

The early research on the effect of delay in feedback provided some highly misleading results that are still widely taught to students of education. Experiments with animals showed quite consistently that any delay in reinforcement reduced the rate at which learning took place. In many experiments, a delay of only five or ten seconds might reduce the rate of learning to zero. From this research, there emerged the doctrine that, in order for reinforcement to be effective, it has to follow closely on the behavior it is to reinforce. This doctrine, unfortunately dignified as a law, became the cornerstone of the development of much of educational technology. Skinner's attempts to develop teaching machines at midcentury were prompted largely by the idea that teachers did not reinforce children either promptly enough or often enough to produce effective learning, but the teaching machine could supposedly do this. Later, the computer was adapted to become a teaching machine and provided virtual immediate reinforcement. Perhaps the very disappointing results achieved with teaching machines can be accounted for partly by the fact that the principles on which they were based, particularly the principle of immediacy of reinforcement, represented vast overgeneralizations from very limited animal data.

First, let us consider the effect of delay in reinforcement or feedback on the development of motor skills. Delay in the reinforcement of motor skills is generally studied through some very simple motor skill that can be studied experimentally in the laboratory. One of the oldest tasks for doing this requires the learner to draw, on a piece of paper, a line three inches long. The subject of the experiment draws a line and then, either immediately or at some later time, is told how well he has done. Sometimes the feedback is delayed until one or more additional attempts have been made to draw such a line on new pieces of paper. In the latter case, the information received is always about the line drawn one or more lines back. Bilodeau (1966), who reviewed such studies, pointed out that the conclusions are clear—subjects have difficulty in utilizing information about how they did two or more lines back in the series. Another point comes out of such studies. The information on whether the line drawn is too short or too long can be most readily utilized if it is given at the time when the person has drawn the line and still has his pencil on the end of the line. If the person holds the pencil in the final position and does not move his hand away, delay of a few seconds in obtaining feedback is quite unimportant, but if he moves his hand away, he has difficulty in using the information provided for improving his performance. The important piece of information that the person has to use in order to profit from feedback is how his hand and muscles feel at the end of drawing the line. The tensions in his muscles appear to be of much greater importance than how long the line looks. If he just raises his hand from the paper and sets it to draw a new line, then he loses touch with what it felt to draw the particular line that he was told was either too short or too long. Feedback can be used about events that can be easily recalled. A point of interest is that this same principle applies to animal learning as well as to human. Rats running mazes will learn well even though reward is delayed at the end of the maze for as much as ten seconds, provided the goal box of the maze is narrow and cramped and does not permit the animal to move during the delay interval. If the goal box permits movements, a delay in reinforcement is very damaging to the acquisition of the maze-running skill. Delay in the provision of information does not damage acquisition, provided that intervening events do not make it difficult for the learner to use the information provided to improve his performance.

The difficulty in utilizing delayed feedback in many motor skills is that one cannot remember exactly what he did so that he can correct his performance next time. In tasks in which one can easily retain information about exactly what he has done, delay in feedback should not be a problem at all. Markowitz and Renner (1964) and Sassenrath and Yonge (1968) reviewed numerous studies in which there has been a delay in feedback and the results have not been damaging to learning. As might be expected, these are all studies in which the task involved was a verbal one. On such tasks, one can easily remember not only what the final product was but also how he arrived at it. For example, give a child a simple arithmetic problem to solve and ask him tomorrow what his answer was, and he can probably recall it immediately. He can also describe just what the problem was and how he arrived at his answer. It is small wonder that giving him feedback, that is, telling him whether he was right or wrong, is just as effective later as it is immediately after he solved the problem. The delay becomes a trivial matter in such a case.

There is an added interesting fact about the effect of delay in feedback on human verbal learning. In many of the studies reported, delay in feedback not only resulted in no deleterious effects on learning, but sometimes an improvement was produced. This is really quite a startling finding in that the effort of much work on the improvement of education has been directed toward cutting down the delay between performance and reinforcement, based on the assumption that such delay is critical. An interesting question is why the delay is sometimes advantageous.

In the case of short delays, Atkinson (1969) has shown that the critical factor appears to be the retention of the response that is reinforced or corrected. A person who has to find out which number is the correct response to a particular nonsense syllable (7 is the right response to the syllable *bix*) may forget what the syllable was and what number he gave if the feedback is delayed as much as twelve seconds. This is very likely to be the case if the interval is filled with some such task as counting.

In cases where there is a longer delay before the individual discovers whether he is right or wrong, or what the right answer should be, other factors are at work. A pupil who works on a problem and is told the next day whether he is right or wrong may have to virtually rework the problem in his head if he is to use the information. Thus delayed feedback may also serve the function of requiring the learner to rehearse his performance, and this rehearsal may facilitate the retention of information related to it. Certainly, there can be no doubt that delays of as long as fifteen minutes in providing feedback related to typical schoolwork are not deleterious and that sometimes delays of hours and days may be advantageous.

Verbal Directions and the Guidance of Skills

Teachers have long believed that one can tell a person how to perform a motor skill. The golf instructor tells the novice after he has whacked a rapid drive down the fairway "Now note how I moved the hips through with the swing of the club and that I followed through with the drive so that the club came to a stop above my head." The golf professional then asks the novice to swing the club, and, while the novice is doing this, the professional accompanies his performance with a flow of advice. Almost every instructor in a sport or other motor skill area is likely to give a considerable amount of verbal directions as he goes through the motions of demonstrating the skill. Holding (1965) has attempted to summarize the extensive research in the area, which often gives the appearance of being contradictory. Holding is able to bring some order into the findings by showing that the value, or lack of value, in giving verbal information during the demonstration or performance of a skill depends on particular circumstances.

Let us begin by considering the case in which the person performs the skill. In a very complex skill that is rapidly performed, such as the swing of a golf club, the verbal guidance of the instructor is useless. In skills that can be performed slowly, much more success is likely to be derived from verbal guidance, because the performer can stop and think at each stage and the directions can indicate precisely what is to be done. Holding points out that a skill such as backing up a truck is one in which the person teaching how to do it can indicate in absolutely clear terms what the learner should do or what is wrong with his performance. If the driver becomes flustered, it is very easy for him to stop, collect his wits, and think over the entire task. This is to be contrasted with the teaching situation encountered by the golf instructor, who has the greatest difficulty in explaining, verbally, what the novice should do or how he should correct his performance. Movements of the hips defy accurate verbal description. Also, one cannot accurately describe such matters as speed of movement or how tightly one should grip a golf club.

Holding points out that the verbal description of motor tasks is something of an art. He suggests that sometimes colorful verbal analogies may have value in guiding behavior. If a child learning to ride a bicycle is told that he should let the bicycle steer itself, the child may then know that he has to relax and avoid sudden turns of the handle bars. Tell a child playing a long note on the violin that he has to play it as though he loved it so much that he could not bear to part with it, and it may help him to understand the nature of the task. Holding points out that the concoction of effective verbal analogies is a part of the art of teaching and one cannot provide simple formulas for concocting them.

Motivational Aspects of Feedback

Up to this point in the chapter, the emphasis has been on the information provided by feedback, but feedback has other aspects besides the strictly intellectual. Ask a person in a laboratory to draw a line he judges to be three inches in length on a clean sheet of paper, then give him a new sheet of paper and ask him to do it again, and carry on the procedure for as many trials as the subject will go. If he is told nothing after each performance, he will not proceed very far before he starts to protest the apparent stupidity of the entire procedure. He soon says he is bored, asks how long he has to keep it up, and is very likely to refuse to cooperate. A very different form of behavior is manifested when he is asked to perform the same task but after each trial is told how well he is doing. He may be told simply that the line is too short or too long, or that it is a particular amount too short or too long. An alternative procedure is to tell him after so many trials whether he has tended to make the line too short or too long over the average of those trials. Any of the procedures cited will result in very sustained performance of the subject, who then treats the task as a challenging game. He will show improvement on the task, and the improvement has the effect of energizing behavior. Knowledge of results has the effect of maintaining behavior on tasks that would otherwise be considered dull and uninteresting.

This is a phenomenon on which there has not been adequate experimentation. One might suspect that programmed learning, with its frequent feedback of information at the end of each small task, would have the effect of maintaining behavior at the tasks, but there is no evidence that children working on such tasks continue to pursue them with any particular vigor. Children take well to teaching machines for short periods, but over longer periods seem to become bored with them. The value of frequent feedback found in the case of very dull tasks may not be present in the case of tasks that are much more interesting in themselves. Perhaps one should conclude that when dull, rote learning tasks are to be mastered, the behavior of pupils can be maintained by providing frequent feedback. This is often accomplished in the classroom by turning the task into a game—for instance, a spelling contest. The spelling bee is really nothing more than an attempt to convert a dull, routine, and repetitive learning task into a game in which there is frequent feedback concerning performance. The learning of addition, multiplication, and other skills calling for repetition and rehearsal is often encouraged in the elementary school by procedures that provide frequent feedback and friendly competitiveness.

In more complex problem-solving tasks, the inherent interest in the task may maintain behavior. Give children the task of exploring what are the poisonous contaminants of foods sold in the stores, and it may be difficult to divert their attention to other topics. Feedback is not the only condition that sustains activity in the intellectual sphere. Attention is well maintained if the individual is able to obtain interesting information, structure it, organize it, and add to his store of knowledge. If he encounters difficulties along the way and finds himself unable to understand that which he seeks to understand, then, without help, he may give up the task. The intervention of the teacher at such a time, when the student would otherwise give up, is an important condition for maintaining behavior related to the acquisition of knowledge. However, intervention on the part of the teacher in such a situation is different from providing feedback. The role of the teacher is to structure the information so that the child can fit it into the system of knowledge he already possesses. In Chapter 8, it was pointed out that man is a creature who takes in and structures information. This taking in and structuring information is an important factor in maintaining learning behavior.

Grades and the Record System

Grades today represent a kind of feedback given to the student that supposedly has motivating properties. Grades have a long history and have been used for all kinds of purposes. Grades supposedly not only are for transmitting information to the pupil, telling him how he is doing, but they are also used to inform parents, and teachers in later grades, about the quality of the pupil's work. A fascinating history of grading systems has been written by Cureton (1971). Cureton points out that the first examining systems in schools in the early 1800s, and hence grades, were based on oral examination procedures. Pupils practiced penmanship for the purpose of learning to write, but the quill pens were too awkward to sharpen and maintain to permit written examinations. The pupils in these early schools were typically ranked in terms of their performance. The introduction of the metal pen, about 1828, revolutionized the entire examination procedure.

In the late nineteenth century, examinations and grades also often served a different purpose than they do today. Cureton describes the procedure adopted in some schools in which the effectiveness of the system was determined through the examination of both pupils and teachers. In such cases, the teachers were given an oral examination by the superintendant, in public, before the entire school board. Teachers had to obtain a given percentage score in order to be retained.

The percentage system of grading in education came into being in the last half of the nineteenth century. The underlying idea was that 100 per cent signified perfection, but it was only much later that teachers began to realize that perfection was a matter of judgment and not the absolute and objective standard many had believed it to be.

Later in the century, the percentage system was replaced, in some institutions, by a category system. Cureton writes that the University of Georgia in 1891 used a three-category system and, in the same year, a Virginia academy introduced a six-category system, with the students being given grades of *optimus, melior, bonus, malus, pejor,* and *pessimus.* Cureton also discovered that the six-category system turned out to be more like a three-category system because, for all practical purposes, only the top three categories were used. Indeed, the grade of *bonus* was considered to be a disgrace.

Early in the present century, considerable dissatisfaction was expressed with the percentage system of reporting grades. Research studies showed that when an essay examination was marked by several different teachers, the same paper might receive grades differing by as much as 50 percentage points. Neither the zero point nor the 100 per cent mark represented established agreed-on standards. Indeed, the percentage scale was a very subjective scale. Also, the scale assumed that one could discriminate differences involving 1 per cent along the scale, and clearly no teacher could make discriminations that fine. As a result of this wave of criticism, many schools adopted a five-point grading system, some using letter grades and others using numerical designations. The practice of grading on the curve came into being with the adoption of the letter-grade system. The influence of great statisticians such as Francis Galton and Karl Pearson led people to believe that the normal curve was the natural curve for the distribution of achievement and that letter grades were merely a reasonable means of designating areas within the normal curve. Not everybody was happy with this application of statistical concepts, and many took the view that as the higher levels of education were approached the distribution of grades should become more skewed. These advocates believed that although the grades of the first-grader should be normally distributed, with a balanced number of *A*s and *F*s, and *B*s and *D*s, the grades of graduate students should be skewed to the top range, with most students obtaining grades of *A* and *B*.

Grades given in the customary letter form do not transmit much information to the student. They provide inadequate feedback. The letter grade tells him something about how he performed in relation to others, but it is of doubtful value in the subsequent guidance of his behavior. When the grades given the student are transmitted to the guidance counselor or to the home-room teacher in subsequent years, they provide no more information than they provided the student. The parent may be able to conclude from the child's grade either that all is well or that something seems to be wrong.

The typical grade merely indicates how the child stands in relation to

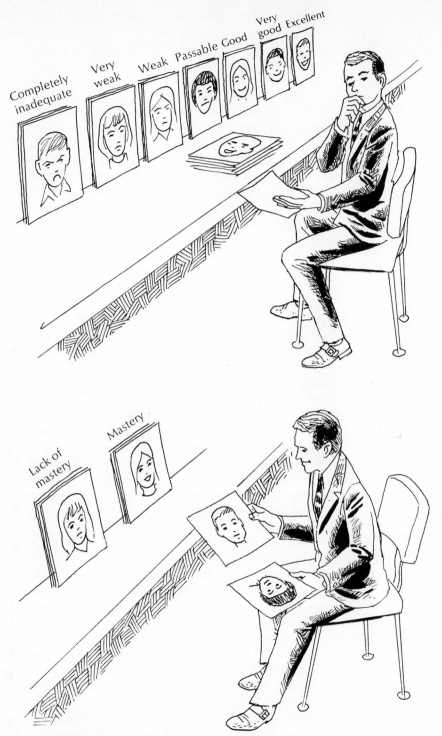

Grades put pupils into slots. How many useful categories of achievement are there?

the other children in his class. A child is given a grade of C in his fourth-grade arithmetic work, but what can the fifth-grade teacher know about the child from seeing this grade? About all the teacher can tell is that the child performed like the average child in the arithmetic phases of his work. The fifth-grade teacher may know only in a vague general way what the children accomplished in the fourth grade. She may know that the children supposedly learned how to solve problems of long division, but she can only guess whether the average child had mastered long division, could undertake it haltingly, or could not do it at all. What the grade is likely to suggest to the fifth-grade teacher is that this is a child to whom she can give grades of C, because this is the kind of grade he has been getting—hardly a very useful kind of suggestion.

In actual practice, school grades provide even less usable information than is indicated here. Teachers often make personal decisions about grades, which contaminate the little information they can give. One teacher may decide that a grade shall indicate the progress of the child in relation to his level of achievement at the beginning of the school year. A teacher who does this may give two children an A, one of whom was the most advanced child in the class and the other the most backward. It was the fact that the most backward child made a great amount of progress that gave him an A. Such grades are utterly confusing, because the two grades of A mean very different things and carry with them no information concerning how they should be interpreted. Another factor that makes grades difficult to interpret is that they often represent a system used to punish or reward pupils. A child's grade in arithmetic may be lowered because he was particularly ornery during the last week of the semester. A child's grade may be raised because he was particularly cooperative with the teacher. Now such lowering or raising of the grades does not lower or raise the achievement of the pupil. What it does is to provide a system of rewards to the pupil while providing misinformation to those who attempt later to interpret the grades. If school grades are to work, then they should reflect as far as possible the actual performance of the student.

Because grades refer to performance, or should refer to performance, they should ideally be tied to well-defined levels of proficiency. At the present time, they cannot be made to do this, perhaps because subject matter is a very complex and not too well organized body of knowledge, and a single letter or percentage grade cannot summarize what the pupil can and cannot do. Some of the newer experiments with record keeping are attempts to overcome these deficiencies.

Let us consider a record system, complete with all modern inventions, that will permit the teacher to keep track of the performance of each pupil. In order for such a system to operate, it is necessary that the entire curriculum be divided into identifiable units. The units should probably be numbered. When a student finished a unit satisfactorily, then this piece of information would have to be entered in the record system. The records could be kept by name or number. Presumably, the units

316
. . . .
Information Feedback,
Rewards and
Punishments, and the
Guidance of Learning

could be grouped together into categories. For example, all the units of work related to fractions might be grouped in the fraction group. After the computer had recorded the satisfactory completion of all the units related to fractions, the information would be summarized by the computer, indicating that the work had been completed. Such a grouping would appear to be necessary, because without it the teacher would be overwhelmed by detailed data every time he asked the computer to report back all the information available about the work completed by a particular pupil. Indeed, the main difficulty in developing such a system is that it is likely to be used to record data in overwhelming quantities and inundate the teacher with data every time information is called for about a particular pupil. Useful data systems have to provide data in a quite concise form and have to have some capacity for summarizing the data transmitted to the memory system.

Although the computer has a very large memory system, teachers and other human beings have only a limited capacity for using data in the making of decisions. If more data are provided than a human being can readily use in making a decision, he is likely to disregard the data. This has been the problem of executives whose decision making is backed by a vast quantity of computer-stored information. The executive often finds himself flooded with information, which he then ignores.

Computer systems for keeping the records of the work accomplished by pupils are still in the experimental stage. None existing is developed to the point where one can say that it provides an improvement over the old-fashioned teacher's gradebook. The gradebook does not have much to recommend it, but the newer systems have not solved the problem of the large-capacity computer versus the limited-capacity user.

The limitations of data systems with respect to the teacher's needs become even more pronounced when the system is used for providing data to counselors or other persons. The teacher may well be familiar with just what subject matter is included in each category, but others may not be.

Feedback and Rewards

Previous sections considered the direction of the course of learning through the giving of information. A second condition that influences learning is that commonly described as rewards. A difficulty in discussing the topic of rewards separately from the previous topic is that rewards carry some information as well as provide the recipient with objects of high value. The information given during the course of learning is intrinsic to the task itself. In learning to throw a basketball free-throw, the learner sees the ball either pass through the hoop or miss it. The outcome provides information related to the throw that is intrinsic to the very task itself. A child solves an arithmetic problem and is told "The correct answer is 247." This feedback on the correctness of the solution is specific to the particular problem. One would not give that answer to the next problem and probably not to any other that day. One may, of course, also look over the pupil's shoulder and say "Right," which is short for saying "Your answer of 247 is right." The feedback is still quite specific to the particular problem. But what are commonly referred to as rewards are events not intrinsic to the task. Suppose I offer a child a nickel for every problem he solves correctly; the money given is not specific to the particular problem. It may also provide him with information about which problems he solved correctly if, after he has attempted each problem, I either reward him for a correct solution or do not reward him for failure. Then the reward carries with it information about the correctness of his solution. Rewards often do not carry this kind of information, as when a child works at his problems throughout the semester and receives a prize at the end of the semester for solving more problems correctly than any other child. In such a case, the reward carries no information that has not already been given to the student.

What are referred to here as rewards are objects or situations that are highly sought after, and not just as consequences of particular performances. A child who has been told "The right answer is 247" is only interested in hearing that announcement following problems for which the correct answer is 247. In contrast, the child is always delighted to hear someone say to him "Here is a dollar." The child does not try to persuade his parents to say to him "The right answer is 247," for this statement has relevance only when it follows attempts to solve particular classes of problems, but he may attempt to trick his mother or father into saying "Here is a dollar." The one statement, providing informational feedback, is intrinsic to and a component of the situations in which it is used; the other, the reward, is a highly sought after condition that is not intrinsically and necessarily tied to the performance of specific skills.

Objects classified as rewards are also often received without being contingent on particular behaviors. Thus gifts of objects and money are received at Christmas and are appropriate. A Christmas card that carried only the words "You're right" would not be sent, or, if sent by a madman, would probably be rejected.

Although informative feedback and rewards are different categories of events, they influence learning and can be used to exercise some control over learning. Informative feedback provides guidance and sometimes energizes behavior. The presence of rewards energizes behavior and sometimes also provides information that influences learning. The difficulties of disentangling these two components are great, and at present experiments cannot be devised to study the two components separately.

The point has also been made that feedback not only provides information but has motivational properties, too. Teachers have long believed that whereas grades may provide the student with information about how he is doing, they also either spur him on to further effort or discourage him from even trying. There can be little doubt that the student who receives consistently good grades is encouraged and energized by the feedback. What about the student who receives poor grades and who is told regularly that he is failing or that he is near to failing? This is a problem that cannot be easily studied directly, but it can be studied indirectly. There have been many investigations of the effect of criticism on student learning. These have been summarized by Beller (1973). The general conclusion is that mild criticism is useful and helpful to the student, but that severe criticism can be demoralizing and reduce the student's level of effort. Translated in terms of grades, this might suggest that giving a grade of *D*, with suggestions concerning how the student might do better next week, might spur him on to further effort, but giving a near failing or failing grade might well reduce his level of effort. Some programs in schools wisely avoid this whole issue by assigning students only those tasks for which they have the necessary preparation to succeed. In such programs, the records consist of lists of what each student has accomplished, and not what grades he has achieved in a uniform curriculum.

Situations Using Rewards to Control Learning

Monetary rewards and other rewards have long been used informally to control learning. Parents commonly offer money to their children for achieving above a specified level. Rewards appear in the form of scholarships and sometimes in the form of prizes. Psychologists who have viewed the use of such devices have pointed out that such incentives for learning influence only the very few students likely to win them. Most students realize that they are not in competition for such material benefits and are uninfluenced by them. This observation has suggested to psychologists that a more equitable distribution of rewards might influence more learners to expend greater effort.

Several proposals have been made in this connection. One is that all pupils be paid for their work, much as the employees of a factory are paid for the work they do. Such a proposal suggests that the pay earned by the pupil be adjusted to his achievement, much as pay is adjusted in ordinary life. Psychologists point out that this system is, to a degree, already operative in countries that pay their college students a living wage to attend colleges and universities. Both Canada and Great Britain give college students a stipend and pay their fees, but the wage is dependent on their having at least passing grades and continues only so long as they stay in school. The pay is not tied to their level of accomplishment, perhaps because the wage is minimal. A similar system has been proposed for the high school, with the idea that the dropout might be more willing to stay in school if he were paid to stay there. At the time of writing, no plan has yet been adopted that actually pays pupils for the work they do in school.

Those who argue for paying pupils for school achievement say that schoolwork is just as much work as is a job in industry. If industry can pay its workers, then surely the schools can, too. If there is nothing wrong

The teacher thinks she is reinforcing the child for "attending" to the teacher. Is he being reinforced for doing nothing, or for not moving, or for being relaxed, or for daydreaming?

with paying a factory worker, then there is nothing wrong with paying a student in school. Critics are likely to point out that there is a real and important difference between the work of a person in a factory and the work of a pupil in school. The one contributes to the gross national product, but the other does not. Then it may be pointed out that the service worker, such as the physician, is paid but does not contribute to the gross national product. There is still an important difference between the work of physicians, lawyers, social workers, and so forth and the work of the pupil in the schools. The pupil does not contribute a service but receives a service. Payment to receive a service presents an unusual situation, though not completely unique. Some people do have health insurance so that when they are sick they are paid as long as they are in the hospital. Such patients are virtually paid to receive a service.

Rewards may not necessarily involve money. Many who would be very hesitant to pay money to pupils for any learning they undertake are less hesitant to endorse proposals that pupils be rewarded with privileges. Teachers have long pursued this practice at the lower elementary-school grades. A child is rewarded for behaving well during mathematics study by being allowed to work in the art corner for twenty minutes. Teachers generally recognize that some activities are highly preferred over other activities, and the pupil is persuaded to engage in the less preferred activities by being promised that he will be allowed to engage in one of the more preferred activities. The strongest argument against this system is that it assumes that certain activities are necessarily dull and that pupils have to be coerced into engaging in them. Many fine teachers would take issue with this position. Although mathematics is generally considered to be a dull subject, the author has visited a class in which the children were sitting on the edges of their chairs keyed up in excitement over the mathematical ideas the teacher was discussing. When there is a good teacher, there is not a dull subject. One might even say that there is no such thing as a dull school subject—only dull teachers who make the subject dull.

The reward system described in the previous paragraph often is not very effective because the rewards are too remote. A child is told that if he works well all morning, then he can feed the fish in the afternoon, or engage in free reading, or whatever else. The reward is likely to be a little remote from the activity to be effective as an energizer of behavior. One way to make the reward more immediate is to hand out tokens, immediate rewards for quite small units of work, that can be used later to purchase privileges. A pupil who earned ten tokens might be able to purchase with them ten minutes in the painting corner or perhaps twenty minutes of free reading.

The use of token systems in educational settings has been quite widely studied, and these studies have been reviewed by O'Leary and Drabman (1971). Ayllon and Azrin (1968) have also provided a colorful description of the use of tokens in hospital settings. Unfortunately, most of the studies have been undertaken with individuals who present special learning problems, for instance, the mentally retarded and the emotionally disturbed. There is great danger in generalizing from these studies to normal children. One also suspects that the publication of such studies is selective, with those yielding positive results being published and those that produce negative results either not being submitted for publication or being rejected by publishers. Journal editors do not like to accept studies giving negative results, and for this reason what appears to be evidence of positive worth follows the announcement of all new techniques.

The results of such studies generally show that token economies can be used successfully to control gross forms of behavior such as disruptive behavior or staying-in-one's-seat behavior or looking-at-one's-book behavior. These behaviors can be increased by giving tokens contingent on their occurrence when the tokens have some value to the pupil. The tokens are typically turned in for privileges or for small toys or trinkets. The studies reported by O'Leary and Drabman (1971), with just a few exceptions, indicate that the use of tokens does not produce any permanent change in these gross forms of behavior. Indeed, children whose behavior is controlled through a token system during the afternoon do not show any improved behavior during the morning session. The papers on the subject provide numerous suggestions concerning how conditions could be arranged to provide for better generalization of improvements in behavior to new situations, but almost no research has been undertaken to test the validity of these suggestions. More generalization would be expected with normal children than with the populations typically studied. Mentally retarded children are well known to have difficulty in transferring what they learn in one situation to the solution of problems in new situations. Another related problem is reported by Meichenbaum et al. (1968), who found themselves confronted with girls who said "If you don't pay us, we won't shape up."

Because most of the children involved in such studies spend much of their time engaging in behavior unrelated to academic learning, it is hardly surprising that the token system does often result in an improvement in their academic learning. This does not mean that ordinary children, who do not have such problems, would improve academically by the introduction of a token system. Such children in a well-run school are busy learning and do not present the problems of the mentally retarded or the emotionally disturbed. Unfortunately, many who advocate the widespread use of token systems in schools have never seen a well-run classroom, in which such devices would have no role to play. Token systems may well be a crutch for the poor teacher, but use of them would have the unfortunate effect of marking programs thus run as incompetently managed.

Magnitude of Reward

There can be no doubt that rewards have the effect of energizing behavior. Anyone who has ever run a Cub Scout troup knows that the offer of a prize for a Cub who sells the most Christmas cards (or whatever is sold) increases the amount of energy devoted to the project. Rewards are not the only way of energizing behavior, but they are one way, and because they are readily manipulated they become a means that the school can easily use. This does not mean that the school should use a reward system but only that rewards *can* be used to energize behavior. However, the energy invested in learning should not be equated with the amount learned. Although complete apathy may make for a situation in which little learning takes place, the overenergetic child may learn less than the child who goes about his work with a typical amount of vigor.

Atkinson and Wickens (1971) have summarized some of the most significant work related to the effect of the amount of reward on the amount of learning, these studies dealing with tasks called **paired-associate tasks.** In these tasks, a person learns to say a particular word in response to a word that is given. The subject is presented with the first word of a set of pairs of words and tries to guess what the second word is. He is then shown both words together. Thus he sees the word *street*, then he has time to guess what the second word is, and then he sees the word again together with the word he was to guess, *street–man*. The second word in the series is then presented, followed by the complete second pair. In this way, he works through the list of pairs. Of course, the first time he works through the list he has no idea of what the second word in each pair should be. The second time through he may be able to guess a few correctly. Slowly he is able to reach the point of being able to give the second word when the first is given. The technique requires that the experimenter introduce certain other controls into the procedure. The order of presentation of the pairs has to vary. Otherwise, the learner simply acquires a list of responses that are given in a prescribed order and he does not learn to associate the second word with the first.

Atkinson and Wickens, after reviewing the research, came to the conclusion that if the learning of certain items is rewarded, typically with money, and the learning of other items is not rewarded, only the rewarded items are learned. This finding is an important one and parallels the observations of teachers who have worked in school systems in which there are rewards for particular learning activities. These teachers report that when a reward system is introduced (generally in the form of tokens to be traded later) pupils will learn only activities tied to the reward system. A child in such a setting, asked to undertake a task because the teacher suggests that it may be a useful one to learn is likely to refuse to learn if he discovers that no rewards are offered. The implication is that when a reward system is introduced into a learning situation the pupils cease to be concerned with learning, as such, and become concerned with obtaining the rewards. Those who propose that learning in school be controlled by the money system will have to find means of overcoming this difficulty that is injected into the learning process if the money system is going to work.

Most programs of education are based on the hope that students will ultimately become independent learners, highly motivated to learn for themselves. The hope is that such learners will find the task of learning intrinsically worthwhile and that there will be no need to energize learning by means of rewards that are not a part of the learning process itself. The introduction of material rewards into the learning process may make it impossible to achieve this goal. Of course, some may argue that it may well be that there are individuals who are not able to become self-energized learners, but this is very unlikely.

A second type of problem is also discussed in the same review. An alternative procedure for distributing rewards is to give the paired-associate task to some subjects with all the items rewarded and to other subjects with none of the responses rewarded. Under such conditions, there is no difference between the rates at which the lists are learned. The presence of a reward has no effect on learning.

The results reviewed by Atkinson and Wickens were obtained mainly by experimenters using college students, and the results are not consistent with those derived from working with younger children. Studies reviewed by Benowitz and Busse (1970) have shown that young children learn more rapidly when they can obtain, through learning, small trinkets, prizes, and other objects highly sought after by the children. Material rewards are effective at the lower age levels even though they do not seem to have an effect on the learning of college students. Presumably, such children would learn only the items rewarded if some items to be learned were rewarded and others were not. The rather small increase in learning produced by rewards in the children hardly seems worthwhile in view of the dangers that result from tying rewards to learning.

What the data seem to suggest is a picture of learning corresponding roughly to the following sketch: At all levels of development, learning takes place automatically, if the information enters the perceptual systems and has certain characteristics, regardless of whether a reward system is or is not introduced. In the young child, the use of rewards may hold him in the learning situation longer than he would be likely to remain otherwise and rewards may energize behavior; the educated adult, in the form of the college student, does not benefit from the introduction of ulterior rewards, because he will remain for long periods in the learning situation. Now this does not mean that rewards should necessarily be used when teaching young children. Indeed, whatever may be gained by the use of rewards is probably lost by the negative effects, except perhaps in the case of the mentally retarded and the emotionally disturbed. There are alternative procedures that can be used to maintain children at a learning task. One of these is to plan learning so that the young child in the lower elementary grades is not confronted with the same task for more than a short time. A continuous variety of tasks will have the effect of maintaining attention, and this procedure is used by most teachers, though perhaps not to the degree that would make teaching as effective as it might be. For example, in being taught to read in the first grade, a child may spend some time matching printed words with objects; then he may spend ten minutes running words through the languagemaster, which says the word aloud as the child sees it on the card; then he may work in a group with the teacher putting labels on a display; and perhaps later he may work on telling a story that the teacher types out in large type. Such

324

· · · · · · · · · · · ·

Information Feedback, Rewards and Punishments, and the Guidance of Learning a program that has a great variety of activities through which the skill is acquired has little difficulty in maintaining the attention and goal orientation of the children. On the other hand, where there is no such variation in activity, the interest of the children quickly declines, they become restless, and, ultimately, disruptive behavior ensues. Rewards, as we have defined them here, in the form of trinkets, tokens, or any other material object are quite unnecessary for the development of an effective educational program.

Some Effects of Delayed Rewards

A matter of considerable interest is the effect of delayed reward, in contrast with immediate reward, on learning. Although there is some evidence that the behavior of young children is energized by the offering of rewards, and thereby learning is somewhat increased, the effect of delay in reward on the learning as such has not been investigated to the point where conclusions can be drawn. Yet there are many experimental programs in effect at the present time in which delayed rewards are offered for pupils' performance. The author knows of one school district in which the performance of pupils over an entire semester wins for them points that can win a bicycle for the child who earns more than a certain number. The reward is delayed, but the points or tokens earned may have many of the properties of a material reward. A problem that has been studied very extensively in this general area is the choice of reward that children make when they have to choose between a delayed reward and an immediate reward. If the rewards are equal, children will obviously choose the immediate reward, but the delayed reward may become more attractive than the immediate reward if it is of greater magnitude.

A particularly interesting finding, which has turned up in many studies reviewed by Walls and Smith (1970), is that children from disadvantaged backgrounds do not respond to delayed rewards, although a middle-class child may be expected to choose a delayed reward if it is larger than the immediate reward. In a typical study, children may be offered the choice between a small candy bar immediately after finishing a task and a bar three times the size that they could obtain a week later. In some of the studies, money has been used, and there have been children who preferred seven pennies a week later rather than five pennies on the completion of the work. Some researchers have used very short delays of only a few minutes, with essentially the same results. The tendency for the disadvantaged to avoid choosing deferred rewards is not a peculiarity of the American culture, for the effect has been found by investigators abroad. The phenomenon is widespread, and it is also of significance in the use of reward systems in schools.

The problems presented for education by this phenomenon are substantial. Much of education itself is undertaken because of the anticipation of a long-delayed reward. Children are told that if they stay in high school, they are assured of a union card and a good job, but the delay in the delivery of the reward is several years for the entering freshman. It is hardly surprising that a substantial percentage of high-school students are dropouts and never receive that delayed reward. Even in the case of vocational training, in which the goals are more immediate to the participants, there is still a delay before the student can obtain employment. The system used in other countries, in which school may be continued on a part-time basis in the factory while the student holds a part-time job in the same factory, may overcome the difficulties of keeping the student in school to attain a delayed reward. In the part-time work and part-time school system, some of the rewards are immediate.

The reason for the poor response of the culturally disadvantaged to the delayed reward is a matter of considerable interest. The most promising interpretation seems to be that the disadvantaged fail to learn concepts related to time and because of this lack are unable to plan for their future. The educated person is so familiar with time concepts and with planning into the future that he has difficulty in conceiving of a human being who would not have this capacity. Those raised in the ghettos of the great cities provide many evidences of a deficiency in their ability to handle time concepts. They show little capacity for arriving at school on time, and some eventually become unemployable because they are not able to meet the time requirements of a job in such matters as arriving on time, doing work on schedule, and keeping to the schedule for coffee breaks and lunch.

An interesting question is the kind of training that will develop the time sense needed for adjustment to a complex civilization. Walls and Smith point to some research indicating that individuals can slowly learn to appreciate delayed rewards, and this represents a beginning in time-sense training. The training technique used has generally involved providing rewards for tasks with longer and longer delays.

Another kind of explanation of the phenomenon that may also have validity is that disadvantaged children have no internal control. This explanation implies that the disadvantaged child is controlled by immediate circumstances. He sees the small candy bar that is offered as an immediate reward, his behavior is controlled by the presence of the bar, and he asks for it. He could ask for the larger and delayed reward only if his behavior could become controlled internally and if he were to reject responding to the candy bar immediately offered. It should be pointed out that the development of internal controls is closely related to the development of a time sense, because internal controls are used largely in planning future behavior. A person who has good internal controls shows it by his ability to defer immediate action in order to plan more effective action, and this involves an appreciation of the future.

Aversive Conditions

Situations that are said to be **aversive** are the opposite of those said to be rewarding. The rewarding situation is one that is sought after, that is approached, generally one that has value regardless of the task the

326
. . . .
Information Feedback,
Rewards and
Punishments, and the
Guidance of Learning

person is performing, and is sought after by any avenue that may reach it. Aversive conditions, on the other hand, are those that are not sought after and are generally avoided. Just as there is some uniformity in the situations that are rewarding for different individuals, so too are there situations that are aversive for most individuals. The most universally aversive situation is one that causes pain. Nearly all individuals avoid situations in which they expect to receive painful stimuli, although there are a few who respond differently and who may actually seek out certain pain-producing situations. Such persons are called masochists.

Rewards, at the most primitive level, involve the satisfaction of basic needs, such as the satisfaction of hunger, the provision of a warm environment, and the relief of thirst. Aversive conditions, at the most primitive level, involve the inflicting of bodily damage. These are powerful conditions that, all through history, have been used to control behavior. The slow growth of civilization has resulted in these primitive rewarding and aversive conditions being replaced by much more subtle conditions for behavior control. Children today are rarely coerced into conformity by offers of food, because few children are ever hungry for any long period of time. They are much more likely to be coerced through offers of special privileges and often with money. Punishment is rarely physical, but other aversive conditions such as social disapproval and isolation are used as means of controlling behavior.

Rewards are used largely to direct behavior. Jim's father says "If you get at least a *B* this semester in English, I will give you a dollar." The object of this admonition is to use a reward for the purpose of channeling behavior into the study of English rather than into other activities. Aversive conditions are commonly used to punish; that is, an aversive condition is provided in the hope that it will suppress the response that it follows. Punishment meted out by the law is an attempt to suppress a response frowned on by society. The announcement that aversive conditions exist if a person enters a particular area sometimes is used to keep persons out of particular localities. A sign such as "Very High Voltage—Do Not Enter" controls behavior in this particular way.

Rewards and aversive conditions are related to a degree in an interesting way. The withdrawal of an expected reward can have a marked punishing effect. Indeed, many parents punish through withdrawing anticipated rewards, and so rewards become a means of punishment. Teachers also use rewarding situations in this way, as when a teacher says "You have been very disorderly today, so there will be no recess."

The withdrawal of expected rewards also has sometimes quite unexpected results. There is a well-known phenomenon, demonstrated many times in the laboratory, called **frustrative nonreward.** Suppose that a four-year-old is given the task of finding out which of several buttons will deliver a marble. He eventually discovers that the third button delivers a marble each time it is pressed twice. This makes him happy, but then the experimenter quietly throws a switch and cuts off the reward mechanism. The child pushes the button twice and gets no reward. His typical reaction is likely to be that he will push the button with a greatly increased vigor. This is the situation of frustrative nonreward, and the result is increased vigor of performance. The same kind of phenomenon can also sometimes be observed when a child is working a series of problems and solves each one quite easily. Then he hits upon one he cannot solve, and his leisurely pace of work becomes replaced by a vigorous and concentrated effort.

Although frustrative nonreward is a well-established phenomenon, one cannot make recommendations concerning how it should be used by the teacher in the classroom. The challenge that can sometimes be produced by being confronted with a difficult task is probably of a very similar character. Such challenges are believed to have motivating properties in at least some students. One suspects that in order for them to be challenging, the person must have had a history of success. The frustrative nonreward phenomenon occurs only after a history of reward and does not occur after long experience of failure.

We have discussed the situation in which an expected reward does not appear, but what happens when an expected punishment does not take place? The withdrawal of an expected reward is punishing, but the withdrawal of an expected punishment has only very slight rewarding features, if it is rewarding at all. Indeed, in most experiments that have been undertaken, the removal of an expected punishment has had no rewarding characteristics.

There can be no doubt that punishment can be used to increase learning under some conditions. There are even studies in which reward alone has been less effective than either punishment alone or combinations of reward and punishment in the case of kindergarten children, (Witte and Grossman, 1971). The issues related to punishment are primarily ethical and pertain to our views on the kind of world in which we would like to live.

Punishment and the Suppression of Responses

The loss of the ability to make a response, through the processes commonly described as forgetting, is widely considered to be an undesirable feature of the way that life is arranged. This may generally be the case, but there are many circumstances in which one may wish that a response would just vanish. Problems of discipline are problems in which the teacher wishes that a response habitually made by a child would not occur. The clinician seeks to find means whereby responses that plague the life of a patient could be "forgotten." The traditional method of handling these problems has been punishment. Teachers punish in the hope that responses can be eradicated. A century or more ago, the behavior of the insane was often punished by beating in the hope that thereby the devil would be driven out. Legislative bodies and rulers have also long taken the position that punishment is the best method of eliminating unwanted responses. Let us now turn to what scientists have to say about the use of punishment and its effectiveness.

Whether punishment is or is not effective has been controversial from two separate points of view. On the one hand, scientists who have been interested in the effects of punishment on behavior have had to engage in research for nearly fifty years to settle the central scientific issues. Indeed, until midcentury, the data were far from clear concerning the effects of punishment. On the other hand, there has been extended discussion, over thousands of years, concerning the justification of punishment. Should an individual be permitted to punish another individual, or under what circumstances is punishment justifiable? These are the important ethical issues.

Punishment in schools has long been justified on the grounds that it is the only technique that can be widely applied to control undesirable aspects of pupil behavior. There is really not much evidence to support such a point of view. Rosenshine and Furst's (1971) collection of studies shows little evidence that teachers who use punishment most are the most effective in producing learning. Anyone who has ever observed extensively in schools knows that teachers who engage in much punishing behavior do not even necessarily have more orderly classes than those who avoid punishment. Some of the most orderly classes ever observed by the author were handled by teachers who never raised their voices but who controlled events in a quiet, firm, and organized way. Educators have generally taken the position that punishment is a quite unnecessary technique that characterizes the incompetent classroom manager. There can be little doubt that teachers who do spend much time punishing pupils are those who would be rated low on most criteria that have ever been chosen as criteria of effective teaching. Many who engage in punishing behavior simply lack alternative techniques of handling the numerous incidents that occur in the classroom. All too often they are teachers who lack self-control.

Another argument is commonly raised against the use of punishment. The argument is an ethical one, that a person does not have the right to make the life of another unhappy, unless there is overwhelming reason to do so. The argument, originally attributed to Dewey, is that school is not just preparation for life, but it is a part of life itself—and life should be pleasant. This is a persuasive position, particularly in the present era when it has become recognized that children, as well as adults, have rights as human beings. There is much to be said for this argument. Also, if school is not considered to be a model for life, where are children going to find a good model they can use in shaping the adult world, as they will ultimately have to do?

At this point, the question may be raised whether a school can be effectively run with almost no punishment. The fact is that there are classrooms and a few schools run on this basis. The author has visited many classrooms where the most punishing event that occurs is a frown of disapproval on the part of the teacher. Such classrooms are orderly, but there is no rigid enforcement of order just for the sake of order. A pupil may leave his seat to obtain help from another pupil or to consult a reference work at the back of the room. Such a classroom is to be contrasted with others in which the most trivial departure from rules is immediately heavily punished. These two kinds of classrooms do not appear to differ in terms of the amount of serious work going on. In the one with the relaxed atmosphere, generally there is less hostile and disruptive behavior on the part of the pupils, and rarely does a pupil trip another or throw a spitball. Both classrooms have internal forces operating that make for some degree of orderliness, but they are entirely different. In the one, the pupils fear the teacher and see him as a basically hostile figure. In the other, the teacher is seen as a representative of reasonableness and an organizer of activities, not primarily as a punisher.

Solomon (1964) finds that mild punishment generally produces a suppression of the response on which it is contingent. As the degree of the punishment increases, the punishment has a more and more permanent suppressive effect on the contingent response. If the punishment is sufficiently strong, the effect may be to produce a completely permanent suppression of the response. If the subject learns an avoidance response after being very severely punished, then that avoidance response may be permanent. An animal that learns to avoid a section of a box because it receives a very powerful shock in that location may continue to show an avoidance response as long as it lives. Such permanent effects of punishment only occur when an electric shock of great strength is used. The shock is generally such that it is fatal to some of the animals in the experiment.

The results of research suggest that punishment is not a practical procedure in civilized society for producing the permanent suppression of a response, because the punishment that will do this is likely to be far more severe than can be humanely administered. On the other hand, mild punishment may provide the suppression of a response for a short time, and this temporary suppression may be long enough to permit an alternative response to occur and to be rewarded. Reprimands provide such temporary suppression of a response. Unfortunately, the teacher who uses them often provides the child with no alternative, so the response occurs again very shortly and then the child is reprimanded again. An overactive child, who becomes restless and disrupts the work of the children around him, can sometimes be given an outlet for his energies in such tasks as collecting or distributing books or cleaning the chalk board. Such activities eliminate the disruptive aspects of the child's behavior and harness his energies for useful purposes. The alternative is seen in the behavior of some teachers who will reprimand the same child twenty or thirty or even more times each class period.

A crucial factor in determining whether there is a permanent effect or whether the effect is transitory is whether some alternative response is rewarded. If there is an alternative that produces a reward, then the effect of punishment is much more likely to be positive.

The effect of punishment also depends on the degree to which the response to be suppressed has been poorly or thoroughly learned in the past. Smoking is a difficult response to suppress partly because it usually has been practiced for years. Even severe punishments for the smoker, such as showing him the lungs of people who have died of lung cancer, may have little effect on the habit. Punishment is likely to be most effective in the case of habits that have been only recently acquired.

Another interesting finding is that animals and human beings become habituated to punishment. If punishment is to have a consistent effect, it has to be regularly increased. The author can remember visiting a class where a teacher engaged in a daily punishing routine of shouting at the children, handing out minor punishments related to restrictions on their freedom, and withholding rewards. The children seemed little disturbed by the teacher's performance, though the adult visitors watching the class found the situation almost unbearable. Needless to say, the numerous petty punishments handed out by the teacher had virtually no effect in controlling the behavior of the children.

The threat of remote punishment probably has little effect on the disruptive behavior of the child. The teacher who says to the child in the early morning "You have done that once too often. You must stay in after school" is not likely to exert much control over the behavior of that child. The punishment is too remote. If punishment is used at all, it should be mild and immediate.

Some psychologists have taken the position that punishment should not be used for the suppression of responses because there are side effects that are much more serious than the behavior it is desired to suppress. Those who have advocated such a position have come mainly from the ranks of clinicians, and they have put forward their case on two grounds. They point out that most of the reprimands by parents and teachers involve telling a child that he is bad. They claim that a child frequently confronted with the idea that he is bad may end up believing he is bad. Those who believe they are bad may be expected to behave badly. People do tend to produce behavior consistent with the concept they have of themselves. Insofar as this is true, the circumstances of punishment may have a long-term ill effect. However, for such an effect to take place, punishment would have to be frequent and persistent over a long period. Occasional punishment would not produce this undesirable side effect.

The second argument of the clinician is that the prolonged use of punishment produces a permanent high level of anxiety and also persistent feelings of guilt. This is the problem of many neurotic individuals, whose whole lives may be dominated by overwhelming feelings of anxiety, as if life were lived under the threat of a great impending doom. Here there is danger in arguing that the behavior of the neurotic represents what happens to normal children, to a lesser degree. There is danger in generalizing from the behavior of disturbed people to the behavior of the typical child.

Now there can be no doubt that excessive punishment can have undesirable side effects, but excessive rewards also have unfortunate consequences (see Jones, 1968). The spoiled child is one whose behavior has been entirely manipulated by rewards. When he does not have his own way and hence cannot immediately obtain the rewards he wants, he becomes sulky or tearful or disorganized. The over-rewarded person is often greedy and highly possessive of the rewards he has accumulated. In some ways, the over-rewarded person may become as great an antisocial force as the person who has been excessively punished.

Finally, it must be mentioned that punishment is a complex social phenomenon. The teacher who gives the appearance of being a punishing figure is setting an example for the children in the matter of social management. Children who grow up in punishing environments may conclude that the only technique for social management is punishment, for they have not seen any other technique. In addition, the administration of punishment probably has an effect on the punisher. Ultimately, a callous and insensitive attitude may develop. Punishment is always a hostile and aggressive act, and there is some evidence that the free exercise of aggression results in the ever freer exercise of aggression. In the human being, aggression easily gets out of control. Each of us should be continuously on his guard lest aggressive tendencies be channeled into unproductive activities.

332
. . . .
Information Feedback,
Rewards and
Punishments, and the
Guidance of Learning

Summary

1 All events that have the property of increasing the probability that a particular behavior will occur are called positive reinforcers. However, the term covers a variety of phenomena, for events following a response that change its rate of occurrence do this for many different reasons.

2 An important aspect of some reinforcing events is that they carry information to the behaver. This kind of information is called knowledge of results. Information may be given before or after a person makes a response. Sometimes it makes no difference whether information is given before or after a response is made, but sometimes there are advantages in providing the information after the response is made. Sometimes information has to be given before responding.

3 A first stage in the performance of a motor skill has to be a stage of attention. In the case of typing, the typist has to attend to the material to be typed. Misperception is a major source of typing errors. Typing involves a motor set; that is, the individual readies himself to strike the appropriate keys. Once the typist has made the decision to strike a key, he cannot stop the motion in progress. Action involves the assembly of a program in the nervous system and the setting in motion of the program. It takes time to intervene and stop the program once it has started. The internal programs of beginning typists are quite short action programs, involving no more than the typing of single letters. As skill is acquired, the individual produces programs involving groups of letters that are run off as groups. An expert may run off whole groups of words at one time.

4 The halting typing of a single word by a beginner is intimately controlled by information. Information is needed before the task is begun about what the task involves. Then there is information used while the task is in progress. In addition, there is knowledge of results, which shows the individual what he has accomplished. The terminal feedback may result in the modification of the internal program so that it will function more effectively next time. The learner also uses concurrent feedback, that is, information that provides guidance while the task is in progress. Learning involves the slow elimination of cues that are needed for guidance early in learning but that would interfere with more advanced stages of the skill.

5 Improvement in the performance of a skill takes place by two

means. The teacher may indicate procedures that have to be followed to improve the skill. The learner may also improve his own internal motor programs.

6 The role of learning by observation has long been a controversial issue. Individuals do have a capacity for observing a performance, assembling an internal program to perform the skill, and then executing the skill. The task of learning by observation is not an easy one, for the observer may not know what to look for, and the skill may be performed so rapidly that the actions involved are difficult to identify. Despite these difficulties, there is no doubt that some skills can be learned largely by observation. There is some evidence that animals other than man have some capacity for learning from other members of their own species. Learning by observation must be regarded as a form of perceptual learning that takes place independent of the reinforcements provided. Some such learning is regarded as incidental learning.

7 The early research on reinforcement left the strong impression that reinforcement has to be provided immediately after the response for it to be effective. Indeed, so strong was this impression that it was an important factor in Skinner's proposal concerning the need for teaching machines. Supposedly, teachers could not reinforce pupils quickly enough or often enough to be effective. In motor skills, there does seem to be a strong case for the immediacy of reinforcement. At least, reinforcement should occur before movements other than the one to be reinforced have taken place. Delayed feedback is ineffective in the case of motor skills because the learner has difficulty in remembering exactly what he did. In tasks in which the learner can easily recall what he did, verbal tasks being an example of such tasks, reinforcement can be delayed without damaging the acquisition of the skill. In some types of human learning, delayed feedback has been found to be superior to immediate feedback. There is a possibility that delayed feedback may result in recall, and recall can function very much like an additional learning trial. In academic work, contrary to the position taken by Skinner, delays of feedback of fifteen minutes are not deleterious, and even delays of hours or days may be advantageous.

8 Guidance is often advantageous in the learning of motor tasks, particularly if the task can be performed slowly and provide time during which directions can be given by the instructor. There appears to be something of an art in providing verbal guidance of motor tasks. Picturesque language that conveys precise meaning may be crucial in providing good instruction. The use of effective verbal analogies in the giving of such instruction may be the mark of an effective teacher.

9   Feedback has motivational components in addition to providing information. Individuals will continue to perform very dull tasks if they are given information about how well they are doing. Some tasks may not be so dependent on frequent feedback to energize behavior. Problem-solving tasks, which may be inherently interesting, may be able to energize the behavior of the problem solver even though feedback may be quite infrequent.

10 Grades represent feedback. In the nineteenth century, percentage systems were introduced and, later, category systems, of which the letter-grade system is an example. From the discovery that many aspects of nature reflect the normal curve, the idea developed that grades should also reflect a similar distribution. The grade thus came to indicate how the child stood in relation to other children and did not indicate what the child could or could not do. Grades indicating relative performance provide very little information of use in helping the individual child. These grades are also often contaminated by such personality factors as cooperativeness. Grades should, ideally, be related to well-defined levels of proficiency. This can be done only if the curriculum is divided up into a number of identifiable units and the record of the student indicates the units he has passed at some acceptable level of proficiency. Such records tend to be voluminous and present a record-keeping problem that probably has to be handled by a computer. Teachers using such data systems are likely to be flooded with more data than they can easily use. Records and grades have motivational properties that also need to be understood.

11 Feedback has been regarded as having two components. One is the informational component, and the other is the reward component. Rewards are highly sought after situations that do not carry any great amount of useful information. Rewards are not intrinsic to the situation in which they are given. A dollar given as a reward does not have to be given in a particular situation. On the other hand, the statement "You are right, the answer is 17!" is appropriate only when the answer is 17. Rewards have been widely used to keep students in a learning situation, notably in situations having little intrinsic attraction for the student. Some psychologists have suggested that all pupils be paid to learn, to see if this procedure might keep students in school. Nobody knows what would be the effect of paying students for some-

thing other than goods or services. Less radical systems of rewards offer pupils the opportunity for undertaking preferred activities if they will undertake activities they do not like. Token systems have also been suggested. There is no doubt that token economies can be used to control certain gross forms of behavior, for instance, to keep students in their seats. There is little evidence that the changes thus produced have any permanence. There is little evidence that such systems have any great impact on academic work. There is also the possibility that students in such systems end up by working only at the activities for which tokens are provided. Experiments show that when some components of a task are rewarded and some are not, learning takes place only on the components for which rewards are given. There is no evidence that monetary reward systems will develop independent learners. A successful educational system must be one that develops self-energized learners. Children learn without any rewards extrinsic to the learning task, if such tasks are properly constructed.

12 Since many of the rewards related to education are long delayed, the effect of delaying a reward is of some interest. Research has shown that, although middle-class children may respond well to delayed rewards, disadvantaged children do not. A positive response to delayed rewards may require that the individual have a well-developed concept of time.

13 Aversive situations are those that are avoided and, at the most primitive level, involve pain. The withdrawal of an expected reward can have very aversive effects. The withdrawal of an expected reward may have the effect of energizing behavior. This is known as the effect of frustrative nonreward. Punishment may have the effect of improving learning, but there are ethical issues involved in its use.

14 Punishment is an attempt to suppress or eradicate behavior through the use of aversive conditions. There is clear evidence that punishment does have the effect of supressing a response and, when extremely severe, may permanently prevent a response. Nevertheless, there are strong arguments against the extensive use of punishment in schools. Perhaps the most justifiable condition for punishment is when the punishment suppresses a response long enough for a more appropriate response to be learned. Human beings and other creatures may become habituated to punishment. Although punishment may have bad side effects, rewards also have undesirable secondary effects if used to excess to control behavior.

336
• • • • • • • • • • •
Information Feedback,
Rewards and
Punishments, and the
Guidance of Learning

Let us begin by giving some brief consideration to what is meant by an **attitude**—an issue about which there is considerable controversy in the literature. Definitions are many, but the one adopted here is that an attitude is a readiness to respond in such a way that behavior is given a certain direction. A person who has a positive attitude toward democracy responds positively to democratic institutions and practices and negatively to authoritarian procedures. Some of the expressions of his positive democratic attitude are found in the opinions he holds and expresses and also in the kinds of actions in which he becomes involved. The expressions of attitude are not the attitude itself, which must be conceived to be the underlying tendencies in his personality. A common expression of attitude is an **opinion.** The expressions of the attitude generally have organization; that is, they are characterized more by consistent elements than

11

The Learning and Modification of Attitudes

by inconsistencies. One cannot observe the attitude directly—only its manifestations. In technical terms, the attitude is a theoretical construct, that is, a concept that does not correspond to anything directly observable.

Primitive forms of attitude are seen in the very young child's acquired tendencies to approach certain situations and avoid others. Even at the early childhood level, attitudes always have an evaluative component that leads to approach or avoidance.

One speaks of a person's attitudes, and also of his **values.** The terms are closely related. In contemporary psychology, a person's values are considered to be the organizations of his attitudes. For example, a person has positive attitudes related to making money, owning a fine house, driving an expensive car, having a lot of money in the bank, and buying only the best. One might say that the value system of this person, reflected by these attitudes, is an economic one. Another person's life might be dominated by religious values. Such a person might show positive attitudes toward helping the poor, supporting religious organizations, giving away his money except for what he needs for necessities, and living a simple and unassuming life. Attitudes *may* be organized into a value system, or they may not be. The attitudes of some may show no organization and may even have inconsistent elements. Thus although one person may have a positive and supportive attitude toward all minorities, another may have positive feelings toward one minority group and negative feelings toward others. Rokeach (1968) points out that values appear to have broad motivating properties and imply goals in life. A person preoccupied with religious values is unlikely to end up as a banker and a person preoccupied with economic values is unlikely to become a simple parish priest.

A distinction must also be made between attitudes and **interests.** The distinction made here is based on the differentiation made by Getzels (1969), who introduces the matter by pointing out that one may have a positive attitude toward Eskimos but have no particular interest in them. An interest, he states, "impels an individual to seek out particular objects, activities, skills, understanding, or goals for attention and acquisition" (p. 470). Interests provide driving forces in broad directions. Attitudes may have actions attached to them, but they do not carry the same driving force as interests.

Components of Attitudes

Attitudes cannot be pictured as simple structures underlying behavior, for research has shown them to be extremely complicated. The analysis of the components presented here is derived largely from an article by Katz and Stotland (1959). Although this is somewhat old and has been followed by prolific research, a more convenient classification of attitude components does not seem to have evolved.

Katz and Stotland take the position that attitudes have three basic components—**cognitive, affective,** and **action components.** Let us consider each of these separately, beginning with the cognitive component.

Every attitude is based to some degree on beliefs, some of which represent true and valid knowledge and some of which represent suppositions that are quite untrue. All beliefs, regardless of whether they are valid or invalid, constitute the cognitive component of an attitude. Many of the strong attitudes that play a powerful role in politics are based on beliefs that are nothing short of nonsense. In recent times, such beliefs as that all pacifists are communists, all liberals are socialists, all conservatives are facists, and so on, represent cognitive components of very commonly held attitudes. The fact that the components do not represent anything corresponding to the truth has nothing to do with the fact that attitudes are built on them. Many of the most unfortunate attitudes, particularly attitudes toward minorities, are based on falsities. Attitudes of whites toward blacks and Orientals have been typified by such quicksand foundations.

The cognitive components of an attitude may be broad or narrow. They may also be strong or weak. A person may have a preference for a particular political party but know so little about the political issues that he is quite unable to justify his preference. In such a case, the cognitive component is both narrow and weak. A person may have a prejudice against a particular minority, and this prejudice may be backed up by an enormous amount of misinformation. In this case, the cognitive component is broad and weak. Sometimes attitudes are built on a solid foundation. A person may have a strongly negative attitude toward the kind of diet typically consumed by Americans. His negative attitude may be based on substantial and valid data showing that it is deficient in certain important trace minerals and lacks some of the substances necessary for good nutrition. In such a case, the cognitive component of the attitude is broad and strong. Education is concerned with building attitudes on the basis of broad and strong cognitive components and with the removal of attitudes that rest on a flimsy foundation and are generally aspects of man's worst behavior.

The affective component of attitudes pertains to the aspects of attitude that have to do with liking or disliking particular objects or events. A positive attitude toward, say, the Democratic Party, involves a liking for the party, a wanting to do things for the party, a feeling of comfort when the party wins, and so forth. Some attitudes may have virtually no cognitive base at all and may represent little more than an affective component. One may have a positive attitude toward dark-haired blue-eyed people, for no apparent reason of which he has knowledge, though an observer might point out that the basis for this liking is the fact that one's own coloring is dark hair and blue eyes. Most of the devices used for measuring attitudes are designed to measure the affective component of attitudes. These devices are commonly extended questionnaires that ask questions pertaining to the extent to which one endorses particular ideas or behaviors or how one feels about them. A classical device for measuring attitudes toward a particular minority group asks whether one would be willing to accept a member of the group as a member of the same community, as a neighbor, or as a relative by marriage. Through such questions, the device probes the extent to which an individual accepts or rejects the members of the minority.

Attitudes may have tied to them action components, though not necessarily so. For example, secondary-school programs often include the objective of developing a favorable attitude toward democracy and democratic institutions. These programs provide a sound cognitive base for the attitude, and the affective component may develop to where the student feels a warm appreciation of democracy and democratic institutions. Those who plan such programs and related curricula hope that the positive attitudes will also have an action component, particularly manifested by voting behavior. Of what value would be a positive attitude toward democracy if the individual did not participate in the basic democratic process that takes place at the ballot box? The evidence seems clear that the school and the other educational forces in the community have not been as successful as might be hoped in developing an action component of the attitude, for the evidence is clear that the American adult has a very poor record as a participant in the democratic process. Although many other countries provide data showing that as many as 90 per cent of their adults vote in elections, the percentage voting in the United States is rarely above 70 per cent.

Most attitudes related to important issues of the day have no action component tied to them, so they result in virtually no effective action. Perhaps the most serious of these no-action-component attitudes is in the area of environmental pollution. Everybody is against pollution and for a cleaner and healthier world, but few take action to achieve the goal so universally endorsed. Hardly anyone is willing to give up his car or his fireplace or willing to have his clothes washed in soap in place of detergents.

For these reasons, a knowledge of a person's beliefs, opinions, and preferences provides little basis for knowing how he will act, for these can be surprisingly independent of action.

Function of Attitudes

Although one can hardly conceive of a person who has no attitudes, the function that attitudes have is still not clearly understood. McGuire (1969) has provided a very detailed analysis of the various functions attitudes may perform, and this discussion follows his analysis. It is probably more correct to speak of the functions of attitudes than to imply that they have a single function. Probably the most common function they have is that of being instrumental in achieving a particular goal. The junior executive finds himself agreeing with his superiors on all the political and social issues of the day. Soon he speaks and acts like the conservative and influential company he keeps. The attitudes that he first expresses,

The teacher on the top has little effect in developing the behavior shown on the bottom. What could the teacher do to be more successful in this respect?

and then slowly acquires, represent instrumental means of achieving particular ends. These behaviors and the attitudes that underlie them are, of course, frequently reinforced by the company he keeps, and the promotion ladder provides high incentives for maintaining the attitudes and occasional significant reinforcements. Such attitudes are likely to be of the greatest importance to him in achieving his occupational goals. Attitudes expressed for utilitarian purposes may have a transitory life, or they may become permanent parts of behavior.

A second function of attitudes is that of providing a simplified set of rules for responding to the world. The traditional Moslem, who has been raised to view all non-Moslems as persons of inferior status, has learned a rule for handling a very complex world in a very simple way. The rule relieves him of the need to avoid discriminating between one non-Moslem and another, for the rule prescribes uniform treatment of them. The rule underlying the behavior is essentially the manifestation of an attitude. Certainly, in the political field, opinions and their underlying attitudes represent simple ways of handling complex problems and issues. It is much easier to vote with a party on all issues than to consider each issue separately and come to an individualistic conclusion on each issue of how to cast a vote. Attitudes toward one's country, embraced in the concept of patriotism, provide simple rules of behavior that are, at this time, being questioned concerning their adequacy as a basis of reacting to the issues of the day. The simple rules of behavior inherent in traditional patriotic attitudes made the task of the government very simple, for the government could easily predict how the electorate would respond. Governments oppose discarding the simple rules of traditional patriotism partly at least because it makes governing a vastly more difficult task than it ever has been. The present trend of educated youth is to show the love they have for their country in much more complex ways and through much more complex attitudinal structures than has been the case in the past. Whether an orderly society can be developed under such conditions remains to be seen.

A third function of attitudes suggested by McGuire is that they have expressive functions, permitting the individual to develop and grow in ways that involve real gratification. A person who did *not* have strong and positive attitudes toward some aspect of his environment would be truly wishy-washy, incapable of finding any great rewards in life. Attitudes represent the channels through which behavior can realize important goals. The religious leader's positive approach to religion is essential for the success of his career. The most successful men in politics are those whose positive attitudes with respect to political issues can be readily identified. Much of the evil in civilizations of the past and present can be ascribed to strong and irrational attitudes that have guided behavior. One example is Hitler's fanatical hate of the Jews and of communism, which he had crudely linked together in his distorted mind. In the case of Hitler, his expressed attitudes on these matters were not chosen coldly for political purposes but were the result of a deep, pathological hate, with which he became completely preoccupied. Hitler's attitudes had the effect of creating for himself a unique self-identity, but more socially acceptable attitudes of a milder nature can also serve this important purpose. Certainly, the identity of the economist John Kenneth Galbraith is created partly by his well-known attitudes toward present-day capitalism. J. William Fulbright has a special identity because of his views on foreign policy.

A fourth function of attitudes appears to be what has been called the ego-defensive function. The poor white laborer in the South can feel that he is *not* the most inferior person on earth by becoming hostile to blacks and referring to them as inferior beings. The object chosen for such a purpose in the development of the attitude is a matter of convenience. In other communities, the object of a similar attitude might be Latin Americans or Americans of Oriental origin. If the individual can convince himself that he is superior to group X, then he no longer feels at the bottom of the social ladder. Of course, the group designated as inferior does not have to be inferior, but only has to be imagined as inferior. The attitude can then be further bolstered by taking actions that will best prove the inferiority of the group in question. For example, many of the laws passed in the last century that denied the right of blacks to an education were of this character. If the black was not inferior in fact, then he was going to be made inferior through discriminatory education. One can understand that such attitudes, based on inner factors in the individual rather than on objective factors in the situation, are particularly difficult to change. Reality has nothing to do with the attitude, but reality is modified by the attitude to make it correspond to a wished-for condition. Such an attitude is not going to be readily changed by providing information that the downtrodden group is not really inferior, because those who hold the attitude are going to make them inferior by whatever means are at their disposal. If the group holding the attitude is denied the opportunity of relegating the other group to an inferior position, then the people involved may seek out some other means of overcoming their underlying feelings of inferiority.

Dissonance: A Key Concept in Understanding Attitudes

An important concept that has guided the more recent development of the model of man as an information-processing system is **dissonance.** The concept was originally given prominence by Festinger (1957), although he did not originate it. This concept has had a long period of evolution in the behavioral sciences and, despite the fact that it has been the focus of extensive research, still cannot be defined with complete precision. However, many scientific concepts have had a long history of evolution before a satisfactory definition has been achieved. For example, by the year 1800 many interesting experiments had already been performed with electrical phenomena, but understanding of the nature of electricity and the precise meaning of the concept had to await J. J. Thomson's demonstration of the existence of subatomic particles.

Let us initiate this discussion of dissonance, as a psychological concept, by discussing some examples of it—much as the scientist in the year 1800 would have initiated the discussion of electricity by pointing out common examples of electrical phenomena, such as lightning, the spark produced from a Leyden jar, and the ability of a rubbed piece of amber to pick up small particles as though it were a magnet. Aronson (1968) has pointed out that dissonance theory has long classified the phenomena that fall within its scope into four main categories, as follows:

Logical dissonance: A soldier at the front believes that his company will be wiped out, but he also believes that he is going to live through it all. The two sets of beliefs are logically inconsistent, for he has no basis for believing that his fate is going to be different from that of anyone else. Another common inconsistency of beliefs is found in scientists who believe that all events are strictly determined by the events that preceded them and that the universe is completely orderly and, at the same time, believe that there is a Divine Being who can prevent events from occurring in an orderly sequence and who may be a nonphysical cause of events. The two sets of beliefs are logically inconsistent, but there are ways in which the persons involved attempt to resolve the inconsistency.

Cultural dissonance: A professor gives all of the students in his class a grade of either *D* or *F*. In the American culture, this is inappropriate behavior in that custom requires that there be a certain kind of distribution of grades. In the case of our professor, there may be nothing dissonant for him about his action, but the students are likely to perceive the action as highly dissonant; that is, there is an inconsistency between the customs of academic culture and what has happened to them in the particular class.

Dissonance between a person's broad plans of behavior and a particular action: Most behavior appears to be guided by broad plans in the educated individual. A person who acts as though guided by a broad plan to be honest may sometimes, under pressure, behave in a dishonest way. Under such conditions, dissonance is produced. The individual is likely to feel very uncomfortable about the dissonant act and will attempt to overcome the dissonance in various ways.

Dissonance between past and present experience: An example of dissonance between past and present experience is found in the case of an associate who has always treated one in a courteous and kindly way and who, one morning, treats one with rudeness and abruptness.

Now a point to note about all dissonant situations is that they produce some tension in the person who experiences the dissonance. The soldier who tells himself that he is going to survive, even though nobody else in his company will, may try to resolve the dissonance by saying to himself "Perhaps some of the others may survive, too." Soldiers are typically convinced that it is the other fellow who is going to die, but when things get tough and it seems clear that the whole unit is likely to be wiped out, each has difficulty in maintaining the view that his own life will have some special protection. Such a view involves more dissonance with his assessment of the situation. A student faced with the dissonance between the customs of the college in assigning grades and the low grades assigned by a particular professor is likely to march into the dean's office and demand action. A person who is generally honest, but who accepts a bribe to arrange for the ballots in an election to be destroyed, may feel very uncomfortable about what he has done. He is shaken by the dissonance between his act of dishonesty and the concept he has of himself based on his past behavior. He can resolve the dissonance in many ways. One way is to tell himself that the election was of no importance anyway. Another is to tell himself that the election will be at least as fair as the previous one. Still another might be for him to take the position that the election had been unfair anyway.

The occurrence of dissonance is motivating, in that it generally leads to some kind of action that removes the dissonance. Sometimes the action taken to remove the dissonance may be just a minor reappraisal of the situation. If I hear that the mild and gentle Professor Jones has been arrested for beating his wife, I am likely to resolve the dissonance that confronts me by saying that Jones must have become mentally ill. There is no dissonance between Jones being mentally ill and Jones beating his wife, although there is dissonance between Jones being in a good state of mind and Jones beating his wife.

Now let us look at the use of the concept of dissonance from another vantage point. Aronson, like many other writers in the field, points out that the word *dissonance* lacks precision, even though there are a number of situations that define it quite roughly. Aronson suggests that dissonance can be much better defined as a situation in which there is a conflict in expectancies. A person who expects himself to be honest, but who behaves in a dishonest way, shows a conflict between his expectancy and what actually happens. In all dissonance, there is either a discrepancy between a number of expectancies or between expected events and actual events.

What Aronson proposes is that the concept of dissonance be replaced by the concept of violation of expectancy. Though we accept, here, this definition, we will continue to use the word *dissonance* because of its common usage in the field. Another related set of terms must be mentioned, namely, those of **cognitive consistency** and **cognitive dissonance.**

Dissonant relationships may exist between what are called cognitions. This term is not from common language but is derived from the technical language of psychology. The word comes originally from the Latin word *cognitio,* meaning *know.* A cognition is anything you think you know, regardless of whether your knowledge is right or wrong. Thus pieces of correct information are included in cognitions, and so also are any pieces of misinformation one may foster. What are commonly referred to as beliefs are cognitions, and so too are opinions. The opinions that constitute the core of our attitude system are cognitions. In a sense, anything stored in man's information system, right or wrong, verifiable as knowledge or unverifiable, is a part of the system of cognitions, or a part of the cognitive system.

The elements in the cognitive system may have many different relationships with one another. They may be in a relationship of dissonance of the kind discussed in this chapter. They may be in a relationship of consonance; that is, the one cognition may be related to another element and the two elements may fit together. A six-year-old child says "I know the man next door is a gangster because he is always going out late at night and he is mean to kids." The two cognitions represented by the statements "He is always going out late at night" and "He is mean to kids" represent two cognitions in consonance. Both statements may be quite untrue and the conclusion blatantly false, but the cognitions exist as stored elements in the child's cognitive system. They are in consonance in that they both lead the child to drawing the same conclusion, namely, that the man is a gangster.

Some elements in the cognitive system may be in neither a relationship of consonance nor one of dissonance. They may be just irrelevant to each other. I know that bananas are yellow, and I also know that most saucepans are made of metal. These two pieces of information have no relevance to each other; they have a relationship of irrelevance. In this chapter, our main center of interest will be on the elements in the cognitive system that are in a relationship of dissonance.

Let us begin this discussion by considering a problem that has long intrigued psychologists. The problem is whether individuals do or do not avoid exposing themselves to information that is dissonant with the cognitions they have already stored. An excellent summary of research on this problem has been done by Berscheid and Walster (1969). The earlier research produced very inconclusive findings. Psychologists had expected to find clear evidence that individuals would avoid listening to speeches expected to include information that was inconsistent with the cognitions they already possessed. The general idea was that Republicans would choose to listen to Republicans and Democrats to Democrats. However, sometimes the tendency to expose oneself selectively in this way was evident, and sometimes it was not. Experiments were typically undertaken with quite sophisticated audiences consisting of college students. A common technique was to measure some aspects of the attitudes of the students and then to provide them with a choice of titles of articles they could read. The question asked by the research worker was whether the students would avoid choosing the titles that suggested the dissemination of information contrary to their beliefs. For example, a group of conservative students might have a choice between reading an article on "The Role of the Stock Market in a Free Enterprise System" and "Ways in Which Labor Can Improve Its Collective Bargaining Position." The expectancy was that a conservative student would choose to read the first of these two articles, because it would be likely to present information in consonance with his own cognitions, and that he would avoid choosing the second article, lest the information arouse in him a state of dissonance. States of dissonance are regarded as being aversive conditions, that is, conditions that the individual tends to avoid, or remove, or move away from.

Although studies can be found, here and there, that support the hypothesis that individuals avoid exposing themselves to information that is at variance with information they already possess, the bulk findings have been negative. Now this does not negate the finding of the type that Democrats go to lectures by Democrats and that blood donors go to hear lectures on the importance of giving blood. People are selective in what they expose themselves to for a number of different reasons. A Democrat attends lectures by Democrats perhaps because his friends go or because it is sponsored by an organization to which he belongs. He probably goes, not because he wants to hear the information, but because a good turnout is important in order to provide a good showing for the party in the public eye. People expose themselves to information similar to what they already possess partly because social circles to which they belong limit the information to which they are exposed.

Most studies undertaken have a limitation imposed by the fact that their subjects were college students. College students, because they are more knowledgeable than most, are probably more secure than most in their beliefs. If I hear a piece of information that is contrary to the beliefs I have built on a solid basis, I am not likely to be disturbed by the information. In other words, the item of contrary information does not produce much dissonance, if it produces any at all. If somebody tells me that the world was created only five-thousand years ago, I am not likely to experience much dissonance, because I am not likely to accept the statement as information. The evidence to the contrary is so overwhelming that any small piece of information supporting the idea that the world was recently created is hardly likely to carry much weight. If the statement comes from a person whom I otherwise respect as a source of information, then I may experience some brief moment of dissonance before I write off the whole incident by saying to myself "That guy must be pulling my leg." Informed people are likely to experience little dissonance when exposed to information contrary to their beliefs, but what happens to those who have much less confidence in what they know? Surely, they should experience much more dissonance when faced with an item of conflicting knowledge. This has been the topic of a series of studies reviewed by Berscheid and Walster.

The evidence for this latter hypothesis is positive, but at this time not overwhelming. In some studies, there is a fairly clear case that those who are confident of themselves are more likely to expose themselves to potentially dissonant information. Most of the studies have used college students as subjects, and this factor has probably weakened any effect that exists. One would expect that experimentation with uneducated groups, difficult to involve in experiments, might produce a much stronger effect.

Berscheid and Walster point out another factor that seems to play a part in exposure to dissonant information. They suggest that very often individuals do not want to expose themselves to dissonant sources of information involving people because they fear that the sources themselves, that is, the people disseminating the information, may not like them. Some evidence supports this position. The author can state that he has known many individuals involved in the peace movement of the 1960s who avoided meeting individuals representing the extreme right largely because they were afraid of being rejected. They expected to be called "pinko" or "red," though one suspects that this would not have happened. Perhaps what they feared as much as anything was that the rightist would be polite to them but would think hostile thoughts. Human relations are very complicated, and subtle elements involved play a role in what information the individual decides to expose himself to.

The research discussed up to this point has been concerned only with the matter of exposure and says nothing about what information the individual retains once he has been exposed. The problem of whether information in consonance with beliefs is more or less readily retained than information in dissonance is a problem that has not yet been adequately investigated. There are very real difficulties in studying this problem. One is that information in consonance with beliefs is already information that has been partly learned.

Attitude Change

The literature on attitude change and the conditions that produce it is so large that only the expert can be expected to be familiar with original studies. Many excellent summaries have been made. A highly technical summary has been provided by McGuire (1969), and this chapter has been largely molded around what he says. A much less technical account has been written by Triandis (1971), who has himself made many research contributions to the area. A small popular book by Karlins and Abelson (1970) provides a summary of practical suggestions concerning actions that are effective in changing attitudes.

The research literature on attitudes is far richer in material on how attitudes are changed than on how attitudes are formed in the first place. The reason for this emphasis is that many serious problems in our society can be attributed to the fact that attitudes are formed that run counter to the development of a democratic society, and the schools have the task of rectifying these ill-formed attitudes. Most people would agree that a democratic society cannot operate in an atmosphere of prejudice—in which people are denied basic rights because their skin is of a particular color, or because they speak a language other than English, or because they are poor, or because they belong to a minority religious group. Although the law has attempted to block many avenues through which prejudice has traditionally channeled its evil effects, the basic problem in the movement toward a true democratic society is still the elimination of the prejudices that run counter to democratic ideals.

Many different techniques have been used successfully for producing attitude change. The nature of attitudes is such that a condition that will produce effective change in one attitude will not produce effective change in another. For example, mention was made earlier that there are some attitudes in which the object of the attitude is chosen, not on the basis of any real knowledge, but because the object is there. Attitudes toward minority groups are of this character. The hostility expressed toward a particular minority might just as well have been expressed toward another minority group, except that one minority group rather than the other happened to be there. Such an attitude is not based on particular knowledge about the minority group and for this reason is not readily changed by the prejudiced person being given information about the group. On the other hand, if I am prejudiced against a particular religious group because I believe its members to be narrow-minded in their ways, my prejudice may be changed if I am provided clear evidence that they are not at all narrow-minded, but liberal in their ways.

Let us focus attention on verbal techniques for the changing of attitudes, because these are the ones that are most widely studied and also those that teachers use. Let us begin by looking at factors related to the source of a message designed to change attitudes. Then we will move on to a consideration of the characteristics of a message that make it persuasive, followed by a discussion of the medium through which the message is transmitted. Finally, we will present some of the information available concerning what is known about the characteristics of a receiver that makes him either influencible or uninfluencible.

The source: The term **source** requires brief discussion. If a teacher says that the President of the United States is in favor of open housing, in the hope of changing attitudes with respect to this issue, and provides quotations from presidential messages, then the source of the message is the President, not the teacher. In such a case, the teacher is the medium through whom the message is communicated, that is, the channel of communication. Sometimes the source of a communication is the teacher himself, and pupils in classes also are important sources of communications, all of which *may* influence attitudes. The characteristics of sources that may influence attitudes may be divided up in many ways. McGuire, borrowing from predecessors in his field, suggests that a convenient classification of source characteristics is into the categories of **credibility, attractiveness,** and **power.**

Credibility has two main components. One of these is the perceived competence of the source of the message. The other is the perceived trustworthiness of the source. Note that a distinction is being made here between how competent a source is in relation to producing the particular message and how competent he is believed to be by the receiver of the message. The word *perceived* is used by sociologists and social psychologists rather loosely, for it does not involve so much the process of perception as it does the belief system of the receiver of the message. Competence is also distinguished from trustworthiness. A competent source may be viewed as one that may deliberately mislead and hence be highly untrustworthy.

The findings generally show that the judged competence of a source is an important factor in determining whether the message will or will not change attitudes. In this connection, a change in attitude refers to a change in the opinions that the receiver may express or endorse. The judged competence of a source is of considerably greater importance than is the judged trustworthiness of a source in this respect, but trustworthiness does appear as a significant factor in some studies. The data give support to the notion that a politician who has acquired a reputation for expertise in some area may have success in changing the attitudes of the electorate even though he is known as a slippery character of questionable honesty. An interesting question is what a communicator should do if he knows that he is a low-credibility source and yet wants to change the views of those who are to receive his message. Karlins and Abelson (1970) have a suggestion of what to do in such a predicament, based on some quite substantial data. They suggest that in such circumstances the communicator would best remain unidentified until after he has made his communication. He may also be effective if it is clear that he is arguing against his own best interest. Apparently, delay in the identification of the credentials of the source allows the message to have an effect, an effect that is not readily reversed when the credentials of the source are disclosed. Another factor is involved in this phenomenon, namely, that the acceptance of the message may result in the acceptance of the source. Messages influence beliefs about the source.

Finally, Weiss (1971) points out that, of the news media, television has the highest credibility. Weiss implies that this high credibility is not necessarily due to accuracy of reporting on television but may be due to the vividness with which real events can be directly seen. Weiss (1971) points out that the high credibility of television exists despite the fact that television does not have an overwhelmingly good record in terms of accuracy.

The second source characteristic of importance in the present connection is attractiveness. One aspect of attractiveness is the extent to which the individual who is the source is similar to the receiver. People are so constituted that they are attracted to individuals similar to themselves, but this also means that they tend to expose their minds to the talk of similar people who reflect their own ideas. There does seem to be some tendency for people to adopt the ideas of those similar to themselves, but the data are confused by the fact that sometimes individuals may adopt attitudes of those who represent opposite characteristics. The most notable example of the latter is the well-documented fact that some of those held in Hitler's concentration camps, who were beaten and tortured by the guards, ended up by becoming advocates of the same brutal methods. Some people acquire the attitudes and behaviors of those that persecute them. It is as though an individual, by identifying with his persecutor, is able to convince himself that he no longer belongs to the persecuted group. Marlowe and Gergen (1969) have summarized the literature on personal attraction, and so too has Byrne (1971).

Familiarity is an important factor in much attitude change. The familiarity effect is seen in the fact that individuals tend to acquire the attitudes of the group to which they belong and slowly move toward the group norm. Belonging to a group also has complex effects that play a role in attitude change. A group to which one belongs has the ability to provide many rewards if group standards are conformed to. Those who do not conform are likely to be ostracized or otherwise punished. There is also another factor. Any objects that are repeatedly presented tend to become more and more liked. This is true regardless of whether the objects are nonsense syllables, animals, or pieces of artwork. Probably much the same thing happens when one hears the same ideas expressed again and again by the members of a group to which one belongs. Mere familiarity with ideas gives them a degree of acceptance they do not have when presented for the first time.

The power of the source is a factor that has only recently been studied in any depth by social psychologists and sociologists. Let us consider what this term means in the context of attitude research. A teacher has some power as a source, for the teacher can control the rewards and punishments in the classroom situation. The boss in a business may have considerable power over the employees with whom he has close contact. In the politically controlled state, run by Big Brother, those who operate the state's bureaucracy may have such power that they can virtually require the citizen to express certain views. Under such conditions, one speaks of the **forced compliance** of those who behave in the way they are required to behave. There seems to be no doubt that forced compliance can be a strong factor in producing attitude change. If I am required to say, aloud and daily, in a public situation, that Dictator Doakes is a wonderful man, I slowly come to believe that Dictator Doakes is a wonderful man. I may also be required to recite in public the sayings of Dictator Doakes, and as I do this I slowly come to believe in them.

The effectiveness of a power figure in changing attitudes is highly dependent on his use of rewards and punishments. Psychologists interested in operant conditioning have interpreted this as supporting their position that learning takes place insofar as there are reinforcers operating, but the support is only superficial. A review of the problem by Insko (1967) shows some interesting facts. First let us consider the case of a reward given to an individual after he has been forced to express an opinion contrary to his own beliefs. Many situations have been devised in which individuals are forced to do this. One is the debate. An experimenter can arrange a debate and so devise his experiment that a debater is required to support a position that he would not ordinarily endorse. The undertaking of this act tends to change his attitude so that it becomes more favorable toward the position he has been required to take. This is a subtle forced-compliance situation. In another type of situation, one can arrange for a person to make a statement that he would not ordinarily make. For example, in one technique subjects engage in a long, tedious, and extremely monotonous and boring task. As these individuals finish the task and leave the room, they are required to tell the next person who is to do the task that it is fun to do. They are paid to do this. The act of saying the task was fun results in an improved attitude toward the task.

In such situations, subjects can be given either large or small rewards for performing in the particular manner prescribed. The typical finding has been that a small reward is far more effective in producing a change in belief or attitude than a large reward. Those paid twenty dollars to say that the dull task was fun tended to acquire a liking for the task by saying that they liked it but those paid one dollar showed an even greater change. Now this finding is not in accordance with the operant position, in that most research on positive reinforcements within the operant model shows that larger rewards produce at least as good learning as smaller rewards.

Although the operant model of learning fails to account for this interesting phenomenon, the dissonance model of attitude change offers a quite convincing explanation. The dissonance model implies that the motive to change belief is dissonance. If I am offered a large reward for saying "The task was fun," then I can also say to myself "Well, I don't really believe that the task was fun, but I am saying it was because I am being well paid to say this." If the reward is small, I cannot rationalize the inconsistency between what I say and what the task was actually like. If I cannot rationalize the inconsistency, there is dissonance. I can then remove the dissonance by forgetting that the task was really boring and telling myself that it was really fun. This is the reason that there is considerable evidence that small rewards, used in forced-compliance situations, produce greater change in attitudes than do large rewards. In order to obtain the experimental effects, the difference between the large and the small reward has to be considerable, with the large reward being twenty to a hundred times larger than the smaller.

Much the same effect that is produced by small and large rewards is occasionally found in experiments comparing mild and severe punishments. As has already been pointed out, there can be no doubt that severe punishments can produce a permanent inhibition of behavior, but there are occasions in which a minor punishment can produce a greater effect than a more severe punishment. The very severe punishments that produce an effect are generally such that they cannot be humanely administered by a civilized community. Within the range of punishments that can be administered, milder punishments may sometimes be more effective than the less mild ones. Suppose a child wants to go out of his yard and explore the neighborhood and is severely punished for it. He may still continue to want to explore the neighborhood. He does not explore the neighborhood because he fears the punishment, but he does not change his desire to explore, because there is no dissonance. On the other hand, if the consequence of exploring the neighborhood is mild reprimand, then he may continue to want to explore the neighborhood, but as soon as he sets foot outside of the yard he experiences dissonance between his desires and the anticipated reprimand. He can resolve the dissonance by saying to himself "What's so great about exploring the neighborhood?" What he has done is to reduce the dissonance by reducing the desire to explore outside the yard. Hence, although the threat of punishment may keep the child inside the yard for a time at least, the mild punishment may have the effect of reducing the desire for the prohibited behavior. Dissonance theory has been quite effective in predicting the difference in the effect of mild and moderate punishment in some situations.

The power of the source will also have an effect insofar as the source can scrutinize the receiver of the message. McGuire cites numerous studies in which this effect is quite evident, and it is one of considerable interest not only to those in education but also to those who formulate public policy.

Message characteristics: The results obtained from study of the characteristics of the source have been far clearer and more definitive than the results of research on message characteristics. Perhaps the reason for this is that measuring techniques have been better developed in the area of people characteristics than in the area of characteristics of verbal materials. One can measure the prestige of a source much more easily than one can measure the style characteristics of a message.

One of the commonest sources of appeal is that of the message providing some kind of threat to the receiver. Recent attempts by governments abroad and the American Cancer Society at home to stop the use of cigarettes have involved messages containing threats—"If you do not stop smoking, this is what will happen to you." The message then shows the plight of the person with lung disease. Another area in which threat is designed to produce attitude change is in the use of automobile seat belts. Recent materials distributed in schools on the dangers of using drugs have also included the element of threat and the supposed response of fear on the part of the pupil. A very important and practical problem is the extent to which the introduction of threat and the supposed arousal of fear are effective in producing either changes in attitude or changes in behavior. Should one tell the child about the very worst consequences of the use of drugs or should one take an approach that lays less emphasis on the dramatic?

Although the opinion is commonly expressed that the more threatening a message is, the more it is likely to be effective, the results of research do not lead to such a firm conclusion. McGuire has reviewed dozens of studies and can only make the statement that the studies show a general trend. The effect of threat seems to depend on which aspect of behavior is involved. It makes a difference whether one measures a change in the person's intention to give up smoking or whether one measures if he did or did not give up smoking. The use of an element of fear appears to influence intention but not the act itself. The stronger the threat, the more the intent is likely to be modified, but strong threats have no greater effect on the act to be undertaken or suppressed than mild threats. Thus messages about the terrible effects of smoking are likely to lead people to say that they intend to give up smoking, but they are not likely to change their smoking habits.

The research in this area also includes some studies in which increased threat seems to have had a negative effect. There is a possibility that strong threat may be so anxiety provoking that the individual avoids thinking further about the matter. In the late 1950s, the Federal government attempted to enlist the support of the public in building underground bomb shelters, and the literature on the subject emphasized the horrors of atomic warfare. The response of the public was to ignore the materials. The interpretation given to this response was that attending to materials describing the horrors of atomic warfare was so anxiety producing that people tended to avoid having their anxieties raised to such a pitch.

The role of information in producing attitude change is complex. Some attitudes have a strong base of information, but some do not. This point has already been made in the earlier statement that attitudes have a cognitive component that may be weak or strong. In fact, the same attitudinal position may be held with and without a strong cognitive component. For example, a person might have opposed the Vietnam War on the basis of extensive knowledge of the military situation, information about the virtual impossibility of achieving military victory without destroying the countries involved, and study of the history of the Southeast Asian countries. Another person might have held an identical attitude because he was a dedicated opponent of all violence. The latter person might have had no knowledge of the Vietnam situation and even little knowledge of the arguments that pacifists use in supporting their position. Because the knowledge base varies from person to person, even when virtually the same attitude is involved, one can well understand that the giving of information may have many different effects on attitudes, depending on the particular person involved. Much also depends on the emotional basis of the attitude.

The style of presentation of the message designed to change attitudes has been extensively investigated. A long discussion of these researches by McGuire may be summarized as follows:

1. Clarity of presentation has little to do with how much it results in opinion change. Indeed, clarity as a factor in any educational presentation has not shown itself to be a decisive factor, except, perhaps, where a message is so garbled that it cannot be understood at all. One suspects that a message that lacks clarity forces the listener to work harder to comprehend the message, but the information retained from the message may be

unaffected. If information is to change an attitude, then the information has to be received, but whether it is received with difficulty or is easily received would appear to be of little consequence. There are, of course, studies that show that clarity is a factor, but the finding is not typical.

2. Another factor that has long been believed to determine the effectiveness of a communication in producing attitude change is the dynamic quality, emotionality, and humor. In keeping with this belief, some politicians use emotionally toned words or introduce humor. Research on such factors is limited, but the results do not suggest that such factors play an important role.

3. There is some evidence that when the listener is left to draw his own conclusions, the message is more likely to influence attitudes than when the conclusions are handed to him. McGuire points out that Freud was the first to suggest this to be so, but he cites seven recent research studies that uniformly support this conclusion.

4. Arguments can be presented in a straightforward way, or they can be presented together with a refutation of opposing arguments. The merits of either of these positions do not come out as a clear factor, and there is some evidence that the less intelligent are confused by presentation of refutations of opposing arguments, though the more intelligent may show more attitude change from this procedure.

5. Repetition of a message appears to facilitate its effect, perhaps in line with Hitler's dictum that if a lie is repeated often enough then the public will begin to believe it.

6. There is quite substantial evidence that a large discrepancy between the position of the source and the position of the receiver results in greater attitude change than a small difference. Let us state this in terms of a practical issue. Suppose that one were interested in converting an audience to the position that capital punishment should be abolished. One would do better to take the position that capital punishment, for whatever crime, should be unequivocally abolished than to take the more moderate position that it should be reserved for just a few rare crimes such as piracy. In many respects, this conclusion is surprising, for the common belief is that one does best in changing the attitudes of others by presenting a position not too different from the others' position. The finding that a firm and very different position from that of the receiver produces the greatest change is consistent with dissonance theory. A very different position of the source from that of the receiver produces greater dissonance in the receiver than does a moderately different position. However, if the difference is made extreme enough, then it may cease to be effective. One suspects that the inability of either the extreme political right or the extreme political left to gain many converts may be a result of the fact that the extreme positions held are viewed as being nothing short of ridiculous. For example, the famous position taken by the policy makers of the John Birch Society that President Eisenhower was an agent of the Communist conspiracy was quickly dubbed by the public as being sheer nonsense. A considerable divergence of the opinion of the source

from that of the receiver may give the receiver the impression that he is listening to a fresh and different viewpoint, but an excessive divergence may tell the receiver that he is listening to nonsense.

Channel factors: Now let us turn from message factors to channel factors. Educators do not generally speak of channel factors but rather of media and media factors. The message always comes through some medium, and the properties of the medium may influence the extent to which a message is persuasive. Marshall McLuhan is credited with the famous saying that "The medium is the massage," meaning that those who receive a message may become so preoccupied with the medium itself that the message transmitted by the medium may be lost. Thus one may watch the television screen and not be particularly concerned with what he is watching. The argument is that one attends to the television, the medium, rather than to any message conveyed.

Of particular interest in this connection is the effect of the mass media on changes in attitudes. This has been an extensively studied problem, partly because the managers of the mass media are interested in determining whether they have a service to offer political parties. McGuire has provided a detailed review of the very large number of studies undertaken in this connection. He points out that the criterion of change used in such studies generally loads the dice in favor of the media. For example, some of the studies merely were concerned with demonstrating whether the receivers of a message transmitted through a mass-medium channel retained it or not. Perhaps retention of the message is necessary for attitude change, but it is not a sufficient condition for attitude change. Even with the use of such weak criteria, the studies have shown that the mass media exercise surprisingly little influence on attitudes, and it is hard to find a study showing any real impact in this respect. Although the mass media themselves have long suggested that they exercise control over public attitudes, historians have also been able to find little supporting evidence for the position. Historians point out that Franklin Roosevelt was elected despite the fact that an overwhelming body of the press was against him. Truman was also elected under similar circumstances. Such findings have not deterred political parties from pouring very large sums of money into the use of media in the hope of swaying public opinion on the political issues of the day.

One can demonstrate that the mass media are effective in disseminating information. The studies of *Sesame Street* show clearly that children learn from mere exposure to the television medium (see Ball and Bogatz, 1970). In cases in which attitude change is dependent on a change in the underlying knowledge component, then this can obviously be changed through the mass media.

An interesting point, in relation to education, is the relative effectiveness of the mass media in contrast with face-to-face persuasion situations. The two situations involve very different conditions of learning. In the face-to-face situation, the source can adjust to the responses made by the receiver. The person in the role of message source can see what his message is doing. If he sees antagonism, he may be able to change his position enough to obtain a more receptive audience. The television speaker, addressing vast audiences, has to make judgments concerning the way in which the audience is going to respond. Of course, the audience includes many diverse groups who will respond very differently to the message. With some of these groups, the television speaker may be making correct judgments, but with others he will be wrong. Because of the diversity of the audience, the television speaker will make compromises, attempt to endorse several positions, and perhaps attempt to provide each listener with some statements to which he will respond. The result is often a speech filled with inconsistencies that will not persuade any person to change his attitudes. This dilemma is particularly acute when a country is highly divided into many factions, each one of which the speaker may attempt to appease. In addition, there is evidence (Weiss, 1971) that the mass media have been quite ineffective in building images of politicians. The fact-to-face communicator does not have to face these difficulties. He probably will choose small homogeneous audiences, as he does in a political campaign in addressing small neighborhood gatherings in individual homes. He specifically avoids bringing together the ghetto inhabitants with the inhabitants of suburbia, but meets them separately and has very different interactions with them. He may also avoid certain groups, taking the position that it is not useful to attempt to persuade them to see things his way. He will probably concentrate his time on those groups whom he is most likely to be able to persuade.

The teacher has certain advantages over the politician in face-to-face attempts to change attitudes. One of these is that pupils are not likely to have as fixed attitudes as the adult population. Attitudes are in the formative stage in the elementary-school child. The teacher can engage in the formation of attitudes, which may be a much easier task than changing attitudes already well established.

Receiver factors: The traditional position in educational psychology has been that an active receiver is one who is most likely to learn. This is the position taken by Thorndike, half a century ago, and more recently by Skinner and his followers. However, evidence has already been presented that learning does occur under conditions that do not necessarily involve any great activity. Individuals do learn by being exposed to films and television broadcasts that call for only a minimum of activity on the part of the learner. Persons do acquire large components of some motor skills through nothing more than observing the skills being performed. Attempting to perform the skill before the person fully understands what has to be done may result in poor performance and frustration. Action and the attempt to produce the response have to come at the time when the individual knows enough to be able to produce a response that resembles the one to be acquired. Workers in the area of attitudes initiated much research expecting to find that an active recipient of a message, who had to work with it and perhaps draw inferences from it, might show more attitude change than one who passively listened to or watched the message as it was presented.

McGuire has summarized the very extensive research on the effect of active participation on the part of the receiver and the degree to which the communication results in attitude change. The evidence seems clear that little is gained by receiver activity. Active receivers of messages, who have to work with what they are given, show no more attitude change than those who receive the message quite passively as listeners or viewers.

One of the most widely studied receiver factors is influenceability. Ordinary experience leads one to assume that some individuals are more easily influenced than others. Those who tend to be influenced by another person attempting to persuade them to assume a new attitudinal position are, of course, conforming to the opinions of the person who is attempting to influence them. The question arises whether these individuals are generally the most conforming individuals in other situations. McGuire concludes that there is a trend in this direction; that is, there is a tendency for individuals to be more or less conforming to the opinions of the group in which they happen to find themselves. Another way of saying this is that the opinions and attitudes of some individuals have chameleon-like properties, tending to become colored by surroundings.

Influencibility is related to some situational factors. Karlins and Abelson (1970) point out that individuals who are deeply attached to a group are not likely to be influenced by communications that come into conflict with group norms. Motivation to maintain membership in the group is also motivation to maintain attitudes that the group endorses. This phenomenon is one of great significance in the case of the adolescent, who is highly motivated to be accepted by his peers. The need for peer-group membership of the adolescent is such that he is unlikely to be influenced by communications that conflict with group norms. Thus the adolescent who belongs to a street gang is unlikely to be influenced by those who might wish him to hold attitudes other than those held by the gang.

An interesting matter in relation to education is the question of whether some ages are more influencible than others. The traditional view has been that the younger the child, the more he is likely to be influenced by the adult. In the discussion of this question, one must keep in mind that the concept of influencibility is tied to the concept of attitude change and not to the concept of attitude formation. Attitudes are probably most easily formed in the young child, in whom attitudes can be developed without first the necessity of eradicating old biases and prejudices. Attitude change is another matter. The evidence indicates that children tend to increase in influencibility about up to the age of nine years. After that age, there is increasing resistance to change. The data suggest that the elementary-school years may be those during which the teacher can exert the greater influence on the development of attitudes. Why attitudes become more difficult to change after the age of nine is a matter for speculation. One view is that the child learns defenses that prevent his attitudes from being changed. As the child grows older, he may also learn counterarguments to use against those who might attempt to change his position. A child raised as a pacifist might not know how to answer a third-grade teacher who says "It is all very fine to be a pacifist in theory, but what would one do if the country were to be invaded?" At that age, he might even be persuaded that, under some conditions, the only course of action would be to fight. If the child were just a few years older, then he would know exactly what the counterarguments would be and could come up with a strong defense against most of the arguments offered to the pacifist position.

The last point that has been made suggests that there would be a negative relationship between intelligence and influencibility. The person with a well-developed intelligence has many well-developed rationalizations for his beliefs and is much more skillful in producing counterarguments. This is what has generally been found in research, but the finding is an oversimplification of the actual situation. Presumably, the intelligent person is also more likely to be swayed by logical and sound argument than is the less intelligent. If this is so, then one would expect that the more intelligent individuals would be less moved by appeals to emotion but more influenced by rational persuasion.

Finally, the point must be made that women in our society are more influencible and suggestible than men. This is hardly surprising in view of the fact that women have been assigned, by men, a role in which they are rewarded for believing what men tell them to believe and for doing what men tell them to do. There is no reason for thinking that women are inherently more suggestible and influencible than are men, even though the phenomenon is seen even in elementary-school children. One suspects that as the Women's Liberation Movement has impact, the effect will vanish.

An aspect of influencibility that has been much discussed in recent years is authoritarianism. Adorno et al. (1950) developed a measure of what they called the authoritarian personality. This measure they found to be related to anti-Semitism and political conservatism. The scale for measuring authoritarianism, known as the **California F-Scale,** became the basis of hundreds of studies during the decades that followed its publication. Although Adorno and his associates viewed the California F-Scale as measuring a single dimension, it now seems clear that they were dealing with a complex of variables. One component of this complex is a variable described by Rokeach (1960) as open-mindedness—closed-mindedness, having certain obvious relationships to the influencibility factor. Both Adorno et al. and Rokeach agree that the closed mind is one that is threatened by new beliefs. The closed mind is not only tightly compartmentalized but is highly dependent on outside authority.

Although Adorno et al. viewed the authoritarian personality as reflecting an extremely conservative position, later studies, reviewed by Deutsch (1968), have shown that those who are politically left may suffer from the same closed-mind syndrome. There are also cultural factors involved. The lower socioeconomic groups tend to be unbending and intolerant on noneconomic issues, such as internationalism and ways of expressing patriotism, but they tend to be receptive of new ideas in the economic area. These more recent studies suggest that authoritarianism and closed-mindedness are not simple unitary traits but combinations of characteristics. A person may be open-minded with respect to one issue but closed-minded with respect to another.

Retention of Attitude Changes

Research as far back as the 1930s conducted by L. L. Thurstone, as well as a large volume of later research, has shown that attitude changes produced by particular experiences tend to shrink with the passage of time. In the typical study, changes in attitudes have been studied over a period of one to three months. Why this happens is a matter of considerable interest.

The most plausible explanation for this slippage is that the experience that produced the change slowly faded from memory. For example, in some of the early studies of attitude change, a film was shown that presented a minority group in a favorable light, and the purpose of showing the film was to change the attitudes of the viewers toward the particular minority group. Such a film presentation was shown to change the opinions about the minority group as expressed through tests of attitudes. The change in attitude, determined by measuring the attitude toward the minority before and after viewing the film, was then shown to slowly shrink with the passage of time. The change in attitude was dependent on what the viewers learned from the film, and what they learned from the film would slowly be forgotten with the passage of time. As the content of the film was forgotten, the influence of the film on attitude would also fade. The transitory effect of the film has to be pitted against the other experiences to which the viewers have been exposed for their entire lives. Suppose, for example, that a child has been told by his parents during his entire life that members of minority group X are "no good." After six or more years of hearing this, he is then shown a film that presents a contrary opinion, and his attitude shows a slight shift toward a more favorable position. Two weeks after seeing the film, he can remember little about the film, but he still remembers vividly what his parents have told him, because they had voiced the same opinion so many times.

Theories of Attitude Change

This chapter has already touched on theories of attitude change, but a full exposition of the topic would require a book. Two major works devote several hundred pages to the problems of theorizing in this area (see Insko, 1967, and Kiesler et al., 1969). Although one cannot here even give a summary of the theorizing that has been done in this field, it may help the student to point out that this chapter has touched on two different approaches to the construction of theories of attitude change. One of these is dissonance theory of attitude, a component of a more general theory known as **cognitive consistency theory.** This type of theorizing has been very successful in stimulating research and, in fact, is the underlying basis of much of the research during the last decade. It has also had some value in explaining certain odd facts, such as why a small reward is more effective than a large reward. The theory is far from being as precisely stated as one would like it to be, but this is a fault shared by most psychological theorizing. Many have pointed out that psychologists are good at collecting information and findings but have not been very successful at putting the findings together into a theory. The field of attitude change is no exception. The theories that have been developed have had only limited success in explaining many different findings within a common framework.

A second kind of theory of attitude change is that with roots in contemporary theories of learning. The operant view of learning has been used by some as a basis for understanding attitude change. The position is that new attitudes are formed because new behaviors are reinforced. The strength of the position comes largely from studies in the forced-compliance category, in which a person is required to make a statement or perform an act contrary to what he would ordinarily perform. The act or statement is then reinforced. The evidence shows that behaviors that are reinforced tend to represent more and more the attitudes of the individual. To state that it is the reinforcement that is producing the attitude change is, undoubtedly, a gross oversimplification of very complex events. A more complex explanation tied to learning theory that introduces other data is that the individual required, for example, to make statements with which he does not agree may think about the statements and begin to see them in a different light. A person asked to make a statement favorable to a politician with whom he disagrees may begin to see the reasons why the politician takes the positions he does. He may see merits in them that he had not previously seen.

A Unified Program of Attitude Development and Change

Although there is some tendency for the individual to work toward producing consistency in his internal organization of attitudes and the beliefs, and sometimes the knowledge on which they are based, a very discordant environment works in the opposite direction. The child sees adults engaging sometimes in honest behavior and sometimes in dishonest behavior. He sees adults advocating a larger slice of the gross national product for themselves, yet opposing others who also seek the same. He sees them advocating democracy and yet not voting, and also endorsing the most authoritarian administration in schools. He sees them demanding that the children share things, but not offering to share what they have with the poor. The child emerges from such a background with numerous specific rules for behavior, such as that one is generous with a friend, one is stingy with a stranger; one says one is in favor of democracy, one does not necessarily vote; one attempts to obtain all the money one can by any legal means, and so forth. Behavior governed by numerous separate and distinct rules that are little related to each other is behavior at a disjointed and immature level. Behavior is more mature in those who are able to substitute broad general rules or principles for numerous specific rules. A person who understands the need for supporting democracy in all the ways that it has impact on the individual is a much more mature person than the individual who has learned only to support specific aspects of the democratic process and not others. An important objective of education is to enable the student to bring together many of the specific rules he has learned in his inconsistent environment and to organize them under more encompassing rules. A child must learn to see that the duty to vote, the duty to obey the law, and the need to conduct a committee by democratic methods are all part of the package of being a citizen in a democracy. Education has this integrative function in a highly inconsistent world. The school that does not perform this kind of integrative function is providing only the most primitive form of education.

Although it is easy to say that the school should perform this kind of integrative function, the fact is that the school environment is just as inconsistent as the rest of the world in which the child lives. In addition, schoolbooks typically neglect the important issues of the day. If a Dickens were to write today, his books would almost certainly be banned from the shelves of school libraries. Important issues of the day are rarely touched on, except insofar as the teacher injects a personal opinion here and there into his comments. Yet the great issues of the day, such as those involved in the balanced use of the environment and the development of social responsibility, are not going to be handled by occasional editorial comments. Material related to such issues and the building of related attitudes should certainly appear in kindergarten and be systematically introduced into every grade throughout school. There is no reason why textbooks at the elementary-school level should not focus on these issues and on other issues of equal social importance. Consider, more specifically, the issue of pollution and the maintenance of a balanced environment. Problems related to this matter could be introduced into the lowest-level readers. Science teaching, even in the first and second grades, could give some attention to the problem. The writer recently saw a science teacher demonstrate that a candle would not burn for more than a few moments when covered with a glass. He explained that the flame consumed the oxygen under the glass and that when all the oxygen had been consumed the flame went out. The teacher never drew the attention of the children to the smoky dirty interior of the glass left at the end of the experiment. He never realized that he had before him a very fine demonstration of air pollution. He could have discussed in the class why the candle produced so much "smog" when the candle was covered (incomplete combustion).

In a unified program on the environment, the social studies could play an important role, and the social studies teacher should bring out the importance of legislation. Pupils might well conduct studies on the individuals and groups in their community who produce pollution, with or without breaking laws. The teaching of English could, at times, focus on the problems of the environment, for the children could write reports on the studies they had made. Perhaps even the parents could become involved in the program, developing projects through the Parent-Teacher Association in which the children might become involved. A program that attacks a problem on every curriculum front is more likely to have success than the present procedure of devoting one unit a year to a problem.

What has been said in this section is particularly relevant to the teaching of attitudes. If attitudes are to be learned in the school, then every phase of the school program should contribute to the development of the attitudinal objectives. If positive attitudes toward democratic living are a goal, then the school must provide good examples of democratic procedures and, more important still, must avoid the arbitrary exercise of authority. If the school is to foster humane attitudes toward others, each interaction in the school, between teachers and pupils, teachers and teachers, and pupils and pupils, should be an effort to demonstrate humaneness, and the curriculum itself should be designed to foster humane attitudes. Only a unified effort to build attitudes has much chance of having a lasting effect.

One area of attitudinal development, which has not been discussed up to this point, is the development of positive feelings toward learning as an activity. Various simple recipes have been proposed for this purpose. Mager (1968), for example, is for the development of approach tendencies toward the subject matter of the school but has few suggestions concerning how this should be done, except for removing aversive conditions. This is a gross oversimplification of the kinds of actions that need to be undertaken. The author has visited classrooms in which there were virtually no aversive conditions operating but the children were dawdling through assignments. The work was not in any way unpleasant, but it challenged none and aroused enthusiasm in none. The mere elimination of aversive conditions does not necessarily produce enthusiastic learners who will learn to value learning in itself.

In order for genuinely positive attitudes to be developed toward schoolwork, the work has to be related to the satisfaction of important needs in the pupil. For some, it will be necessary that the schoolwork provide a challenge, but for others it may be necessary that schoolwork become an avenue for satisfying social needs or other need structures. The solution has to be, to a large degree, individual.

Summary

1 The early foundations of attitude are seen in simple approach and avoidance tendencies. Attitudes develop as complex structures underlying approach and avoidance behavior. Attitudes are not directly observable. Values are organizations of attitudes. Values have broad motivating properties and imply goals in life. Interests involve action components related to the objects involved. A person acts in relation to his interests, but attitudes may not involve any significant action components.

2 Attitudes are complex and involve three components, although any one component may be extremely weak. First, there is a cognitive component, in that attitudes always involve some beliefs that may be either true or false. Attitudes are often based on beliefs that are sheer nonsense. Education is concerned with building attitudes on the basis of a solid foundation of established knowledge. Second, attitudes have an affective component, that is, a component involving liking or disliking. Many attitudes involve little more than irrational likes and dislikes. Third, attitudes may have attached to them action components. A person may vote because he has strong attitudes related to the responsibility of the citizen in a democracy. On the other hand, he may have attitudes strongly favoring democracy, but he may fail to vote. In the latter case, the attitude lacks the necessary action component. Education seeks to build attitudes that have appropriate action components, but the development of such components is an aspect of attitude education for which few techniques have been developed. The control of environmental pollution is an example of an area in which attitudes with strong cognitive components have been developed but in which action components are largely lacking.

3 Attitudes may be instrumental in achieving particular goals. Attitudes may also provide a simple set of rules for responding to a very complex world. A third function is to provide an avenue of self-expression through which the individual may find gratification and achieve new fulfillment. A fourth function of attitudes is to provide ego defenses. Many race attitudes develop to serve this kind of function.

4 An important concept in the understanding of attitudes is that of dissonance. Psychological dissonance may be a result of logical or cultural inconsistencies in a situation. It may also be a result of discrepancies between broad plans of action and particular acts, or between past and present experi-

364
· · · · · · · · · · ·
The Learning and
Modification of Attitudes

ence. The existence of dissonance is motivating in that it leads to some kind of action if the dissonance is to be resolved. A useful definition of dissonance is that it involves a situation in which there is a conflict in expectancies, that is, when one event is expected and another occurs. The terms *cognitive consistency* and *cognitive dissonance* are sometimes used. Elements in the cognitive system may be either in consonance with one another or they may be dissonant.

5 Although Democrats go to hear Democrats and blood donors go to hear lectures on why one should give blood, most of the studies undertaken have involved college students, and these studies have provided no substantial evidence that individuals avoid exposing themselves to information dissonant with the information they already possess. The possibility exists that college students may be so secure in their own beliefs that they experience no dissonance when exposed to views contrary to their own. There is some evidence that those most confident of themselves are the least concerned about exposing themselves to sources of information that might produce dissonance.

6 Very large numbers of studies have been undertaken on conditions that facilitate attitude change. One group of studies has investigated the characteristics of the source of a message that facilitates attitude change. A major source characteristic is credibility, which has two components, perceived competence and perceived trustworthiness. The competence aspect is much more important than the trustworthiness component in producing attitude change. If the source has low credibility, then the source had better remain anonymous until after the message has had impact. In the case of media, television has the highest credibility, despite the fact that it does not have an overwhelmingly good record in terms of accuracy.

7 The attractiveness of a source is important in that individuals tend to expose themselves to sources to which they are attracted. Familiarity appears to be an important factor in attitude change, because individuals tend to expose themselves to familiar persons and slowly acquire the attitudes of those persons. The group to which one belongs also has the capacity for providing rewards for showing conformity of beliefs.

8 An important factor in attitude change is forced compliance. An individual required to perform in a particular way tends to modify his attitudes to make them consonant with the way of acting. Many experiments on forced compliance, some undertaken by operant psychologists, illustrate this phenomenon. Forced-compliance studies generally involve a reward

for undertaking the required behavior. A small reward is generally more effective than a large reward, a fact that fits dissonance theory rather better than it does the operant position. A similar phenomenon is found in *some* studies comparing severe and mild punishment in which mild punishment was more effective than severe punishment. These studies contradict the more typical findings from research on punishment.

9 Threat implied in a message has a complex relationship to the effects of the message. The main effect of strong threat is to influence the intent of the receiver, but it is not likely to influence his actions.

10 The role of information in producing attitude change is complex. Much depends on the extent to which the attitude is or is not based on information. The effect of new information on an attitude is quite unpredictable.

11 The effect of the style of a message on attitude change has been investigated from many angles. Factors that do not seem to have a positive effect are clarity, emotionality, and humor. Attitude change is more likely to be achieved if the listener is left to draw his own conclusions. The more intelligent listeners are more likely to be influenced when opposing arguments are presented and then refuted. The less intelligent listeners are likely to be confused by presentation of both viewpoints, even though one is refuted. Repetition of a message adds to its effect. A large discrepancy between the attitude of the receiver of the message and the attitude reflected by the message produces more attitude change than when the discrepancy is smaller.

12 The effect of the mass media on the changing of attitudes appears to be quite minimal, despite the fact that they have relatively high credibility. Even very large amounts of television time have failed to produce marked changes in attitude toward politicians.

13 Individuals differ in the extent to which they are influenced by others. Children tend to increase in influencibility up to about the age of nine. Situational factors also play a part. One is likely to reject new ideas that come into conflict with the norms of the group to which one belongs. Women are more influencible than men, but this is probably a result of the role assigned to them in society. Attempts have been made to measure certain aspects of influencibility. The closed mind, uninfluenced by encounters with new beliefs, reflects a component of the authoritarian personality. The closed-mind syndrome seems to typify extremists of all kinds in the political sphere.

14 Attitude changes produced by some source of influence tend to dissipate as time passes. An explanation offered for this is that the message producing the change in attitude is slowly forgotten. As the message is forgotten, the effect it had on attitude disappears.

15 Extensive effort has been made to build a theory of attitude change. Two major theoretical positions hold the field. One is the operant position, which views attitude change as a matter of reinforcing behaviors related to the attitude to be developed. A second theoretical position is based on dissonance theory.

16 The systematic education of attitudes in schools requires that the program of the school have some unity with respect to the attitudes to be changed or developed. One of the most important attitudes to be developed is a positive one toward learning and toward an intellectual approach to problem solving.

367
. . . .
Summary

The Social Nature of Man

Psychologists have long had difficulty in identifying the characteristics of man as a species. Indeed, it has been only recently that psychologists have come to appreciate the great differences that exist among species and to be cautious in generalizing from what is known about one species to what is known about another. The notion that studies based on rats or pigeons could be justifiably generalized to the human species was widely held at midcentury. Since that time, evidence has accumulated that generalizations across species should be made only when the greatest cautions are observed. Evidence has further accumulated that, even within a species, substantial differences in the laws of behavior may be found (see Lockard, 1971). Man is very distant on the evolutionary scale from any

12

....

Learning and Social Development

other living creature. Although he belongs among the primates, he did not descend from any living primate. The hominids, from which modern man arose, left behind only a few bones from which their form could be reconstructed. The earlier ancestors of man left no trace in the clay of time. What this means is that there are no species living that are sufficiently near to man that one can study them in order to discover species characteristics. The nearest are the other primates, but these are extremely distant relatives, most of them still living in trees. It has probably been ten- to twenty-million years since man had ancestors that lived in trees. The baboon is one of the few primates that lives on the ground, and it has been valuable as a source of information about ground-living primates, but these creatures are still very distant relatives.

Despite the remote relationship between the modern lower primates and modern man, some understanding of the human species has been derived from the study of the other primates. At least all primates seem to share certain characteristics. Most primates live in groups and spend substantial amounts of time each day in social interaction. These interactions involve playful behavior and also behaviors that are collectively referred to as grooming behaviors. They are not sexual behaviors but form a special basis for interaction among members of the species. Nevertheless, there is a relationship between the playful behavior of the younger members of a primate species and subsequent sexual behavior. Harlow (1961) has shown that infant rhesus monkeys raised in isolation from one another are not able to adequately perform sexually when they reach maturity. A playful social interaction appears to be necessary for subsequent reproductive activities. Animals raised in isolation are never able to engage in reproductive activities. Now let us be cautious at this point and not jump to any unwarranted conclusion that man raised in isolation would be unable to reproduce. He might be able to because man has some potential for learning through verbal communication. But that is all a side issue. What is important is that man belongs to a group of species who have high innate social needs and when these needs are not satisfied trouble may result. What is not known is whether man has higher innate social needs than, say, the chimpanzee, the baboon, or the gorilla. We do know that early man lived much like the gorilla, in small bands, and also like the gorilla did not engage in warfare with other groups. Warfare and other antisocial tendencies did not appear until sometime after primitive technologies emerged (Clemente and Lindsley, 1967).

The human and related species are to be contrasted in their social needs with other species that have very low social needs. Most common laboratory species, including pigeons and rats, manifest little social behavior, and contact between members of the species is limited mainly to sexual behavior and maternal behavior.

The field of social development is one of the most extensively studied in the whole field of psychology. The vigor of this scientific area is seen in the fact that the second edition of the *Handbook of Social Psychology* consists of five volumes and each volume is nearly a thousand pages long. For this reason, a single chapter on social development can touch on only one or two topics of central interest to the student of education. This author pondered long on which topics to include in this chapter before deciding on those that seemed to have great importance for education. The chapter emphasizes the topics of moral development and the control of human aggression. If children can develop moral principles of a kind that make civilized life possible, and if they can learn *not* to show socially disruptive amounts of aggressive behavior, then a better world will emerge.

In the present era, it is becoming clear that the home and the out-of-school environment of the child are not developing the social behavior and skills needed for a democracy to operate smoothly, and both the school and the society itself must look at themselves and at the problem if our kind of society is to survive. Particularly evident is the extreme hostility of many who attend schools. Enormous amounts of damage are done to school property, and some of this hostility is directed toward other children. The dangers produced by the latter are such that there are many high schools today where it is unsafe for a girl to use the washroom. Knifings in schools are not uncommon, and disruptive behavior may make it virtually impossible for children to learn in many classes at the junior and senior high-school levels. The social development of youth has obviously moved in directions that, if the trend continues, may permit only anarchy to exist. Some reversal of this trend is clearly necessary, and the schools will have to make their contribution. The position taken here is that every aspect of society has to share in the social education and social development of the young, for it seems clear that, without the cooperation of all, little is going to be accomplished.

Moral Judgment and Moral Development

Psychologists have found it much easier to study moral judgment and the development of moral judgment than to study the development of moral behavior shown in acts of altruism or other forms of helping or loving behavior. The judgments that are made about what a person considers to be good or bad can be studied through the techniques that have been developed for the study of other aspects of cognitive psychology. Moral judgment is a matter of *knowing* what is considered to be right or wrong, in terms of the norms set by society.

The classic research in this area was undertaken by Piaget (1948), and many of his findings still stand today undisputed. Piaget recognized that the child is exposed to a world in which certain acts are punished and other acts are praised and rewarded. The young child does not understand why punishments are meted out for some of the things he does but not for others. The adult may attempt to give explanations of why punishments are given, but these explanations are typically beyond the understanding of the preschool child. It is hardly surprising that, on the basis of what he observes, the child comes to the conclusion that certain acts are called wrong because they are punished. This is the reverse of the mature adult's understanding of the situation. Such an adult understands that certain acts are punished because they are wrong. The child comes to his reverse conclusions because he has no understanding of what is cause and what is effect. Piaget has pointed out that this confusion of cause and effect is very common in early childhood.

The schools have long played a role in moral development, and this role must be distinguished from that played by churches. Schools have long fostered the morality reflected in the United States Constitution and have attempted to persuade students that the only acceptable way of promoting social change is through the channels provided by our form of constitutional government. Moral positions such as the concept of equal rights of all citizens have been taught, though often without too much effect on pupil behavior. The idea that the schools teach moral values is not in any way new. Our reflections here are designed to provide a better basis for the teaching of morality than has generally been provided.

The four-year-old child is not capable of formulating the more complex principles through which an adult comes to classify an act as right or wrong. For example, many of the rules related to what is right and what is wrong have to do with property rights, and the young child has not learned the rules related to those rights.

It is not surprising that Piaget found that the concept of intent does not enter into the moral judgment of the very young child. As children approach the elementary-school years, they begin to introduce intent as a basis for determining the rightness or wrongness of an act. They then give a person credit for trying to do what was right even though it turned out to be wrong. This involves a level of abstraction that the younger child is unable to achieve. One difficulty is that the concept of intent implies that the same act may be right or wrong, depending on the intent of the doer. If a child trips another, the act is wrong if intentional but not wrong if accidental. This is a subtle distinction not dependent on observable properties of what happened at the time of happening.

Piaget's description of the development of moral standards has been developed further by Kohlberg (1958). Kohlberg presented a series of problems involving decisions with moral implications to children of different ages. From his data, he derived a series of stages of moral development that he has since refined, experimented with, and to some degree validated in cross-cultural studies. The present version, published by Kohlberg and Turiel (1971), is the basis for what is said here. The system involves six stages of moral development, plus an early premoral stage in which there is no moral basis for any action. When moral behavior begins, six distinct phases can be discerned.

Stage 1. This corresponds to the earliest stage described by Piaget in which the physical consequences of an act determine whether it is good or bad. At this stage, there is a primitive deference to power and authority, in that power and authority have control over the rewards and punishments.

Stage 2. Action that is right is action that satisfies one's own needs and, to a lesser extent, the needs of others. There is a bargaining element in morality at this stage: "If you do what is good for me, then I will do what is good for you." Relations between children at this stage involve a notion of fairness in how people should treat one another, but there is no concept of justice.

Stage 3. Action has to be in accordance with the expectations of the various groups to which the individual belongs. He not only conforms to the social order but manifests loyalty, even giving up some immediate source of satisfaction for the sake of the group.

Stage 4. Respect for authority and the maintenance of the social order become important. Doing one's duty is the very essence of right behavior. The fixed rules of society have to be obeyed, and good behavior involves showing respect for authority.

Stage 5. Although the behavior involved in stage 4 is very commonly observed, that in stage 5 is far more rare. It involves the sophisticated idea that right action involves both the rights of the individual and the rules and standards agreed on by the rest of society. There is an understanding that values are relative but that there have to be constitutionally agreed on rules of conduct. Rules of conduct are not fixed eternal standards, as they are in stage 4, but even though they are represented by laws, the laws can be changed. Kohlberg describes the morality at this stage as the morality of the United States Constitution.

Stage 6. At this stage, there is reliance on what are believed to be carefully thought out universal principles that are self-chosen and arrived at by decisions of conscience. These are principles that involve the concept of the equality of rights of all human beings, a belief in the dignity and worth of the individual, and the idea of universal justice. They are highly abstract, not concrete as are the Ten Commandments.

The six stages show a steady decrease in the amount of arbitrariness in morality, an increase in the level of abstractness of the concepts involved, and an increase in the degree of personal responsibility. Kohlberg takes the position that the typical level of morality achieved in the American citizen is represented by stages 3 and 4. Only a few ever achieve stages 5 and 6, and many do not achieve even stage 3. The adult world of the American culture is represented by all stages of moral development, with a predominance of people in the middle range. An interesting point to note is that the average level is below that represented by the Constitution, even in high places.

Kohlberg and Turiel (1971) and Turiel (1973) have considered the issue of how education can raise the level of morality. They take the position that children do not acquire new levels of moral behavior either by being told what to do, or how to behave, or by being corrected. These are the traditional ways in which churches have attempted to change moral standards, and most religious educators would agree on their ineffectiveness. Kohlberg and Turiel take the position that, at each stage, the individual has to discover the possibility of new ways of thinking about morality and that these discoveries permit him to move to the next stage. What the teacher has to do is to produce conditions that permit children to make these discoveries for themselves. Such conditions include focusing attention on real-life moral issues and conflicts, helping the child to use his reasoning to arrive at various solutions, and then evaluating the solutions. The child has to be helped to see flaws in his reasoning, inadequacies in his solutions, and consequences that he did not first envisage. Then he is helped to improve on his solutions. Although the usual techniques of providing stories of exemplary characters or of preaching are quite ineffective, stories from history may serve to bring out moral dilemmas that students can discuss.

There is some evidence that the stages of morality are not culturally determined, in the sense that different cultures might produce a different series of stages. Kohlberg and Turiel report that similar stages have been found in people in Great Britain, Israel, Taiwan, and Mexico. It should be noted that children brought up under disadvantaged conditions, in various parts of the world, remain typically at stages 1 and 2. Such individuals, not uncommon in our own culture, may be very common in a primitive community.

As with all taxonomies having a relationship to the work of Piaget, the assumption is made that a person has to complete each stage before he can proceed to the next stage. A child cannot be raised so that he can go directly to stage 6 but has to start at stage 1 and then proceed to stage 2 and so forth. Furthermore, the developing individual does not necessarily and automatically move from one stage to the next but must have the experiences necessary to promote the transition. The experiences do not direct the child where to go in his thinking but permit him to discover, for himself, a new approach to moral problems.

The development of moral judgments is also related to the development of guilt feelings. Aronfreed (1968) regards guilt as an experience of anxiety triggered by the recognition that an act is harmful to another person. Aronfreed points out that guilt may also have components of fear. A person not only develops a state of general anxiety in relation to an act he has performed, but he also may fear the consequences of his act. Guilt is a very general state of anxiety, a general feeling of malaise, but fear is an emotional response related to some specific unpleasant consequence that is expected.

Thus a child's moral judgments have not only cognitive components but they also have emotional components that make them extremely complex responses. The cognitive and the emotional components are interlocked.

The growth and education of the child permit him to develop progressively more complex rules for evaluating the rightness or wrongness of an act. Older children may evaluate acts, not in terms of their immediate effects, but in terms of long-term consequences. To do so requires a conception of time that a very young child does not have.

Altruism

Psychologists have hesitated to study altruistic behavior until recent times partly because there is considerable difficulty involved in defining this category of events. Macaulay and Berkowitz (1970) have discussed the attempts to wrestle with this problem and cite a range of definitions. They point out that at one extreme there are psychologists who define an altruistic act as any act that benefits another individual. If this definition is pushed to the extreme, then the bacteria that live in my intestines and manufacture vitamin B elements are altruistic in relation to me. At the other extreme are those who say that an act is altruistic only if it is undertaken with the intent to help another or do service or provide succorance. The latter definition would classify as altruistic a behavior that harmed another but was undertaken with good intentions. The concept of intent has always been difficult for psychologists to handle, for it is hard—and usually impossible—to determine what a person's intentions are. One generally does better to use the concept of expectancy, because the expected outcomes of an act can be determined much more readily. I can state precisely what I can expect to result from giving a sixteen-year-old a brand-new car and a credit card for unlimited amounts of gasoline, but my intent may have included all kinds of vague ideas such as that the beneficiary of this gift will like me better, that I will be happier, and so forth. Expectancies can be stated quite precisely. For example, I can state that my expectancy is a one in four chance that the sixteen-year-old will become involved in an accident within a year. From the point of view of this discussion, an altruistic act is an act performed in relation to others such that its expected consequences are judged by the performer to be beneficial. The definition avoids the issue of whether the act is undertaken in anticipation of rewards or punishments. This definition has limitations, and even though it is a convenient one in dealing with altruistic behavior of children of school age, it does not include within its scope more primitive forms of altruism in the preschool child.

It must be quite evident to the reader that the form in which altruistic behavior manifests itself is related to the stage of moral development. At stage 1, a child might share his toys with another child because he knows that if he does not, he will be punished, and if he does, he may be rewarded. This level of altruistic behavior is a far cry from that of, say, St. Francis of Assisi, who shared whatever he had with anyone who had less than he because for the other person to have less was demeaning to him. The behavior of St. Francis, deeply rooted in the concept of the universal brotherhood of man and the concept of sharing as a road to personal fulfillment, is in accordance with morality at stage 6.

Studies of altruism have typically been based on a much less sophisticated concept of morality than Kohlberg's, perhaps because a simple theory often provides a good channel for starting research.

The oldest theory of altruism is that it is behavior that occurs because it carries with it rewards. This was a popular view in the early nineteenth century, promoted by the philosopher Jeremy Bentham. More recently, such a view, stated in a more sophisticated form, has been embraced by such psychologists as Aronfreed (1968). One of the great difficulties of this position is that often no reinforcing events in the history of the development of altruistic behavior can be found, and none sufficient to maintain it. Individuals may continue to undertake altruistic acts that produce observable punishments, so where are the reinforcers? Aronfreed tries to overcome this difficulty by proposing that there are hidden reinforcers in the form of satisfactions not observable to the experimenter. In doing so, Aronfreed has to abandon the attempt to limit himself to objective data as the operant psychologist attempts to do. A simpler solution is to abandon the concept of the operant psychologist that reinforcements are needed to maintain altruistic behavior.

Bryan and London (1970) have brought together some of the material on the reinforcement of altruistic behavior. They refer to experiments demonstrating the obvious fact that children offered a piece of gum for performing an altruistic act tended to perform that act more frequently. The act was to share their marbles with another child, involving no great loss on their part in comparison with the gain achieved by winning the gum. This is quite a trivial case to study. Much more significant for the purposes of understanding altruistic behavior are those instances in which there is no obvious payoff and no evident reinforcement for maintaining behavior.

Bryan and London (1970) point out that theories of the effect of rewards on the maintenance of altruistic behavior generally have to introduce the concept of **empathy,** a theoretical concept that can to some extent be intuitively understood. Empathetic theories of altruistic behavior assume that a person who performs an altruistic act sees the other person respond in a way suggesting pleasure. The pleasure-related response of the other individual produces a related pleasure response in the performer of the act, called an affective response.

When a person responds in the same way that he believes another person is responding, he is said to be engaged in empathetic behavior. Allport (1968) points out that empathy has long been a riddle in psychology in that nobody has been able to explain how it comes about. Some have proposed that there may be an innate tendency for one human being to reproduce what another does, but others have strongly disagreed with this position and have made rather unconvincing attempts to explain empathetic behavior in terms of conditioning. The study of empathy, in recent times, has involved experimental studies of imitation, or **modeling behavior.** The person whose behavior is imitated is referred to as the model. The person who does the imitating is the observer. When the model is reinforced for some aspect of behavior, then the observer is said to be vicariously reinforced. Many of the early studies of modeling behavior, conducted by Bandura and Walters (1963), focused on the problem of modeling aggression, a matter discussed later in this chapter. Studies have been undertaken on the conditions in which altruistic behavior is modeled by an observer. Some of these studies have been undertaken with children, but in some studies adults "off the street" have been the subjects, and in such a case one might expect morality at a level of stage 3 or stage 4. In other studies, the subjects have been college students, who might perhaps be expected to be at more advanced stages. A factor that has not been adequately explored is the effect of the relationship between the model and the observer. It probably makes a difference whether the model is a stranger to the observer, or a familiar person, or what sociologists refer to as a significant person.

Experimentation in such an area often is difficult because the child brings to the experiment all kinds of behaviors that have been learned previously. The background of the child, which cannot be easily controlled, makes the experimenter's data difficult to interpret or even uninterpretable. For example, Bryan and London cite a number of experiments in which children who were exposed to a model who demonstrated "giving" behavior then showed an increase in giving behavior. Just how can the behavior of the children be interpreted? One simplistic interpretation is that the children copy the behavior of the model. A slightly more complex interpretation is that the children see the model as showing them the rules to be followed in this particular situation. The children long ago discovered that the best thing to do in new situations is to watch what the adults do and then do likewise. At a still more complex level, it might be hypothesized that the children have in the past been rewarded for manifesting generosity and that they have an established tendency to be generous. The behavior of the models often has the result of releasing behavior that has already been learned, much as the presence of food may initiate eating, even in people who are not particularly hungry. Many of the data cited by Bryan and London simply show little more than that children follow what seem to them to be the rules of the situation in which they find themselves.

The data on modeling suggest that a model who preaches has very little impact on the behavior of children (Bryan and Walbek, 1970). This is to be contrasted with exemplary behavior on the part of the model, which has considerable impact. Very little of the laboratory data provide any indications of the permanence of the effect of seeing a model display generosity. Presumably, single instances of generosity would have very little impact on a viewer. Another question is the extent to which a display of generosity on the part of a model will result in the display of generosity by the observer in other situations and in private situations.

An interesting issue raised by Bryan and London is how children respond to the highly inconsistent behavior of adults in this respect. Children see adults preaching generosity but often behaving in a niggardly manner. They also see adults preaching greed and the importance of competition but practicing generosity in their private lives. The research evidence on this point suggests that children are not at all concerned by the lack of consistency of behavior in this respect. Perhaps the situation is similar to that in the area of moral development already considered, in which the rules deduced by the child are very specific rules. A child knows that the rule is that one does not swipe a piece of the adults' candy when an adult is around, but at other times one can. A child may also conclude that adults engage in generous behavior from time to time, but when they will do this is quite unpredictable. Other conclusions may be drawn by the child, such as that the adult may be counted on to be generous when in public situations, such as giving in church, but cannot be counted on to be generous in the milieu of the family. The rules that the child draws from his observations of adult behavior may not be the rules that the adult hopes the child will draw. Nevertheless, they may be good, objective deductions from the behavior observed. These rules appear not to be based on what the adult says. One suspects that the child simply does not attend to exhortations by the adult.

The social environment of the child seems to be of the greatest importance in the building of altruistic and succorant behavior. The generous child is one raised in an environment characterized by giving. It should also be noted that much giving behavior is dependent on economic circumstances. The poor may give great love and affection to their children, but their economic circumstances limit the extent to which they can provide examples of the giving of possessions or money. One suspects that the children of the poor learn to give love, but cannot learn the giving of possessions, and may have difficulty in giving away their wealth if they should become wealthy.

Generosity is related to age in children, though the relationship is not of overwhelming magnitude. Both sharing behavior and giving behavior increase at least through the elementary-school years. Bryan and London give emphasis to an idea derived from Elvin Staub that generosity, as a form of behavior, becomes complicated during the school years by the concept of deservedness, perhaps related to a move from morality stage 2 to morality stage 3. Generosity is believed to be more appropriate toward some individuals than toward others because individuals differ in the extent to which they deserve to be the recipients of generosity. What is shared is also influenced by whether the person feels highly entitled to the property or whether he acquired it for reasons other than those of good performance.

Experiments on the modeling of altruistic behavior in adults are of interest, particularly because they bring out the inadequacies of training. Of special interest are the studies related to what is known as the **bystander effect.** This effect is demonstrated by incidents in which a person in a public situation appeals for help, or is in obvious need of help, but none of the onlookers take steps to provide the assistance called for. Latané and Darley (1970) have studied this phenomenon and have provided an explanation of why help is not provided in these situations. What happens is that the individual, seeing another in distress, takes his cue on what to do by looking at the other persons present. Thus each person waits to see whether any of the others will act. None do because each is cued to be inactive by the inactivity of the others. This is a stage 4 level of moral behavior, in which the expected behavior of the group and the standards set by the group determine what is right or wrong. An interesting fact is that a person faced with the same situation when alone is much more likely to take action on his own initiative, for he is not paralyzed by the inactivity of others. Kaufmann (1970b) also provides some indirect evidence indicating that if helping behavior is a legal requirement then it is more likely to occur than if there is no such legal pressure. The phenomenon considered here, and the large number of cases reported in the newspapers where needed help was not given, suggests that the schools have the important task of raising morality above stage 4.

Many institutionalized forms of giving also seem to depend on what the giver believes to be typical behavior. Macaulay (1970) showed that if a person sees another donate to a cause, he is more likely to make a contribution. Macaulay also showed that the stubborn refusal of a model to contribute also sometimes increased donations by observers in a backlash effect.

Most studies of altruism in adults show that development typically does not proceed beyond stage 4 morality, but at least one study strikes a more optimistic note. Fellner and Marshall (1970) studied the behavior of those who gave kidneys to a relative or friend. The altruism involved in giving up a part of one's body is particularly interesting, because such an act of giving runs counter to the basic need to protect one's body against anything that might threaten its integrity. An interesting finding was that nearly all of the donors and prospective donors studied made a split-second decision on the matter when they were first approached. The person making the approach did not ask for an immediate decision, but the donors preferred to make up their minds immediately and made no effort to weigh the alternatives. One might have expected them to have made inquiries about the long-term risks and about what would happen to the receivers if a donor were not found. The donors made the decision before they had all the facts laid before them and were actually asked to decide. The instantaneous character of this decision, almost like the instantaneous decision one might make in a matter that might save his own life, suggests that deep needs are involved. The research gives a very positive view of man's potential as a social creature.

Another interesting outcome of this research was the finding that, after surgery, those who had lost a kidney reported a strange kind of spiritual rebirth. They talked as though the giving of a kidney had somehow made them more worthwhile human beings and their lives now had a fullness and happiness they never had before. The giving of a kidney had fulfilled them. The act of giving appears to have a special role in the mature development of man, perhaps by moving him to a higher level of morality.

Aggression — A Species Characteristic

The term aggression has a great variety of meanings. The essence of the meanings is that aggression involves an action on the environment of a vigorous nature, generally more vigorous than is absolutely necessary. The aggressive salesman works to influence his client with more vigor than is probably necessary. The aggressive child dominates his playmates in a way that is unnecessary for the continuation of their game. In the broadest meaning of the term, one can view all actions of the individual directed toward the environment as aggressive — a view that equates acting on the environment with aggression. In this chapter, we will be concerned mainly with problems produced by forms of aggression in which one individual acts with unnecessary vigor on another individual, that is, with social aggression. One extreme form of unnecessary expenditure of energy is warfare.

A distinction must be made between hostility and aggression. A salesman may be aggressive, but he is not necessarily hostile. A person may have deep-seated hostility and brood over the way he hates the world, but he may show little aggression toward the world. Aggression is always a manifest behavior, but hostility may be internal, and because hostility is internal it is difficult to define. In our discussion, we will be concerned primarily with aggression, because aggression involves observable behavior that can be identified and studied scientifically.

Within the definition of aggression given here, primates would be viewed as being aggressive creatures, in that they spend their long waking hours doing things to the environment or doing things to one another. Under natural conditions, they are not hostile to one another and inflict few painful acts on members of their own species. However, under the crowded conditions of close captivity, such as occur in zoos, primates may show almost unbelievable cruelty to other members of the colony. This behavior is in marked contrast with the amiable lives that these same primates lead in an open and free environment. Why they behave so in captivity is not known. One theory is that the crowded conditions increase the number of contacts between the animals beyond the point where these contacts can be tolerated. Another possibility is that dietary deficiencies disturb behavior. It is of interest to note that other animals show this same captivity problem when confined in zoos and also other forms of abnormal behavior, such as eating their young. One wonders whether some of the more destructive behaviors of man may be a result of circumstances similar to captivity that hold men prisoners within the warp and woof of civilization (Clemente and Lindsley, 1967).

Primates, like primitive men, are aggressive in the sense that they explore their environment with vigor and even invent simple tools so that they can do things to their environment that they could not do otherwise. As with other species, attacks on their own kind are rare. Primates that do make such attacks very rarely press them to the point where serious injury or death occurs. A species that destroyed its own kind would be rapidly eliminated. In nature, aggressive behavior toward one's own species always has strict limits placed on how far it may go. Dogs do attack dogs, but dogs rarely kill dogs. An animal attacked by a member of its own species always has the choice of fighting or giving up. If it gives a signal showing that it gives up, then the attack will end. In many animals, the give-up signal consists of exposing the most vulnerable part of the body. A dog may do this by lying on its back and exposing its belly. When this signal is given, the attacking dog withdraws. Most species have a sign of this kind that stops an attack from members of its own species, but the human species does not. Presumably, man does not have such a universally recognized signal because his remote ancestors, living in trees, did not engage in attacks on their own species and hence had no need for such a signal.

Man's capacity to kill his own kind appears to be unique among living things. Richardson (1960) has estimated that during the period from 1820 to 1949 roughly fifty-nine million people were killed through attacks of human beings on other human beings. Of this number, about a fifth, twelve million, were killed outside of armed conflict or in some way unrelated to armed conflict. A majority of these were murdered (almost ten million), and a majority of those murdered were murdered by a relative in their own homes. A point of interest to note in connection with this is that those who argue against the control of all guns say that people need them to defend themselves, but the fact is that relatively few murders are committed by outsiders breaking into the houses of strangers. Most murders are family affairs, and the control of the distribution of guns would probably reduce the number of family murders without adding appreciably to the hazards of living. Man is a very dangerous creature, dangerous not only to all other species with which he "shares" the planet but particularly to his own species. Let us consider briefly how this may have come about.

A few million years ago, the ancestors of man left the trees and took to living on the plains of Africa. Until a few years ago, the date of this event was placed at about two-million years ago, but more recent data suggest that ten-million years would be a better figure (see Clemente and Lindsley, 1967). These ancestors of man are called hominids, meaning that they were manlike creatures, though they were considerably different from modern man. The early hominids probably had some primitive tools, for other primates show a capacity to invent tools, as when they use rocks to crack nuts. The change from living in trees to living on the plains also brought with it a major change in diet. The tree-living primate is fundamentally a vegetarian and a fruit eater. Such food is readily accessible, and a fine sense of color vision enables him to discriminate the ripe fruit from the unripe at a distance. Tree-living primates do experi-

Predators have natural weapons used for killing game. They also have natural inhibitions that prevent them from using these weapons to exterminate their own species.

But man invented weapons without developing inhibitions about using them against his own species.

Education must help man learn to limit the uses of the dangerous objects he has invented.

ment with eating small amounts of meat, but the availability of fruits and nuts hardly encourages the primate to become carnivorous. When man's ancestors took to life on the plains, the situation was different. Suitable vegetable foods were not plentiful, but small game was. Man not only became a hunter, but he also became the inventor of weapons with which game could be more easily secured. Virtually nothing is known about the order in which weapons were developed, for the earliest relics come from a much later period, the Stone Age, which occurred about 10 thousand years ago. By the time of the Stone Age, man had come to approximate modern man closely in bodily form and brain size. It is probable that Stone Age man had as much mental capability as modern man, but he did not have the linguistic skills or the accumulated knowledge that would permit him to think with the skill of modern man. Stone Age man lived in small family groups. He used spears for hunting and developed a device for throwing a spear that was essentially a means of extending the arm. He ate not only meat, but roots that he sometimes placed in hot water to cook.

The slow cultural development of first the early hominids and then man resulted in the development of dangerous weapons to satisfy his carnivorous needs, but early man did not use these weapons against his own species. There is no reason for believing that Stone Age man engaged in warfare between family groups. Indeed, early man seems to have lived much like his primate ancestors in a state of peaceful coexistence between scattered family groups (see Clemente and Lindsley, 1967). Space on the surface of the earth was sufficient for the roving groups of hunters to engage in the activities needed for survival without coming into conflict with one another. Cave man was not able to accumulate surpluses of wealth that might arouse the envy of others. The killing of two deer in a day was no better than the killing of one, for the meat would not keep, but once man learned to cultivate crops the situation was completely altered. It involved a technology that Stone Age man did not possess. The cultivation of crops requires an understanding that the planting of a seed will produce a complete plant—a piece of knowledge difficult for early man to acquire because it required him to piece together events taking place over a span of many months.

Once early man began to raise crops, the way was opened for the accumulation of wealth. Some invented more effective tools than others for the cultivation of the land and were able to raise more food than they required, and perhaps some worked longer hours toward the same goal. The result was that some men accumulated surpluses, which they were able to use to buy the services of other men and to buy luxuries difficult to come by. It must not have been long before communities formed, dominated by the more successful of the agriculturalists, and some of these communities, or perhaps their leaders, saw the possibilities of seizing the accumulated wealth of one or more of the neighboring communities. The weapons that had been developed so successfully for the bringing down of game were now used for warfare. Man became a species with weapons of great power for killing but with no inherent mechanism that would prevent these weapons from being used against himself. Man thus became the one species that engages in widespread destruction of his own kind. This destruction has not, until recent times, threatened to destroy the species, which is perhaps why the problem has not been much worried about until recent times. Richardson, in his study of deadly quarrels from 1820 to 1945, found that the percentage of deaths inflicted by human beings on each other was about 1.6 per cent of all deaths, but deaths indirectly due to warfare probably have amounted to about 10 per cent of all deaths.

Now the point to note is that because man, unlike other animals, has not evolved innate forms of behavior to prevent his species from destroying itself, he will have to invent them if he is to survive. Attempts to do this by the invention of the League of Nations and the United Nations Organization were steps in the right direction but do not appear to have been sufficient to prevent man from self-destruction. The main hope of species preservation rests at this time with what can be accomplished through education and the various institutions that participate in education, but effective educational programs will depend on knowing much more about the nature of aggression and the techniques most effective in bringing it under control. Let us consider some of the research findings derived from studies of human aggression.

Research on Conditions That Result in Aggression

Child-rearing patterns and aggression: One would intuitively expect there to be some relationship between child-rearing practices and the amount of aggressive behavior that the child learns to produce, but this relationship has been difficult to study. A part of the difficulty derives from the fact that some components of aggression are innate. Zigler and Child (1969), who have given considerable thought to this problem, list numerous demonstrations showing that, in a variety of species, more aggressive or less aggressive strains can be bred. They also have assembled evidence showing that babies differ from birth in the extent to which they are active and that activity is a basic component of aggression, for one could not conceive of an aggressive child who was passive. If this conclusion is correct, then one would expect that the most aggressive parents would have the most aggressive children, because some related traits would be inherited. However, if one did not know that the trait was inherited and found a correlation in this respect between the behavior of the children and that of their parents, one would not know whether the correlation was a product of heredity, or learning, or a combination of both. This is one facet of the old problem of the extent to which personality characteristics are inherited or acquired. In view of the difficulty of separating genetically determined and acquired factors, research on the problem of identifying the effect of child rearing has been difficult.

Zigler and Child have reviewed the literature on child rearing and later child behavior with respect to the topic at hand. They cite considerable evidence to show that punitiveness on the part of the parents is related to aggression on the part of the child. Punitiveness is generally appraised by what the parents say about themselves. Aggression on the part of the child may be measured in terms of his behavior in a school setting or his behavior in artificial situations such as those involving doll play. Another factor that contributes to a similar relationship is when parents have no interest in the child, particularly when such an attitude is accompanied by hostility. On the other hand, there is evidence that firm, but not punitive, control by parents results in less aggression. Perhaps such control results in the parents not allowing the child to manifest aggression, which fits with the suggestion that aggressive behavior must be controlled if one does not want to see much of it during adulthood. Related to this is the finding that extreme permissiveness on the part of the parents produces aggressive children (Kaufmann, 1970a), again emphasizing the importance of learning and child-rearing conditions in the development of aggression. The traits of parental behavior considered here also interact in their effects. If a parent is both permissive and hostile, then more aggression is observed in the child than if the parent is permissive and nonhostile or permissive and warm.

Models of aggression: This discussion brings us back to the concept of modeling, for the parent provides a model that may be imitated by the child, who is in the observer role. Bandura and Walters (1963) conducted pioneer work on the effect of a model in producing aggressive behavior in young children. Their work, together with later work, has been reviewed by Bryan and Schwartz (1971). In the typical laboratory study in this area, a child is exposed to a film in which aggressive behavior is manifested by an adult. The child is then placed in a doll-playing situation, and the degree of aggression against the doll is measured in some way. The studies do show quite clearly that aggression manifested in the film is followed by similar behavior toward the doll. Studies also show that children will model behavior involving courage and self-sacrifice. It seems quite certain that children will model a wide range of different behaviors. Few of the studies have been arranged so that they involved aggression toward other human beings. Bryan and Schwartz could find only two such studies, one with adults and one with children. In both cases, the viewing of a film resulted in an increase in aggressive behavior toward the other human beings in the experimental situation.

The effectiveness of the model in producing behavior in the observer depends on what happens to the model for doing whatever he does. Experiments have been conducted in which films were shown of models who were either rewarded, punished, or suffered no consequences. Observers do not usually imitate models who are punished, but rewarded models and nonrewarded models have the effect of causing the observer to behave in the same way as the models do.

Bryan and Schwartz also point out that a child who views a film in which an adult attacks a doll shows immediately thereafter heightened aggression not only toward dolls but also in a variety of other situations. The effect appears to be an immediate heightening of aggressive behavior in general.

Let us emphasize again the fact that it is easy to give a simple interpretation of modeling behavior and to say that the observer just learns the response manifested by the model. What probably happens is much more complex. Consider the case in which a child views a film of an adult performing violently toward an object such as a doll. When the motion picture is over, the child is given a doll to play with and begins hitting it. Now the child did not learn to hit the doll by seeing the film, for the child learned long ago how to do this. The film triggered the behavior rather than taught the behavior. Some psychologists state this by saying that the film **releases** the response.

Another interpretation of modeling behavior is based on the idea that much behavior is controlled by social norms. A child may not ordinarily consider hitting a doll, but if he sees people hitting dolls he may conclude that this is the appropriate way to relate to dolls. Models, particularly if there are many models observed, provide the norm for deciding whether behavior is or is not appropriate.

An important limitation of the studies of modeling is that they deal with immediate consequences of the behavior of the model and have rarely been concerned with long-term effects, which may be quite different from short-term consequences.

Aggression cues: Kaufmann has been able to muster some evidence that the presence of objects suggestive of aggression, such as guns, will increase such remote behaviors as verbal aggression. This raises the long-debated issue of whether movies or television programs depicting violence "teach" violence. The data suggest that the showing of such materials may increase the amount of strong language, or perhaps the vigor of one's reactions to others, through releasing these responses. This is far different from learning a violent response. There are probably rare instances in which a person commits a crime because he has learned how to commit the crime from television, but this may well be balanced by the good achieved through people learning, through the same programs, that there are ways of preventing oneself from being robbed or from being swindled. One suspects that the numerous programs showing the operation of confidence men have taught some of the public how to avoid falling for such tricks.

Another situational factor that determines the amount of aggression is the social situation in which the person finds himself. A person who is part of a cohesive group is more likely to react strongly and aggressively toward a person outside the group who hurls an insult. For this reason, a member of a gang who, alone, might behave as a civilized person may sometimes behave with uncalled-for violence when provoked to a mild degree by an outsider. This phenomenon was seen in an extreme form in Cleveland in February 1971, when members of a motorcycle gang visiting an automotive show attacked people outside of the gang, and within a few minutes some people were murdered and others were brutally mutilated.

Some effects of prolonged exposure to television violence: The facts cited up to this point appear to be consistent, and tempt one to generalize and say that a civilized and benign society would surely be one in which children saw few models of aggressive behavior. However, the data are greatly limited in value by the fact that they refer to the immediate consequences of brief exposure to acts of violence. What happens with longer exposure and what are the long-term effects? Only one study, by Feshbach and Singer (1970), could be found that provided any data to answer such questions.

In the Feshbach and Singer study, the television viewing of boys aged nine to fifteen was closely controlled. The boys were either in private residential schools or in homes. The programs viewed by the boys involved six hours per week over a period of six weeks. One group of boys viewed such programs as *Gunsmoke, Have Gun Will Travel*, and *The Untouchables*. The other group viewed such programs as *Ed Sullivan, Gidget, Lassie*, and *My Favorite Martian*. The boys were rated daily for the extent to which they showed a great variety of aggressive behaviors including fighting, insulting another, being rough or careless with property, and using profanity toward someone. The boys also rated one another for various aspects of aggression and took a number of tests both before the experiment started and at the end.

The results of the experiment do not agree well with the laboratory studies from which one might be tempted to predict that those who saw television programs manifesting aggression would show more aggression in their lives. The opposite occurred. The boys who saw violence on television showed a reduction of aggression in their own behavior. The difference between the two groups cannot be ascribed to any lack of interest and boredom on the part of those who saw nonviolent programs, for they rated these as highly as the other group of boys rated the violent programs.

Feshbach and Singer suggest that the violent television programs seemed to have a cathartic effect. They suggest that these programs may have enabled the boys to find a vicarious outlet for pent-up aggressions.

A point to note is that the findings of this study are contrary to those of the Surgeon General's committee report (1972) on this topic. The discrepancy can be accounted for by the fact that the studies reviewed in the latter report were all concerned with the immediate effects of the television programs, such as might be studied in the course of an experiment taking no more than an hour, but the Feshbach and Singer study involved the long-term effects of prolonged exposure.

If the findings of Feshbach and Singer can be repeated, then the effects of exposure to filmed violence must be considered to be perhaps different on a long-term basis and a short-term basis. There is also the possibility that the key to the difference may not lie in whether exposure is long or short. It is possible that violence is much more likely to be triggered by exposure to aggressive behavior on the part of persons with whom the observer closely identifies. Boys may not identify closely with characters from another age such as are shown in most television programs. One can say that exposure to some filmed materials presenting violence leads to violence but not always. When it does and when it does not is a matter that has to be investigated.

Some Thoughts on the Control of Aggression of Man Toward Man

This final section cannot present a program for education that will surely result in a reduction in the amount of aggression that human beings will direct toward their own species, but it can present a few ideas concerning the form that such a program might take.

Because education begins in the home, let us consider the steps that can be taken there to begin building a nonviolent society. The data on the effects of excessively authoritarian or excessively permissive parental behavior seem clear, and although one may exhort parents to assume a pattern of behavior between these two extremes, such exhortations may not be particularly effective. A more easily controlled factor may be the attitudes that the parents have toward violence. All too often in our society, parents are proud of the fact that their son is tough, "all boy," and "knows how to hit back." The small boy is expected to fight with other boys and is even encouraged to boast about the scraps he has won. Violence is commonly encouraged in the preschool child as a means of settling disputes. A parent may even feel his own ego to be enhanced through having a tough son. The father may not be able to lick some of the people he would like to lick, but at least his son can. Surely, nonviolent approaches to the settling of human differences should provide the very foundation for an orderly society. Too often, the home not only fails to provide this foundation, but rather provides a foundation of violence. The change needed calls for a fundamental change in the early moral values inculcated in the child.

A point to note about the typical encouragement of violence in the preschool boy is that it does nothing to move him to a higher level of moral development. It represents a stage 1 or stage 2 of moral development. Yet it is through the moral dilemmas he must face in relating to other children that he may achieve a higher level of moral development.

The role of the school curriculum in developing a nonviolent society has not been given the consideration it deserves. School curricula in most countries devote much time to a discussion of the violence of the past, and history is often taught as though it could not be anything else than the story of violence. Because armed conflict is a part of man's history, the facts cannot be, and should not be, hidden from the growing generation. The presentation of the facts does not mean that there has to be glorification of the violence involved, but the history books of every nation tend to honor its own role in the conflicts of the past. Many schools that would like to stress alternative nonviolent attempts to provide solutions to international problems often find themselves up against strong criticism from members of the community in which they are located. Many a high school cannot stage a United Nations Day without being confronted by hostile criticism. Opposition comes from individuals in the community operating at morality stages 3 and 4. They view history as a subject that should be taught in precisely the way it always has been taught in order to produce an unchanging society. History can be used as a means of ensuring that students' behavior will conform to the way of life prescribed by people at morality stages 3 and 4, who emphasize conformity with authority, fixed rules, and the maintenance of a social order exactly as it is.

Of course, there are some enlightened communities where schools are encouraged to explore new ways through which a better and less violent world can be built.

If Kohlberg is correct in his analysis of moral development, then the greatest difficulty in changing the high-school curriculum to emphasize nonviolent approaches to international, national, and personal problems is that the curriculum is controlled largely by people at stages 3 and 4. In order for change to be brought about there would have to be more people at stages 5 and 6, stages at which the founding fathers were when they wrote the United States Constitution. There is no good reason why most individuals should not proceed to the highest stages of moral development, but it is probably going to require an educational system different in many respects from the one we have today. It also may require profound changes in religious education.

Finally, a point must be brought out that was originally raised by Lorenz (1966). Lorenz, as a biologist, has been impressed by the fact that many animals have ritualized aggression in forms that do little harm to their species. For example, deer engage in combat with horns so large and clumsy that they have little chance of inflicting real injury. Lorenz proposes that much more can be done to ritualize aggression in the human species. He notes that international sports events represent a kind of ritualization of international aggression. Sporting events in the local community may serve a similar function. We need to know much more about the effect of such ritualization on the behavior of the onlooker before endorsing the proposal. Does watching the competitive behavior of two hard-hitting football teams enhance or reduce the aggressive behavior of the onlookers? Lorenz hopes it will result in a reduction, but it may not. This approach to the reduction of harmful social aggression should be explored, as should every other.

389
• • • • • • • • • •
Some Thoughts on the
Control of Aggression of
Man Toward Man

Summary

1 Although man as a species is only remotely related to other living species, he does behave in ways similar, in some respects, to those of other primates. Most primates are highly social creatures, spending much of the day in social interaction. A playful social interaction among young primates appears to be essential for proper sexual development. The social needs of man are in sharp contrast with the lack of social needs found in some other species.

2 The school has typically assumed responsibility for education in the areas that are neglected by the informal sources of the child's education. The social education of the modern student is obviously deficient in many respects, and much of the social inadequacy found in modern society reflects inadequate moral development.

3 Moral judgment is a matter of a person knowing what he considers to be right. Moral behavior is doing what is right in terms of some standard. The classic work in the area is that of Piaget, who found that children have entirely different conceptions from the adult of what makes an act right or wrong. The young child sees an act as wrong because it is punished. Schools do attempt to teach moral values in that the United States Constitution represents a moral position. The concept of equal rights represents a moral position with respect to all human relationships.

4 Further development of Piaget's work has been undertaken by Kohlberg, who has distinguished six stages of moral development, preceded by a premoral stage. The six stages divide into three main stages. The stages show a steady decrease in the arbitrariness involved in morality and a progressive increase in the amount of personal responsibility involved. Not all individuals move through the complete stages of moral development. The typical American citizen stops development, in this respect, in the middle stages. Only a few ever attain stages 5 and 6.

5 Education has some potential for raising the level of moral development. Higher stages are achieved by presentation of problems that offer a challenge and lead to new ways of thinking about moral issues. Little, if anything at all, is accomplished in the area through preaching. The child has to be helped in thinking about such problems and must be helped to improve on his solutions. The stages in morality do not seem to be culturally determined, in that children raised in very different cultures move through the same stages of

moral development. The level of moral development reached in some cultures is probably higher than in other cultures.

6 An altruistic act is one undertaken with the expectation that the recipient of the act will benefit from it. The characteristics of altruistic acts depend on the level of moral development of the person performing the acts. A person at stage 2 performing a moral act may do it because he sees it as part of a bargain and expects later returns. At stage 6, altruism does not involve marketplace concepts. The oldest theory of altruism is that pleasure results for the person who performs the altruistic act. Although altruistic acts may be increased in frequency by payoffs, such findings generally require quite complex theories to make them intelligible. The concept of empathy has been widely used to help understand such behavior. A model may influence the altruistic behavior of an observer. Children do not seem to be particularly concerned about the moral inconsistency of adults, perhaps because the child is still at the stage of viewing morality as an arbitrary affair not based on any universal principles. The generous child is one raised in an environment characterized by giving. The generosity shown by a child depends on his stage of moral development. Inadequacies in moral development are clearly brought out in the bystander effect. A call for help is more likely to be answered by a sole bystander than by one of a group. A member of a group waits to see what the others will do before he acts, because most members of a group are at a stage of moral development where group standards are the basis of right and wrong.

7 Although moral development does not typically proceed beyond stages 3 or 4, at least one study strikes an optimistic note. Kidney donors not only gladly give a part of their bodies to help another but describe the event as a great spiritual experience. Perhaps the experience is such that it helps to move the donor to a higher stage of moral development.

8 Aggression is a vigorous action on the environment. Of particular importance is when the vigorous action is against other human beings. A distinction should be made between hostility and aggression, for aggression does not necessarily involve hostility. Most primates other than man show little aggression against their own species, though they are quite aggressive toward their environment. However, other primates do show aggressive and damaging behavior toward their own species when they are forced to live under crowded conditions. Man's capacity to kill members of his own species appears to be one of his unique characteristics. Armed con-

· · · · · · · · · · · ·

flict is a major category of such killing within the species, but murder within the family has also been quite common. Unlike other species, man does not have any innate control over social aggression and no natural inhibitions against the destruction of his own species. As man evolved from the stage of being a tree-living primate to an inhabitant of the plains, he invented dangerous weapons but he did not develop controls over the use of these weapons. An important problem for education is the development of internal controls within each individual that will prevent dangerous or deadly aggression toward his own species.

9 Studies with different species have shown that more aggressive or less aggressive strains can be bred. This suggests that there is an inherited component of aggression. There is also evidence that child-rearing practices exert an influence. Parental punitiveness appears to raise the level of aggression. Ignoring the child also has a similar effect, particularly when coupled with hostility. A model may raise the level of aggression in an observer, but this may be merely the releasing of aggression rather than the learning of aggression. Modeling behavior may also reflect the fact that much social behavior is controlled by social norms.

10 The effects of exposure to violence on television remain controversial. Although modeling studies suggest that the viewing of violence may increase violent behavior, at least one significant study suggests that the long-term effect may be different.

11 The development of a generation of nonviolent human beings will require the cooperation of all forces that have impact on the child. Much of the behavior of the parent will probably have to change, particularly that of endorsing violence on a minor scale. History will probably have to be viewed in a rather different light from the way it is viewed in typical schoolbooks. There will also have to be efforts made to raise the level of morality beyond stage 4. There is a possibility that substitutes may be found for violent behavior.

Learning and Social
Development

The purpose of the book up to this point has been to bring together scientific findings having implications for education. Some of this knowledge has already had impact on education, although the impact has not always been of the most direct kind. Teachers, without knowing they are doing so, reflect the advances that have been made in the behavioral sciences. A teacher who refers a child to a clinic for possible diagnosis of brain damage is showing the impact of scientific knowledge; so, too, is the teacher who visits the home of a child in order to explore possible reasons for the child's failure to make progress in reading. The influence of research is also seen in the teacher who complains that the materials in a particular unit of work are badly sequenced and need reordering. These common responses on the part of the teacher would not have occurred half a century ago except under very exceptional circumstances. The

13

The New Technology of Education

results of behavioral research are seen in the way in which teachers analyze classroom problems, in the way they evaluate instructional materials, and in the way they handle the day-to-day problems of the classroom. The impact of scientific knowledge, in this respect, is subtle, for it is the kind of impact in which scientific knowledge becomes a part of the common knowledge of the culture. The physical sciences, too, have a subtle impact. Every housewife is familiar with a scale of temperature, and baking and cooking are tied to the use of such a scale, yet such scales were developed primarily as scientific instruments for scientific purposes. Scientific discoveries slowly become integrated into the lives of the people of the culture in which they take place.

In the case of the behavioral sciences, a major impact on practice is found in the way the sciences come to view man. As the sciences change their view of man, so, too, slowly does the educated citizen acquire the new view that emerges. Perhaps the greatest single impact that the behavioral sciences have had on teaching is in the concepts of man that they have generated. For example, teachers view children from underprivileged homes not as children who do not want to learn but as children whose academic difficulties are a result of environmental circumstances over which the children have no control. This view has displaced the view that such children are inherently stupid or that they lack the moral fortitude necessary for school achievement. This volume has been concerned to a great extent with building a conception of man that may influence the way in which teachers will attempt to solve the problems they encounter in the classroom. An important point to note is that this kind of influence is somewhat removed from the problem of developing a technology of education, a problem that must now be considered.

Let us begin this discussion by considering what is meant by the term **technology.** One speaks of the technology of smelting metallic ores, the technology of producing glass and ceramic articles, the technology of building, the technology of printing, and so forth. The common core of all of these activities is that they involve routines designed to result in some useful product that cannot be easily produced on a commonsense basis. Most technologies involve procedures that have evolved over long periods of time. The technology of smelting, for example, probably began several thousand years ago when men first discovered that throwing a chunk of heavy rock into the fire sometimes resulted in a small lump of copper being found in the ashes next day. The open fire was eventually replaced with a primitive furnace, probably consisting of a large hole in a rock. Later, the techniques were extended from the smelting of copper to the smelting of iron ore and other metallic ores. The blast furnace was finally evolved a little more than a century ago and permitted the producer to determine whether the product was to be soft iron or hard steel.

Metal technology, like most other technologies, evolved before the advent of the scientific age. The inventions involved in these technologies were made by practically oriented men of great creative genius. None of the technologies emerged suddenly; all of them have a history of slow development over a long period of time. Unfortunately, the history of technology as it appears in high-school history gives the false impression that sudden great inventions result in the big technological developments of history. For example, high-school history books leave the impression that Watt invented the steam engine. Watt did not invent the steam engine at all (see Lilley, 1966), but he did make important modifications in the steam engines of his day that led to a far more useful device than had been previously available.

Lilley points out that the steam engine, before Watt, had evolved from the water wheel, which had been a great source of power back as far as Roman times. The early steam engines were designed around the water wheel. What they did was to use heat to expand steam to lift water to a higher level, much as some coffeepots do. The raised water was then allowed to fall over a water wheel. This type of engine was very inefficient. The next step was to use steam, not to push water to a higher level, but to push a piston, and it was this type of engine that Watt managed to improve. Historians who have studied the record see a continuous line of development from the water wheel of Roman times to the modern reciprocating engine. Whatever activities can be considered to constitute an educational technology also show the same continuous development over long periods of time.

If the term *technology* is used in the educational sphere in the way it has been used in other areas of human activity, then it must be viewed as encompassing all those recognized activities that constitute well-accepted aspects of education. Thus there is a technology related to the use of printed materials in schools. This technology includes the design of these materials and the conditions under which they are used in the school setting. There is also a limited technology related to the selection of content for inclusion in printed materials. The latter technology includes such rules as Herbart's dictum that learning should start with the familiar and move to the unfamiliar and should begin with the simple and move to the complex. The technology also involves the use of what is known about the difficulty of words and the relation of sentence structure to the ease with which the material is understood. Other elements in the technology of education are the ideas that praise should be used rather than punishment and that there are individual differences that have to be recognized if teaching is to be effective. Aspects of the technology of education constitute the classroom management procedures involved in educational practice.

Historical Antecedents of Contemporary Educational Technology

Although some writers of the time appear to assume that educational technology is a recent invention, whatever is being accomplished today has a continuous history with a long sequence of developments. The book on the subject by Saettler (1968) describes a history back to the early Sophists of 500 B.C. What is known about practical procedures for teaching is not a recent discovery. The expository methods of the Sophists might perhaps be contrasted with the Socratic method, in which the student to some extent directs his own learning by seeking answers to significant questions. The approaches of the Sophists and of those who pursued the Socratic method represent differences in procedure related to the achievement of different goals. Thus, even from the earliest days, various technologies were produced for achieving different goals. The earliest aspects of technology developed were those that would be described in modern times as teaching methods. Later developments involved the invention of procedures for the duplication of materials for the student and teacher. The early forms of printing involved the cutting of print in the surface of blocks of wood, together with some ornamentation, and these blocks could then be used for making many copies of the documents engraved on them. Manuscript copying was, of course, a common occupation of those who spent their lives in monasteries, but it hardly provided a means for the widespread dissemination of educational materials.

Gutenberg did not invent the printing press, as many commonly say he did. What he can be given some credit for inventing is type that could be set up for printing and then be disassembled and reused. Dutch printers had almost certainly already used movable type on a small scale, but Gutenberg was able to incorporate the idea into the consummation of an ambitious project—the printing of the Bible. Like all contributions to technology, Gutenberg's represented one step forward in a long sequence of steps that included the development of small type castings, the means for producing paper, and the production of inks. Gutenberg received support for his enterprise because it was coupled with the great educational enterprise of disseminating the Bible. The success of the printing press, in this respect, established it as the prime development of all time of educational technology.

Experimentation with the format in which subject matter was presented was common in the Middle Ages. The best-known example of such experimentation was the catechism, a step-by-step systematic development of the ideas to be mastered. The catechisms of monastic education resemble the step-by-step presentations of modern programmed materials. The idea that subject matter needs to be analyzed by the teacher and then organized in an optimum sequence is a very old idea that has been many times rediscovered by those concerned with education. The concept of sequencing of subject matter played an important part in the thinking of the philosopher Johann Frederick Herbart, who had a profound influence on the development of educational ideas. Maria Montessori also viewed the problem of sequencing as a matter of crucial importance in preschool and elementary-school instruction. Many of the Montessori materials represent attempts to provide carefully sequenced materials. Thus children learn to classify materials before they engage in

396
• • • • • • • • • • •
The New Technology of
Education

ordering materials into scales. The present emphasis on the sequencing of subject matter is just a continuation of a long tradition.

The technology of behavior related to teaching placed emphasis, in the early stages of its development, on developing procedures for the teacher to follow and materials for the student to study. Only within the last century has there come to be some recognition that a technology of education has to take into account still other factors. Perhaps the most significant of these is the behavior of the pupil. Not much more than a century ago did some educators come to recognize that pupils were not like empty vessels to be slowly filled with the elixir of knowledge, but that pupils had purposes of their own of which account had to be taken if learning was to proceed with efficiency. Slowly there evolved a conception of the learner as a person who had to play an active and central role in the direction of his own learning. The old technologies of education had little to say about how to arrange effective learning for a person who was to choose his own goals and largely direct his own activities.

The view commonly held until as late as the present century was that the child had the responsibility to learn whatever the adult proposed and that failure to learn could only happen if the child did not try hard enough. According to this conception of the nature of the child, academic failure was moral failure. The treatment for failure was punishment, which was supposed to result in the child becoming sufficiently motivated to accomplish the goals set for him. Teachers who held this theory were not discouraged from applying it when the failing child, punished for failing, continued to fail. The theory and its related practices were abandoned, not so much because of obvious ineffectiveness, but because research slowly produced a changing conception of man. Teachers and others concerned with education came to recognize that individuals of school age differ in their capacity to learn and that such differences are important.

Much of the technology of present-day education, that is, its practices and procedures, evolved before research related to human behavior had even begun. Even some of the more modern aspects of educational technology have been developed without any impact from the behavioral sciences.

Perhaps the most important single technological development related to education in recent years has been the development of motion pictures and film strips. Most of this has occurred because manufacturing firms have seen the schools as a new market, but it has had only the most limited support from scientific research. Surprisingly little is known about how children respond to motion pictures, what attracts their attention in them and what they ignore, and what they ultimately retain. There has been some agreement that the passive role of the pupil observer is not a desirable one, and various attempts have been made to convert this role into a more dynamic one, but these have not been very successful. One technique has been that of stopping the film in various places and then presenting the pupil with a problem to solve related to what he has seen and heard. Projection devices have also been simplified so that the children themselves can operate the equipment. The advantage is that with such equipment all children do not have to view the material simultaneously, but each child can show it to himself when he is ready. Parallel developments in the area of speech and sound have also had impact, the most sophisticated devices being the language laboratories, which were highly fashionable in the 1960s, but many of which have fallen into disuse in recent times.

An overall evaluation of such mechanical and electronic devices cannot be given. As a minimum contribution, one can say that they have provided some variety in classroom procedure, and this is excellent. They have probably made the classroom a more interesting place. How effective they are as teaching devices is controversial, for often they are used as substitutes for effective teaching. The teacher may spend the afternoon running films through the projectors because that is the easy thing to do.

Educational technology is not, in itself, good or evil. The author would reject strongly the position taken by Skinner (1971) that the evils of an industrial and manufacturing technology can be counteracted by the development of a behavioral technology that is somehow expected to provide a balance. A technology of behavior has already shown itself to be capable of propagating extraordinary evils. Anyone who doubts this statement should read the article on the subject by Wolf and Jorgensen (1970), which documents some of the nefarious purposes for which a technology of behavior has already been used. They cite, for example, the project undertaken in Southeast Asia on the control of the behavior of native populations. The recommendation of the project was that the behavior of natives could best be controlled through the control of food, but that food control could not be used effectively until all crops and other sources of food had first been destroyed. The behavioral sciences have great capacity for establishing new milestones along the path of human disgrace. The impact of behavioral technology is not necessarily going to be good.

Technology of education, as it has emerged in recent years, has been developed along two distinct lines. The predominant source has been operant psychology and must be traced to Skinner's interest in the development of improved ways of controlling learning in the classroom. Skinner's (1954) original conception of how this should be done involved the idea that the kind of equipment used to control learning in the laboratory should provide an excellent means of controlling classroom learning. The adaptation of this equipment led to the development of what have been called **teaching machines,** though these machines were eventually to involve much more than simple adaptations from the laboratory. The idea of using mechanical devices for the control of pupil learning was not new, having been advanced much earlier in the century by Pressey (1932). However, Pressey drew his analogy for the new technology of education from industry, whereas Skinner thought in terms of adapting labora-

398
. . . .
The New Technology of Education

tory procedures to educational use. Both Pressey and Skinner assumed that a technology of education should be based on scientific knowledge and seemed to imply that a technology could not be developed without such knowledge. This assumption is obviously nonsense in view of the fact that most educational technology, like that of other fields, was developed long before scientific knowledge had been developed. Whether, at this stage of educational development, scientific knowledge is crucial to educational technology remains controversial. Ultimately, such knowledge must surely become important, but there is probably still much scope for educational invention that is only remotely related to basic science.

Operant psychology makes assumptions about the nature of man that are not acceptable to many persons of scientific competence. Hence there are alternative viewpoints that can supply the basis of a technology. Psychologists engaged in research on perceptual problems and on problems related to man's ability to receive, organize, and retain information offer one alternative. Those concerned with such problems have viewed the pupil in the classroom as a creature who seeks out information, actively organizing the information discovered. Such models of pupil behavior have generally been described in the literature of pedagogy as **discovery models of learning.** Around such models of pupil behavior a limited but new technology has also begun to emerge.

Technology Related to the Operant Model of Learning and to Other Earlier Models

The operant approach to the development of an educational technology has been intimately related to attempts to build machines to handle aspects of instruction. Sidney Pressey began during World War I to develop mechanical devices that would test and instruct at the same time. Pressey did not envisage that machines would take the place of many traditional instructional procedures but believed that they would supplement the more typical procedures. His position is to be contrasted with that of some of the recent enthusiasts for teaching by machine who have taken the position that the teacher is obsolete and will soon be replaced by a mechanical device. Nearly forty years after Pressey's early experimentation with his classroom devices, Skinner (1954) quite independently came to the conclusion that what was needed to improve education was proper instrumentation related to teaching. Skinner was unaware of the fact that his proposals were not new. Later, as he became cognizant of the work that had preceded his, he began to ponder the question of why the early devices had not produced the revolution in schools about which Pressey had written. He came to the conclusion that the reason was that the Pressey machines had come before a science of learning could have provided the knowledge necessary for designing them correctly. Skinner believed that by midcentury a body of knowledge had been built and that his devices would succeed where others had failed.

Skinner built teaching machines on the basis of principles of learning derived from a study of lower organisms, particularly pigeons and rats. The two main principles incorporated into their design were that the learner should always have to perform the response himself, in contrast with just choosing a response, and that feedback or reinforcement should be immediate. Skinner was probably much too quick in generalizing these principles to all of human learning behavior, for the fact is that they have not proven themselves to be particularly valid. Human beings do learn by merely watching other human beings, and without making the responses to be learned, and reinforcement is often more effective when it is delayed. Skinner's machines were ingenious but not designed on the basis of any well-established scientific principles of human cognitive learning. Indeed, it is doubtful whether they would have been any less effective if designed on the basis of commonsense. Whereas the Pressey machines had merely asked the pupil to make a choice between answers presented and then told him whether his choice was correct, the Skinner devices required the pupil to construct an answer and then the machine showed the pupil the answer he should have given. Skinner, like other operant psychologists who followed him, believed the difference to be important, but in practice it has not been shown to be so. Skinner was also quite concerned with designing machines that would not permit the learner to cheat, but this also has turned out to be a matter of no great consequence.

Certain newer concepts related to the design of teaching machines can be viewed as of much greater consequence. One important concept is that of the adaptivity of machines. A review of the development of this concept is provided by Stolurow (1961). Teaching machines are more or less adaptive to the needs of the learner; no machine, and perhaps no teacher, is completely adaptive to the learner's needs. For example, if a pupil said to me "I want to know more about the civilization of the Upanishads!" I can probably do nothing to help him. I do not know who the Upanishads are. I do not know whether they are living today or died out long ago. Generally, I am able to adapt by suggesting places where he can locate information and sometimes by giving him information. If he does not understand the material to which he is referred, then he can come back to me and I will send him to more easily understood sources. Any effective teacher has to be at least partially adaptive in this respect, and the designers of teaching machines have attempted to make their devices adaptive to the learning needs of the pupil.

In a sense, teaching machines are inevitably minimally adaptive, in that they provide teaching related to fixed objectives. Unlike the human teacher, they are not adaptive to the objectives of the pupil but only adaptive in how the objectives are achieved. A pupil who tells the teaching machine that he doesn't want to learn the addition of fractions, or any other aspect of mathematics, cannot expect any positive help from the machine. The teacher, who is somewhat more adaptive in this respect, may be able to offer constructive suggestions, perhaps giving him some problems to work on that interest him and will eventually require some mathematics for their solution.

Adaptivity in teaching machines is generally limited to keeping track of how the pupil is doing on a series of problems and changing the instructional program to help the pupil overcome difficulties he encounters. The type of device that provides the greatest flexibility in doing this is the computer that has been arranged to function as a teaching device. The computer can feed information to the learner, present him with problems, check his answers, and decide whether he has or has not demonstrated skill in solving the problems. If he has not demonstrated adequate skill, then he can be given additional information or he can be helped to correct his errors. If he has solved the problems successfully, then he can be introduced to new information and a new set of problems. The machine can even offer the pupil a range of topics to study.

The statement is commonly made that teaching machines, unlike live teachers, make no assumptions about learners, but this is a specious claim. Although machines make no assumptions, the designers of machines do, and the machines reflect the assumptions built into them. Such machines are generally built on the basis of the assumption that correct education is that which takes the pupil through a prescribed intellectual routine, diagnoses the difficulties he has along the way, and, by various means, ensures that certain specific goals are achieved. The assumption is implicit that the pupil makes few, if any, significant choices. At the best, he can choose among the limited array of repertoires provided by the machine. Because machines are built after the designer has made very important assumptions about the nature of the learner, they operate within a very limited and prescribed area of education, but perhaps an area within which they have legitimate functions.

The Ordering of Subject Matter and the Design of Curricula for Machine Teaching

The idea that the elements in a curriculum should be arranged in the best order, if teaching is to be easily accomplished, is an idea that has long intrigued teachers and educational planners. The catechisms of the Middle Ages were attempts to order subject matter in ways believed to be effective for teaching. In the last few decades, there has been an interest revived in this problem, largely because those interested in machine teaching are preoccupied with questions of efficiency, and the ordering of subject matter is believed to have potential for contributing to effective education. In addition, the approach of operant-conditioning psychologists to the learning of skills involves the analysis of the skills into components that should be learned in a definite order. The operant psychologists have typically attempted to apply to the classroom the techniques they have used in the laboratory. In addition, other psychologists, notably Gagné (1970), have taken the position that learning involves the acquisition of a hierarchy of skills and that the only path to effective learning is to start instruction with the skills at the bottom of the hierarchy and slowly move to the top. Thus, in the acquisition of reading, the pupil has to be able to discriminate common simple shapes, such as squares and circles, before he can begin to discriminate the complex forms involved in the recognition of letters and words. Later, he will learn to recognize words by using information derived from the context and perhaps using no more of a cue than the first letter of the word that is being recognized.

The typical example given of how subject matter, if properly organized for teaching, falls into a hierarchy is in mathematics. One can easily understand that addition has to be learned before multiplication, that number series have to be learned before addition, and that the concept of number has to be acquired before any of these. All this makes sense and has provided the basis for many studies showing that mathematical concepts are better acquired in some orders than in others. Curriculum developers have tended to assume, on the basis of studies of mathematics and mathematics teaching, that all subject matter can be arranged into the best order for teaching purposes. Now there can be no doubt that subject matter can be arranged in orders that seem reasonable to both learners and teachers, but whether there is one optimum order is an open question in most subject matter fields. The order that can best be justified may depend on many factors, including the age of the learner.

Because instruction by means of a teaching machine requires that the subject matter be divided into units to be presented and that the units be presented in a particular order, some means has to be found for doing this. The usual basis for ordering subject matter for this purpose is intuition. The subject-matter expert looks over the material to be formulated into a program to be run through a machine and arrives at an order he believes is a useful one for instructional purposes. The process is basically intuitive in that the structure of most subject matter is not particularly evident and certainly very complex.

In a program to be presented by machine, information is presented in units called **frames.** The size of a frame has long been controversial. Skinner and many of his followers have taken the position that a frame should include only a small amount of information. Others have suggested that this is an ineffective way to teach, suggesting instead that each frame include a substantial amount of information, perhaps as much as that provided by several hundred words. The argument is that the large unit of information gives the learner an overall concept of what he is attempting to learn and a broad grasp of what it is all about. The small unit of information may be dull and uninteresting, and its significance may escape the learner. The notion that the unit should be small comes from animal training, which generally involves taking the animal through small steps of the skill to be learned. However, human beings have the capability of

402

. . . .

The New Technology of Education

grasping complex situations and do not necessarily have to have them broken down into small components.

In programmed learning, each presentation of information is followed by an exercise in which the learner has an opportunity to use the information he has been given. This, of course, is a revival of the old idea that activity related to whatever is to be learned is important. In programmed learning, the activity is an attempt to perform either a component of the skill to be acquired or the complete skill. Then, after the performance has been completed, the learner is given an evaluation of his performance. This is referred to as **reinforcement** by operant psychologists, who have also held the questionable belief that reinforcement should occur without delay. When computer-based teaching machines are used, the device may keep track of a pupil's progress. If it does this, then it may provide additional study for those who have less than a certain percentage of correct answers.

The programming of materials for presentation through teaching machines led to asking whether the machine is really necessary at all. Those who doubted the necessity of the machine proposed that the material be presented in book form. Various devices were proposed in connection with the book form of programmed learning that would prevent the pupil from seeing the answer until he had completed the problem. The simplest of these devices involved no more than a piece of paper, slowly moved down the page of the text as the pupil worked, which prevented him from uncovering the answer to each problem until he had entered it on the sheet.

In the early 1960s, there was a proliferation of textbooks published in programmed form. Materials thus presented tended to be extremely bulky and, for this reason, quite costly. A pupil taking a first course in a foreign language might have to purchase as many as three volumes of such materials, a factor that limited greatly the use to which such materials could be put. Just because of the cost, enthusiasm for programmed textbook materials was quite brief and their use is declining. There is also perhaps a second reason to account for their limited use—the absence of any literary skill in their production. They tend to be humorless, dull, and lacking in any of the real skills of the writer.

All kinds of variations have been introduced into teaching machines. Some machines have the capacity of showing motion pictures as a part of the instruction provided. Some can show slides. Some may show pictures and have a recorded voice narrative. The learner may solve problems by pointing to the correct picture, because many devices have been developed that permit the machine to record which is pointed at. Thus the subject matter may be presented in a variety of forms, and these devices do provide great flexibility in this respect. The subject matter does not have to be presented in the verbal form that constitutes the main material used in textbooks.

Nevertheless, the point must be made that programmed materials designed for teaching machines, like all materials produced by the new

403

• • • • • • • • • •

The Ordering of Subject
Matter and the Design
of Curricula for Machine
Teaching

technology, are always removed one step from the real world. There is a fundamental difference between seeing an experiment undertaken in a film presentation and seeing the same experiment undertaken before one's own eyes. In the real situation, the student can examine the materials involved, do the experiment again with certain variations, check on whether the results just represent some artifact, and obtain a great diversity of information that he could not obtain from a film. Even the most realistic materials presented in films and other devices are one step removed from the real world, but education should bring the pupil into close contact with the real world. It should not provide only substitutes.

Computed-Assisted Instruction

The concept of teaching by machine has resulted in a proliferation of invention, but most of this invention is of experimental interest only. Many devices permit experiments on teaching to be undertaken with a high degree of experimental control, and, although they may not be ready for use in the classroom on a regular basis, they should not be written off as useless. There is also the possibility that experimental devices may ultimately become of value for day-to-day use in the classroom. However, teachers have difficulty in finding out just what is the status of these experimental devices, because they are promoted by Madison Avenue techniques. For example, a company interested in promoting its computer system for use in instruction in schools used prime advertising time on a television network to tell the audience that its system taught more efficiently than any other method. The president of the same company is quoted as using similar promotional lines at the ceremony opening the facility that was going to handle the teaching system. All this is unfortunate and may serve to prevent such devices from serving whatever useful purposes they may be found to have.

In computer-assisted instruction, the pupil sits at a terminal. The information he receives from the computer may be typed out on a teletype, or it may appear printed on a screen much like a television screen. The pupil types his responses on a standard typewriter keyboard. The pupil can work best if he has some familiarity with the typewriter keyboard, but in giving the answers to mathematics problems, for which such terminals have been mainly used, the pupil probably only has to type out a number to give his answer. If the answers are to be given in words, then they involve very few words. At present, it is not feasible to present problems that require long answers, for computers have difficulty in handling and analyzing sentences of any length, except for those that form part of a standardized repertoire of sentences with which the responses can be matched. Single-word responses are those that the computer can best analyze, next to numbers. In contrast, the verbal outputs of computers can be extensive, for the devices are capable of printing out hundreds of lines a minute. Perhaps, in this respect, computers are much like human beings—good at producing verbiage but quite poor at receiving verbal in-

404
• • • • • • • • • •
The New Technology of Education

formation and analyzing it. Human beings may well have a tendency to design machines that include inherent human weaknesses.

One of the most ambitious and best-documented programs of computer-assisted instruction is described in a volume by Suppes et al. (1968). The program took place mainly in schools near Stanford University in California, and the experiments were confined to the elementary grades. The content taught was mathematics and spelling. The program was an adjunct to more typical instruction and consisted of lessons lasting four to six minutes. Pupils were assigned to the teletype booth, one at a time, to take their lesson on the teletype. A very careful initial orientation was necessary in order to overcome anxieties related to the new method of instruction. Pupils had to learn that information would come to them through the teletype and that they would type out their answers on the machine. They learned to type out their names when they first entered the telephone booth and then to type out numbers indicating their answers to problems. The materials used in the instructional program are described as "drills" and were, presumably, supplemented by regular classroom instruction.

Just what to make of this particular experiment and the findings is difficult to say. The responses of pupils to working on the teletype tended to be favorable, though some pupils were highly negative and the report calls attention to instances of "crying," which are described as "normal" school behavior. How normal this is beyond the first grade is questionable. One would generally expect children to respond favorably to a new gadget in a gadget-oriented society. In a way, the experiment plays with loaded dice in that exposure to the teletype was brief, and most children will respond positively to any variation in the usual classroom routine. Classrooms typically lack sufficient variation in activities, but whether computer-assisted instruction is the best way to introduce variation is a matter for study. Another serious question that may be raised is whether the complicated and expensive equipment used in the experiment does anything much more than present rather typical workbook materials through a mechanical channel. It is very hard to see from the account of the study how the teletype terminal and computer equipment provided any real advantage over the old-fashioned workbook. Indeed, many might say that the old-fashioned workbook, together with a device permitting the pupil to check his answers, might have advantages of simplicity and ease of use. The idea that machine teaching prevents the pupil from looking up the answer before he has solved the problem is a point of doubtful strength in its favor. Some of the promoters of machine teaching have emphasized this point, but there is little evidence that pupils using workbooks cheat themselves out of education by looking up answers rather than solving problems. Common observation in the classroom suggests that they do not.

A point to be noted in the present connection is that workbooks can be arranged so that pupils who fail to achieve mastery of particular units of work can be given additional help. The type of programmed text known as a Crowder text is of this character. A pupil using such a text reads a page or more for information, attempts to solve a problem, and then checks his answer. Beside his chosen answer is a number indicating the page to which he is to turn. If he has not solved the problem correctly, then he is given some pointers about where he went wrong and is referred back to the problem. When he solves the problem correctly, he is allowed to proceed with the next unit of work. Books and workbooks do not have to manifest the inflexibility they have in the past but can be designed to undertake all kinds of teaching procedures.

Perhaps a more serious objection raised about the entire procedure in the Stanford project is that the workbook has long been regarded as one of the inferior procedures used in teaching. The teacher's reliance on the workbook often results in a degeneration of classroom procedures. The pupils work the problems, and the teacher sits and watches. Often everybody likes the procedure. The pupils are happy because the teacher is "off their backs," and the teacher is happy because the pupils are busy and do not cause too much trouble. The teacher also does not have to think up answers to difficult questions the pupils may ask. The procedures have the virtue of eliminating tensions but have little else to recommend them. Pupils engaged in workbook assignments do not ask interesting questions and rarely have the opportunity to explore issues except those raised by the workbook. The Stanford project mechanizes this kind of procedure.

A final question that has to be raised in the evaluation of computer-assisted instruction is cost. At the time of writing, the cost is far above that of conventional teaching. The enthusiastic supporters of the enterprise take the position that cost will decline as computers become more widely used, but this prediction is of doubtful validity. Experience up to this point indicates that as computers become more complicated and can come nearer to undertaking highly useful teaching functions, they also will become more expensive. For example, in order to develop computer-assisted instruction further, it is necessary to have a machine that will permit the pupil to communicate freely with the machine in ordinary language. Such a device can be built, but the expense involved is likely to be enormous. There is no basis to the argument that computers can correct the work of pupils quite cheaply, for the use of paraprofessionals in the classrooms has already provided a cheap means of undertaking such chores. An even cheaper method is to let the pupil score his own tests, an activity that he will engage in competently so long as he is not under pressure to compete with other children.

There are other questions that need to be raised in relation to computer-assisted instruction. Although the human being is likely to be fascinated by a mechanical gadget for a short time, one wonders how long pupils would remain intrigued with learning in isolation. Man is a primate and, like most primates, does not typically enjoy activities undertaken in isolation. He likes group work and group participation. The isolation booth of the computer terminal is not well designed in terms of man's nature. Perhaps the booth permitting two pupils to work together might be better designed in terms of human qualities. Although much thought has been given to problems of attaining academic goals, little concern has been shown for the matter of how to achieve them in ways compatible with man's essential nature. The isolation booth of the computer terminal seems to be particularly poorly designed in this respect.

Overall Evaluations of Programmed Instruction

Programmed instruction and the design of teaching machines developed in a flurry of enthusiasm. Leaders in the movement proclaimed that the new development would increase the rate of learning by many times, some even predicting that through use of such devices doctoral degrees would commonly be acquired by the age of twelve. Kindness leads us to avoid documenting the latter statements in detail and telling who said what and on what occasion. Enthusiasm for a new development is good provided it does not interfere with sober evaluations of what is actually being accomplished. Studies soon began to accumulate comparing the outcomes of programmed instruction and the outcomes of machine instruction with those of instruction along more traditional lines. Hundreds of studies, mainly doctoral dissertations, were done in the 1950s and early 1960s, and although no single one of these studies is of any great significance, the studies taken altogether provide a consistent picture.

Hartley (1966) reviewed studies of programmed instruction undertaken up until the mid-1960s. Of the 162 studies located, 37 per cent favored the use of programmed materials, 49 per cent showed no significant difference between programmed methods and traditional methods, and 14 per cent favored the traditional procedures. Zoll (1969) reviewed studies in mathematics that made similar comparisons. Of these thirteen studies, three showed a significant difference favoring the programmed procedures, three showed a significant difference favoring the traditional procedures, and seven showed no significant difference. The trend of the studies is typical of studies conducted in education. Whatever is considered the new method has a slight edge over what is considered the more obsolete method. This trend reflects a novelty effect more than anything else. Both learners and teachers respond with enthusiasm to new methods of instruction and, for a short time, pursue them with renewed energy. Unfortunately, the initial enthusiasm wears off and so too does the apparent efficiency of the new invention. Students learn through the use of programmed materials and through machine teaching, of that there can be no doubt, but these new devices cannot be credited with any startling efficiency in comparison with the older methods. This should not lead the reader to say that the new methods should necessarily be discarded, for they can provide a variation in activity in the classroom, and variation generally promotes learning. Any device that shakes the routine of the classroom out of a rut is likely to be advantageous and help to keep both pupils and teachers alive. Classrooms filled with virtually dead pupils and dead teachers lack, more than anything else, variation in the procedures and tasks undertaken.

The discussion up to this point should not be interpreted as implying that the evidence is now in and it can be stated conclusively that programmed instruction or teaching-machine instruction is no better or no worse than traditional instruction. There are difficulties associated with making such comparisons that are not evident on the surface and that were not evident to most of those who have undertaken the research in the area. The difficulties have become apparent as the research has proceeded. Let us consider briefly what some of these difficulties are.

One difficulty has already been noted, namely, that a new instructional method tends to evoke positive responses from learners so long as the method is new. The novelty effect is a plague for the educational researcher, though a boon to the teacher, who can arouse new interest in pupils by varying procedures. Another difficulty involves the way in which materials are developed for the experimental comparison. Suppose that an experimenter is going to compare the effectiveness of teaching a unit on the addition of fractions by two methods, one involving a programmed text and the other involving a presentation by the teacher followed by the pupils' attempts to solve some problems of adding fractions. The lessons are prepared in the two forms, but let us suppose that the person who does this is not very good at writing programmed materials. This immediately produces a bias in favor of the traditional method of teaching. The writer of the materials might also have been very good at writing programmed materials, in which case the bias would have been in the opposite direction. There is inevitably bias of this sort. Also, however good one set of materials may be, there is still the possibility that a better set of materials might be written for the other method. Experiments of the kind considered are primarily comparisons of the cleverness of the writers of materials rather than comparisons of methods. What this means is that studies comparing two methods do not give very clear answers concerning their relative virtues. The best one can conclude from the studies of programmed learning is that the new method does not seem to provide any very striking improvements over the older methods. The differences are certainly not the striking ones predicted by the early enthusiasts.

Other difficulties are shared by all studies that compare two methods of teaching. One of the most imporant of these is that teachers have prejudices and are likely to favor one method over another. In some studies, teachers may be assigned to the method they prefer, but who can genuinely say he prefers a new method he has never tried? Also, most studies compare the effectiveness of teachers who are using an old method with which they are thoroughly familiar with the effectiveness of teachers using a new method with which they have had little experience. A teacher needs time with a new method to gain the experience required to use it to full advantage. One suspects that experience with a method continues to produce gains in quality of teaching perhaps over many years.

Another difficulty faced by such studies is that there may not be simple answers to the question "Which method is best?" Many research workers have long suspected that some methods are more effective with certain groups of students than with others. For example, very slow learners require an enormous amount of repetition in teaching. They have difficulty in transferring information to permanent memory, and repetition helps them in this connection. There is, perhaps, the possibility that pupils highly rigid in their thinking may respond more positively to very structured teaching than do more imaginative pupils, who may require more opportunities to think freely. Bracht (1970) has summarized some of the studies indicating that the effectiveness of a teaching method is influenced by the characteristics of pupils. Some positive evidence suggests that the phenomenon is a real one. For example, Bracht touches on the very substantial evidence that, in the case of attitude change, high IQ students change more if some effort is made to present both sides of an argument, with refutation of the "wrong" side. The low IQ students seem to become confused when both sides are presented.

The Social Goals of an Educational Technology

The immense enthusiasm that has been shown toward the development of an educational technology is strange in view of the fact that it is taking place at a time when there is considerable disillusionment concerning the value of technology as a whole. At the present time, there is much more concern with matters related to the control of the ill effects of modern technology than there is any rejoicing with the bounties that it may have brought us. Many seek to escape from the impact of technology, some by returning to simpler ways of life involving the growing of their own foods, some by purchasing only products that will not harm the environment, and some by seeking political action that will reverse the trend toward destruction of the planet. The search to escape from the evils that technology has brought represents one of the vigorous movements of the day. There is a paradox in the fact that educational technology is being promoted with enthusiasm in an age characterized by disillusionment with the world that technology has produced.

Technology, in itself, is neither good nor bad. It can serve many ends, and the ends may sometimes be worthwhile. However, one cannot pass over lightly the point made by Mumford (1970) that most of the great advances and developments in the humaneness of man have come from sources other than technology. Great ideas, such as the idea that man should be free or that all men should receive an education, did not emerge as a result of any technological development but were the result of the development of a conception of what is worthwhile in life. Athens' contribution to posterity was not a contribution to the building trades but a contribution to how man viewed himself and the universe. The worthwhile contribution of technology has been in matters related to the provision of food, shelter, clothing, and health rather than a direct contribution to the mind of man or to the development of the political institutions that make civilized life possible.

Let us consider some of the more obvious potential sources of negative effects of the new educational technology. One of the obvious ones is that it is likely to be designed to eliminate any kind of pupil initiative. The kind of program designed by Suppes et al. (1968) in the field of computer-assisted instruction illustrates this. The behavior of the pupils in the booth equipped with the computer terminal is completely dominated by the program on which the computer is run. When events in a classroom are completely dominated by the teacher, one is likely to comment that such a classroom is very old-fashioned and out-of-date. The use of a computer to perform the same class of actions does not make the classroom any more up-to-date. Presumably, those who design such classrooms consider them avant garde rather than obsolete—a very curious viewpoint. The unfortunate feature of this situation is that the pupil is submitting himself to a situation in which he virtually renounces all control of what happens except for quite trivial aspects of his actions. From this author's viewpoint, the situation has features that have little place in a well-designed educational program. Education, from the author's point of view, should concentrate on giving the pupil opportunity to make decisions for himself and for him to be very independent of machines and other people in the decisions he makes. Education should provide opportunities for pupils to make significant decisions related to what they are going to accomplish and what they are going to learn. An educational program in which all significant decisions are made by adults is hardly education but would be more appropriately described as indoctrination or training. Educators have long held out the hope that schools would become places where pupils and teachers work together. The kind of technology that is given the greatest support at this time is one in which teachers are the planners and pupils are those whose behavior is controlled by the planners. What a caricature of education!

Andrews and Karlins (1971) have pointed out that education based on behavior-control principles is designed to produce adults who will fit docilely into an industrial system and who will have little concern for making decisions for themselves. In such an "advanced" world, the people of Russia, China, and the United States will all be cogs in their great industrial machines. The peoples of the different countries will probably differ only in some of the things they say but not in what they do and not in what controls their behavior. Peoples will not be slaves to a class, or slaves to a state, but slaves to the technology that has acquired control over every phase of their lives.

Related to this overwhelmingly serious criticism of modern educational technology is the fact that educational technology has been, to a

410
• • • • • • • • • • •
The New Technology of Education

marked degree, tied to the goal of the efficient achievement of traditional objectives. The objectives may have little significance for the new generation. The high-school diploma is, for many, a means of becoming eligible to belong to a union, but what is learned in high school may have nothing to do with what it takes to be an efficient union worker. Furthermore, the high-school curriculum may have little to help workers enrich their lives outside of work. The usual attempts to introduce English literature have little long-term value for students who turn to television for recreation and who are unlikely to read books for pleasure. The learning of mathematics is probably "irrelevant" to most students, who will not even have to work out the amount of change coming to them in the supermarket, for the cash register does this automatically. Most mathematics taught to the masses is taught so that the few will have the background needed in some college science courses. For the others, it has little functional value in their lives. Machine methods of handling numbers have taken over for man most of his mathematical tasks of only a generation ago. The pupils can see that education in the modern world is not there to enrich their lives, but that it is only a prolonged ritual that will enable them to obtain a union card. The present emphasis of educational technologists on finding efficient ways of teaching mathematics is hardly a channel of innovation likely to endear education to the modern generation. Most of the more significant problems of education are not those of how to make education more efficient but how to change its goals and purposes so that it will enable a person not only to enjoy education as one of life's great experiences but to see education as a source of enrichment for his entire life.

This leads to the question of why educational technology has fallen into the same rut as other technologies and with at least as devastating potential side effects. Why has not educational technology sought to enhance man's freedom through education? Why has not educational technology sought to convert education into a wonderful, inspiring, and freedom-giving experience?

The answer to this question is not simple, but one of the major factors in the unfortunate trend of much innovation in education is that it is to a great extent politically sponsored. The largest single set of enterprises directed toward educational innovation is the chain of regional laboratories funded by the Federal government. These enterprises, as Chase (1970) points out, are largely engaged in the development of educational materials and these materials are designed almost exclusively for the purpose of achieving traditionally endorsed objectives with greater efficiency. These organizations, as Chase also points out, exist to serve a public purpose, and, although they have their own boards controlling them as corporations, they are subject to review and evaluation by the United States Office of Education. The result is that their programs must conform to government policies. Now government policies are only rarely concerned with social change but are generally directed toward making the system, as it is, run more smoothly by eradicating the problems produced by elements that do not function well within the system. Educational technology has become the tool that government can use to help eradicate behavior that prevents the system from running smoothly.

For this reason, the major direction of effort of the government-sponsored educational technology has been to develop educational tools that can be used to produce conformity in the main nonconforming sections of our society. The poor, the underprivileged, the black, the Latin Americans, the Eskimos, and the Puerto Ricans belong to this category. These are the groups that the government sees as misfits, and it views the problem as one of educating them in such a way that they will conform to the rest of society. The problem is viewed as though it were one of modifying some of the human components in the great industrial machine so that these components will fit better. Education, through the new technology, is viewed as the means whereby some degree of uniformity in the human component can be achieved.

There is, of course, nothing new in a government developing a technology for particular political purposes. Indeed, much of technology has developed so, typically to the detriment of man. The Romans developed the metal industries as a means of arming the legions and extending imperial power. The nobility of the medieval period developed the use of the horse for military purposes, inventing both the stirrup and the horseshoe. In contrast, the so-called barbarians were the main developers and exploiters of first the water wheel and later the harnessed horse and iron plow—devices from which the great bulk of humanity benefited. History gives us little hope that a government-developed technology will be of any great value to the people, for such technologies have generally served only the most immediate ends of a relative few. Whether a federally sponsored technology in education can do anything more than achieve some goal of producing uniform educational products remains to be seen. That such a technology can be developed there seems to be little doubt, but there are real doubts whether such a technology can genuinely contribute to the overall quality of life. Indeed, it might be expected to produce a deterioration.

Needed Trends in Educational Technology

The developments in education that have been considered in this chapter have been criticized because of their tie to very short-term political goals, and the reader has a right to ask what the alternatives are. In considering these, the point must first be made that the author is not against all technology in the educational field. In education, as elsewhere, technology may serve worthwhile goals of the mass of humanity, or it may serve the purposes of the few and be damaging to the many. Technology may also serve the immediate goals of the many but have damaging side effects that are not identified until much harm has been done. The author believes that an educational technology is needed that serves the mass of humanity on a long-term basis, and that it should be an instrument

412
• • • • • • • • • • •
The New Technology of Education

whereby man builds up his individuality. In the development of this technology, the greatest sensitivity should be shown to possible harmful side effects, and no project should evolve without some attempt being made to assess potential damage as well as potential worth.

The technology of education needs to be more closely associated with the independent type of invention occurring outside of the federally sponsored machinery for educational progress. There is a need, for example, to develop a technology related to the open classroom. In particular, there is a need to develop rich sources of materials that children can explore. There may well be a greater need for this than there is for the rather dull packaged material that constitutes the main product of the so-called educational industry. A few manufacturers are producing interesting classroom exhibits and related materials that children can explore and that they can be given the choice of exploring or not exploring in a free environment. The design of a classroom in which there are real opportunities for exploration, rich sources of information that the pupil can consult, and opportunities for making significant decisions offers a real challenge to the educational technologists who have not become preoccupied with turning out pupils to meet very precise specifications.

One of the chief deterrents to such a program is cost, and this is a serious deterrent at a time when there is so much preoccupation with the matter of producing more education for the same or less money. The affluent American society has not learned that good education is expensive and is far different from the cheap mass-production model. A rich educational environment means not only the ready availability of extensive sources of information but also very large quantities of natural objects for the children to study and work with. These facilities, in turn, mean that there has to be a far better pupil–teacher ratio than there has been in the past and also better-qualified teachers.

Closely related to this kind of development is the development of situations in which pupils can make real and significant choices. Almost nothing is known about what children learn when they are given amounts of time during which they have to choose among learning activities. Such periods should be times to make explorations that the pupil has wanted to make, but the environment must provide real alternatives for exploration. The alternatives also must not be blind alleys. A pupil who chooses to study the balance of life in a tank must be helped to continue this exploration and to pursue at subsequent times the problems he has encountered. Too often, such free exploration periods are terminated with some statement by the teacher that enough time has now been wasted and it is time to get back to real work. There are problems of space and money related to equipping a school that will provide the kind of educational environment envisaged, but a beginning needs to be made in working out the details.

An educational environment that teaches the child to be free and independent must also make him recognize that some aspects of community life require conformity to regulations and self-discipline. He must come to recognize this limitation on his freedom as a necessary evil, but one to be kept to a minimum. Just as teachers and pupils have to arrive on time in order to have an organized school, so too do workers in factories and other places have to submit to similar controls. However, the pupils must learn, through the example provided by the school, that one submits to such controls only temporarily and for the purpose of enjoying opportunities for freedom. The school should be the place where the alienation from society produced by such controls exercised on a massive scale comes to be resolved. This must be accomplished through the pupil becoming not the willing recipient of such controls, as he is at present, but one who accepts them on occasion, with reluctance, as a means of achieving more worthwhile goals.

How far children can learn to avoid becoming subservient to a controlling technology of the world of work and the world of governmental control remains to be seen. No serious and extensive effort has, as yet, been made in this direction, and most of the recent effort in educational reform has involved a trend in the completely opposite direction, which, over the years, can be expected to increase alienation of youth. The political pressures are all in the direction of producing an education that will bring man more and more under the control of the great machine, or monster, he has created. Perhaps education must seek to free itself from such control as a first step.

One step that schools can begin to take as a part of their own liberation process is to end meaningless educational requirements. For example, many unions require their members to have high-school diplomas, even though the education provided by high schools has no relevance to performance on the job. The purpose of the requirement has been to exclude members of minority groups from the union. The result, of course, is not only social injustice but a degradation of education. Under such circumstances, students can hardly be expected to see a high-school education as anything more than a political gimmick of questionable morality. If students are to view education as a life-relevant activity, then education must cease to be a mere political tool of power groups but must become a means of personal self-development in a society where man truly values freedom from unnecessary control.

Related to this matter is a matter long ago discussed by John Dewey, namely, the extent to which the school can become a model for society by providing opportunities for learning the democratic process. Unfortunately, the school has become much more a model of a factory than a model of a free and democratic state. This is an area in which sociologists and social psychologists need to devote efforts to the development of social organizations within the school that will provide useful experiences. Certainly, the traditional systems of student government appear to be as obsolete as much of the rest of the curriculum.

Such problems are not going to be solved overnight. Large sums of

414
• • • • • • • • • • •
The New Technology of Education

money need to be made available to particular schools, over long periods of time, to work out experimental procedures. Perhaps twenty years is not too long a period for the evolution of a highly different form of school system and a technology of education entirely different from the present one, with its preoccupation with developing a packaged curriculum to be used for producing a uniform pupil product.

415

Needed Trends in
Educational Technology

1 Research in the behavioral sciences has impact on education in providing a conception of man that guides the educational process. In addition, this same body of knowledge has played a role in the development of a technology of education.

2 Technologies consist of well-developed and well-tried procedures that are effective in achieving certain practical goals. Most technologies existed, albeit in a primitive form, long before the scientific era. Most technologies showed a steady development over the centuries, and educational technology has been no exception. The technology of education has had a long history in that many effective procedures for instruction were developed long before psychology emerged as a science. Perhaps the greatest of all developments in the history of educational technology was the invention of the printing press. The history of education has also shown that most of the modern controversies about teaching methods have roots in much earlier controversies. The methods of teaching of the Sophists and the followers of Socrates find their modern counterparts in expository teaching and discovery teaching. The scholars of the Middle Ages were preoccupied with finding the best order in which to present subject matter, as are the designers of programmed materials today. Nevertheless, the behavioral sciences have enriched our concept of how to teach effectively and have been particularly emphatic in stressing the need to recognize individual differences among pupils.

3 Perhaps the major technological development in the educational field in recent years has been the development of film strips and motion pictures and the use of sound recordings. These have introduced some variety into the pupils' environment, and that alone may well justify their use. Too often, they are used as substitutes for a direct contact with the real world.

4 Educational technology, like all other technologies, is not in itself either good or bad. The virtues it may have depend on the use to which it is put. Although technologies seem to ultimately benefit mankind, in their initial stages they often do no more than benefit the privileged. Examples can be given of immoral applications of the behavioral sciences.

5 The predominant development of educational psychology in recent years has been along operant lines. However, such a development is based on assumptions about human behavior that some would not accept. The operant approach has been intimately related to the development procedures for instruc-

tion and the reinvention of the teaching machine. An important concept related to the design of such machines is that they should be adaptive to the needs of the learner. Teaching machines differ in the extent to which they are thus adaptive. In a sense, teaching machines are minimally adaptive in that they provide teaching related to fixed objectives, which may not be the objectives of the student. The computer is the basis of the most adaptive teaching machines. Teaching machines are based on major assumptions about the nature of learners, one of which is that learners are not in a position to make significant decisions.

6 Problems related to the ordering of subject matter have long been studied by teachers and research workers. Catechisms represented some of the earliest attempts to order subject matter in a way that produced the most effective learning. In more recent times, attempts have been made to identify hierarchies of skills. The developers of programmed learning have attempted to divide subject matter up into ordered sequences of frames. In most programs, a frame constitutes a very small amount of knowledge and the resulting overall program tends to be extremely bulky and quite costly. This has been one of the reasons why such materials have not been widely used. Another is that the materials have tended to show little literary skill in their production. Teaching machines have been developed that incorporate the use of different media. Nevertheless, such materials tend to be a step removed from the real world.

7 Computer-assisted instruction represents a type of teaching-machine system with a high degree of flexibility in what it can do. It is still at the experimental stage, but it is a valuable device for conducting research on teaching. A major limitation of such systems is that they can analyze only very limited communications from the student. They can provide teaching situations with a very high degree of control over how teaching takes place, and hence different methods of teaching can be compared. There is little evidence to show that computer-assisted instruction can make any notable contribution to classroom learning, but perhaps the utility of such devices has not yet been adequately explored. To some extent, computer-assisted instruction is very much like that provided by traditional workbooks, but the workbook has often been criticized as a method of teaching. The cost of instruction by computer is high and is more likely to increase than to decrease.

8 Numerous studies have now been made comparing programmed with nonprogrammed or traditional instruction. The overall differences found hardly seem to support one method over another. Students learn by programmed instruction and by machine-controlled instruction, but not with the speed anticipated twenty-five years ago. Teaching machines may be able to introduce some variation into classroom procedures and produce a novelty effect. There are basic difficulties in conducting research that compares two methods of instruction or two sets of materials for instruction. One can never be sure that each is an equally good representative of what can be produced. The question "Which teaching method is best?" may not be a useful one to ask. A teaching method that is effective in achieving a particular objective with one student may be ineffective with another.

9 Educational technology is receiving impetus at a time when there is a great disillusionment with the effects of technology. The negative aspects of other aspects of technology are being closely watched, but educational technology is regarded by its promoters as being wholly good in its outcomes. Much of educational technology is designed to produce a uniform educational product. Through such a formula the hope is that social misfits will disappear from the scene. Some people have doubts whether an educational technology that accomplishes such goals is particularly useful. An alternative would be the development of an educational technology that would free man from many of the controls that the rest of technology imposes on him.

A

Adams, J. A., 1967. *Human memory.* New York: McGraw-Hill.

Adorno, T. W., et al., 1950. *The authoritarian personality.* New York: Harper.

Ainsworth, M. D. S., and Bell, S. M., 1970. Attachment, exploration, and separation: Illustrated by the behavior of one-year-olds in a strange situation. *Child Development,* **41,** 45–67.

Allport, G. W., 1968. The historical background of modern social psychology. In G. Lindzey and E. Aronson (Eds.), *The handbook of social psychology.* Vol. 1. Reading, Mass.: Addison-Wesley, pp. 1–80.

American Association for the Advancement of Science, Commission on Science Education, 1965. *The psychological bases of science—A process approach.* Washington, D.C.: the Association.

Anderson, R. C., and Hidde, J. L., 1971. Imagery and sentence learning. *Journal of Educational Psychology,* **62,** 526–530.

• • • • • • • • • • • •

References

419

Anderson, R. C., and Myrow, D. L., 1971. Retroactive inhibition of meaningful discourse. *Journal of Educational Psychology Monograph*, **62**, No. 1.

Anderson, R. C., Kulhavy, R. W., and Andre, T., 1971. Feedback procedures in programmed instruction. *Journal of Educational Psychology*, **62**, 148–156.

Andrews, L. M., and Karlins, M., 1971. *Requiem for democracy.* New York: Holt, Rinehart & Winston.

Annett, J., 1961. *The role of knowledge of results in learning: A survey.* Technical Report, NAVTRADEVCEN 342–3. Port Washington, N.Y.: Naval Training Device Center.

Annett, J., 1969. *Feedback and human behavior.* Baltimore: Penuiin Books.

Aronfreed, J. M., 1968. *Conduct and conscience.* New York: Academic Press.

Aronson, E., 1968. Dissonance theory: Progress and problems. In R. P. Abelson et al. (Eds.), *Theories of cognitive consistency: A sourcebook.* Chicago: Rand McNally, pp. 5–27.

Ashton-Warner, S., 1963. *Teacher.* New York: Simon & Schuster.

Atkinson, R. C., 1969. Information delay in human learning. *Journal of Verbal Learning and Verbal Behavior*, **8**, 507–511.

Atkinson, R. W., and Wickens, T. D., 1971. Human memory and the concept of reinforcement. In R. Glaser (Ed.), *The nature of reinforcement.* New York: Academic Press, pp. 66–120.

Ausubel, D. P., 1963. *The psychology of meaningful verbal learning.* New York: Grune & Stratton.

Ausubel, D. P., and Robinson, F. G., 1969. *School learning: An introduction to educational psychology.* New York: Holt, Rinehart & Winston.

Ayllon, T., and Azrin, N., 1968. *The token economy: A motivational system for therapy and rehabilitation.* New York: Appleton-Century-Crofts.

B

Baker, E. L., 1973. The technology of instructional development. In R. M. W. Travers (Ed.), *Second handbook of research on teaching.* Chicago: Rand McNally, in press.

Baker, R. L., and Schutz, R. E. (Eds.), 1971. *Instructional product development.* New York: Van Nostrand Reinhold.

Baldwin, T. L., McFarlane, P. T., and Garvey, C. J., 1971. Children's communication accuracy related to race and socioeconomic status. *Child Development.* **42**, 345–357.

Ball, S., and Bogatz, G. A., 1970. *The first year of Sesame Street: An evaluation.* Princeton, N.J.: Educational Testing Service.

Bandura, A., and Walters, R. H., 1963. *Social learning and personality development.* New York: Holt, Rinehart & Winston.

Beller, E. K., 1973. Research on early education. In R. M. W. Travers (Ed.), *Second handbook of research on teaching.* Chicago: Rand McNally, in press.

Benowitz, M. L., and Busse, T. V., 1970. Material incentives and the learning of spelling words in a typical school situation. *Journal of Educational Psychology*, **61**, 24–26.

Bereiter, C., and Engelmann, S., 1966. *Teaching disadvantaged children in the preschool.* Englewood Cliffs, N.J.: Prentice–Hall.

Berlyne, D. E., 1965. *Structure and direction in thinking.* New York: Wiley.

Berlyne, D. E., 1970. Motivational problems raised by exploratory and epistemic behavior. In S. Koch (Ed.), *Psychology: A study of a science.* Vol. 5. New York: McGraw-Hill, pp. 284–364.

Berscheid, E., and Walster, E., 1969. Attitude change. Part II. In J. Mills (Ed.), *Experimental social psychology.* New York: Macmillan, pp.121–231.

Bidwell, C., 1973. The social psychology of teaching. In R. M. W. Travers (Ed.), *Second handbook of research on teaching.* Chicago: Rand McNally, in press.

Bilodeau, I. McD., 1966. Information feedback. In E. A. Bilodeau (Ed.), *Acquistition of skill.* New York: Academic Press, pp. 255–296.

Bishop, C. H.., 1964. Transfer effects of word and letter training in reading. *Journal of Verbal Learning and Verbal Behavior,* **3,** 215–221.

Bjork, R. A., 1970. Positive forgetting: The noninterference of items intentionally forgotten. *Journal of Verbal Learning and Verbal Behavior,* **9,** 255–268.

Block, J. H. (Ed.), 1971. *Mastery learning: Theory and practice.* New York: Holt, Rinehart & Winston.

Bloom, B. S., (Ed.), 1956. *Taxonomy of educational objectives. Handbook I: Cognitive domain.* New York: David McKay.

Bloom, B. S., 1964. *Stability and change in human characteristics.* New York: Wiley.

Bloom, B. S., 1968. *Learning for mastery.* Los Angeles: Center for the Study of Education and Instructional Programs, University of California.

Bloom, B. S., 1971. Mastery learning. In J. H. Block (Ed.), *Mastery learning: Theory and practice.* New York: Holt, Rinehart & Winston, pp. 47–63.

Bloom, L., 1970. *Language development: Form and function in emerging grammers.* MIT Research Monograph No. 59. Cambridge, Mass: MIT Press.

Borg, W. R., 1964. *An evalution of ability grouping.* Cooperative Research Project No. 577. Washington, D.C.: U.S. Office of Education.

Bormuth, J. R., 1971. Readability, measurment of. In L. C. Deighton (Ed.), *The encyclopedia of education.* Vol. 7. New York: Macmillan, pp. 361–368.

Bosco, J. J., 1970. *Social class and the processing of visual information.* Final Report, Project No. 9–E–041, U.S. Department of Health, Education and Welfare. Kalamazoo, Mich.: Western Michigan University, ED 041 345.

Bower, G. H., Lesgold, A. M., and Tieman, D., 1969. Grouping operations in free recall. *Journal of Verbal Learning and Verbal Behavior,* **8,** 481–493.

Bower, T. G. R., 1966a. Slant perception and shape constancy in infants. *Science,* **151,** 832–834.

Bower, T. G. R., 1966b. The visual world of infants. *Scientific American,* **215(6),** 80–92.

Bracht, G. H., 1970. Experimental factors related to aptitude-treatment interactions. *Review of Educational Research,* **40,** 627–645.

Brackbill, Y. (Ed.), 1967. *Infancy and early childhood.* New York: Free Press.

Brackbill, Y., and Fitzgerald, H. E., 1969. Development of the sensory analyzers during infancy. In L. P. Lipsitt and H. W. Reese (Eds.), *Advances in child development and behavior.* New York: Academic Press, pp. 173–208.

Briggs, L., 1970. Sequencing of instruction in relation to hierarchies of competence. In L. Briggs, *Handbook of procedures for the design of instruction.* Pittsburgh: American Institutes for Research.

Broadbent, D. E., 1958. *Perception and communication.* New York: Pergamon Press.

Broadbent, D. E., 1970. Psychological aspects of short-term and long-term memory. *Proceedings of the Royal Society of London,* **B175,** 333–350.

Broadbent, D. E., 1971. *Decision and stress.* New York: Academic Press.

Brown, R., and McNeill, D., 1966. The "tip of the tongue" phenomenon. *Journal of Verbal Learning and Verbal Behavior,* **5,** 325–337.

Bruner, J. S., 1969. Processes of growth in infancy. In A. Ambrose (Ed.), *Stimulation in early infancy.* New York: Academic Press, pp. 205–228.

Bryan, J. H., and London, P., 1970. Altruistic behavior by children. *Psychological Bulletin,* **73,** 200–211.

Bryan, J. H., and Schwartz, T., 1971. Effects of film material upon children's behavior. *Psychological Bulletin,* **75,** 50–59.

Bryan, J. H., and Walbek, N. H., 1970. Preaching and practicing generosity: Children's actions and reactions. *Child Development,* **41,** 329–353.

Buckley, N. K., and Walker, H. M., 1971. *Modifying classroom behavior.* Rev. ed. Champaign, Ill.: Research Press.

Bugelsik, B. R., 1956. *The psychology of learning.* New York: Holt, Rinehart & Winston.

Buros, O. K. (Ed.), 1965. *The sixth mental measurements yearbook.* Highland Park, N.J.: Gryphon Press.

Byrne, D., 1971. *The attraction paradigm.* New York: Academic Press.

C

Cain, L. F., and Willey, R. de V., 1939. The effect of spaced learning on the curve of retention. *Journal of Experimental Psychology,* **25,** 209–214.

Callahan, R. E., 1962. *Education and the cult of efficiency.* Chicago: University of Chicago Press.

Carthy, J. D., and Ebling, F. J. (Eds.), 1964. *The natural history of aggression.* New York: Academic Press.

Chall, J. S., 1967. *Learning to read: The great debate.* New York: McGraw-Hill.

Chall, J. S., 1970. Learning andnot learning to read: Current issues and trends. In F. A. Young and D. B. Lindsley (Eds.), *Early experience and visual information processing in perceptual and reading disorders.* Washington, D.C.: National Academy of Sciences, pp. 14–32.

Chase, F. S., 1970. The lavoratories: 1970 and beyond. *Journal of Research and Development in Education,* **3(2),** 104–120.

Chomsky, N., 1965. *Aspects of the theory of syntax.* Cambridge, Mass.: MIT Press.

Clemente, C. D., and Lindsley, D. B. (Eds.), 1967. *Aggression and defense: Neural mechaniams and social patterns.* Berkeley, Calif.: University of California Press.

Cofer, C. N., and Appley, M. H., 1964. *Motivation: Theory and research.* New York: Wiley.

Cohen, D. K., 1970. Pooitics and research: Evaluation of social action programs in education. *Review of Educational Research,* **40,** 213–238.

Cole, M., and Maltzman, I. (Eds.), 1969. *A handbook of contemporary Soviet psychology.* New York: Basic Books.

Craik, F. I. M., 1970. The fate of primary memory items in free recall. *Journal of Verbal Learning and Verbal Behavior,* **9,** 143–148.

Cratty, B. J., 1970. *Perceptual and motor development in infants and children.* New York: Macmillan.

Cruickshank, D. R., Broadbent, F. W., and Bubb, R. L., 1967. *Teaching problems lavoratory.* Chicago: Science Research Associates.

Cureton, L. M., 1971. A history of grading. *National Council on Measurement in Education Special Report,* **2,** No. 4.

D

Dale, P. S., 1971. Language learning, early. In L. C. Deighton (Ed.), *The encyclopedia of education.* Vol. 5. New York: Macmillan, pp. 322–327.

Day, H., 1968. Role of specific curiosity in school achievement. *Journal of Educational Psychology,* **59,** 37–43.

Deese, J. E., 1970. *Psycholinguistics.* Boston: Allyn & Bacon.

Dellas, M., and Gaier, E. L., 1970. Identification of creativity: The individual. *Psychological Bulletin,* **73,** 55–73.

Denenberg, V. H., 1970. *Education of the infant and young child.* New York: Academic Press.

Deutsch, M., 1968. Field theory in social psychology. In G. Lindzey and E. Aronson (Eds.), *The handbook of social psychology.* Vol. 1. Reading, Mass.: Addison-Wesley, pp. 412–487.

Dick, A. O., and Dick, S. O., 1969. An analysis of hierarchical processing in visual perception. *Canadian Journal of Psychology,* **23,** 203–211.

Downing, J. A., 1967. *Evaluating the initial teaching alphabet.* London: Cassell.

Downing, J. A., 1971. Initial teaching alphabet. In L. C. Deighton (Ed.), *The encyclopedia of education.* Vol. 5. New York: Macmillan, pp. 89–94.

Dreeben, R., 1973. The school as a workplace. In R. M. W. Travers (Ed.), *Second handbook of research on teaching.* Chicago: Rand McNally, in press.

E

Ebel, R. L., 1965. *Measuring educational achievement.* Englewood Cliffs, N.J.: Practice-Hall.

Eccles, J. C., Ito, M., and Szentágothai, J., 1967. *The cerebellum as a neuronal machine.* New York: Springer-Verlag.

Ellingson, R. J., 1967. The study of brain electrical activity in infants. In L. P. Lipsitt and C. C. Spiker (Eds.), *Advances in child development and behavior.* Vol. 3. New York: Academic Press, pp. 53–97.

Ellis, H. C., 1965. *The transfer of learning.* New York: Macmillan.

Ellis, H. C., 1969. Transfer and retention. In M. H. Marx (Ed.), *Learning: Processes.* New York: Macmillan, pp. 379–478.

F

Fellner, C. H., and Marshall, J. R., 1970. Kidney donors. In J. Macaulay and L. Berkowitz (Eds.), *Altruism and helping behavior.* New York: Academic Press, pp. 269–281.

Ferster, C. B., and Skinner, B. F., 1957. *Schedules of reinforcement.* New York: Appleton-Century-Crofts.

Feshbach, S., and Singer, R. D.,1970. *Television and aggression: An experimental field study.* San Francicso: Jossey-Bass.

Festinger, L., 1957. *A theory of cognitive dissonance.* Stanford, Calif.: Standford University Press.

Fitts, P. M., and Posner, M. I., 1967. *Human performance.* Belmont, Calif.: Wadsworth.

Fitzgerald, H. E., 1968. Autonomic pupillary reflex activity during early infancy and its relation to social and nonsocial visual stimuli. *Journal of Experimental Child Psychology,* **6,** 470–482.

Flanders, N. A., 1970. *Analyzing teaching behavior.* Reading, Mass.: Addison-Wesley.

Flavell, J. H., 1963. *The development psychology of Jean Piaget.* Princeton, N.J.: Van Nostrand.

Flom, M. C., 1970. Experience in the development of visual coordination. In F. A. Young and D. B. Lindsley (Eds.), *Early experience and visual information processing in perceptual and reading disorders.* Washington, D.C.: National Academy of Sciences, pp. 291–230.

Foster, H. L., and Newman, A. P., 1971. Language problems of inner-city children. In L. C. Deighton (Ed.), *The encyclopedia of education.* Vol. 5. New York: Macmillan, pp. 334–338.

Fowler, H., 1965. *Curiosity and exploratory behavior.* New York: Macmillan.

Fowler, W., 1962. Cognitive learning in infancy and early childhood. *Psychological Bulletin,* **59,** 116–152.

Furth, H. G., 1971. Linguistic deficiency and thinking: Research with deaf subjects. *Psychological Bulletin,* **76,** 58–72.

G

Gagné, R. M., 1970. *The conditions of learning.* 2nd ed. New York: Holt, Rinehart & Winston.

Gates, A. I., 1917. Recitation as a factor in memorizing. *Archives of Psychology,* **6,** No. 40.

Gerlach, V. S., Schutz, R. E., Baker, R. L., and Mazer, G. F., 1964. Effects of variations in test direction on originality of test response. *Journal of Educational Psychology,* **55,** 79–83.

Getzels, J. W., 1969. A social psychology of education. In G. Lindzey and E. Aronson (Eds.), *The handbook of social psychology.* Vol. 5. Reading, Mass.: Addison-Wesley, pp. 459-537.

Gibson, E. J., 1965. Learning to read. *Science,* **148,** 1066–1072.

Gibson, E. J., 1969. *Principles of perceptual learning and development.* New York: Appleton-Century-Crofts.

Gibson, E. J., and Walk, R. D., 1960. The "visual cliff." *Scientific American,* **202(4),** 64–71.

Gibson, E. J., Osser, H., and Pick, A. D., 1963. A study of the development of grapheme–phoneme correspondences. *Journal of Verbal Learning and Verbal Behavior,* **2,** 142–146.

Gibson, E. J., Osser, H., Scheff, W., and Smith, J., 1965. *A basic research program in reading.* Final Report, Cooperative Research Project No. 639, U.S. Office of Education. Washington, D.C.: Department of Health, Education and Welfare.

Gibson, J. J., 1966. *The senses considered as perceptual systems.* Boston: Houghton Mifflin.

Gladstone, R., 1969. Age, cognitive control, and extinction. *Journal of Experimental Child Psychology,* **7,** 31–35.

Glaser, R., and Cox, R. C., 1968. Criterion-referenced testing for the measurement of educational outcomes. In R. A. Weisgerber (Ed.), *Instructional process and media innovation.* Chicago: Rand McNally, pp. 545–550.

Goodman, M. E., 1964. *Race awareness in young children.* New York: Collier Books.

Gordon, I. J., 1969a. *Early child stimulation through parent education.* Final Report to the Children's Bureau on Project No. PHS R-306, R-306(01). Gainesville, Fla.: Institute for Development of Human Resources, University of Florida, ED 038 166.

Gordon, I. J., 1969b. *Human development from birth through adolescence*. 2nd ed. New York: Harper & Row.

Green, R. L., Bakan, R. F., McMillan, J. H. and Lezotte, L. W., 1973. Research and the urban school: Implication for educational improvement. In R. M. W. Travers (Ed.), *Second handbook of research on teaching*. Chicago: Rand McNally, in press.

Gronlund, N. E., 1968. *Constructing achievement tests*. Englewood Cliffs, N.J.: Prentice-Hall.

Gronlund, N. E., 1970. *Stating behavioral objectives for classroom instruction*. New York: Macmillan.

Guilford, J. P.,1956. The structure of the intellect. *Psychological Bulletin*, **53**, 267–293.

Guilford, J. P., 1967. *The nature of human intelligence*. New York: McGraw-Hill.

H

Haber, R. N., and Hershenson, M., 1965. Effects of repeated brief exposures on the growth of a percept. *Journal of Experimental Psychology*, **69**, 40–46.

Haith, M. M., Kessen, W., and Collins, D., 1969. Response of the human infant to level of complexity of intermittent visual movement, *Journal of Experimental Child Psychology*, **7**, 52–69.

Halford, G. S., 1970. A theory of the acquisition of conservation. *Psychological Review*, **77**, 302–316.

Hall, J. F., 1971. *Verbal learning and retention*. New York: Lippincott.

Harlow, H. F., 1959. Learning set and error factor theory. In S. Koch (Ed.), *Psychology: A study of a science*. Vol. 2. New York: McGraw-Hill, pp. 492–537.

Harlow, H. F., 1961. The development of affectional patterns in infant monkeys. In B. M. Foss (Ed.), *Determinants of infant behaviour*. London: Methuen, pp. 75–97.

Harlow, H. F., and Harlow, M. K., 1965. The affectional systems. In A. M. Schrier, H. F. Harlow, and F. Stollnitz (Eds.), *Behavior of nonhuman primates*. New York: Academic Press, pp. 287–334.

Hartley, J., 1966. Research report. *New Education*, **2(1)**, 29–35.

Hebb, D. O., 1966. *A textbook of psychology*. 2nd ed. Philadelphia: Saunders.

Heckhausen, H., 1967. *The anatomy of achievement motivation*. New York: Academic Press.

Hellyer, S., 1962. Supplementary report: Frequency of stimulus presentation and short-term decrement in recall. *Journal of Experimental Psychology*, **64**, 650.

Hemphill, J. K., Griffiths, D. E., and Frederiksen, N., 1962. *Administrative performance and personality*. New York: Bureau of Publications, Teachers College, Columbia University.

Herriot, P., 1970. *An introduction to the psychology of language*. London: Methuen.

Holding, D. H., 1965. *Principles of training*. New York: Pergamon Press.

Homme, L., 1971. *How to use contingency contracting in the classroom*. Rev. ed. Champaign, Ill.: Research Press.

Howe, M. J., 1970. *Introduction to human memory*. New York: Harper & Row.

Hubel, D. H., and Wiesel, T. N., 1959. Receptive fields of single neurones in the cat's striate cortex. *Journal of Physiology* (London), **148,** 574–591.

Hull, C. L., 1943. *Principles of behavior.* New York: Appleton-Century.

Husén, T. (Ed.), *International study of achievement in mathematics: A comparison of twelve countries.* Stockholm: Almqvist & Wiksell.

Hutt, S.J., Lenard, H. G., and Prechtl, H. F. R., 1969. Psychophsiolgical studies in newborn infants. In L. P. Lipsitt and H. W. Reese (Eds.), *Advances in child development and behavior.* New York: Academic Press pp. 127–172.

I

Inhelder, B., and Piaget, J., 1958. *The growth of logical thinking from childhood to adolescence.* New York: Basic Books.

Insko, C. A., 1967. *Theories of attitude change.* New York: Appleton-Century-Crofts.

J

Jackson, P. W., 1968. *Life in classrooms.* New York: Holt, Rinehart & Winston.

Jenkins, J. G., and Dallenbach, K. M., 1924. Obliviscence during sleep and waking. *American Journal of Psychology,* **35,** 605–612.

Johnson, D. M., 1955. *The psychology of thought and judgement.* New York: Harper.

Jones, M. R. (Ed.), 1968. *Miami symposiun on the prediction of behavior, 1967: Aversive stimulation.* Coral Gables, Fla.: University of Miami Press.

Jones, R. M., 1970. *System in child language.* Welsh studies in Education Series, Vol. 2. Cardiff, England: University of Wales Press.

Judd, C. H., 1908. The relation of special training to general intelligence. *Educational Review,* **36,** 28–42.

K

Kagan, J., 1970. The determinants of attention in the infant. *American Scientist,* **58,** 298–306.

Karlins, M., and Abelson, H. I., 1970. *Persuasion.* 2nd ed. New York: Springer.

Katz, D., and Stotland, E., 1959. A preliminary statement of a theory of attitude structure and change. In S. Koch (Ed.), *Psychology: A study of a science.* Vol. 3. New York: McGraw-Hill, pp. 423–475.

Kaufmann, H., 1970a. *Aggression and altruism.* New York: Holt, Rinehart & Winston.

Kaufmann, H., 1970b. Legality and harmfulness of a bystander's failure to intervene as determinants of moral judgment. In J. Macaulay and Berkowitz (Eds.), *Altruism and helping behavior.* New York: Academic Press, pp. 77–81.

Kendler, T. S., and Kendler, H. H., 1970. An ontogeny of optional shift behavior. *Child Development,* **41,** 1–27.

Kennedy, W. A., and Willcutt, H. C., 1964. Praise and blame as incentives. *Psychological Bulletin,* **62,** 323–332.

Kiesler, C. A., Collins, B. E., and Miller, N., 1969. *Attitude change.* New York: Wiley.

Kjeldergaard, P. M., 1968. Transfer and mediation in verbal learning. In

T. R. Dixon and D. L. Horton (Eds.), *Verbal behavior and general behavior theory.* Englewood Cliffs, N.J.: Prentice-Hall, pp. 67–96.

Klare, G. R., 1963. *The measurement of readability.* Ames, Iowa: Iowa State University Press.

Kleinsmith, L. J., and Kaplan, S., 1963. Paired-associate learning as a function of arousal and interpolated interval. *Journal of Experimental Psychology,* **65,** 190–193.

Kohlberg, L., 1958. The development of modes of moral thinking and choice in the years 10 to 16. Unpublished doctoral dissertation, University of Chicago.

Kohlberg, L., and Turiel, E., 1971. Moral development and moral education. In G. S. Lesser (Ed.), *Psychology and educational practice.* Glenview, Ill.: Scott, Foresman pp. 410–465.

Krathwohl, D. R., Bloom, B. S., and Masia, B. B., 1964. *Taxonomy of educational objectives. Handbook II: Affective domain.* New York: David McKay.

L

Latané, B., and Darley, J. M., 1970. Social determinants of bystander intervention in emergencies. In J. Macaulay and L. Berkowitz (Eds.), *Altruism and helping behavior.* New York: Academic Press, pp. 13–27.

Lenneberg, E. H., 1967. *Biological foundations of language.* New York: Wiley.

Lenneberg, E. H., 1969. On explaining language. *Science,* **164,** 635–643.

Leventhal, G. S., 1964. Reward magnitude, task attractiveness, and liking for instrumental activity. *Journal of Abnormal and Social Psychology,* **68,** 460–463.

Lewis, M. Q., and Bartz, W. H., 1970. Learning and the memory stores. *Journal of Experimental Psychology,* **86,** 465–466.

Lilley, S., 1966. *Men, machines and history.* New York: International Publishers.

Lindeman, R. H., 1967. *Educational measurement.* Glenview, Ill.: Scott, Foresman.

Lipe, D., and Jung, S. M., 1971. Manipulating incentives to enhance school learning. *Review of Educational Research,* **41,** 249–280.

Lockard, R. B., 1971. Reflections on the fall of comparative psychology: Is there a message for us all? *American Psychologist,* **26,** 168–179.

Longstreth, L. E., 1970. Tests of the law of effect using open and closed tasks. *Journal of Experimental Psychology,* **84,** 53–57.

Lorenz, K., 1966. *On aggression.* New York: Harcourt, Brace, & World.

M

Macaulay, J. R., 1970. A shill for charity. In J. Macaulay and L. Berkowitz (Eds.), *Altruism and helping behavior.* New York: Academic Press, pp. 43–59.

Macaulay, J., and Berkowitz, L. (Eds.), 1970. *Altruism and helping behavior.* New York:Academic Press.

Mager, R. F., 1962. *Preparing instructional objectives.* Palo Alto, Calif.: Fearon.

Mager, R. F., 1968. *Developing attitude toward learning.* Palo Alto, Calif.: Fearon.

Markowitz, N., and Renner, K. E., 1964. Feedback and the delay-retention effect. *Journal of Experimental Psychology, 72, 452–455.*

Marlowe, D., and Gergen, K. J., 1969. Personality and social interaction. In G. Lindzey and E. Aronson (Eds.), *The handbook of social psychology.* Vol. 3. Reading, Mass.: Addison-Wesley, pp. 590–665.

Marshall, H. H., 1969. Learning as a function of task interest, reinforcement, and social class variables. *Journal of Educational Psychology, 60, 133–137.*

Marsland, R. L., 1970. Implications for therapy. In F. A. Young and D. B. Lindsley (Eds.), *Early experience and visual information processing in perceptual and reading disorders.* Washington, D.C.: National Academy of Sciences, pp. 457–464.

Mason, W. A., 1968. Early social deprivation in nonhuman primates: Implications for human behavior. In D. C. Glass (Ed.), *Enviromental influences.* New York: Rockefeller University Press and Russell Sage Foundation, pp. 70–101.

Matteoni, L., 1971. Reading instruction: Reading instruction and language deprivation. In L. C. Deighton (Ed.), *The encyclopedia of education.* Vol. 7. New York: Macmillan, pp. 412–418.

Matthews, G. V. T., 1968. *Bird navigation.* Cambridge Monographs in Experimental Biology No. 3. London: Cambridge University Press.

Maw, W. H., and Maw, E. W., 1965. *Personal and social variables differentiating children with high and low curiosity.* Cooperative Research Project No. 1511. Newark: University of Delaware, ED 003 274.

McAshan, H. H., 1970. *Writing behavioral objectives: A new approach.* New York: Harper & Row.

McGuire, W. J., 1969. The nature of attitudes and attitude change. In G. Lindzey and E. Aronson (Eds.), *The handbook of social psychology.* Vol. 3. Reading, Mass.: Addison-Wesley, pp. 136–314.

McLaughlin, B., 1965. "Intentional" and "incidental" learning in human subjects. *Psychological Bulletin, 63, 359–376.*

McNeil, J. D., and Popham, W. J., 1972. The assessment of teacher competence. In R. M. W. Travers (Ed.), *Second handbook of research on teaching.* Chicago: Rand McNally, in press.

McNemar, Q., 1969. Lost: Our intelligence? Why? In L. E. Tyler (Ed.), *Intelligence: Some recurring issues.* New York: Van Nostrand, pp. 259–277.

Mechner, F., 1967. Behavioral analysis and instructional sequencing. In P. C. Lange (Ed), *Programed instruction.* The 66th Yearbook of the National Society for the Study of Education. Part II. Chicago: the Society, pp. 81–103.

Meichenbaum, D. H., Bowers, K. S., and Ross, R. R.,1968. Modification of classroom behavior of institutionalized female adolescent offenders. *Behavior Research and Therapy, 6, 343–353.*

Miller, L. B., 1969. *Experimental variation of Head Start curricula: A comparison of current approaches.* Research Grant No. CG8199 from Office of Economic Opportunity, Annual Report. Louisville, Ky.: University of Louisville, ED 041 618.

Miller, L. B., et al., 1970. *Experimental variation of Head Start curricula: A comparison of current approaches.* Research Grant No. CG8199 from Office of Economic Opportunity, Progress Report No. 5. Louisville, Ky.: University of Louisville, ED 041 617.

Mumford, L., 1970. *The myth of the machine: The pentagon of power.* New York: Harcourt Brace Jovanovich.

Munsinger, H., and Weir, M. W., 1967. Infant's and young children's preference for complexity. *Journal of Experimental Child Psychology*, 5, 69–73.

Murray, H. A., et al., 1938. *Explorations in personality*. New York: Oxford University Press.

Mussen, P. H., Conger, J. J., and Kagan, J., 1969. *Child development and personality*. 3rd ed. New York: Harper & Row.

Myers, K. E., Travers, R. M. W., and Sanford, M. E., 1965. Learning and reinforcement in student pairs. *Journal of Educational Psychology*, 56, 67–72.

Myklebust, H. R., 1964. *The psychology of deafness*. 2nd ed. New York: Grune & Stratton,

N

Nakamura, C. Y., and Boroczi, G., 1965. Effect of relative incentive value on persistence and response speed. *Child Development*, 36, 547–557.

Neisser, U., 1964. Visual search. *Scientific American*. 210(6), 94–102.

Newman, H. H., Freeman, F. N., and Holzinger, K. J., 1937. *Twins: A study of heredity and enviroment*. Chicago: University of Chicago Press.

Nickell, M., and Travers, R. M. W., 1963. Effects of different reinforcers: A comparison across age levels. *Psychological Reports*, 13, 739–746.

Nixon, J. E., and Locke, L. F., 1973. Research on teaching in physical education. In R. M. W. Travers (Ed.), *Second handbook of research on teaching*. Chicago: Rand McNally, in press.

Norman, D. A., 1969. *Memory and attention*. New York: Wiley.

Nottebohm, F., 1970. Ontogeny of bird song. *Science*, 167, 950–956.

Nuttin, J., and Greenwald, A. G., 1968. *Reward and punishment in human learning*. New York: Academic Press.

O

O'Leary, K. D., and Drabman, R., 1971. Token reinforcement programs in the classroom: A review. *Psychological Bulletin*, 75, 379–398.

Osgood, C. E., 1949. The similarity paradox in human learning: A resolution. *Psychological Review*, 56, 132–143.

Overing, R. L. R., and Travers, R. M. W., 1966. Effect upon transfer of variations in training conditions. *Journal of Educational Psychology*, 57, 179–188.

Overing, R. L. R., and Travers, R. M. W., 1967. Variation in the amount of irrelevant cues in training and test conditions and the effect upon transfer. *Journal of Educational Psychology*, 58, 62–68.

P

Paivio, A., 1969. Mental imagery in associative learning and memory. *Psychological Review*, 76, 241–263.

Paivio, A., 1970. On the functional significance of imagery. *Psychological Bulletin*, 73, 385–392.

Paivio, A., and Csapo, K., 1969. Concrete image and verbal memory codes. *Journal of Experimental Psychology*, 80, 279–285

Palermo, D. S., 1970. Imagery in children's learning: Discussion. *Psychological Bulletin*, 73, 415–421.

Peterson, L. R., and Peterson, M. J., 1959. Short-term retention of individual verbal items. *Journal of Experimental Psychology*, 58, 193–198.

Piaget, J., 1948. *The moral judgement of the child.* Glencoe, Ill.: Free Press.

Piaget, J., 1954. *The construction of reality in the child.* New York: Basic Books.

Piaget, J., and Inhelder, B., 1969. *The psychology of the child.* New York: Basic Books.

Popham, W. J., 1969. Objectives and instruction. In R. E. Stake (Ed.), *Instructional objectives.* AERA Monograph Series on Curriculum Evaluation, No. 3. Chicago: Rand McNally, pp. 32–64.

Posner, M. I., and Keele, S. W., 1973. Skill learning. In R. M. W. Travers (Ed.), *Second handbook of research on teaching.* Chicago: Rand McNally, in press.

Pressey, S. L., 1932. A third and fourth contribution toward the coming "industrial revolution" in education. *School and Society,* **36,** 668–672.

Puff, C. R., 1970. Role of clustering in free recall. *Journal of Experimental Psychology,* **86,** 384–386.

R

Rabin, A. I., 1965. *Growing up in the Kibbutz.* New York: Springer.

Rachman, S., 1967. Systematic desensitization, *Psychological Bulletin,* **67,** 93–103.

Raths, L. E., 1969. *Teaching for learning.* Columbus, Ohio: Merrill.

Razik, T. A., 1965. *Bibliography of creativity studies and related areas.* Buffalo: State University of New York.

Reed, H. B., 1946. Factors influencing the learning and retention of concepts. I. The influence of set. *Journal of Experimental Psychology,* **36,** 71–87.

Reese, H. W., 1968. *The preception of stimulus relations.* New York: Academic Press.

Richardson, A., 1969. *Mental imagery.* New York: Springer.

Richardson, L. F., 1960. *Statistics of deadly quarrels.* Pittsburgh: Boxwood Press.

Riesen, A. H., 1970. Effects of visual enviroment on the retina. In F. A. Young and D. B. Lindsley (Eds.), *Early experience and visual information processing in perceptual and reading disorders.* Washington, D.C.: National Academy of Sciences, pp. 249–258.

Risley, T., 1968. Jenney Lee: Learning and lollipops. *Psychology Today,* **1(8),** 28–31, 62–65.

Robinson, H. M., 1971. Reading instruction: Research. In L. C. Deighton (Ed.), *The encyclopedia of education.* Vol. 7. New York: Macmillan, pp. 406–412.

Robinson, J. P., and London, P., 1971. Labeling and imaging as aids to memory. *Child Development,* **42,** 641–644.

Rokeach, M., 1960. *The open and closed mind.* New York: Basic Books.

Rokeach, M., 1968. *Beliefs, attitudes, and values.* San Francisco: Jossey-Bass.

Rosenshine, B., and Furst, N., 1971. Research on teacher performance criteria. In B. O. Smith (Ed.), *Research on teacher education: A symposium.* Englewood Cliffs, N.J.: Prentice-Hall.

Rusk, R. R., 1933. *A history of infant education.* London: University of London Press.

S

Saettler, P., 1968. *History of instructional technology.* New York: McGraw-Hill.

Sassenrath, J. M., and Yonge, G. D., 1968. Delayed information feedback, feedback cues, retention set, and delayed retention. *Journal of Educational Psychology*, **59**, 69–73.

Schaefer, E. S., 1970. Need for early and continuing education. In V. H. Denenberg (Ed.), *Education of the infant and young child*. New York: Academic Press, pp. 61–82.

Schwab, J. J., 1962. The concept of the structure of a discipline. *Educational Record*, **43**, 197–205.

Scott, J. P., 1967. The process of primary socialization in canine and human infants. In J. Hellmuth (Ed.), *Exceptional infant*. Vol. 1. Seattle: Special Child Publications, pp. 467–514.

Scott, J. P., 1969. The social psychology of infrahuman animals. In G. Lindzey and E. Aronson (Eds.), *The handbook of social psychology*. Vol. 4. Reading, Mass.: Addison-Wesley, pp. 611–642.

Shackle, G. L. S., 1961. *Decision, order and time in human affairs*. Cambridge, England: Cambridge University Press.

Sheppard, W. C., 1969. Operant control of infant vocal and motor behavior. *Journal of Experimental Child Psychology*, **7**, 36–51.

Shouksmith, G., 1970. *Intelligence, creativity and cognitive style*. New York: Wiley.

Silberman, C. E., 1970. *Crisis in the classroom*. New York: Random House.

Simon, A., and Boyer, E. G. (Eds.), 1970. *Mirrors for behavior II: An anthology of observation instruments*. Philadelphia: Research for Better Schools.

Skinner, B. F., 1953. *Science and human behavior*. New York: Macmillan.

Skinner, B. F., 1954. The science of learning and the art of teaching. *Harvard Educational Review*, **24**, 86–97.

Skinner, B. F., 1957. *Verbal behavior*. New York: Appleton-Century-Crofts.

Skinner, B. F., 1959. *Cumulative record*. New York: Appleton-Century-Crofts.

Skinner, B. F., 1969. *Contingencies of reinforcement: A theoretical analysis*. New York: Appleton-Century-Crofts.

Skinner, B. F., 1971. *Beyond freedom and dignity*. New York: Knopf.

Smith, F., 1971. *Understanding reading*. New York: Holt, Rinehart & Winston.

Solomon, R. L., 1964. Punishment. *American Psychologist*, **19**, 239–253.

Spence, J. T., 1966. *A study of certain factors affecting children's school performance*. Austin, Texas: University of Texas, ED 011 086.

Spence, K. W., 1956. *Behavior theory and conditioning*. New Haven, Conn.: Yale University Press.

Sperling, G., 1960. The information available in brief visual presentations. *Psychological Monographs*, **74(11)**, Whole No. 498.

Standing, L., Sell, C., Boss, J., and Haber, R. N., 1970. Effect of visualization and subvocalization on perceptual clarity. *Psychonomic Science*, **18**, 89–90.

Stefan, S., 1970. Phonemic recording of digital information. *Journal of Experimental Psychology*, **86**, 398–406.

Sticht, T. G., 1971. Failure to increase learning using the time saved by the time compression of speech. *Journal of Educational Psychology*, **62**, 55–59.

Stolurow, L. M., 1961. *Teaching by machine*. U.S. Office of Education, Cooperative Research Monograph No. 6. Washington, D.C.: U.S. Government Printing Office.

Stone, L. J., and Church, J., 1968. *Childhood and adolescence*. 2nd ed. New York: Random House.

Suppes, P., Jerman, M., and Brian, D., 1968. *Computer-assisted instruc-*

tion: Stanford's 1965–66 arithmetic program. New York: Academic Press.

Surgeon General's Scientific Advisory Committee on Television and Social Behavior, 1972. *Television and growing up: The impact of televised violence.* Washington, D.C.: U.S. Government Printing Office.

T

Talland, G. A., 1965. *Deranged memory.* New York: Academic Press.

Taylor, W. L., 1953. "Close procedure": A new tool for measuring readability. *Journalism Quarterly,* **30,** 415–433.

Thomas, H., 1965. Visual-fixation responses of infants to stimuli of varying complexity. *Child Development,* **36,** 629–638.

Thorndike, E. L., 1927. The refractory period in associative processes. *Psychological Review,* **34,** 234–236.

Tolman, E. C., 1932. *Purposive behavior in animals and men.* New York: Century.

Torrance, E. P., 1965. *Rewarding creative behavior.* Englewood Cliffs, N.J.: Prentice-Hall.

Towle, T. O., and Jennings, J. W., 1969. Conditional exploration in domestic rats. *Psychological Reports,* **25,** 63–69.

Travers, R. M. W., 1967. Perceptual learning. *Review of Educational Research,* **37,** 599–617.

Travers, R. M. W., and Myers, K. E., 1966. Efficiency in rote learning under four learning conditions, *Journal of Educational Research,* **60,** 10–12.

Travers, R. M. W., Reid, I. E., and Van Wagenen, R. K., 1963. *Reinforcement: A review of selected research.* Final Report: Part I, Office of Education Contract No. 2-10-010. Washington, D.C.: U.S. Department of Health, Education and Welfare, ED 003 055.

Triandis, H. C., 1971. *Attitudes and attitude change.* New York: Wiley.

Tulving, E., 1967. The effects of presentation and recall of material in free-recall learning. *Journal of Verbal Learning and Verbal Behavior,* **6,** 175–184.

Tulving, E., and Osler, S., 1968. Effectiveness of retrieval cues in memory for words. *Journal of Experimental Psychology,* **77,** 593–601.

Turiel, E., 1973. Stage transition in moral development. In R. M. W. Travers (Ed.), *Second handbook of research on teaching.* Chicago: Rand McNally, in press.

Tyler, R. W., 1934. *Constructing achievement tests.* Columbus, Ohio: Bureau of Educational Research, Ohio State University.

Tyler, R. W., 1950. *Basic principles of curriculum and instruction.* Chicago: University of Chicago Press.

Tyler, R. W., 1969. *Basic principles of curriculm and instruction.* Chicago: University of Chicago Press.

U

Underwood, B. J., 1957. Interference and forgetting. *Psychological Review,* **64,** 49–60.

Underwood, B. J., 1969. Attributes of memory. *Psychological Review,* **76,** 559–573.

Uzgiris, I. C., 1967. Ordinality in the development of schemas for relating to objects. In J. Hellmuth (Ed.), *Exceptional infant.* Vol. 1. Seattle: Special Child Publications, pp. 315–334.

V

Valverde, F., and Ruiz-Marcos, A., 1970. The effects of sensory deprivation on dendritic spines in the visual cortex of the mouse: A mathematical model of spine distribution. In F. A. Young and D. B. Lindsley (Eds.), *Early experience and visual information processing in perceptual and reading disorders.* Washington, D.C.: National Academy of Sciences, pp. 261–289.

Vinacke, W. E., 1952. *The psychology of thinking.* New York: McGraw-Hill.

Von Senden, M., 1960. *Space and sight.* Glencoe, Ill.: Free Press.

W

Walcher, D. N., and Peters, D. L. (Eds.), 1971. *Early childhood: The development of self-regulating mechanisms.* New York: Academic Press.

Walen, S. R., 1970. Recall in children and adults. *Journal of Verbal Learning and Verbal Behavior*, **9**, 94–98.

Walk, R. D., and Gibson, E. J., 1961. A comparative and analytical study of visual depth perception. *Psychological Monographs*, **75(15)**, Whole No. 519.

Wallen, N. E., and Travers, R. M. W., 1963. Analysis and investigation of teaching methods. In N. L. Gage (Ed.), *Handbook of research on teaching.* Chicago: Rand McNally, pp. 448–505.

Walls, R. T., and Smith, T. S., 1970. Development of preference for delayed reinforcement in disadvantaged children. *Journal of Educational Psychology*, **61**, 118–123.

Watson, J. B., 1925. *Behaviorism.* New York: People's Institute.

Watson, J. S., 1969. Operant conditioning of visual fixation in infants under visual and auditory reinforcement. *Development Psychology*, **1**, 508–516.

Weinberg, M., 1970. *Desegregation research: An appraisal.* Bloomington, Ind.: Phi Delta Kappa.

Weiskrantz, L., 1970. Visual memory and the temporal lobe of the monkey. In R. E. Whalen, R. F. Thompson, M. Verzeano, and N. Weinberger (Eds.), *The neural control of behavior.* New York: Academic Press, pp. 239–256.

Weiss, W., 1971. Mass communication. In P. H. Mussen and M. R. Rosenzweig (Eds.), *Annual Review of Psychology*, pp. 251–307.

West, L. J., 1969. *Acquisition of typewriting skills.* New York: Pitman.

Wickelgren, L. W., 1969. The ocular response of human newborns to intermittent visual movement. *Dissertation Abstracts*, **29**, 4373-B.

Wickelgren, W. A., 1968. Sparing of short-term memory in an amnesic patient: Implications for strength theory of memory. *Neuropsychologia*, **6**, 235–244.

Witte, K. L., and Grossman, E. E., 1971. The effects of reward and punishment upon children's attention, motivation, and discrimination learning. *Child Development*, **42**, 537–542.

Wolf, E. R., and Jorgensen, J. G., 1970. Anthropology on the warpath in Thailand. *New York Review of Books*, **15(9)**, 26–34.

Wolpe, J., 1958. *Psychotherapy by reciprocal inhibition.* Stanford, Calif.: Stanford University Press.

Wood, R., and Skurnik, L. S., 1969. *Item banking.* Slough, England: National Foundation for Educational Research in England.

Woodworth, R. S., 1958. *Dynamics of behavior.* New York: Holt, Rinehart & Winston.

Y

Yarbus, A. L., 1967. *Eye movements and vision.* New York: Plenum Press.

Z

Zigler, E., and Child, I. L., 1969. Socialization. In G. Lindzey and E. Aronson (Eds.), *The handbook of social psychology.* Vol. 3. Reading, Mass.: Addison-Wesley, pp. 450–589.

Zimbardo, P. G., 1969. *The cognitive control of motivation.* Glenview, Ill.: Scott, Foresman.

Zintz, M. V., 1970 *The reading process.* Dubuque, Iowa: W. C. Brown.

Zoll, E. J., 1969. Research in programmed instruction in mathematics. *Mathematics Teacher,* **62,** 103–110.

434
• • • • • • • • •
References

Index
of Names

436

· · · · · · · · · · ·

Index of Names

438

· · · · · · · · · · ·

Index of Names

439
· · · · · · · · · · ·
Index of Names

443

444
• • • • • • • • • •
Index of Subjects

448

. . . .

Index of Subjects